CAIRO TO KABUL

Afghan and Islamic Studies presented to Ralph Pinder-Wilson

Ralph Pinder-Wilson

edited by

Warwick Ball and Leonard Harrow

MELISENDE
LONDON

Cairo to Kabul
Afghan and Islamic Studies presented to Ralph Pinder-Wilson

First published 2002
by Melisende
an imprint of
Fox Communications and Publications
39 Chelmsford Road
London E18 2PW
Tel: 020 8498 9768
Fax: 020 8504 2558
e-mail: M106040@cs.com

ISBN 1 901764 12 5

Printed in England by the St Edmundsbury Press

CONTENTS

ACKNOWLEDGEMENTS

The editors gratefully acknowledge the generosity and support of the following who helped make this publication possible: Sheikh Nasser Sabah al-Ahmed al-Sabah, Kuwait, The Altajir World of Islam Trust, Bonhams & Brooks, Christie's, The Iran Heritage Foundation, Dr Nasser D Khalili, the Council of The Society for South Asian Studies (The British Academy), whom Ralph Pinder-Wilson has supported and worked with since its inception, and several anonymous donors.

We would also like to thank the help of the following in the preparation of this work: Wendy Ball, Manijeh Bayani, Josephine Bayliss, Antony Bream, Deborah Freeman, Rachel Maxwell-Hyslop, Venetia Porter and Wak Kani.

NOTE ON SPELLING

The papers in this volume are by scholars from a wide range of disciplines. To avoid a lengthy debate about the merits of varying systems of transliteration and the spelling of foreign words and terms, the spellings of such terms and the use of any transliterated characters have been left as presented by the contributors.

SUBJECT CONCORDANCE

A. REGIONS

B. CHRONOLOGICAL

C. SUBJECTS

Ralph Pinder-Wilson

Charcoal drawing byAntony Bream

RALPH PINDER-WILSON
An Appreciation

A fascination with Persian art led me as a rather raw high school student in the 1960s to purchase *Persian Painting of the Fifteenth Century* by a certain Ralph Pinder-Wilson. The paintings, together with Ralph's wide-ranging introduction and commentary, appeared at that time very remote, evoking both an exotic civilisation and a world of scholarship that seemed very distant from a provincial Australian high school. It certainly helped stimulate a life-long interest in all things Iranian and oriental.

But it also meant a certain amount of trepidation when, some ten years later, I arrived in the British Institute of Afghan Studies in the summer of 1977 armed with little more than a grant, a Landrover and a wish to carry out field work in Afghanistan. Having someone of Ralph's calibre and reputation at the Institute (where he became Director in 1976) made an immense difference, not only to the Institute but to odd strays such as myself who passed through, as he helped to guide and focus my interests and energies. Always having time and patience for many a young researcher in Kabul, Ralph's academic stature, his phenomenal knowledge—together with his kind and approachable nature—was a constant source of encouragement and inspiration.

Indeed, the Pinder-Wilson years in Kabul are amply reflected in this work in papers by Finbarr Flood, Jonathan Lee, David Mac Dowall (at that time Hon Secretary of the Institute) and Willem Vogelsang, as well as myself. These years are certainly warmly remembered by all who passed through. All received a warm welcome and were treated with equal courtesy, whether it was the Institute cook or a visiting ambassador. Many doubtless recall the image of Ralph of a morning hurrying across the compound, white rabbit like, muttering 'I'm late, I'm late' in a manner that disguised the very effective and efficient organisation that went into managing the Institute's affairs over several difficult years in what is still one of the most difficult countries in the world. Hence, a major campaign of preservation work was carried out at the Buddhist stupa at Guldara and three seasons of excavations (directed by Svend Helms) at Kandahar were successfully completed. In addition, numerous other smaller-scale research projects, field-work and expeditions were all only made possible by the often very complex bureaucratic negotiations and logistic arrangements that Ralph managed, being as he was equally adept in Afghan ministries, the Kabul bazaar, the Embassy, and the ever-watchful Council back home. Rachel Maxwell-Hyslop, one of the many who came through Kabul at that time, recalls how 'in 1978 [when] I was working in the Kabul Museum ... an expedition to Bamiyan and Balkh was organised by Ralph. [The group included Peter Fraser, John and Sheila Boardman, Lionel Sackville and Bill Maxwell-Hyslop]. Ralph organised everything with great efficiency and we all profited from his detailed knowledge of Buddhist art and architecture and Afghan archaeology and history. I have stayed and worked in all the British Schools of Archaeology—Athens, Rome, Ankara, Amman, Jerusalem, Baghdad and Tehran and Kabul. The memories of the latter are outstanding. Ralph had an extremely difficult job largely due to the political situation, but he triumphed over every difficulty with extraordinary courage and consideration for everyone. The fact that British scholars were able to work and travel in Afghanistan up to the time of the Russian invasion was largely due to Ralph.'

Whilst Ralph made the Kabul Institute the beginning a number of people's academic careers, it formed but one later chapter of his own, and his academic background was far broader, started long before and continued long after. His academic career did not end when he left the Kabul Institute at the time of its closure in 1982 following the Soviet invasion—far from it, for he is still active today, in his ninth decade, with two major works being published this year 'Ghaznavid and Ghurid Minarets' in *Iran* and (with George Scanlon) *Fustat Glass of the Early Islamic Period.*

Ralph once mentioned in Kabul his desire to 'retire' after Afghanistan to the Deccan in India and study little known gems of Sultanate architecture. In the end this did not eventuate, instead he 'retired' to a number of active research and consultancy positions studying major Islamic collections in Britain and the Gulf. This interest is reflected in studies of manuscripts and collections in this volume by John Carswell, Anna Contadini, Yolande Crowe, Ernst J Grube, Jens Kröger, David Matthews, Annemarie Schimmel, Avinoam Shalem, Eleanor Sims and Rachel Ward. But India has remained a constant life-long interest ever since he joined the Indian Army at the beginning of his career. Hence it is particularly gratifying to find this reflected in a number of papers relating to India in this volume by Barbara Brend, David Fleming, Finbarr Flood, David Matthews, and Mehrdad and Natalie Shokoohy.

India was a first and perennial interest, but it also marked the beginning of another life-long interest: Iran. Ralph once recalled that he joined the Indian Army in order learn Persian (at the same time continuing a family tradition: his grandfather was a captain in the East India Company Navy). Consequently, it was in Persian studies that he made his mark, and the contributions relating to Iran from Patricia Baker, David Fleming, Jennifer Scarce and Avinoam Shalem in this volume are a tribute to this. Ralph is not only a recognised major authority on Persian painting, but for many years was an active Council member of the British Institute of Persian Studies, being instrumental in, amongst other things, instigating the Institute's excavations at Siraf. The director of Siraf, David Whitehouse, recalls that as a member of the team in the first season, between October and December 1966 when the other members of the team were very young and totally unfamiliar with the ways of Iran, Ralph in his quiet way somehow managed to keep everyone more or less on track. He was indispensable in many ways: he spoke Persian (and was, therefore, the liaison with the quartet of experienced workmen borrowed from Persepolis, one of whom treasured a letter of recommendation from Herzfeld!), he was well acquainted with the more presentable of our finds, and he was never heard to complain about the very basic living conditions. The team lodged, of course, in the guest quarters of the shaikh's fort, a ramshackle building that dated from the early years of the 20th century. Ralph's Siraf days are acknowledged in this volume by contributions from three former members: Warwick Ball, Jennifer Scarce, who describes the stucco panels in this fort, and of course David Whitehouse himself.

He also brought Middle Eastern excavation experience to Siraf extending back very many years, having previously participated in the excavations at the Fatimid site of Fustat in Egypt and the Umayyad (and earlier) site of Harran in southern Turkey. His contribution to Fustat, Fatimid studies and the Islamic glassware that came out of it was significant: it is gratifying to note that his and George Scanlon's *Fustat Glass of the Early Islamic Period* appears at the same time as this volume, and the present volume also includes further Fatimid studies by Edmond de Unger, Ernst J Grube, George Scanlon and Rachel Ward, as well as glass studies by Patricia Baker, Stefano Carboni and David Whitehouse.

Ralph's earlier work on the Harran dig near the beginning of his career in 1959 was fondly remembered by another doyen of Near Eastern archaeology, Robert Hamilton, in his book *Letters from the Middle East by An Occasional Archaeologist:* 'Ralph Pinder-Wilson is the nicest person imaginable, who carries kind-heartedness almost to the point of caricature. ... Ralph and Donald have established a kind of Marx Brothers partnership, designed to get a laugh out of most of the operations that constitute our existence—including such tiresome processes as classifying pottery, cleaning coins and ordering the meals. They keep up a duet of idiotic burlesques on scientific or archaeological or any other kind of jargon, and manage to be very funny. Ralph especially proves to have the subtlest and slyest humour, speaking always with his very gentle diffident voice, and saying things which sound perfectly serious and thoughtful until you realize that they are preposterously absurd, and extraordinarily funny.'

At the time of the Harran excavations Ralph had by that time been a member of the Oriental Department of the British Museum since 1948. He joined the Museum immediately after serving in the Indian Army and graduating from Christ Church, Oxford, where he had studied Persian and Arabic. Ralph worked at the Museum until his appointment as Director in Kabul in 1976—joining at the time of the Indian Exhibition of 1947-48 and leaving just after the time of the Paintings from the Muslim Courts of India Exhibition in 1976. It was a heyday for the Oriental Department, with people such as Douglas Barratt, Basil Gray, William Watson and others forming a part of it. Rachel Ward, for example, recalls that very soon after he joined, 'In 1948 in an interdepartmental exhibition held in Gallery 33 (now the Hotung Gallery) Ralph included a Mughal jade dish encrusted with gems which had been given to the museum just before the war by Percy Thomas Brooke Sewell, an Englishman living abroad. It so happened that Brooke Sewell visited the exhibition during a visit to London in 1948 and was thrilled to see his dish on display. He went to see the Keeper of the Department, Basil Gray, and from then on became a generous supporter of the Department helping make purchases during his lifetime and leaving a fund and bequest on his death in 1958. The Bequest continues to fund the majority of the purchases of the department.'

Ralph's characteristic generosity and attention to younger members of the profession is also fondly remembered from these years. Josephine Bayliss (née

Lonergan), for example, recalls 'from 1957-1960 I was employed as a museum assistant in the Department of Oriental Antiquities at the British Museum. On my first day when I went to work in the Department, I was taken downstairs to be shown around. The first person I was introduced to was Mr Pinder-Wilson, a neat, quietly spoken man with a black curl hanging down over his forehead. During my time at the Museum I was quite often on duty at the same time with Ralph and often accompanied him to the galleries ... he would show me cards written in Persian, Arabic and Turkish ... He was modest but at the same time totally knowledgeable at many levels. .. I particularly remember a visitor who came into the Museum—I think he was Hungarian and spoke no English. He and Ralph managed to communicate in Latin. I left the Museum in 1960, but Ralph had inspired me during my time at the Museum a lasting interest and desire to learn Persian, and eventually in 1984 I enrolled at SOAS when I met him again. Ralph was always so kind to me when I was young, asking about my family and always taking an interest in me. I will always be grateful to him for his inspiration, which enabled me to enter the golden world of Persian literature.'

As well as taking time off from museum duties to excavate at Harran, Fustat and Siraf, Ralph had a fellowship at All Souls Oxford for a year (1967-8). Robert Hillenbrand recalls that whilst 'he was awarded the Fellowship to enable him to work further on Islamic glass, typically he found time to help someone in a totally different field, namely me. I was just beginning my postgraduate work on Islamic art and when my supervisor (Dr Samuel Stern, a friend of his at All Souls) introduced us he readily consented to exercise a watching brief on my studies for a Diploma in Islamic Art (the first ever offered at Oxford). This involved him moving out of his comfort zone to read a pretty turgid piece on the tomb towers of Mazandaran. Eventually, when the time came for me to submit my DPhil on medieval Iranian tomb towers in 1974, he agreed to examine it, even though this involved him struggling gamely out of hours at the BM with details of rising joints, horizontal joints and brick-end plugs. His encouragement, modestly given, was crucial to me at the beginning of my career. I know he gave similar support unstintingly to others.'

The genesis of this book was a conversation in 2000 with the publisher Leonard Harrow, when both of us agreed that it is high time that a scholar such as Ralph had some form of concrete recognition. This book is, of course, an acknowledgement of a scholar, a mentor and friend. Even more than that it is in appreciation of 'the nicest person imaginable', someone who would always give his time and knowledge unstintingly to others. The variety and breadth of papers in this volume is a reflection, therefore, not only of the scholars concerned. It is a reflection of the interests, scope and scholarly activities of Ralph Pinder-Wilson himself—and a remarkable affirmation of the scholarship he has stimulated over more than fifty years. Even more remarkable than the number of papers represented is the enthusiasm and sheer speed of the response that was elicited (leaving the editor and publisher reeling!): nine months since inception to proof stage, a resounding tribute indeed to Ralph's personality. The same as the gestation of a baby, as Eleanor Sims so appropriately put it. So, we present the result to the deserving parent—but, like Athena, fully grown: the years of labour, upbringing and instruction, the imparting of love, good humour, knowledge, experience and wisdom generally have already been carried out.

Warwick Ball,
September 2001

1 A MIRROR ON THE SOUL PERSIAN ARCHITECTURAL GLASS

Patricia L Baker

Visitors to the 1878 Paris universal exposition were in no doubt. The Persian pavilion was remarkable, perhaps not so much for the artefacts displayed within it but for the architectural decoration of the building itself. This was the third international exhibition where the participating countries could if so desired erect an 'authentic' structure which would speak to the public of the civilisation, art, architecture of the exhibiting country.[1] However, the responsibility of designing the exhibition building to demonstrate this 'authenticity' did not necessarily lie with the exhibitor, and the Persian pavilion like those of Egypt and the Ottoman section were the brainchild of the French architect Jacques Drévet.[2] The exterior of the building itself, a strange ecletic mixture inspired by the 17th century *talar* of Ali Qapu, Isfahan, and a 19th century Shirazi mansion on the lines of the Bagh-i Iram or the Naranjistan, was not the subject of much critical praise. That was reserved for its main hall, the Hall of Mirrors. The exhibition catalogue itself drew the visitor's attention to the interior decoration which

> semblait un immense diamant; des effets de lumière absolument inconnus en Europe jaillissaient du million de morceaux de glace formant les stalactites du plafond[3]

And Charles Blanc[4] described the reaction of visitors:

> Tous les visiteurs de l'Exposition universelle, c'est-à-dire environ dix millions d'hommes, ont vu ou verront ce petit palais de chah, qu'on pourrait appeler le pavillon des Miroirs, comme on l'appelle en Perse. La voûte en stalactites qui recouvre la chambre est revêtue de petites glaces sur ses innombrables facettes. Onze cent mille morceaux de verre étamé ont été mis en oeuvre dans l'ornementation de cette voûte et sur les parois. La couleur des tapis se réfléchissant dans les surfaces prismatiques de la coupole, le mobilier couvert de châles produissant, sur ces myriades des verres, des effets irisés, les lambris divisés en petits damiers, dont les cases, mesurant deux centimètres carrés sont taillées en pointes de diamant pour mieux scintiller, les croisées à vitraux de couleur, doublées d'un châssis à coulisses, également coloré, enfin les rayons qui tombent du sommet de la coupole en se heurtant à des boules rouges ... tout cela forme une luminière sans ombre, une coloration sans merci, un miroitement sans repos, un éblouissement sans pareil.[5]

News of the spectacle spread far and wide and it lived in people's memory for years as is shown by S G W Benjamin's noting in his description, some nine years later, of the audience hall in the Gulistan Palace, Tehran, and a room of the then Minister of Justice completed before 1882, so that readers could envisage exactly the type of decorative embellishment:

> The Persian department at the last Paris Exposition was embellished with a room ornamented with this sort of mirror-work.[6]

---

[1] The first international exhibition to include this facility was that of Paris in 1867, followed by that in Vienna in 1873.

[2] He had been responsible for the design of the 'Persian section' at the 1867 Exposition Universelle, Paris, which consisted of a small pavilion, a replica of a house and an opium factory; Zeynep Celik, *Displaying the Orient: Architecture of Islam at 19th century World's Fairs*, University of California Press, 1992, 53. The Persian display at Vienna in 1873 was shown within a two-storeyed building loosely based in the Safavid style but with an emphatic exterior rather than an 'traditional' emphasis around the courtyard (e.g. at Nain, north-east of Isfahan).

[3] 'Le Livre Chaix (guide de visiteur a l'exposition universalle de 1878)' p. 98, quoted in *Le Livre des expositions universalles 1851-1989* (sic), Paris, 1983, 291.

[4] Writing in *L'Art and l'Industrie de tous les peoples à l'exposition universelle de 1878*, Librairie illustrée, Paris, *c.* 1878.

[5] *Ibid.*, pp. 67-8; this sentiment was echoed by L Simonin 'Sections Etrangères' within the same publication, 486.

[6] S G W Benjamin, *Persia and the Persians*, John Murray, London, 1887, 280.

This decoration was of course *a'inah kari*, small pieces of mirrored glass cut to the required shape by a diamond cutter and/or clippers[7] and then embedded in plaster:

> One of the most beautiful arts of Persia, of comparative recent origin it is true, is the form of *gatch pourée* called *ainâh karree*. The gatch [plaster] ceiling and wall are moulded into the most intricate forms with daring confidence. While the plaster is yet soft, the surfaces, or facets, are inlaid with an incrustation of minute mirrors of every form and often of a very small size. The amount of toil, patience, and skill requisite to inlay a large apartment in this magnificent style is almost incalculable. It is needless to add that the effect is one of bewildering splendor, as if the light were flashed from the polished facets of millions of gems ...[8]

Isabella Bird was just as complimentary wondering why millionaires in the west did not decorate their residences in the technique adding:

> My impression is that this exquisite design was taken from snow on the hillside, which is often fashioned by a strong wind into the honeycomb pattern.[9]

In one respect Benjamin was inaccurate: his comment that the technique was 'of comparative recent origin'. Centuries before Western travellers to Iran had recorded a growing passion for mirrored glass in court circles. Thomas Herbert described a royal Safavid palace at Farahabad, near the Caspian, in 1628 as having windows of Moscovite glass and walls 'adorned with looking glasses, which irradiated the ceiling or roof arched and richly painted'[10] and less than ten years later Adam Olearius was received at the Isfahan court in a room decorated with numerous pictures,

> clothed in a variety of ways, and all in the European style; and below them was nothing but mirrors, large as well as small; so that when one was in the middle of the room, one saw oneself reflected on all sides. They told us that in the Shah's Palace, and the apartments of his women, there was also a mirror-room, but larger and more beautiful than this one.[11]

Bishop Barnabas was similarly struck when he was received in 1721 by Shah Sultan Husain in a pavilion (probably Chihil Sutun, pl. 1.1) in Isfahan with

> a very large open porch, handsomer and more majestic than that of S. Peter's, though not as big. It is completely full of large and small mirrors, marvellously interlaced, and some pictures with fine frames. There are in it 24 columns, the shafts of which must be of wood, but externally are altogether covered with small pieces of looking-glass like the whole porch ...[12]

We know that at least two Safavid court artists had been involved in designing such mirror surfaces for Dust Muhammad, in his 1544 account of past and contemporary court painters, noted that Aqa Jalal al-Din Miraq al-Hasani of Isfahan (fl. 1530-40), and also Mir Musawwir (fl. 1520s),

> adorned an arched *jam-khana* [mirror-house] for Prince Bahram in the most exquisite and masterly manner, making it beautiful as paradise peopled with fair youths and huris.[13]

As Thomas Herbert had already noted this glass was not made in Iran itself for as Jean Chardin noted:

> They [Iranian glassmakers especially Shirazi] have no knowledge of silvering glass, as I have observed; as a result, their glass mirrors are imported from Venice ...[14]

---

7 Seen by the author used by restorers working on the house of Nasir al-Mulk, in Shiraz, autumn 1997.

8 Benjamin *op. cit.*, 279.

9 Isabella Bird, *Journeys in Persia and Kurdistan*, London, 1891, Virago repr. 1988, vol. I, 208 (the subsequent wording follows Benjamin's text, as given above, very closely).

10 Thomas Herbert, *Travels in Persia 1627-9*, ed. William Foster, Broadway Travellers ed., London, 1928, 175.

11 *Voyages ... faits en Moscovie, Tartarie et Perse*, trans. Wicquefort, Charles de Cene ed., Paris, 1727, cols. 740-2.

12 H[enry] C[hick], *A Chronicle of the Carmelites in Persia*, Eyre and Spottiswoode, 1939, vol. I, 557.

13 L Binyon, JV S Wilkinson and B Gray *Persian Miniature Painting*, OUP, London, 1933, 186; grateful thanks to Barbara Brend for drawing my attention to this reference.

14 John Chardin, (Jean Louis de Lorme ed., Amsterdam, 1711, vol. II,

and suggested that metal mirrors were preferred in Iran was because the climate badly affected the mirror silvering.[15] Such imports of mirrors had been noted by other travellers. Richard Hakluyt acting for the English East India Company recommended that 'Looking glasses for women, great and faire ...' as well as English and Venetian drinking glasses found a ready market throughout the Middle East in the late 16th century,[16] a fact not ignored by Venetian merchants, who supplied the Shah directly with 'large crystal mirrors which are unblemished and unbroken; mirrors of middling and small size ...'[17]

The technique of silvering glass was not simple, and the use of mercury in the process made it extremely toxic. After the glass was cast on to flat metal tables[18] and annealed, the sheets were placed on to marble and their surfaces ground a number of times with increasingly fine 'grit' and then polished on a padded bed. Visiting a glassworks in Paris in 1775, Samuel Johnson was totally intrigued especially with the silvering process:

> To silver them, a leaf of beaten tin is laid, and rubbed with quicksilver, to which it unites. Then more quicksilver is poured upon it, which by its mutual [attraction] rises very high. Then a paper is laid at the nearest end of the plate, over which the glass is slided [to minimise air bubbles] till it lies upon the plate, having driven much of the quicksilver before it. It is then, I think, pressed upon the cloth [i.e. weights put on for 24 hours], and then set sloping to drop the superfluous mercury: the slope [of the glass] is daily heightened towards the perpendicular.[19]

It is not precisely known when this mercury method was first employed in Europe but a Murano workshop, Italy, was awarded an exclusive production licence in 1507 for twenty years. Early medieval mirrors used a far simple method of inserting a thin lead sheet behind the glass and frame to provide a reflective surface,[20] or introducing mercury into a blown form, which was then broken so providing a number of small concave mirrors as used to decorate some surfaces in Chihil Sutun (pl. 1.1) and the Hasht Bihisht pavilions in Isfahan. It is unclear which method was used with some or all of the forty tiny plaster mirror-frames found in graves, often by the feet of the deceased, in a large Sasanid necropolis, south of Kufa[21] but lead sheet was definitely used in a small glass mirror held in a limestone frame found in Syria.[22]

Pl. 1.1 Detail of the 17th century mirror-glass surface of the Chihil Sutun talar, *Isfahan (author)*

85; Chardin also noted that the main glass-making centre was in Shiraz, and that Isfahani glass-makers used cullet (broken glass, recycled) as batch.

[15] *Ibid.*, 83.

[16] Richard Hakluyt, *Principal Navigations ...*, Hakluyt Society, London, 1903, vol. III, 270, writing *c.* 1580. This reference to English exports related only to drinking glasses at this time; the main mirror manufacturers at this time were France and the Low Countries. There is no reference to silvering being undertaken in England before 1615, when a Flemish worker was training apprentices in the technique in Southwark, London, and by 1624 perhaps less than 100 plate-blowers, grinders and polishers, 'foylers' and finishers (including their families, 500 total) were in the trade: Eleanor S Godfrey, *The Development of English Glassmaking, 1560-1640*, OUP, 1975, 235-41.

[17] Guglielmo Berchet, *La Republicca di Venezia e la Persia*, Tehran, first ed. 1865, repr. 1976, 64, relating to an order of 1598.

[18] Increasingly during the 18th century the casting technique was employed as much large sizes of uniform thickness of flat-glass could be obtained than from cutting panes from 'crown glass' (spinning the 'open' glass gather) and from 'broad glass' (splitting and flattening blown cylinder forms). (The modern 'float-glass' process was invented in the 1950s by Pilkington Brothers, St Helens, UK.)

[19] James Boswell, *The Life of Samuel Johnson*, Everyman ed., London, 1928, vol. I, 581 (relating to 23 October 1775); see also Jean Haudicquer de Blancourt, *The Art of Glass* (London, 1699) ed. 'Miroirs'. The grinding and polishing processes, and the equipment used are illustrated in D Diderot and J d'Alembert, *Receuil de planches sur les sciences, les arts libreraux et les arts mechaniques*, Paris, 1771, vol. VIII 'Miroitier' pl. I-VI, which accompanied the *Encyclopedie*.

[20] Bruno Schweig, 'Mirrors' *Antiquity*, vol. XV (Sept. 1951), 265-7.

[21] A-M al-Haditti, 'Umm Keshm: a summary report' *Mesopotamia* 30 (1993), 217-40, esp. 228, fig. 29.

[22] W C Braat, 'Two Near Eastern Glasses recently acquired by the Rijksmuseum van Oudheden at Leiden' *Journal of Glass Studies* vol. 8 (1966), 62-3, classified as probably late Roman or Byzantine in date; see also Selim Abdul Hak, 'Contribution d'une découverte archéologique récente a l'étude de la verrerie syrienne à l'époque romaine' *Journal of Glass Studies* vol. 7 (1965), 26-34, noting (but no

By 1850s another technique invented by Justus von Liebig (d. 1873) was increasingly being used in Europe. Marginally less toxic for workers, both methods of applying the silver nitrate (combined with aldehyde and ammonia with heat; or with sugar, nitric acid in the cold method) required detailed attention and application for a successful outcome.[23] The film was laid on the back of the glass and then a copper backing layer applied.

Whatever method was used, the finished product was still expensive in the 19th century. Looking-glasses, as mirrors were called, featured importantly in diplomatic gifts to the Qajar court. In 1817 Russian Czarist gifts to the shah included a tray of cut glass over a metre in length, several *qaliyans* (glass *nargilahs*) and a mirror almost 3 metres tall which immensely pleased the shah 'These mirrors ... are dearer to me than all my own treasures' for as the commentator noted

> 'Glass has, in the estimation of this people [the Persians], a particular value; and, as they never have than opportunity of seeing any other articles of glass than their caleoons, they certainly must have been struck with delight by the sight of a splendid service of crystal, glittering with the brilliancy of diamonds.[24]

And Sir John Malcolm, English envoy, had to supervise the transport of 'gigantic' mirrors from Bushehr to Tehran via Shiraz at the shah's behest. The load entailed the help of over 1,200 men and an outrageous sum of £4,000 in local taxes.[25] Similar gifts of mirrors, a crystal-glass basin and fountain, and a bed frame with glass elements were made by the Russian ambassador in 1820 and 1826.[26] By 1866 the British consul in Tabriz notified Whitehall that over one-fifth of all Russian imports into Iran was glass, and that Bohemian glass formed one-tenth of all European imports into the country.[27]

Obviously, the passion in court circles for mirrored-glass was partly linked to its scarcity and novelty value but perhaps there were other factors. As in Renaissance Europe, for example Italy and the Low Countries, the customer demand for looking-glasses seemed to parallel or compliment an increased awareness in the outward appearance of the individual, the wish of the patron to record his/her likeness for posterity,[28] and there was a similar development in Mughal India with the art of portraiture.[29]

The first known *cabinet de glaces* was commissioned by Catherine de Medici in 1599 which pre-dates by a mere twenty-eight years, the room seen by Thomas Herbert in 1628 mentioned above. The fashion then was introduced into France in the mid-17th century with the famous Galerie de Glaces being installed at Versailles 1678-84. And surely it is this royal connection that largely accounts for its employment in other royal palaces and pavilions throughout Europe,[30] the Middle East and also Northern India. From numerous eye-witness descriptions we know that the first visual impact of Qajar majesty striking foreigners was carefully orchestrated; the Qajar shah and his court staged a spectacle in which brilliance and dazzlement were all important.[31]

---

precise details) two plaster and glass mirrors found near Homs (fig. 21) thought to date from 2nd or 3rd century AD. Finbarr B Flood, 'Light in Stone', *Bayt al-Maqdis: Jerusalem and early Islam*, ed. Jeremy Johns, *Oxford Studies in Islamic Art*, no. IX (ii) (1999), p. 325 notes that the majority of similar glass mirrors found on Palestinian sites, are conventionally dated to 4-5th centuries AD.

23 Encyclopaedia Britannica (15th ed.) 'Mirror'; apart from mercuric poisoning, workers were in danger of explosions as concentrated silver nitrate is used in detonators.

24 T Clark, *A Tour of Asia*, J Souter, London, *c*. 1820, 240-1.

25 The purchase price of the Ardabil carpet, to the Victoria and Albert Museum, London (then South Kensington Museum) at the end of the century was £2500, today's equivalent in excess of £250,000. J W Kaye, *The Life and Correspondence of MG Sir John Malcolm* (Smith, Elder and Co., London 1856) vol. I, pp. 125ff. On 26 May 1810 Sir Gore Ouseley took the Persian ambassador, Mirza Abu'l Hassan Khan, to a mirror factory in London, commenting to the chairman of the East India Company two days later 'I have just found out that the King of Persia is immoderately fond of large mirrors' and that following the visit 'it will be expected that two pair, of the largest dimensions ever seen in the East, should be sent to him': trans. M Morris Cloake, *A Persian at the Court of King George, 1809-1810*, Barrie and Jenkins, London, 1988, p. 243; see also 38-9, 54 for the ambassador's comments on room mirrors and crystal chandeliers in London houses.

26 Herbert Busse, *History of Persia under Qajar Rule (Hasan-e Fasa'i's Farsnama-ye Naseri)*, NY, London, 1972, 161, 175.

27 Abbas Amanat, ed., *Cities and Trade: Consul Abbott on the Economy and Society of Iran, 1847-66*, Ithaca, London, 1983, 246-7.

28 Peter Burke, *Culture and Society in Renaissance Italy, 1420-1540*, Batsford, London, 1972, 190-1.

29 William Finch recorded seeing a (Venetian) mirror glass at the Lahore palace of Jahangir in 1608, and six years later the English East India Company paid for a Robert Young to be taught the 'skill of foyling looking glasses'; he was then sent to Surat to teach the method(s) there; A J Qaisar, *Indian Response to European Technology and Culture*, Oxford University Press, Delhi, 1982, 72-4. By the beginning of the 18th century Mughal palaces were 'ornamented with large mirrors and seem to be made all of crystal': Niccolao Manucci, *Mogul India* ed. William Irvine, repr. DK Publishing, Delhi, 1996, vol. II, 435.

30 E.g. Stockholm, Schönbrunn, Hetzendorf (near Vienna), Charlottenburg, Stuttgart etc.; Serge Roche *et al.*, *Mirrors*, Wasmuth, Tübingen, 1985, 34.

31 For instance, see R Ker Porter, *Travels in Georgia, Persia, Armenia ...*, ed., London, 1821, vol. 1, 325-6.

But why then employ mirror-glass in the context of religious architecture? As visitors to Iran know, the use of architectural glass especially mirror-glass is virtually now synonymous with interior decoration of *imamzadahs* (pl. 1.2), and the temporary *hajlah* road-side stands commemorating the recent death of a young man. We know that the mirror-work in the shrine of Shah Chiragh Sayyid Mir Ahmad, Shiraz was the brain-child of the local governor Farhad Mirza before his recall to Tehran in 1840[32] and possibly as a young child, Abu 'l-Qasim of Shiraz, learnt the skills there which he then exploited several decades later on the *talar* decoration of the Divan-i Qavam (Naranjistan/Asia Institute) in 1302/1884. A year later, in 1885, mirror-glass was installed at the Shrine of Fatimah, Qum, by Hasan Mi^c^mar of Qum.[33] Was it simply a case of employing a painstaking and expensive technique to beautify and embellish the surroundings? Was it also the association with majesty, temporal and spiritual? Or were there aesthetic qualities to be invoked? William Ouseley, brother to the English envoy, Sir Gore Ouseley, drew his readers' attention to the mystical quality of such glass-work and reflected light in his description of rooms in the Qasr-i Qajar, Tehran:

> only serve to excite feelings of mysterious privacy, and might have deserved the Miltonick epithets of 'dim' and 'religious' had the edifice been appropriated to sacred uses.[34]

There is evidence suggesting that medieval European pilgrims carried glass mirrors to 'catch' the supernatural rays of blessing and sanctity emanating from Christian relics and if so, pilgrims to the Holy Land would have followed the practice spreading such ideas into the Middle East. However, mirrors in Islamic society were not always associated with positive beneficial qualities. The Ottoman Turkish poet, Me^c^ali (d. 1535-6) recalled that it was bad luck to look into a mirror after sunset,[35]

Pl. 1.2 Detail of the 19th century mirror glass decoration, Imamzadah Husain, Qazvin (author)

and in 19th century Iran Qazvini cabinet-makers were especially known for making mirror frames with doors:

> fulfilling a traditional need for the Moslems, not to look into a mirror before the morning ablutions. The mirror-doors (*dar-i a'inah*) were therefore made to be closed at night.[36]

Perhaps of more immediate relevance is the significance of the famous Quranic 'Nur' verse (s. 24: 35) in Shi^c^i Islam. In a recent article, Flood has shown that aside from the usual analogies and symbolism of lamp, oil, flame associated with this verse, many leading Shi^c^i Sufis, such as Sahl al-Tustari (d.896) and Tirmidhi (d. 898), stressed the idea that this was an allusion to the light of prophecy, passing from the Prophet Muhammad to his descendants:

> 'This idea had very particular resonance for the Shi^c^i, who developed the idea of *nur Muhammad* as a mark of legitimacy, passing from *imam* to *imam* along the ^c^Alid line ...[37]

There would seem to be in this a possible connection between such ideas and the use of mirror-glass in a religious architectural context. Aside from the increased availability of imported mirror-glass during Qajar times, it could help to explain why it became such a feature of Qajar religious decoration.

32 Herbert Busse, *op. cit.* Among Farhad Mirza's good works in Shiraz, Hasan Fasa'i listed 'Another landmark of his is the mirror mosaic in the shrine of Shah Cheragh Sayyid Mir Ahmad ...' (p. 273).

33 G D Pickett, The Efflorescence of Persian kashi ... (unpublished PhD thesis, London University 1980), Appendix 10. The mirror-glass decoration of the Persian pavilion at the 1873 Vienna Universal Exposition was the work of two Tehrani craftsmen, both called Hassan Ali, according to Hugh Willoughby Sweny: *Reports of the Vienna Universal Exposition 1873*, London, 1874, vol. III, 303.

34 William Ouseley, *Travels in the various Countries of the East ... 1810, 1811, 1812 ...*, London, 1823, vol. III, 362.

35 Edith Ambros, *Candid Penstrokes: the Lyrics of Me'ali*, K Schwarz, Berlin, 1982, 133.

36 Hans E Wulff, *The Traditional Crafts of Persia*, MIT Press, Cambridge Ma., 1966, 88.

37 Flood, *op. cit.*, 342-3.

Perhaps the answer lies in the relationship between the Qajar shah, Fath Ali Shah (r. 1797-1834) court and the famous Sufi master, Shaikh Ahmad Ahsa'i; the two were known to correspond with each other and the shaikh was received in personal audiences during 1808-9.[38] In an address to the shah, Shaikh Ahmad Ahsa'i (d.1826) discussed the resurrection of the Body and Spirit describing how, in his opinion, there were two bodies and two spirits. Employing the analogy of glass, he explained that glass was made of two dense opaque materials, silica and potash, which through heat were both merged and transformed in to a clear glass 'the interior is visible through the exterior, the exterior is visible through the interior' just as the spiritual body after death is homolously distinct from the physical 'corrupted' body. The glass 'is unquestionably the same mineral substance, and yet it is not. It is something other' and cannot be returned to its original ingredients. As for the Spirit, at death the spirit occupies an astral body until the first trumpet sound of the Day of Judgement; at that point it is transformed onto a celestial body to be resurrected. Thus, as with the application of greater heat (spiritual knowledge) 'the glass becomes very fine and brilliant ... If the Elixir of Whiteness (lead oxide?)[39] the philosopher's chemical 'be prepared onto this fine glass, it then becomes a crystal which flames in sunlight ... This incandescent glass is homologous to the astral body ... with which the Spirit enters the Western paradise, the Paradise of Adam, which in further fusion will be transformed into a diamond.'[40] Leaving aside the scientific vagaries, the analogy of glass, crystal, diamonds with their descriptive qualities of 'fineness', brilliance, reflective light, 'inner fire' used to convey ideas of purity, incorruptibility and a spiritual 'light' is intriguing. Could it be that such religious philosophy which found sympathetic listeners in royal circles in 19th century Iran lies behind the use of mirrored glass in religious architecture in Iran, especially *imamzadahs* so inexorably linked with the family of Muhammad and the first Imam? That besides an understandable wish to employ costly and visually attractive decorative techniques in public buildings, religious and secular, there were also implicit symbolic connotations?

[38] *Encyclopaedia Iranica*, 'Ahsa'i, Shaikh Ahmad ibn Zayn al-Din'. By this time the Qajar governor of Kirman was a devoted follower of the shaikh, who also stayed for over a year at the court of the governor of Kirmanshah and visited Qum, Yazd, Isfahan and Mashhad before his return to Kerbala and Mecca.

[39] The addition of a percentage (usually 20-24 percent) of lead oxide to the glass batch makes for a clear, colourless 'white' glass, called lead crystal.

[40] Henry Corbin, *Spiritual Body and Celestial Earth*, trans. Nancy Pearson, I B Tauris, London, 1990, 201; see also *Encyclopaedia Iranica, loc. cit.*

2 THE TOWERS OF GHUR. A GHURID 'MAGINOT LINE'?

Warwick Ball

It has been said that there is 'not a single cluster' of Ghurid buildings. Whilst it is true that there is certainly 'no Ghaznavid or Ghurid equivalent of Marv, Isfahan or Cairo',[1] the large clusters of towers in the remote mountainous Ghurid homeland merit more attention than they have hitherto received, particularly in view of one of the greatest 'towers' of the Islamic world, the Minaret of Jam.

The unusually large number of towers and other fortifications in Ghur attracted the attention in the 19th century of surveyors from the Afghan Boundary Commission and other travellers (fig. 2.1).[2] The work of the Afghan Boundary Commission in the 1880s in particular was the most thorough and comprehensive information-gathering exercise ever undertaken on Afghanistan. Their voluminous results to this day still form perhaps the most important single source for the topography, geography and antiquities of western Afghanistan generally, and still remain under-utilised.[3] Even the Minaret of Jam was reported in their records[4] long before its 'discovery' by Ahmad Ali Kohzad and André Maricq in the 1950s.[5]

The Boundary Commission officers also reported another possible Ghurid minaret and associated remains in Ghur, which remain uninvestigated. These are the ruins of Qalca-i Zarmurgh at Sakhar, southeast of Deh Titan, in the mountainous region to the south of the Shaharak-Adraskand road. News of it first reached the Afghan Boundary Commission in the 1880s, although none of the officers seemed to have actually visited the site. Sahibdad Khan mentions a baked brick minaret 30 metres high and Maitland reports from hearsay an 'ancient city' there. Subsequently, Kohzad reported a Ghurid palace that incorporates the minaret, although again he does not seem to have visited the place, but the existence of the minaret was confirmed on hearsay by Rafat and in the 1970s by an Afghan archaeologist, Zeymal Haidari (personal communication). Kohzad also mentioned another fort, suggestively known as Qal^{c}a-i Sultan, associated with Qal^{c}a-i Zarmurgh.[6]

---

1 Robert Hillenbrand, 'The Architecture of the Ghaznavids and Ghurids', in Carole Hillenbrand (ed.), *The Sultan's Turret: Studies in Honour of Clifford Edmund Bosworth, Volume 2: Studies in Persian and Turkish Culture*, Brill, Leiden, 2000, 124—although Lashkari Bazar, whilst no Isfahan or Cairo, surely surpasses Saljuq Marv in extant monuments.

2 For the Afghan Boundary Commission reports, see note 3, below. Other travellers included General Ferrier, *Caravan Journeys and Wanderings in Persia, Afghanistan, Turkistan, and Baluchistan*, London, 1857, although not all of his descriptions are entirely trustworthy—the meagre remains at Zarni, for example, he describes (p. 248) as 'ruin upon ruin'.

3 Possibly because the only complete original set in the world that I have been able to discover is in the National Library of India. The India Office Library and Records in the British Library, however, have been able to assemble a complete set by microfilming missing volumes. The bulk of the results were published as secret documents as *Records of the Intelligence Party, Afghan Boundary Commission* in 5 volumes between 1887 and 1891 by Maitland, Peacocke and Ridgeway (henceforth referred to as *ABC* I-V). Many of the Boundary Commission Officers further published their own accounts, and the works of Holdich, MacGregor, Tate, A C Yate and C E Yate still remain major source books on Afghanistan. The information from the Boundary Commissions was further incorporated into two more important series of publications: the 6 volume *Gazetteer of Afghanistan*, 1907-14 (updated and re-published as the 5 volume *Historical and Political Gazetteer of Afghanistan*, ed. Adamec, 1972-80), and the 7-volume, originally secret, *Routes in Afghanistan*, 1923-41 (henceforth referred to as *Routes*). There are, in addition, numerous volumes of papers, miscellaneous reports, letters, illustrations and other documents from the Boundary Commission in the India Office Library and Records that contain further valuable information not necessarily appearing in the published volumes (e.g., see note 4, below).

4 Thomas H Holdich, 'Geographical Results of the Afghan Boundary Commission', *India Office Political Dept. Memorandum 76*, 3, and 'Report on Survey Operations in Western and North-Western Afghanistan, in 1884, 1885, 1886, *India Office Political Dept. Memorandum* 77, 24.

5 First reported by Maricq in the *Illustrated London News*, Jan. 10, 56-8, and more fully in André Maricq and Gaston Wiet, *Le Minaret de Djam. La découverte de la capitale des sultans ghorides (XII-XIII siècles)*, MDAFA 16, Paris 1959, although it had also been reported earlier by Afghan archaeologists, e.g., Khalil Afghan, *A^{o}âr-i Hirât*, Kabul 1930, 118-9, and Ahmad Ali Kohzad, 'Along the Koh-i Baba and Hari Rud', *Afghanistan* 9, 2, 1954, 6 (which Maricq and Wiet do not acknowledge).

6 A full bibliography is given in Warwick Ball, *Archaeological Gazetteer of Afghanistan*, 2 vols., Paris, 1982, Sites 974 and 882 (henceforth cited as *Archaeological Gazetteer* followed by site nos.).

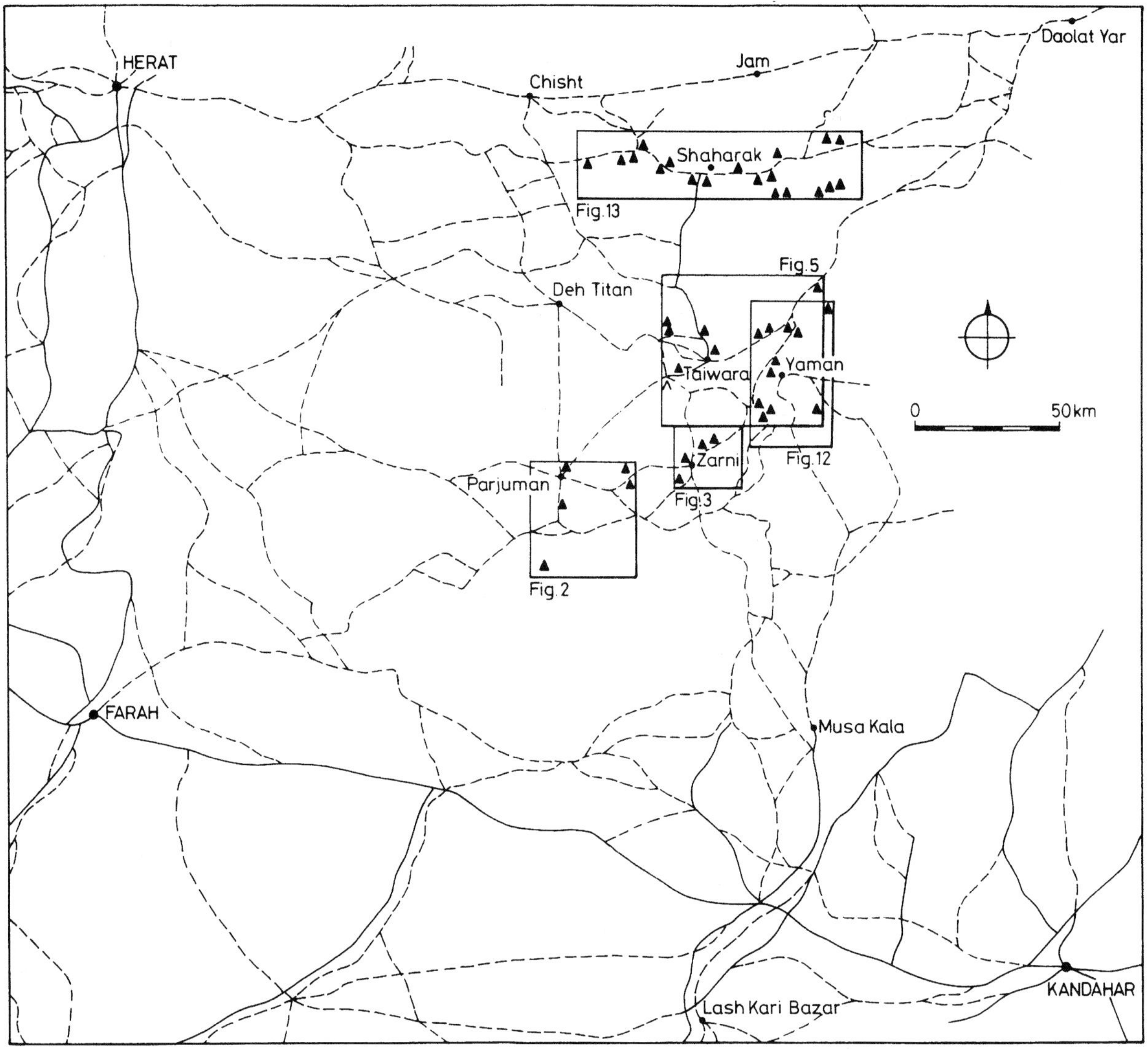

Fig. 2.1 Map of the routes through Ghur, with the fortifications marked ▲.

Pl. 2.1 Qalʿa-i Qaisar (photo: Josephine Powell)

Pl. 2.2 Qalʿa-i Qaisar (photo: Josephine Powell)

Pl. 2.3 Qal'a-i Qaisar (photo: Josephine Powell)

Pl. 2.4 Qal'a-i Qaisar (photo: Josephine Powell)

Pl. 2.5 Qal'a-i Qaisar. Note strategic position overlooking the route (photo: Josephine Powell)

Comparable systems of fortifications occur around the Bamiyan Valley. These offer the closest parallels to the Ghur fortifications, both historically and architecturally, and have been extensively studied.[7] But despite Ghur boasting one of the greatest monuments of the Islamic world, rumours of more, and the existence of large numbers of other towers and fortifications, many of them decorated, no systematic archaeological or architectural studies exist for Ghur. The only relatively extensive archaeological investigation carried out in the region was in the 1950s by Ahmad Ali Kohzad, although even this was nothing more than a reconnaissance that did not attempt to be either systematic or comprehensive.[8] It was with this in mind that fieldwork was undertaken by the present author in 1977 into Ghur, although in the end this too was not as thorough as the monuments deserve.[9] Nonetheless, the results, when combined with the results of the Afghan Boundary Commission surveys, form an important record of these monuments.[10]

The Fortifications

Larwand Region (fig. 2.2)

The Larwand Valley (also called Larband or Darband) is a long valley running exactly north-south, ringed by high mountains. It is well watered, with many rice fields next to the river. Wheat, melons, cucumbers and apples are also grown. In the summer many tents were scattered along the valley, but all belonged to local land-owning Farsiwans practising transhumance; they do not migrate out of the valley. The Larwand River is a tributary of the Farah, and enters from the Mushkan Valley (where it is called the Mushkan River) through a narrow gorge just to the east of the Larwand Pass (also called the Likhto Pass on the

7 Marc Le Berre, *Monuments Pré-islamiques de l'Hindukush Central*, MDAFA 24, Paris, 1987; P H B Baker and F R Allchin, *Shahr-i Zohak and the History of the Bamiyan Valley Afghanistan*, Oxford, 1991.

8 Kohzad, *op. cit.* in *Afghanistan* 6, 1; 6, 2; 7, 1; 8, 4; 9, 1; 9, 2 (1951-54).

9 Some of the results were published in the *Archaeological Gazetteer* and in Warwick Ball. 'Some Notes on the Masjid-i Sangi at Larwand, *South Asian Studies* 6, 1990, 105-10. The field records had an unfortunate history. The field notes lay inaccessible in the British Institute of Persian Studies in Tehran following the Revolution of 1979, and were only recovered in 1992. My entire black and white photographic records of Afghanistan—including those of this work—remained in Kabul following the premature closure of the British Institute in 1982, and have since remained beyond reach or lost. In recent years, however, some prints of these photographs have emerged from various sources. Whilst this hardly makes for an ideal report, it is the recovery of some at least of these records that makes this report possible, whatever the shortcomings.

10 I am also greatly indebted to Bruce Wannell's observations, published as 'Echoes in a Landscape—Western Afghanistan in 1989' in this volume, from his own journey through Ghur in 1989.

map). In the middle of the valley, at Dasht-i Qalᶜa, another river enters from a subsidiary valley to the west that leads to the Borak Pass. The river leaves the valley at the village of Malikan at the north end, leading through a gorge to the village of Parjuman (where it becomes the Parjuman River).

Dasht-i Qalᶜa [11] is the main village in the valley, situated on a high commanding spur overlooking the valley at the junction of two rivers, the Larwand and the Borak, from the southwest. The old quarter-inch *Survey of India* map marks several forts, no longer extant. According to local information it was the site of a large fortress, 'the capital of one of the Ghurid Sultans', that was completely destroyed by the Mongols. Below, on level ground by the river, there was supposedly a *chahârbâgh* built by Sultan Ghiyath ud-Din. Many coins have supposedly been found, and there is a monumental inscription brought from Qalᶜa-i Qaisar (see below).

The Masjid-i Sangi,[12] near the village of Malikan, is one of the most important monuments in Ghur and is well published. It is a 12th-13th century carved stone mosque in the style of northwestern India. According to Kohzad some more stone remains, a cave where coins have supposedly been found, and a scatter of baked bricks and sherds are found in and around Hisar Darra[13] up a side valley to the east of the Masjid-i Sangi. The baked bricks are on top of a mountain, so may have been a signalling tower similar to that overlooking Nili (see below).

To the south-east is the Mushkan Valley. Confusingly, the river is called the Mushkan, even though it is the same as the Larvand. To add to the confusion, the village is occasionally also called Parchuman, as the village and bazaar of Mushkan-i Pa'in is the administrative centre for the Parchuman Woleswali. It is a small but well watered and extensively terraced valley surrounded by spectacularly precipitous mountains, particularly to the east. Both wheat and rice is grown in the terraces. The people are mainly Farsiwan, but the village of Mushkan is about half Pashtu and Pashtu nomads migrate to the valley from the Dasht-i Sakwa. At the village of Sar-i Mushkan, Klimburg in 1958 recorded a possibly Ghurid wooden *mihrab* and pillars in the mosque of Abu Bakr.[14] Some 20km to the south on the road towards Gulistan and ultimately Farah, the map marks three areas of ruins.

The Larwand River leaves the valley to the north and enters the broader Parchuman Valley. At the village of Parchuman there is a large mosque that may be quite old.[15] From here main routes go southwestwards towards Farah and northeastwards towards Taiwara.

The road to Taiwara is dominated to the southeast by the massive fortress of Qalᶜa-i Qaisar, 'Caesar's Castle', 33km north-east of Parjuman where a minor pass crosses over to the Mushkan Valley.[16] This is one of the largest and most elaborate fortifications in Ghur, consisting of inner and outer defensive walls reinforced by circular and hexagonal towers (pls. 1-5), and is one of the very few to figure in history.[17] Construction is of mud on high stone footings. Buildings inside include a mosque, and walls are decorated with triangles impressed into the plaster to form the characteristic lozenge motif of Ghur (pl. 2.5). The fortress is said locally to have been begun by Sultan ᶜAla' ud-Din and completed by Sultan Ghiyath ud-Din. Two hours march to the south more ruins, fortifications and finds of gold coins are reported at Fakhrabad.[18] Nearby is a very small lake with some ruins known as Butgah ('place of the idol') in the middle.

The opposite, northwest side of the valley is guarded by the fortress of Qalᶜa-i Sangi on top of a hill, which once had an aqueduct fed cistern.[19]

Zarni Region (fig. 2.3)

Zarni Valley is fairly wide and surrounded on most sides by low ranges. The valley is very hilly and quite dry, but dotted with small villages surrounded by fields growing wheat and barley. The people are mainly Taimani, but Baluch and Pashtun nomads migrate here in the summer and there is said to be a small Mughal community. Ferrier, travelling through here in the 1850s, mentions 'ruin upon ruin', but both his descriptions and even the routes he took are notoriously unreliable. The only remains in Zarni itself are a ruined tower just to the north of the teahouse on the edge of a gully.[20] It is similar construction to Sang-i Mazar 5 (see below), with exterior impressed lozenge decoration.

[11] *Archaeological Gazetteer* 267.

[12] *Archaeological Gazetteer* 683; see also Ball 1990, *op. cit.*

[13] *Archaeological Gazetteer* 433.

[14] *Archaeological Gazetteer* 751.

[15] *Archaeological Gazetteer* 801.

[16] *Archaeological Gazetteer* 875; see also Wannell, *op. cit.*

[17] Juzjani came from Qaisar—or 'Khissar'—of Ghur on a diplomatic mission to Farah in 622 AH on behalf of the Maliks of Nimruz. See Juzjani, *Tabaqât-i Nâsirî*, transl. H G Raverty, 1888, 233 (henceforth cited as Juzjani).

[18] *Archaeological Gazetteer* 875.

[19] *Archaeological Gazetteer* 879; referred to in *Routes S-W*, 78, as Jam Qalᶜa.

[20] *Archaeological Gazetteer* 1257.

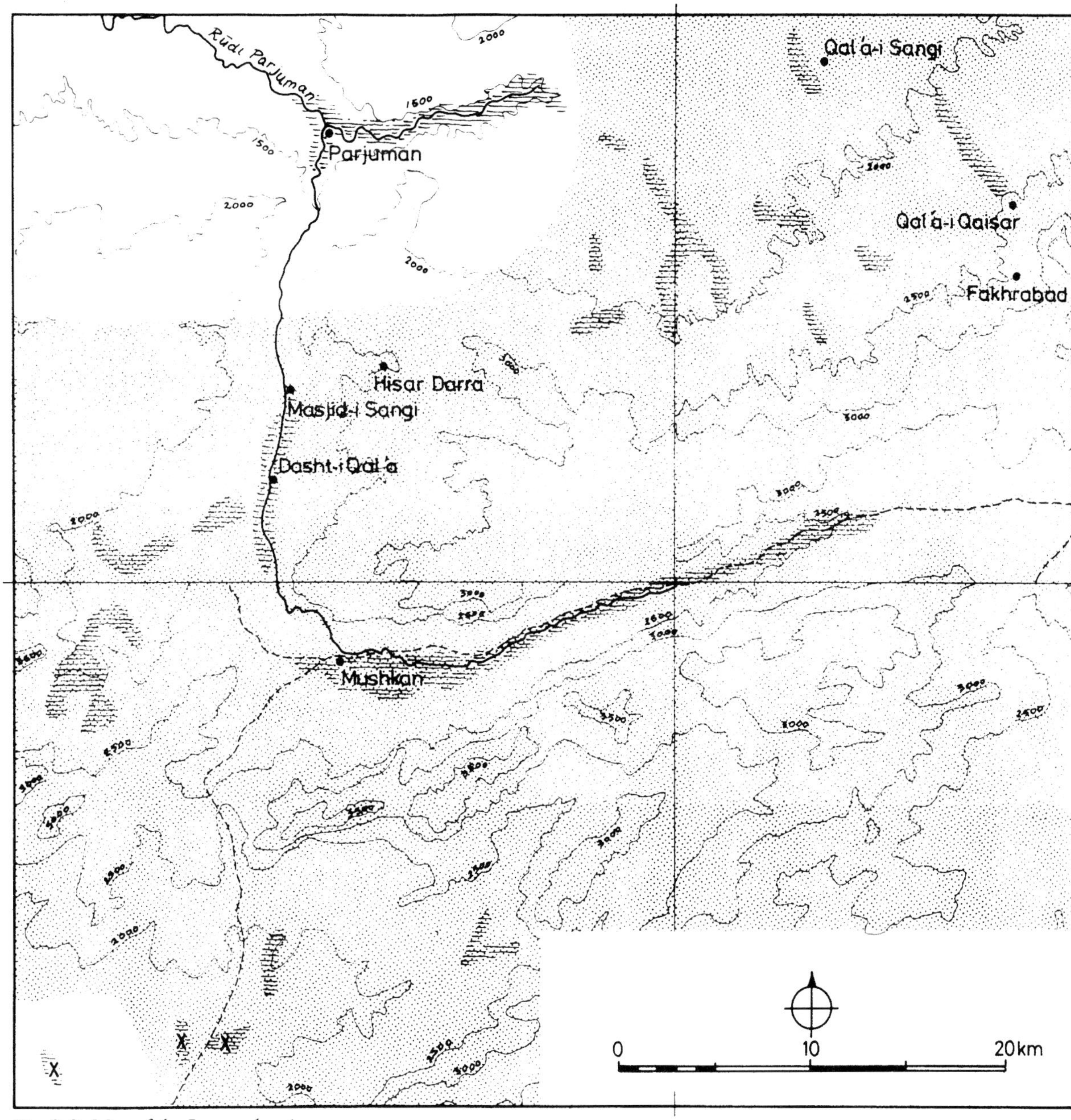

Fig. 2.2 Map of the Larwand region

KEY TO MAPS
- ▫ TOWN
- ■ FORT
- T TOWER
- X RUINS
- • SITES IN TEXT
- VALLEY FLOORS / PLAINS ETC

Pl. 2.6 Sang-i Mazar

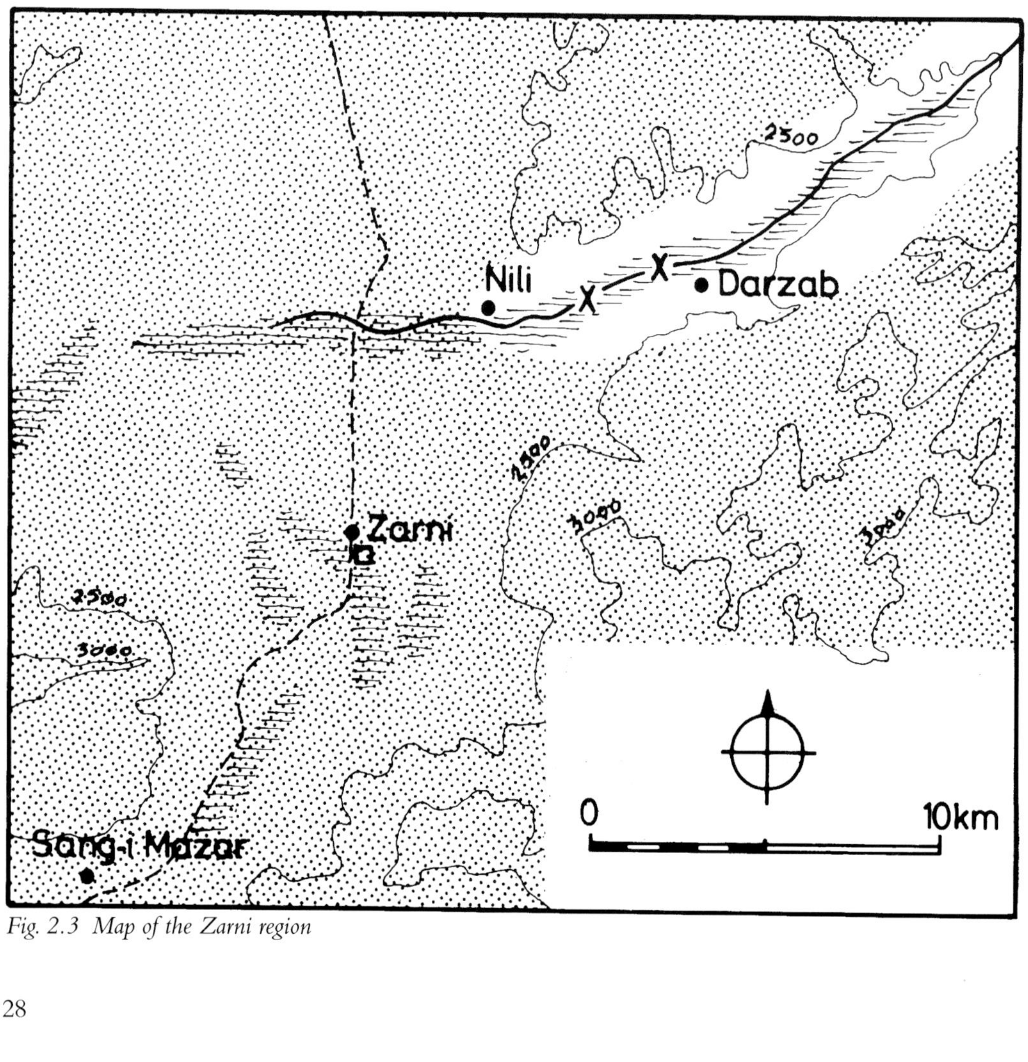

Fig. 2.3 Map of the Zarni region

Guarding the route between Zarni and Mushkan, 12km south of Zarni and 51km from Mushkan-i Pa'in, are a series of five towers at Sang-i Mazar (pl. 2.6).[21] The valley here runs northeast-southwest; the towers are on the hills on the northwest side, just above a stream. The small village of Sang-i Mazar is about 1.5km northeast of Tower 5. Tower 1 was possibly a fort situated on an escarpment above the stream. It is very ruined, now only a single line of very rough stone wall bonded with mud, up to 1.5m in height. Tower 2 (fig. 2.4) was originally a round tower, now consisting of a fragment of a round mud wall on a stone footing up to 3m in height, several hundred metres downstream from Tower 1. It is pierced by regular slits that are opened up inside by a series of semi-circular reveals to form elaborate and distinctive niches, decorated by square and lozenge-shaped impressions on either side (see elevation in fig. 2.4). Towers 3 and 4 are about 1.5km further northeast. Tower 3 consists of two parallel stumps of mud walls, probably originally forming a square tower. Tower 4 is a semi-circle of rough stone wall footings, originally forming a round tower. Some slight mud remains connecting the two suggest that they originally formed a small fort. Tower 5 is a few hundred metres from Tower 4. It is the most impressive and best preserved at Sang-i Mazar: a circular tower, only about half of it now still standing, well constructed of mud-bricks measuring 24 x 40 x 13cm, standing on a large stone footing 3.10m high. The total height of the tower is approximately 12.40m. The exterior is plastered with straw-tempered mud plaster *c.* 5cm thick, decorated with stamped wedges forming lozenge patterns. There are two windows measuring 24 x 52cm.

Verbal reports in Zarni and elsewhere in Ghur speak of the remains of an ancient 'city' in the Nili Valley to the northeast on the route leading to Yaman. Nili[22] refers to the entire valley rather than a specific village, roughly between 10 and 27km from Zarni towards Yaman. It is a rich, well watered and well cultivated valley with many hamlets (pl. 2.7) on a route between Zarni and Yaman. Population is mainly Taimani, with some Pashtun nomads. There is a large cemetery at the first village of Zalargak, 11km from Zarni, and many towers along the length of the valley, beginning at Sanglak and continuing up to the end at the northeast. The seat of the *wakil* is at the village of Mahalla, 23km from Zarni, where there is a *ziyarat* called Khwaja Baba surrounded by trees next to a spring that comes out of the side of the mountain. There are many towers and fortifications along the valley (pl. 2.7)—of which there used to be considerably more

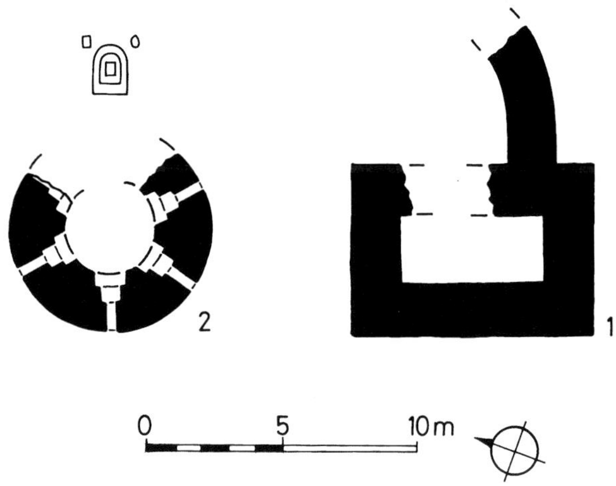

Fig. 2.4 Measured sketch plan of Nili tower 2 (with elevation of the interior niches) and Sayn tower 1

according to local information—but no vestiges of any ancient urban remains: the cemetery at Zalargak is consistent with the present rural character and population of the valley. A large tower-like structure, apparently a 'signal tower', can be observed on top of a mountain to the west (pl. 2.8). According to a local informant,[23] this was a part of an ancient Ghurid signalling system, a line of which once stretched between Chakhcharan and Farah, which could 'carry a message in a single day'.

The following remains were recorded on the ground. Tower 1 is to the northwest of the village of Sanglech, 14km from Zarni (pl. 2.9). It is a small square mud tower possibly later than the others in the Nili Valley, as the finish appears more recent but is rougher. A small cemetery lies on top of the hill just to the north. Tower 2 (pl. 2.10; fig. 2.3) is several hundred metres further northeast. It is a circular tower surviving to a height of 10-12 metres, constructed of mud-brick on a rough stone and mud footing approximately 2m high. Inside, two tiers of slits surrounded by semi-circular reveals survive. Four kilometres further up the valley, on the north side, a series of low mounds form a rough square measuring *c.* 80 x 82m. The stump of a mud wall survives to a height of a metre in one corner. Tower 3 is 6km east of Mahalla on the south side of the Nili Valley. It is the same construction as the others, standing *c.* 6m. high, with lozenge patterns impressed on the exterior mud plaster. Remains of a second tower, also circular, are just visible to the east, which may originally have joined it.

There used to be many more towers in the valley according to local information, but were recently

[21] *Archaeological Gazetteer* 987.

[22] *Archaeological Gazetteer* 775; see also Wannell, *op. cit.*

[23] The Wakil of Nili, Haji Muhammad Nasim Parwana, a descendant of the Shansabani Sultans.

Pl. 2.7 Nili Valley

Pl. 2.8 Signal tower on top of mountain overlooking Nili (photo: Josephine Powell)

Pl. 2.9 Nili tower 1

Pl. 2.10 Nili tower 2

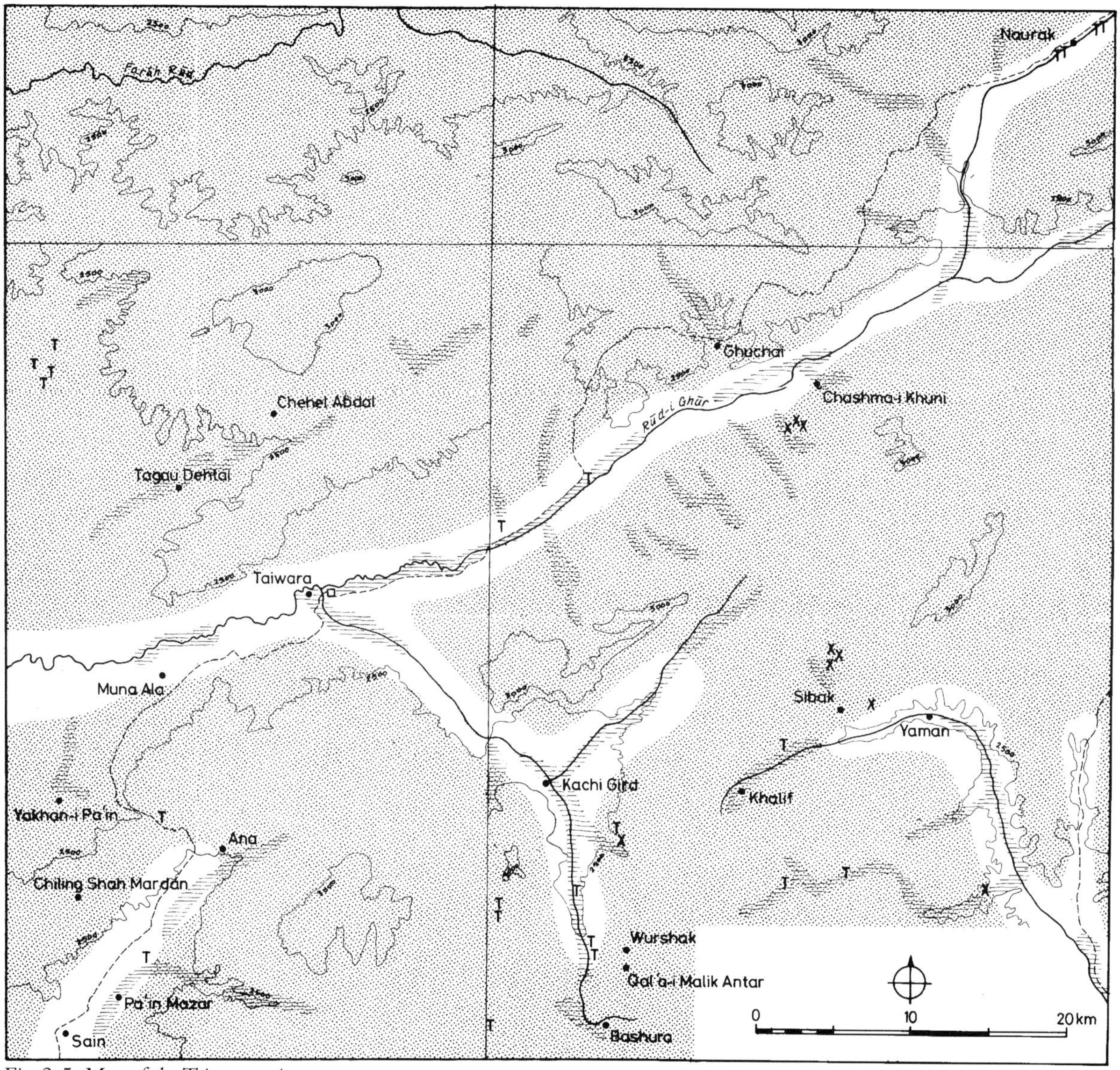

Fig. 2.5 Map of the Taiwara region

demolished to allow for increased cultivation. The remains of one were visible 3km northeast further up the valley towards Yaman (possibly Darzab, below), and remains of perhaps twelve more were visible further down the valley between Tower 3 and Mahalla. Coins have been found in these towers. At Darzab ruins in the form of mounds, where metal objects have been found, are reported by Kohzad.[24]

Taiwara Region (fig. 2.5)

Taiwara is in the middle of a wide, fertile valley watered by the Ghur River. It is the present administrative headquarters for the province of Ghurat, with a modern-looking fort and small bazaar outside it forming the 'capital'. Inside the fort is a small mosque decorated with simple, stamped plaster designs on the interior surfaces. The *mihrab* is especially richly decorated, but does not appear older than 19th century. According to Kohzad there are local reports of ancient remains in the mound underneath the fort.[25]

[24] *Archaeological Gazetteer* 255.

[25] *Archaeological Gazetteer* 1130.

Pl. 2.11 Qalᶜa-i Naurak

The Afghan Boundary Commission reports the remains of several ancient towers at Tagau Dehtai[26] in the Taiwara Valley to the northwest of Taiwara on the road to the upper Farah Rud basin and Deh Turkan, as well as the remains of a citadel at the foot of the Chehel Abdal[27] mountains that bound the north side of the Taiwara Valley. Maps also mark many towers further to the northwest on the route to the upper Farah Rud basin.

The route to the northeast towards Shaharak is guarded by occasional single towers: one just 10km out of Taiwara, another at the end of the valley where the road begins the ascent of the Kotal-i Ghachai, and another at the village of Ghuchai approximately midway between the Taiwara and Naurak valleys. The Naurak Valley is a very broad, flat grassy plain (the Dasht-i Naurak) bounded by low hills. There is little settlement but a number of Taimani transhumant encampments. The eastern end of the plain is dominated by Qalᶜa-i Naurak, a very ruined castle and several towers, 61km north of Taiwara, standing on a rocky bluff (pl. 2.11).[28] The castle is very eroded, consisting of mud walls on a stone footing. The northern end appears comparatively well preserved, consisting of a square projection flanked by two circular corner buttresses. It has four openings in the wall, one above the other, that may originally have been windows, as well as a line of four arrow slits about a quarter of the way up. The east face of the castle has some mud plaster surviving on which were impressed characteristic lozenge patterns. The remains of five further towers, completely separated from the main castle itself, extend to the west. They are very badly ruined, but where discernible they appear to be square. Approximately a kilometre further to the east, where the *dasht* opens out, there were three more very ruined towers stretching for about a kilometre.

The route south-eastwards towards Yaman (see below) is marked by the fortress of Kachi Gird as well as many other ruins and towers towards the end of the valley, that were reported by Kohzad.[29]

The route southwards from Taiwara towards Larwand and Zarni is particularly well fortified by several series of tower complexes. 11km southwest of Taiwara at Muna ᶜAla are eight towers in two groups on either side of the road overlooking the valley, decorated in simple geometric patterns (pls. 12 and 13). One of the towers has quite elaborate decoration in moulded plaster, as well as the more familiar impressed wedges (pl. 2.13).[30] A further 4km southwest, just after the road branches off to Parchuman (see above), ruins of many mud-brick forts and towers standing up to 12m high were recorded by the Afghan Boundary Commission at Yakhan-i Pa'in, connecting with

[26] *Archaeological Gazetteer* 1127.

[27] *Archaeological Gazetteer* 188.

[28] *Archaeological Gazetteer* 767.

[29] *Archaeological Gazetteer* 485.

[30] *Archaeological Gazetteer* 742; *Routes S-W*, 33; possibly those referred to as 'Muhalla' in Wannell, *op. cit.*

Pl. 2.12 Muna ᶜAla

a line of watchtowers (pl. 2.14).[31] To the north are the remains of some tombs. Further southwestwards on this road is the great fortress of Qalᶜa-i Qaisar (described under Larwand, above).

Continuing southwards on the Zarni road a single tower overlooks the road 14km from Taiwara, 4km before the fortifications of Ana, near Waras.[32] These consist of lines of square and circular towers on both sides of the valley. As well as guarding the approaches to Taiwara, Ana also marks a route over to Yaman (see below). On top of the mountain of Chiling Shah Mardan to the west of the Taiwara-Zarni road a shrine associated with ᶜAli was reported by the Afghan Boundary Commission.[33]

Eleven kilometres further south there is a single square tower overlooking the valley, then another 3km further on is the extensive series of fortifications in and around Pa'in Mazar (fig. 2.6, pls. 15-18).[34] The main concentration is a series of nine towers on either side of the river, originally perhaps forming two forts, although any inter-connecting walls have disappeared. There are the remains of 3 or 4 towers further to the west that may originally have been a third fort. All appear parts of what originally must have formed a single extensive fortified complex. The most elaborate towers are those four comprising Qalᶜa-i Chahar Baradar on the east side of the river (pl. 2.16). Tower 1 is square with four circular corner towers and a fifth semi-circular buttress on the north side (fig. 2.7). Construction is of stone and mud for the first 3m, thence mud-brick. The north side is the better preserved, with the remains of four storeys of semi-circular, very low (1.30m high) vaulted rooms visible (fig. 2.7). Both interior and exterior surfaces are plastered with thickly straw-tempered mud plaster, with impressed lozenge patterns on the exterior. There is a revetment wall, possibly incorporating an external staircase up to the entrance, at the southwest corner. Tower 2 is similar to Tower 1 but without any intermediate buttresses and generally better preserved. The corner towers do not appear to be attached to the main body of the central square tower. The interior was divided into two by a mud-brick arch, the springing of which survives on one side. Tower 3 (fig. 2.8) is square with a semi-circular salient on one side and semi-circular buttresses on two other sides. It is very well preserved, although the interior is completely ruined. There are remains of a possible circular tower at the northwest corner. Tower 4 (pls. 2.17 and 18, fig. 2.8) is square with a square salient on one side and a semi-circular buttress on the opposite side. It is also very well preserved on the exterior, although very ruined inside. Curvilinear decoration is cut into the mud plaster on the west and south sides. Approximately 1.5km upstream further north is another series of towers, Qalᶜa-i Zohak, which probably also formed another fort (unvisited).

Some 3km south of Pa'in Mazar are two towers

---

[31] *Archaeological Gazetteer* 1236; *Routes S-W*, 10; Wannell, *op. cit.*, refers to more towers at Yakhan-i Bala.

[32] *Archaeological Gazetteer* 39.

[33] *Archaeological Gazetteer* 207.

[34] *Archaeological Gazetteer* 787.

Pl. 2.13 Muna ʿAla (photo: Josephine Powell)

Pl. 2.14 Yakhan-i Pa'in (photo: Josephine Powell)

Pl. 2.15 Pa'in Mazar from the south—Qal'a-i Chahar Baradar is in the foreground

Pl. 2.16 Qal'a-i Chahar Baradar from the north-west (photo: Josephine Powell)

Pl. 2.17 Qal'a-i Chahar Baradar tower 4

overlooking the village of Sayn.[35] Some coins are said to have been found in the area. Tower 1 (fig. 2.4) is a rectangular tower standing above the valley to the west, *c.* 8m high. Construction is of mud heavily tempered with twigs, on a stone footing 2.3m high. It has a semi-circular salient on one side, surviving only at stone footing level. Tower 2 is a very ruined tower on an adjacent hill just to the east, probably the same plan as Tower 1. Tower 3 is 4km to the southwest at the point where the road leaves the river bed.

Yaman Region (fig. 2.9)

The Yaman Valley lies at the centre of communications between the Upper Hari Rud Valley (Chakhcharan and Daulatyar), the central Ghurat (Taiwara), the Hazarajat and Zamindawar. Accordingly, it is well fortified, particularly on the routes leading westwards to Taiwara and southwestwards to Zarni through the Nili Valley, some of the fortifications of which have been described under those regions. At Yaman itself both the Afghan Boundary Commission and Kohzad describe ruins covering an extensive area consisting of isolated circular or square towers

[35] *Archaeological Gazetteer* 970.

Pl. 2.18 Qalʿa-i Chahar Baradar tower 4 detail

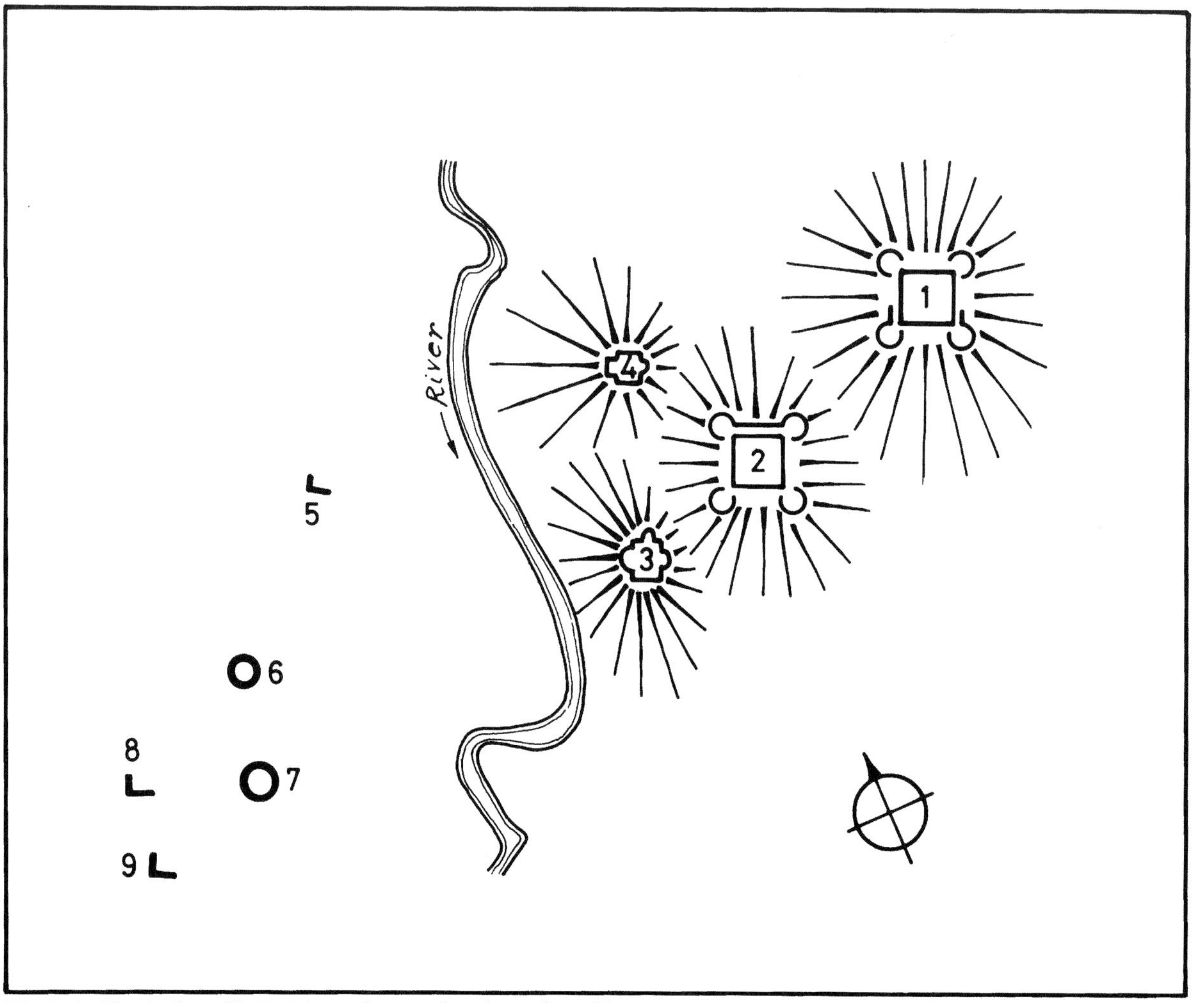

Fig. 2.6 Sketch plan of Pa'in Mazar showing the relationship of the remains

Fig. 2.7 Measured sketch section of Qalᶜa-i Chahar Baradar 1

and small forts. The Boundary Commission also records unusual burials containing burial goods.[36]

The only fortification recorded before the Farah Rud on the route to Chakhcharan to the north is the citadel at Pasaband, mentioned by Kohzad.[37] To the southeast, towards Zamindawar and ultimately Kandahar, maps mark vast numbers of ruins, particularly around the upper Helmand, but this area remains largely unexplored.[38] A little more is known of the remains in and beyond the upper Yaman Valley following the routes westwards to Taiwara and south-westwards to Nili. On the Taiwara route at Sibak, 5km to the west, towers and other remains were mentioned by Kohzad,[39] and at Khatif Kohzad also reported many more ruins and artificial mounds from hearsay.[40] On the route to Nili there is a concentration of remains around Wurshak 13km southwest of Yaman.

[36] *Archaeological Gazetteer* 1239; see also Wannell, *op. cit.*
[37] *Archaeological Gazetteer* 803.
[38] *Archaeological Gazetteer* Maps 104, 105.
[39] *Archaeological Gazetteer* 1103.
[40] *Archaeological Gazetteer* 566.

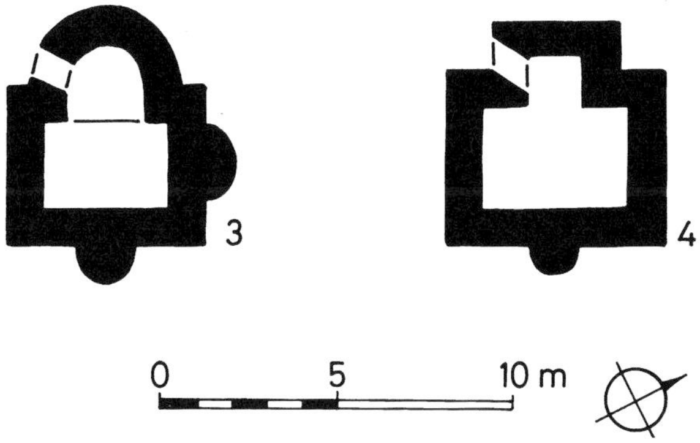

Fig. 2.8 Measured sketch plan of Qalᶜa-i Chahar Baradar 3 and 4

Wurshak itself is a substantial square fort[41] and at Qalᶜa-i Malik ᶜAntar just to the south another fort with 'snake-like' decoration was reported by Kohzad,[42] with many more forts and towers in the vicinity and further south at Bashura.[43]

Shaharak Region (fig. 2.10)

Shaharak is a wide plain rather than a valley, bounded by the Band-i Bayan to the north separating it from the Hari Rud and the Ghurat massif to the south and southeast. It is watered by the Shaharak River, one of the main tributaries of the Hari Rud, which it enters between Obeh and Herat. As such it forms one of the main regions in Ghur with important archaeological remains other than fortifications, such as the Hebrew inscription at Tang-i Azau and the petroglyphs at Tang-o Tizau.[44] Mounds and remains around the administrative centre of Shaharak itself has produced quantities of 'pseudo-prehistoric' painted pottery, probably in fact early Islamic, one of the few evidences of urban remains in Ghur.[45]

Most of the Shaharak remains, however, like elsewhere in Ghur are fortifications, and British officers in the 1880s noted the strategic siting of many of them.[46] The route westwards towards Herat is guarded by lines of towers and fortifications at Pul-i Zuhak, Minara, Palangkhana and Nalbandan,[47] and eroded artificial mounds at Kata Chashma might mark more.[48] Maps mark

[41] *Archaeological Gazetteer* 1234.
[42] *Archaeological Gazetteer* 864; Wannell, *op. cit*, discusses the close association of the Malik ᶜAntar cycle with Ghur.
[43] *Archaeological Gazetteer* 114.
[44] *Archaeological Gazetteer* 1144, 1145.
[45] *Archaeological Gazetteer* 1031.
[46] *ABC* 1, 372.
[47] *Archaeological Gazetteer* 820, 717, 793, 759.
[48] *Archaeological Gazetteer* 537.

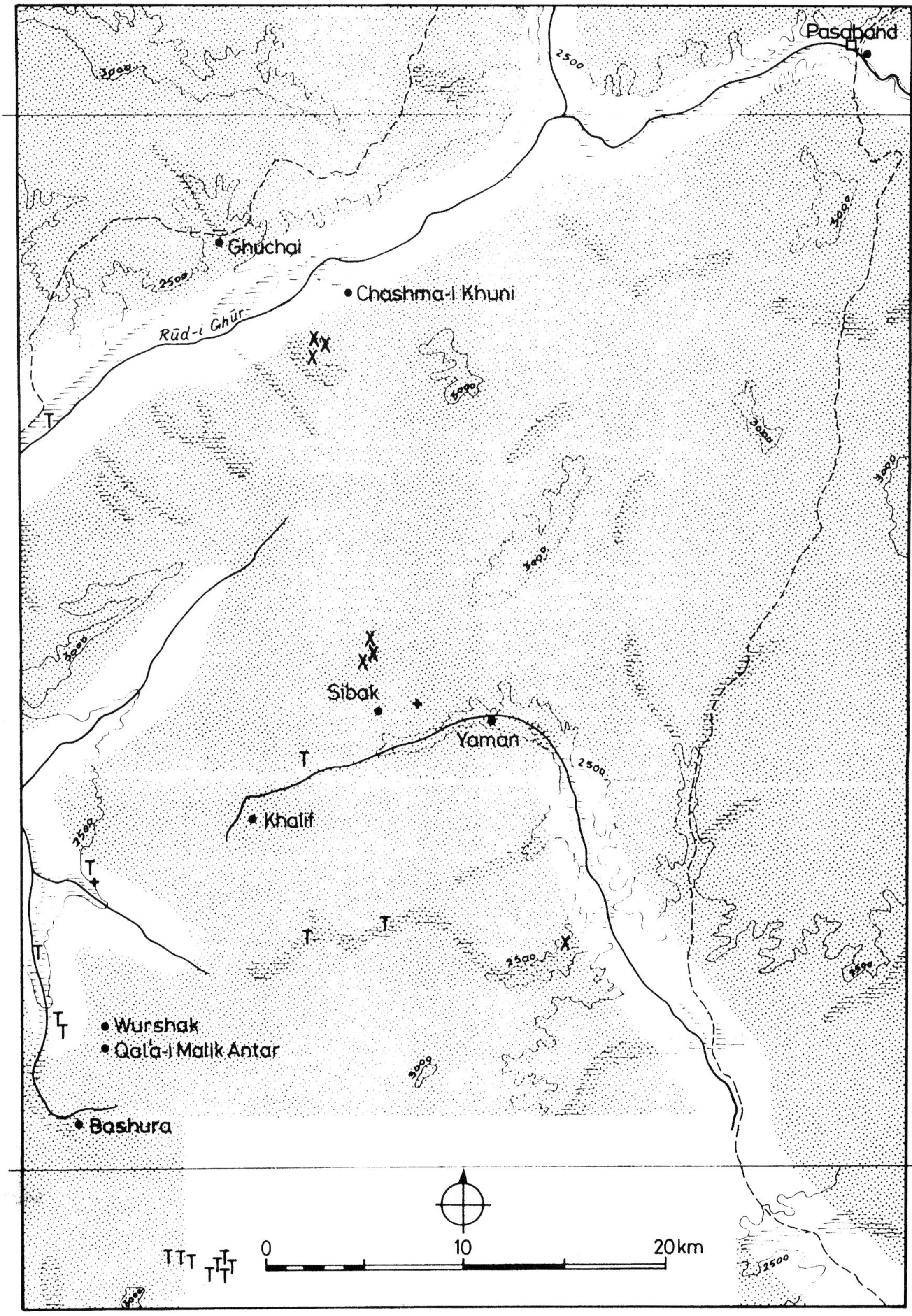

Fig. 2.9 Map of the Yaman region

many more ruins and towers on this route—indeed, the Boundary Commission describes this area as a ruined town.[49] The route to the east towards Chakhcharan and Daulatyar is guarded by more fortifications at Manara, Chehel Gazari, Hauz-i Bangi and Guzarpam,[50] with the map marking very large numbers of towers guarding the northern and especially the southern sides of the valley to the east of Shaharak.

Discussion

The sheer quantity of the remains adds up to one of the most extraordinary archaeological complexes in the eastern Islamic world. Furthermore, due to the impenetrability of the terrain, the recorded remains probably only represent the tip of the iceberg—the consistent reports of the minaret of Qalᶜa-i Zarmurgh are a tantalising reminder of what is still awaiting discovery—and the 1:1,000,000 maps based on satellite images show substantially more towers and other remains (indicated in the maps). The nearest comparable archaeological complex is the Bamiyan region, where similar quantities of fortifications occur and have been subject to more detailed study.[51] Like the Ghur fortifications, those in the Bamiyan region cluster along the valleys and routes, in this case the routes leading in and out of the main centre at Bamiyan. They too usually consist of small forts, fortlets and individual towers, with just the occasional larger more complex fortification such as Shahr-i Zuhak. The decoration of impressed triangles in the form lozenge or diamond patterns are also a pronounced feature at Bamiyan, such as at Darra-i Jandargal, Darra-i Iraq, Darra-i Jalmish, Darra-i Ahangaran, Bamiyan itself, Shahidan, Kakrak and Fuladi.[52] However, none of the more curvilinear plaster decoration recorded at Muna ᶜAla, Yakhan-i Pa'in, Chahar Baradar and elsewhere in Ghur has been recorded at Bamiyan. The Bamiyan fortifications have been dated to the 5th-6th centuries through to the early 13th century, based largely upon ceramics, with the bulk of them falling in to an 8th-10th century group.[53] This corresponds to the period of the ascendancy of the

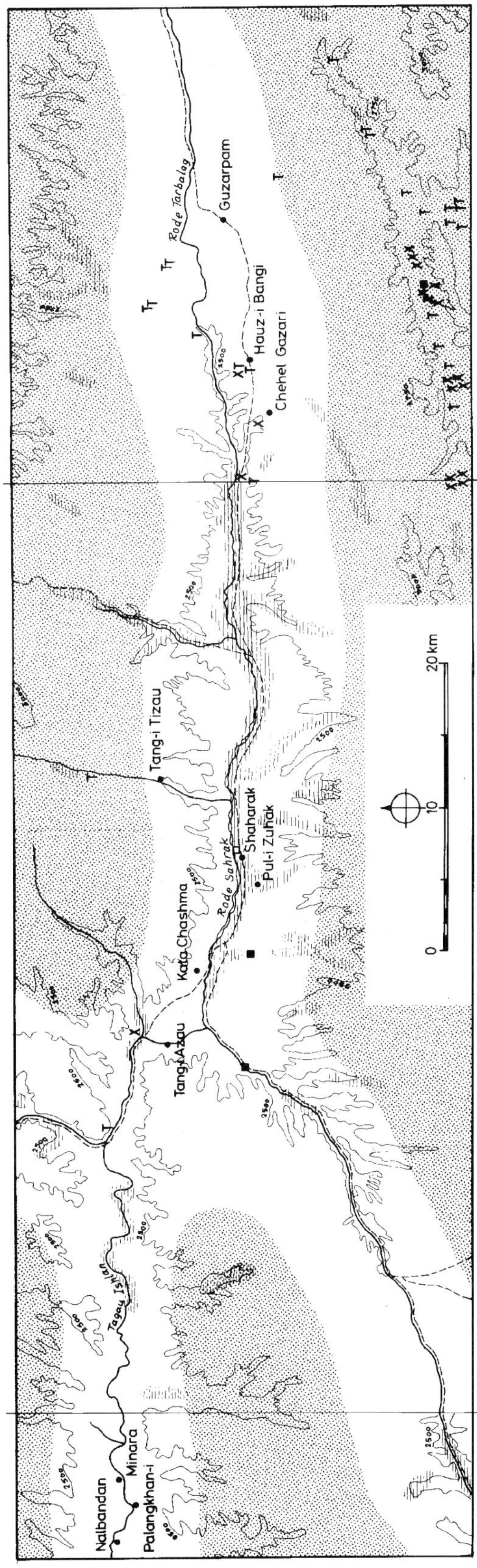

Fig. 2.10 Map of the Shaharak region

[49] *Routes N-W*, 17.

[50] *Archaeological Gazetteer* 704, 195, 419, 403.

[51] Mainly recorded in Le Berre, *op. cit.* See also Baker and Allchin, *op. cit.*, and *Archaeological Gazetteer* Maps 106 and 107 and references, particularly for those fortifications to the west of Bamiyan not covered in Le Berre's surveys.

[52] Le Berre, *op. cit.*, pls. 45, 46, 47, 59, 62, 97, 98, 106, 110.

[53] Gardin and Lyonnet in Le Berre, *op. cit.*, 108-20.

Turkish Kaganate and its dependencies, with their offshoot in eastern Afghanistan, the Turki Shahs.[54]

For the region of Ghur there is no known political structure in the 8th-10th century that is comparable the Turkish Kaganate around Bamiyan that might account for the complex of fortifications. It is true that the Kaganate—never strongly centralised in the first place—had begun to fragment by this period, with the 'Kingdom of Bamiyan' being one of those fragments. Furthermore, all the fortifications of the Bamiyan region appear to converge just on the one place, Bamiyan itself, while the Ghur fortifications converge on a number of distinct localities. Other parts of eastern Afghanistan that, like Bamiyan, were also component parts of the Kaganate, such as Ghazni (Tepe Sardar), did not have comparable systems of fortifications even when they had comparable Buddhist remains. The Bamiyan fortifications, therefore, might be later than the ceramic evidence suggests, i.e., to the period of the Ghurid Shansabani kingdom of Bamiyan in the 12th-13th centuries.[55] However, the ceramic evidence cannot be ignored: all one can say for certain is that both the Ghur and the Bamiyan fortifications systems belong to the same broad architectural traditions, and that the Ghurid dynasty of the 12th-13th century is the only state structure that is common to both.

The Ghurid state was never strongly centralised, consisting of many different clans under different chiefs, all ultimately bound to the Ghurid sultan. In this way Ghur may have been more a confederation than a single state, and the fortified valleys may reflect this with each chief or prince responsible from defending and fortifying his own valley as much against a rival chief as against a common enemy such as the Ghaznavids or Saljuqs—the sources amply support such a picture. Indeed, Ghur had a long tradition of such fragmentation: as early as the Saffarid period, for example, we read that Ghur was divided amongst Muslims and pagans who fought each other from fortified hills and *kushks*, while during ᶜAla' ud-Din's captivity by Sultan Sanjar we read that Ghur broke up and each tribe 'fortified itself in the hills and defiles in which it dwelt.'[56]

Our main source for ancient Ghur, the *Tabaqat-i Nasiri*, is littered with descriptions of and references to the construction of castles, towers and other fortifications in Ghur and Gharjistan.[57] Ghiyath ud-Din, for example, migrated between his summer capital of Firuzkuh and his winter capital of Zamindawar, a distance of '40 leagues', and a 'pillar' was erected every league to mark this route.[58] Whether these 'pillars' were towers or columns is unclear, but the largest concentration of remains are certainly to be found in the region to the southeast of Jam—the Firuzkuh-Zamindawar route broadly—and the remains of possible signal towers or pillars are found overlooking the valleys of Larwand and Nili confirming the *Tabaqat-i Nasiri*. There is also the vast number of uninvestigated remains recorded on maps to the northwest of Zamindawar.[59]

A notable pattern of the Ghur fortifications is that they converge on distinct localities: Larwand, Zarni, Taiwara, Yaman and Shaharak (figs. 2.2-5, 9 and 10). All of these localities are valleys or plains surrounded by mountains, hence easily defendable, and the fortifications dominate strategic routes leading into these valleys. This pattern suggests that each valley might have been the seat of a rival Ghurid chief or prince. However, with the possible exception of Shaharak, urban remains in the centre of these valleys—the actual 'seats' of such hypothetical princes, 'capitals' of such Ghurid mini-states—are conspicuous by their absence. Qalᶜa-i Qaisar is the only remains recorded that might contain accommodation large and grandiose enough for such a purpose, although even here the remains must be seen as primarily military, guarding a major route, rather than residential. *Nowhere in Ghur have any traces of urban remains or actual settlement been definitely recorded*. The question remains, therefore, that if these fortifications complexes were guarding focal points, exactly what were they guarding?

Before answering this question, another puzzling lacuna is apparent. Despite the large and elaborate systems of fortifications defending these focal points, there are virtually none defending what is surely the most important focal point of them all in Ghur: the capital itself of Firuzkuh, modern Jam. There are, of course, some towers on the hilltops immediately surrounding the minaret.[60] But these are not remotely comparable to the very elaborate system of defences with which even a minor locality, such as Zarni, was equipped: there are no lines of towers in either direction along the Hari Rud nor southwards along the

[54] For history see, for example, Deborah Klimburg-Salter, *The Kingdom of Bamiyan. Buddhist Art and Culture of the Hindu Kush*, Naples and Rome, 1989, Chapter III.

[55] For a summary history of the Ghurids, see C E Bosworth, 'Ghurids', *Encyclopaedia of Islam*, 2nd Edition, 1999.

[56] Juzjani, 317-8, 364.

[57] E.g., Juzjani, 320, 331-2, 339-40, 341-2, 355-6, 369-70, 394, 397-8, 403-4, 415, 416-7, 418.

[58] Juzjani, 385-6.

[59] *Archaeological Gazetteer* Maps 104, 105.

[60] *Archaeological Gazetteer* 468.

Pl. 2.19 Base for a yurt in the palace at Khiva

Jam Rud nor along the route northwards.[61] By comparison, the Ghurid capital appears undefended. Neither are there comparative systems of fortifications in Gharjistan, so closely connected to Ghur, or to the north of the Hari Rud generally. They are almost entirely found to the south of the Hari Rud in the historical heartland of Ghur.

This might seem to reopen the old question regarding the location of Firuzkuh, in particular supporting the old hypothesis of locating it around Taiwara with its formidable systems of fortifications. The case for this rests partly on conflicting evidence in the sources, which prefers a location further south, and partly against the impossibility of identifying Jam as a 'city': there are no urban remains and there is no space in any case. But the identification of Firuzkuh with Jam now seems fairly conclusive.[62] A solution, therefore, must take into account not only the identification of Firuzkuh with Jam, but also its lack of comparative fortifications in contrast to other localities as well as the lack of urban remains in *all* localities.

Much of the problem of locating Firuzkuh with Jam has centred around looking for a capital *city*. I suspect Firuzkuh was never any such thing, despite its being occasionally described as a 'city' in the sources. All a capital city need be is the residence of the king: defining a city in the conventional sense, in terms of bricks and mortar, does not necessarily work in this case. Hence, a capital 'city' need be no more than just tents, and Central Asian history has several instances of tented 'cities' and even capitals of nomadic empires, with just the occasional monument to impress the tent-dwellers, such as a victory tower.[63] The Ghurids may well have been part-nomadic, or at least only recently removed from nomadism, just as the Firuzkuhi today in the region are—indeed, the modern Firuzkuhi, a part of the Chahar Aimaq tribe, are a Persian-speaking people who are probably descended from the Ghurids.[64] Might the Ghurids have lived in tents (or yurts)

[61] The only fortification known on the route northwards from Jam into Gharjistan is the minor post at Diwalak, reported by Wannell, *op. cit.*

[62] Giorgio Vercellin, 'The identification of Firuzkuh: a Conclusive Proof', *East and West* 26, 1976, 337-40. For new evidence see also now Ralph Pinder-Wilson, 'Ghaznavid and Ghurid Minarets', *Iran* XXXIX, 2001, appendix.

[63] See Peter Alford Andrews' monumental new study on this subject, *Felt Tents and Pavilions. The Nomadic Tradition and its Interaction with Princely Tentage*, 2 vols., London, 1999.

[64] R N Frye, 'Firuzkuh', *Encyclopaedia of Islam*, 2nd Edition, 1999; 'Firuzkohis', *Historical and Political Gazetteer of Afghanistan*. Vol. 3. *Heart and North-Western Afghanistan*, Graz, 1975, 105-28.

like the Firuzkuhi, despite being great conquerors, leaving no trace of their actual dwellings in the archaeological record? After all, even sophisticated patrons of architecture may live in tents: 18th and 19th century Khiva has brick yurt bases in the courtyards of the palaces and mansions (pl. 2.19), where the khans would live in the winter months (as they only knew how to heat yurts, not houses). Such a hypothesis receives some support in the sources: Sultan Saif ud-Din Muhammad, for example, was seated in his 'pavilion' at Firuzkuh, and 'the Sultan's pavilion was brought out of the city of Firuzkuh' to Sultan Ghiyath ud-Din.[65] The hypothesis is wholly endorsed by the archaeological record—or, in this case, by its absence, a classic case of the dog barking in the night in the Sherlock Holmes story.[66]

The existence of the kind of semi-permanent encampments such as one still finds in Ghur today—encampments, furthermore, that may well have been tribal or princely seats—would also explain the lack of urban remains outside Firuzkuh in otherwise well fortified valleys in Ghur. Hence, the pattern of fortifications suggests Ghurid regional 'capitals' at Larwand, Zarni, Taiwara, Yaman and Shaharak. But this still does not explain why fortifications are entirely lacking at other Ghurid centres equally demanding of fortification, notably in Gharjistan and at Firuzkuh/Jam itself. In suggesting a reason for this, attention is drawn to the map of the routes through Ghur shown in fig. 2.1. This map, taken from the British intelligence *Route Reports* and based mainly on the Boundary Commission Reports, marks all the routes to the south of the Hari Rud. It is likely to be fairly thorough, as it was prepared against the eventuality of a Russian invasion of Afghanistan and India, so shows virtually all usable routes. Two important features are apparent from this map. First is the sheer *numbers* of routes that exist through Ghur: the region is honeycombed by a far greater number of routes than the terrain would suggest today. And second, when the main concentrations of fortifications are plotted onto this map, the fortifications appear to defend the routes leading out of Ghur towards the south and southeast, to Qandahar and the Ghaznavid centres of Lashkari Bazar and Ghazna. One recalls again the vast number of remains northwest of Zamindawar.[67] As an overall pattern, therefore, they are not defending individual valleys and rival Ghurid chiefs against each other. Rather they appear to be something far more comprehensive and inter-dependant, as well as subject to an overall plan: the overall architectural homogeneity of the fortifications has already been stressed, and the line of signalling towers argues for a centralised authority rather than isolated independent bodies. In other words, a vast defensive shield sheltering the Ghurid capital from threats from the southeast.

If so, the towers of Ghur are one of the most impressive systems of fortifications of the Islamic world, a Ghurid 'Maginot Line'. The Ghaznavids were certainly the traditional enemy of the Ghurids, so that concentrating their defences against them certainly makes sense. It is true that after ʿAla' ud-Din's sack of Ghazna in 1173-4 the Ghaznavids no longer posed a threat. But the defences may have been built before then—and the evidence of the Bamiyan fortifications supports an earlier date as we have seen—and the Ghurids may still have not ruled out the possibility of a Ghaznavid revival in any case. The Maginot Line in any case certainly forms an appropriate comparison: like the Maginot Line, the Ghurid defensive lines were ultimately never put to the test, for the real threat when it did come was from a different direction, when the Khwarazm-shahs conquered Ghur in 1215 from the undefended north. A lesson in over-elaborate, over-expensive 'defensive shields' for all ages.

---

[65] Juzjani, 366, 371. Although it is not certain exactly what is meant by 'pavilion', although the implication that it was portable certainly suggests a tent.

[66] A final word must be said about Ghur's greatest tower, the Minaret of Jam. That it was in some measure a victory tower related to Ghaznavid and Ghurid victory traditions is now well established (see T Leiston, 'Mashhad al Nasr' *Muqarnas: an annual on the visual culture of the Islamic world* 13, 1996; Pinder-Wilson, *op. cit.*) This has ultimately been related to ancient Indian tradition, going back to the Mauryan victory columns, a tradition that also probably sees the ultimate origin of Roman victory columns (e.g., Column of Trajan) and a whole range of later related European triumphalist architecture (see Warwick Ball, *Rome in the East*, London, 2000, 287-90.) But apart from this, the 'triumphalist' nature generally of Ghaznavid (and by extension Ghurid) architecture is usually examined within the broader context of Islamic traditions as a whole. But might it make more sense by looking at the tradition in a purely *Turkish* context? After all, the Ghaznavids were relatively recently converted to Islam and were still very close to their Turkish and Central Asian roots. The ethnic origins of the Ghurids are less clear, probably being Iranian rather than Turkish, but a Turkish element was nonetheless still present (Bosworth, *op. cit.*) When one looks at the pre-Islamic Turk inscriptions of Central Asia and the Altai, for example at Karabalghasun (the first Uighur capital) and elsewhere on the Orkhon, they are very triumphalist in tone: many are on stelae erected to commemorate victories (See for example: Denis Sinor, *Cambridge History of Early Inner Asia*, Cambridge, 1990, Chapter 11; D Sinor and S G Klyashtorny, 'The Türk Empire', *UNESCO History of Civilizations in Central Asia*, Vol III, Paris, 1996, 327-48.) The Karakhanid Kalan minaret at Bukhara, as well as perhaps other Central Asian minarets, such as Kunya Urgench, also belongs within this tradition.

[67] *Archaeological Gazetteer* Maps 104, 105.

Acknowledgement

The field work was supported by grants and logistical support from the British Institute of Afghan Studies, the Royal Geographical Society and the Stein-Arnold Fund. I would like to thank John Thorne and Nesar Ahmad who accompanied me in the field. Their assistance—not to mention their good company—made the fieldwork both achievable and enjoyable. I would also like to thank Josephine Powell who has very generously allowed me to use photographs from her own field trips in Ghur—the quality of her photographs speak for themselves and considerably enhance this paper—and Graham Reed who worked up my drawings and field sketches into presentable illustrations.

I owe a particular debt to Ralph Pinder-Wilson, then Director of the Afghan Institute. It was through a shared interest in the Ghurids that Ralph encouraged me to undertake a field trip to Ghur in the first place. Countless discussions since, both in the Institute he presided over and back in the UK, on all aspects of Ghurid history, architectural remains and historical geography have been a constant source of stimulation. This paper in particular, and so much of my academic research generally, has benefited from his guidance, learning, wisdom and encouragement. It is entirely appropriate that this paper and this volume is dedicated to him.

3 THE PILLAR AND THE PICTURES: AN INTERPRETATION OF THE 'DIWAN-I KHASS' AT FATHPUR SIKRI

Barbara Brend

The major buildings of Akbar's palace city Fathpur Sikri are ranged along a ridge. The site was chosen to be near the abode of Salim Chishti, whose prophecy that Akbar would have a son was vindicated by the birth of the future Jahangir in 1569. Building work began at Sikri in 979/1571 and Akbar left the city in 993/1585.[1] The extensive remains include much highly differentiated architecture, some of whose purposes are clear and some less so. A structure which has invited much speculation is known conventionally as the 'Diwan-i Khass', suggesting a private audience chamber.[2] The building is square in plan.[3] Externally there is a horizontal emphasis, two storeys being divided by a surrounding gallery, while a *chhajja* below the roof casts a line of shadow (pls. 3.1 and 2). Central in each of the four facades is a doorway, through which the strangest feature of the building is glimpsed. This is a pillar surmounted by two registers of serpentine corbels which support a round platform at the level of the external gallery (pl. 3.3). The platform, which has an openwork parapet, is linked to the corners of the chamber by four catwalks that run diagonally to meet quarter-circle platforms at the corners of an internal gallery (pl. 3.4). There are rectangular niches in the walls adjacent to the corner platforms. This level is reached by two stairways concealed in the thickness of the wall.[4]

The arrangement of the throne is so developed that it must answer a particular purpose,[5] or perhaps several purposes that were not in conflict. It seems clear that the circular platform was for Akbar's use. Also, it is unlikely that direct communication was intended with persons at ground level. From a seated position in the centre the ground is lost to sight, and it is not to be imagined that the emperor would lean over the parapet in an undignified manner.[6] Thus, contact with other persons would have to come from the corners. It has been suggested that Akbar sat on this throne to hear petitions, or discussion, or to admire jewels. Any or all of these are possible, and it may be said that the emperor's central position would make it particularly easy to turn a cold shoulder to a corner whose propositions were not favoured. It has also been argued, particularly by Nath and by Irwin, that the throne pillar has a cosmic symbolism following ancient Indian tradition. This seems very probable. Also suggestive of Indian symbolism is a feature of the exterior which has not attracted much attention. Surrounding the building but almost hidden in the shadow of the *chhajja* is what amounts to a frieze. The majority of its elements are rosettes, which taken alone might be purely conventional, as the motif is found on other buildings of the palace. However, interspersed with these—and much mutilated— are what appear to be ducks or geese.[7] Taken as a whole the band may thus imply a lotus pool. The question of what precisely this might mean will not be pursued here, but it may serve to show that in suggesting an additional and practical purpose for the throne I do not deny a symbolic dimension. In support of his thesis, Nath has turned to a number of Mughal pictures of tree-houses, his drift being that these are informed by the symbolism of the pillar-throne. I would rather press the argument in the other direction and suggest that the tree-house was desirable,

[1] Michael Brand and Glenn D Lowry (eds.), *Fatehpur-Sikri: a source book*, Aga Khan Program, Cambridge, Mass., 1985, 34-38, 211-213.

[2] Edmund W Smith, 'The Moghul Architecture of Fathpur Sikri' *Archaeological Survey of India*, New Imperial Series, XVIII, N.-W. Provinces and Oudh, III, Allahabad, 4 parts, 1895-8, especially pt. I, 22-24; P Brown, *Indian Architecture (Islamic Period)*, repr. Taraporavala, Bombay, 1956, 96; Saiyid Athar Rizvi and Vincent John Flynn, *Fathpūr-Sīkrī*, Taraporavala, Bombay, 1975; John D Hoag, *Islamic Architecture*, Abrams, New York, 1977, 366-73; R Nath, *History of Mughal Architecture*, Abhinav, New Delhi, 1985, II, 251-69; John Irwin, 'Akbar and the Cosmic Pillar' in *Facets of Indian Art*, eds. R Skelton *et al.*, London, 1986, 47-50; Catherine B Asher, *The New Cambridge History of India: Architecture of Mughal India*, Cambridge University Press, Cambridge, 1992, 63; Ebba Koch, *Mughal Architecture*, Prestel, Munich, 1991; Giles Tillotson, *Mughal India*, Penguin, Harmondsworth, 1991, 108-9.

[3] Smith, pl. LXXVII; Hoag, pl. 485.

[4] Can this be the *Chahar Suffah*, Brand and Lowry, *op. cit.*, 81?

[5] Compare the nearby Anup Talao tank.

[6] Practicalities must be a guide to function. It is clear that the so-called house of the Turkish Sultana with its ornate dado and ceiling is best appreciated lying down.

[7] Smith, pl. LXXXVI, and 23.

and that on the ridge of Fathpur Sikri it had to be realised in stone with a roof in place of a canopy of leaves.

The key picture appears to me to be that painted when Akbar was still a boy—or perhaps a youth—and his father, Humayun, was ruler. 'The young Akbar offers Humayun a picture' (pl. 3.5)[8] by ᶜAbd al-Samad, in the Gulistan Museum, would have been painted between *c.* 1553, when the Mughals were based in Kabul, and 1556, when Humayun died in India: Abkar, born in 1542, appears nearer 11 than 13. On the left of the picture is a two-storey pavilion, with musicians in its upper and lower levels; servants carry refreshments up an external stairway to the upper floor and across a catwalk with a low parapet to where, on the right, the prince and his father are sitting on a platform supported by the branches of a large *chinar*. In the foreground, persons return from a hunt. The picture thus supplies the two-storey structure, the feeder catwalks, and the platform. Presumably, the picture enshrines an event that actually occurred and reflects an arrangement that actually existed. It would seem that at Fathpur Sikri the picture's two-storey pavilion and tree-house were condensed into one structure. The picture's octagonal platform is well furnished. It is carpeted, Humayun has a free-standing throne, there is a small stool or table, and, in addition to the picture presented, three other examples of the arts of the book are indicated. The tree-house is thus a place of retreat; it is loosely associated with music, and dining, but it is devoted above all to the arts of the book.

ᶜAbd al-Samad's picture may be the earliest surviving representation of a tree-house. In that case, the structure may have been invented for Humayun, or it might be a form that he encountered already in use in India or in Kabul. Possibly it owes something to the *machan*, the platform from which an Indian hunter would shoot tiger, if that were already in existence. It does not appear that the idea had currency in Iran in the 15th century, but it enjoys a certain vogue about the third quarter of the sixteenth, and may have been particularly favoured in Khurasan. Possibly the concept was exchanged between India and Iran during Humayun's sojourn in the latter in 1544, but it is not clear in which direction the influence flowed: though the earliest instance may be Humayun's, the preponderance of early examples is with Iran. Persian depictions occur in the frontispieces of manuscripts, which often portray scenes of princely life. Datable to about the 1560s is an example in a *Yusuf u Zulaykha* of Jami in Qazvin style (pl. 3.6), in the David Collection.[9] The right-hand side of a double page shows a young lord with a female companion in a hexagonal tree-house in the branches of a *chinar*. Set in a tiled enclosure, the structure is semi-permanent, since it is reached by a wooden staircase. An oval object is being handed up to the lady; since the left-hand page shows food being prepared, this may be bread? Rather similar is the frontispiece in a *Kulliyat* of Jami in the Russian National Library, which Ashrafi dates to the 1550s or 1560s and sees as Mashhad in style.[10] On the right-hand page a *chinar* grows in a natural setting, and in it sits a middle-aged, kingly figure on a hexagonal platform without parapet. The ladder he had used in his ascent has a more portable appearance. Food and drink are to hand, music is played, the king holds a wine-cup, and he is being handed a manuscript or small portfolio. The left-hand page has food in preparation, a horse, a guard, and an attendant with a large manuscript. A definite date and place of origin is provided by the frontispiece to a *Haft Aurang* of Jami of 979 /1571 made for Ibrahim Mirza at Mashhad, and now in the Topkapi Library.[11] The conception is similar to that of the first example, but the cooks on the left-hand page have moved inside the courtyard. The couple have arrived on horseback; the ladder is portable; the lady is holding a wine flask. Unlike 'Akbar offers Humayun a picture', these do not focus on a particular event, and so the case for their being a representation of reality rather than a pictorial *topos* is less compelling. However, examples which show *chinars* in close association with pavilions suggest that there may have been a attempts to make the imagined real, or to lend stability to flimsy temporary structures. A lacquer cover in the British Museum, datable about 1550 to 1560, shows an open-sided, two-storey pavilion whose upper floor has been built to enclose the upper part of a *chinar* (pl. 3.7).[12] In this, two princely figures are enjoying music, food and wine. A similar but ambiguous juxtaposition of tree and structure is seen in the right-hand side of a double-page picture added to a 15th-century *Khamsah* of Nizami, in the Bodleian Library, which Robinson attributes to Shiraz about 1560, and which was later partly over-painted in India (pl. 3.8).[13] This page shows wine and dancing girls, while the left-hand has another pavilion, cooks, attendants, and horses.

---

8 A U Pope (ed.), *A Survey of Persian Art*, X, 912.

9 B W Robinson, 'Rothschild and Binney Collections', in *Persian and Mughal Art*, Colnaghi, London, 1976, No. 20; Kjeld von Folsach, *Islamic Art: the David Collection*, Davids Samling, Copenhagen, 1990, No. 28.

10 M Ashrafi, *XVI century miniatures illustrating manuscript copies of the works of Jami from USSR collections*, Sovetskii Khudozhnik, Moscow, 1966, 24-5.

11 Filiz Çağman and Zeren Tanındı, *The Topkapı Saray Museum*, tr. and ed. J M Rogers, Thames and Hudson, London, 1986, No. 113.

12 J M Rogers, *Islamic Art & Design, 1500-1700*, British Museum, London, 1983, No. 1, and 39. The dating there suggested, *c.* 1525-50, seems too early for the long-bodied figures and round headgear.

13 B W Robinson, *Descriptive Catalogue of the Persian Paintings in the Bodleian Library*, Oxford University Press, 1958, No. 900.

A drawing which leads us towards a further dimension of the motif is 'Prince in a tree-house' (pl. 3.9), a picture now in the Louvre.[14] This shows the prince sitting on a small, seemingly rectangular platform, which he has reached by an eminently portable ladder. A horse and falconer show how the prince has been engaged; an attendant lord has a flask of wine that a page, who already has a bundle under his arm, will shortly carry up the ladder. Since a note announces that this is a picture of Shah Tahmasp it has generally been dated to the second quarter of the 16th century, most recently by Bahari; however, Makariou has argued convincingly that it is the work of Muhammadi, who was active in Herat in the period 1578 to 1584.[15] A second note, which attributes the drawing to Bihzad is to be rejected so far as the present work is concerned, though it might be interpreted to mean that Muhammadi was copying a drawing that Bihzad had made in Herat when Tahmasp was nominal governor there before his accession. If that were so, Tahmasp might have been the inventor of the tree-house. It is, indeed, easy to understand what its appeal would be to a young prince: while escaping from the everyday world, he retains a sense of majesty. However that may be, a third note opens another vista. Placed on the skirt of a portly figure on the right of the picture, this may again have been added at a later date, but nevertheless it seems significant. Both Bahari and Makariou read this—*mutatis mutandis*—as *piri qapuchi* or 'old gatekeeper'. However, the indefinite *piri* 'an old man' is improbable grammatically and is not justified by the orthography. The note should surely be read *pari qapuchi* 'gatekeeper of the fairy (or fairies)'. Though not making this reading, Makariou sees the visual connection to a picture of about the mid-century in the Freer Gallery of Art which shows a fairy in a tree-house, entertained with music, while food is brought up a stairway at whose foot stands a demon guard (pl. 3.10). This picture she rightly associates with its companion piece, a prince on a throne borne-up by angels, as employing Solomonic iconography.[16] In the frontispiece of an *cAja'ib al-Makhluqat* of 974/1566, in the Cambridge University Library, we see fairies in a tree-house on the left, and Solomon enthroned on the right.[17] From the above, it appears that in Iran about the third quarter of the 16th century the tree-house existed as a *topos*, and may well have existed in fact. In the iconography of contemporary kingship it was a place of refreshment and relaxation, and firmly associate with food, wine, women and song. On a metaphorical level, it could be associated with Solomon and angels or fairies, and was perhaps to be seen as a flying throne. The enjoyment of books is touched on in one example only; however, it may be suggested that a 'throne of the fairies' might perhaps be understood not so much as a jejune fancy but as representing a place for the pleasures of the imagination.

In Mughal pictures the themes of food, wine, music, and the unearthly continue, but women tend to be displaced by books. Mughal histories have a scattering of references which show a world in which the tree-house would not be out of place. Gulbadan tells us that Babur, Humayun's father, would sit writing in a garden in a *chaukandi* containing a *turkhana*: the first appears to be an upper chamber, probably rectangular, and associated with refreshment.[18] References in the *Akbarnamah* of Abu'l Fazl show that the carpenters used by the Mughals could rise to a challenge. Humayun has both a two-storey movable palace, and a pavilion in eight-part format carried on barges.[19] We also learn that in 1564, when Akbar was catching elephants in virgin forest, the carpenters made him a platform for the night; in the morning this was treated as a throne, and Akbar and seated courtiers were regaled with stories of Amir Hamzah.[20] Surely for reasons of safety the platform was at some height above the ground? but were the courtiers on it or round it? It would also be pertinent to know if illustrated folios of the great *Hamzahnamah* were used on this occasion.[21] It might be so, since the session took place in the morning light, while pure story telling could have suited the previous night. Among the Victoria and Albert Museum's holding of these pictures is one that shows the witch 'Anqarut on a throne in a tree (pl. 3.11)—since the throne has legs, it looks as though it may have flown into this position.[22] At the least the picture shows that the idea of a tree-throne was current

14 Ebadollah Bahari, *Bihzad: Master of Persian Painting*, Tauris, London, 1996, fig. 121.

15 Sophie Makariou, 'Une nouvelle page attribuée à Muhammedi dans les collections islamiques du Louvre', *Revue du Louvre*, V, 1999, 104-10.

16 Esın Atıl, *The Brush of the Masters*, Freer Gallery of Art, Washington, DC, Nos. 13 and 12.

17 Robert Hillenbrand, *Imperial Images in Persian Painting*, Scottish Arts Council, Edinburgh, 1997, No. 177 and endpapers.

18 Gulbadan, *The History of Humāyūn*, tr. A Beveridge, repr. Munshiram Manoharlal, New Delhi, 1983, 103. I thank Robert Skelton for guiding me on through Babur, *The Bābur-nāma*, tr. A Beveridge, 663, to Steingass.

19 Abu'l Fazl, *The Akbar Nāma*, tr. H Beveridge, repr. Ess Ess, New Delhi, 1973, I, 647-8.

20 *Akbar Nāma*, II, 343-4.

21 There is no good reason to doubt the dating of 1562-77 given for this vast series of illustrations by Pramod Chandra, *The Ṭuṭi-nāma*, Akademische Druck, Graz, 1976, 66.

22 *Hamza-nāma*, II, Akademische Druck, Graz, II, No. 10, I.S.1512-1883.

in the early part of Akbar's reign, but could it be that the real world served as a model for the imagined, that the painter knew the sort of temporary platform that would be erected on a hunting expedition?

The fantastical world is represented later in the reign in a picture in Los Angeles which shows a feather-clad fairy drinking with a woman in a tree-house.[23] More important are two pictures from Akbar's Lahore period which seem to show tree-houses as adjuncts of normal court life. The first is in the *Divan* of Anvari of 996/1588, in the Fogg Art Museum (pl. 3.12).[24] The picture accompanies a poem which speaks of friendship and wine. The prince in the tree-house is served wine by a youth, while food is prepared below. The central focus is upon an open book in the prince's hand, whose slim format suggests a *safinah* of verse; another book lies before him. Lodged in a *chinar* whose branches have been cut to accommodate it, the tree-house is rectangular, carpeted, and perhaps decorated with mother-of-pearl; it is reached by a reassuringly solid-looking set of wooden steps. Though the setting is the world of Persian literature, the detail insists that the structure could be real. The second example is different in character, since the picture illustrates the distant history of the Mongols. Of necessity, however, Akbar's painters rendered historical events according to the forms of the Mughal court that they knew. Thus, in the *Chingiznamah* copied for Akbar in 1004/1596, in the Gulistan Museum, 'Mangu holds a feast at Qaraqorum' by Miskin must rely principally on the painter's experience of Fathpur Sikri and Lahore (pl. 3.13).[25] Mangu sits in front of a pavilion and before him on two levels of carpeted dais are attendants with food and drink, musicians and dancing girls. The significant fact about the tree-house in this picture is that it is not in use and is, indeed, not needed. It is simply a feature that the painter believes might reasonably be introduced into a courtly scene to fill space. In the upper left of the picture, the tree-house is in quite an old *chinar*, one of whose branches it has forced to grow out horizontally. With steep wooden steps like those in the Anvari, the house itself is commodious with an entrance balcony, and roofed area containing a throne, all surrounded with parapets of wooden lattice.

Examples from the time of Jahangir seem more conventional or symbolic. 'Prince on horseback offering wine to a youth in a tree-house', in the Freer Gallery of Art, is from an Album for Jahangir and dated by Beach to *c.* 1600.[26] With prince, youth, and wine, this revisits themes of the Anvari, but its intention seems to be a piquant reversal: here it is the cup-bearer who is given to drink. This is a conceit with no bearing on reality. The thirsty youth in the tree-house has no other role than to be thirsty, and almost out of reach; we cannot imagine ourselves sharing his platform, not least because it has no steps. Other pictures show Jahangir and his painters looking back at 'Abd al-Samad's masterpiece and pondering it. This is explicit in a marginal drawing in an Album portion in Berlin, though the tree-house is now reached by ladder (pl. 3.14). Food, wine, music, and a book are present; in the side margin an angel or fairy hovers overhead, while the upper margin has a hunter shooting.[27] Another version, possibly of the 17th century, is among pictures on the walls of the Millionenzimmer at Schönbrunn.[28] More enigmatic are two pictures, one formerly in the Binney Collection and one in that of Prince Sadruddin Aga Khan, datable *c.* 1610.[29] Both have a central *chinar* in mountainous country in which live herds of horses. In both, a figure who must be Iskandar is portrayed after a western model, his face in profile, and wearing a Mannerist version of a Greek helmet. In the first picture he is not strictly in a tree-house, but perched in a tree without benefit of platform; he has a hawk on his hand and has evidently paused on a hunt, since we see his horse and a hunter shooting. Below the tree a turbaned personage proffers a book, while a cup-bearer stands ready. In the other picture the hunting elements are absent; Iskandar is in a tree-house whose legs suggest it might sometimes stand on the ground, with him is a youth who hands him a cup; below the tree are musicians, and two figures in discussion about carrying a book up to Iskandar (pl. 3.15). The youth and the man with the book wear turbans of the style of Humayun. Either picture might intend Iskandar's meeting with the learned men of India, from Nizami's *Khamsah*, but this is far from certain. What is clear is that the familiar association of ideas is present:

---

23 Pratapaditya Pal, *Indian Painting*, Los Angeles County Museum of Art, 1993, No. 51 B.

24 Annemarie Schimmmel and Stuart Cary Welch, *Anvari's Divan*, Metropolitan Museum of Art, New York, pl. 2.

25 J Marek and H Knízková, *The Jenghiz Khan Miniatures*, Spring, London, 1963, No. 23.

26 Milo Cleveland Beach, *The Imperial Image*, Freer Gallery of Art, Washington, DC, 1981, No. 16 b.

27 Ernst Kühnel and H Goetz, *Indische Buchmalerei*, Scarabaeus, Berlin, 1924, pl. 24.

28 W Staude, 'Abd us-Samad, der Akbar-Maler und das Millionenzimmer im Schlosse Schönbrunn', *Belvedere*, I, 1931, 155-160, Abb. 90-92.

29 Edwin Binney, 3rd, *Indian Miniature Painting From the Collection of Edwin Binney 3rd: The Mughal and Deccani Schools with some related Sultanate material*, Portland Art Museum, Portland, 1973, No. 50; B N Goswamy and Eberhard Fischer, *Wonders of a Golden Age*, Museum Rietberg, Zurich, 1987, No. 49, M. 162.

tree-house, music, wine, books. As the turban style of the second picture suggests Humayun, or possibly the young Akbar, it may be that either is shown with Iskandar in the mountainous landscape of Afghanistan, whence they both entered India. Thus, whatever may be their ostensible subject, these pictures suggest a meditation on 'Abd al-Samad's work: the tree-throne is the locale where the young Mughal learns to emulate Iskandar.

When Jahangir's painters move to their more overtly symbolic phase we reach 'Jahangir as Lord of Time' of the Freer Gallery of Art (pl. 3.16).[30] A new symbol is used for the throne, but the circular top of the hourglass on its supporting cup surely carries a reference to Akbar's throne platform at Fathpur Sikri. Like that throne also it serves multiple purposes: to display the sun-king, to assert his mythic domination of time, to awe foreigners, and as a place to enshrine the gift of a book—probably the Qur'an given to Sayyid Muhammad in 1618.[31] After Jahangir the motif seems to lose its appeal, but an 18th-century picture in the Chester Beatty Library showing a lord and his retinue resting in a tree-house shows it is not quite forgotten.[32]

I suggest that Akbar wanted a place of seclusion and shade in which to rest and look at books—which would be stored in the wall niches. If its form signalled him to be on the one hand an ideal Indian ruler, and on the other like Solomon, so much the better.

[30] Beach, *The Imperial Image*, No. 17 a, 42.15.

[31] Jahangir, *The Tuzuk-i Jahbngiri*, tr. Alexander Rogers, ed. H Beveridge, repr. Munshiram Manoharlal, New Delhi, 1978, II, 34.

[32] Linda York Leach, *Mughal and other Indian Paintings from the Chester Beatty Library*, Scorpion Cavendish, London, 1995, I, 4.22.

Pl. 3.1 'Diwan-i Khass', Fathpur Sikri, general.

Pl. 3.2 Facade.

Pl. 3.3 Pillar.

Pl. 3.4 Throne platform.

Pl. 3.5 *'The young Akbar offers Humayun a picture', Gulistan Pl. Museum, Tehran. After Pope,* Survey, *X, 912.*

Pl. 3.6 Righthand of frontispiece to Yusuf u Zulaykha, *52.1980, David Collection, Copenhagen. After, Folsach, Islamic Art, No. 28.*

Pl. 3.7 Lacquer upper cover, formerly 1948.12-11.028, British Museum, London, reproduced courtesy of the Trustees of the British Museum.

Pl. 3.8 Righthand of frontispiece to a section of Khamsah, *Elliott 194, 34 b, Bodleian Library, University of Oxford.*

Pl. 3.9 'Prince in a tree-house', OA 7124, Section Islam, Musée du Louvre, Paris.

Pl. 3.10 'Fairies in tree-house', 50.2, Freer Gallery of Art, Smithsonian Institution, Washington, D.C.

Pl. 3.11 'The witch 'Anqarut tempts Iraj' (detail), I.S.1512-1883, Victoria and Albert Museum, London. V&A Picture Library.

Pl. 3.12 'Prince in a tree-house', Divan-i Anvari *of 996/1588, Harvard University Art Museums, Cambridge, Mass. After Schimmel and Welch, Anvari's Divan, pl. 2.*

Pl. 3.13 'Mangu holds a feast at Qaraqorum' (detail), Chingiznamah *of 1004/1596, Gulistan Museum, Tehran. After, Marek and Knízková, Jenghiz Khan Miniatures, 23 b.*

Pl. 3.14 'Tree-house' detail in marginal decoration, Jahangir Album, 24 a, Staatsbibliotek zu Berlin.

Pl. 3.15 'Iskandar in conversation in a tree-house', M. 162, Sadruddin Aga Khan Collection. Courtesy of Prince and Princess Sadruddin Aga Khan.

Pl. 3.16 'Jahangir as Lord of Time', 42.15, Freer Gallery of Art, Smithsonian Institution, Washington, D.C.

4 AN ANTHROPOMORPHIC GLASS RHYTON[1]

Stefano Carboni

An interesting and unusual glass object was purchased by the Eretz Israel Museum in 1993.[2] The piece is an anthropomorphic figurine in translucent yellowish green blown glass with details created in applied glass of the same color. The figure is 19cm high and its diameter at the base is about 8cm. The object is in good condition: only the left arm and fragments of the applied decoration are missing; its surface presents slight corrosion and some weathering, indicating that it was buried for some time before it came to light, but it is preserved in a surprisingly good condition. The glass includes several small bubbles and the pontil mark is visible at the center of the base.

The body of the figurine can be described simply as a cylindrical bottle, slightly compressed in the middle, with a short neck. The top of the neck has an opening and there is a second funnel-shaped spout on the lower part of the body. Consequently, the object is a rhyton, although its shape is rather unusual. The somatic features of the anthropomorphic figure, its robe, as well as the object it holds in its hands were built around the bottle by means of glass applied in the hot-worked technique. The face is a flat oval medallion applied around the bottle's neck, then pinched to give shape to the nose, eyes, and mouth. The face is surmounted by a peculiar headdress terminating in an oval point with two 'flaps' on either side, its upper part extending above the mouth of the bottle. The figurine stands on two feet, its arms flanking either side of the vessel (part of the left arm is missing). The forearms are detached from the body because the figure holds a large object placed on its chest. Several long plaits of hair run along its back from under the headdress to reach the waist. The figure wears a full-length robe suggested by a collar, a belt, and a wavy brim on the back. Two small roundels on the two sides of the chest are likely to suggest breasts. This detail, together with the long plaits, should indicate that the glassmaker meant to represent a female body. The long vertical object the figure holds, placed on its chest above the frontal spout, may look at first like a harp, but a closer inspection reveals it to be a snake (when viewed in profile, it resembles a cobra snake).

This piece is unique, to my knowledge, and is therefore of great interest even if its workmanship is not of the highest quality. All applied attributes are only summarily indicated: its arms and feet do not show fingers and toes; its face has just a hint of facial features; and the remainder of the applied glass is freely and sketchily rendered around the main body.

Yellowish green glass was common to many workshops, in many areas, and in different periods. Like pottery, glass had a wide range of functions in all periods, from plain tableware for everyday use to extremely refined works produced for royal and princely patronage. In the present case, notwithstanding its rarity, the lack of prominent artistic skills on this figurine indicates that it was produced as an affordable item for ordinary use and not for a rich patron. As for its function and meaning, the issue is more complex and will be addressed later.

When I was shown a picture of this object for the first time, my immediate response was that it was likely to be an early Islamic piece, possibly Umayyad. Technical details, such as the applied and pinched glass of the same color point to the late tradition of Roman-Byzantine glass in the Eastern Mediterranean region that greatly influenced early Islamic glass production in the Syro-Palestinian area.[3] The figure, initially interpreted as a musician holding a harp while singing (its mouth seems to be slightly open), may have been in accordance with libation and convivial scenes in settings like caliphal palaces of the Umayyad period, such as Khirbat al-Mafjar.[4] Or, perhaps it may have been related to glass production in Samarra, the ʿAbbasid

[1] This article is adapted from a paper given by the author at a conference on the History of Bukhara, Bukhara, Uzbekistan, 5 October 1993.

[2] Inv. no. MHG 193. It is regarded as possibly Iranian, late Sasanian (6th-7th century AD). See *Journal of Glass Studies*, 37, 1995, 99 and S Carboni and D Whitehouse, *Glass of the Sultans*, New York, 2001.

[3] For a general survey of this production, see for example the catalogue of the exhibition held in Lucerne: *3000 Jahre Glaskunst von der Antike bis zu Jugendstil*, Lucerne, 1981, esp. 110-28. See also the discussion and bibliography of the entry cat. no. 12 in C V Bornstein and P Soucek, *The Meeting of two Worlds: the Crusades and the Mediterranean Context*, Ann Arbor, 1981, 34.

[4] The most complete study on this site is R W Hamilton, *Khirbat al-Mafjar*, Oxford, 1959.

capital, a century and a half later, representing a foreign musician, since its pointed headdress seems to indicate an eastern provenance (original sources mention foreign dancers and musicians).[5] The lack of evidence of rhyta of similar anthropomorphic shape in the Islamic world at that date, however, led me to explore other possibilities outside the Syrian and Mesopotamian areas, extending my research to Greek and Roman art and the Far Eastern artistic traditions. The study confirmed that the object is very unusual and that there are no close parallels for it. In addition, the range of suggestions I collected from colleagues was so large that I had to extend my horizon from Europe all the way to Eastern Asia.

Elfriede Knauer, an expert in Central Asian and Far Eastern art, wrote that the type of musician (such was its identification at the time) strongly reminded her of a glazed terracotta statuette from the late T'ang dynasty, which is datable from the 10th century AD and is presently in the Royal Ontario Museum, Toronto. Its use as a rhyton seemed to Dr Knauer a Central Asian feature and she mentioned that in Chinese sources, Central Asia was the provider of musicians for the imperial court. Therefore, she instinctively would have placed the type in Central Asia, whatever the ethnos of the glassmaker might have been.[6] On the other hand, James Watt of the Department of Asian Art in the Metropolitan Museum could not see any real connection with Chinese art and was suspicious about a Central Asian attribution of this glass figurine.[7] Jessie McNab of the Department of European Sculpture and Decorative Arts in the Metropolitan Museum dismissed the object saying that she had quite a number of similar pieces in her department, which are usually considered Spanish from the 18th or 19th century. She added that the double-gourd shaped bottle was made to appear in animal form and resembled the so-called 'bear-jugs', which represent a bear on its haunches hugging a dog.[8] David Whitehouse of the Corning Museum of Glass shook my belief that the object was produced somewhere in Asia. He wrote that it was a tantalizing puzzle and suggested it might have been produced in Germany in the 15th or 16th century, comparing it to a three-dimensional head of Christ datable to the late 15th century.[9]

An exhibition on ceramics from the area of Samarqand held in Paris and other French cities in 1992-93 included objects from the 8th through the 13th century AD. The first catalogue entry shows an anthropomorphic rhyton in the shape of a naked male figure, made of unglazed earthenware and about 16cm tall. Reported to have been found at Afrasiyab (old Samarqand) and datable to the 7th or 8th century, it does not provide a perfect match for our glass statuette, but the relationship between the two objects is evident.[10] The works are both anthropomorphic-shaped rhyta and have similar dimensions; their two openings are placed above the figures' heads and frontally on the lower part of their bodies. In the case of the earthenware rhyton, the frontal spout represents the phallus of the naked male figure; on the glass statuette, the funnel-shaped opening is definitely pseudo-phallic and helps to give the impression that the supposedly female body, with its breasts and long plaits, belongs instead to a hermaphrodite.

The production of both rhyta and terracotta statuettes—though very seldom in combination—has a long-standing tradition in the regions of modern Afghanistan, Uzbekistan, Turkmenistan, and also Iran which were known as Margiana, Bactria, Sogdiana, and Transoxiana.[11]

Glass rhyta are much less frequently excavated than ceramic ones. Some fragments of the late Sasanian period and a few more early Islamic pieces, however, are known. They usually belong to one of the two large categories in which the rhyta are usually identified; the first category include those shaped as drinking horns (called *bālogh* in Persian).[12] For example, one object from the early Islamic period in the Victoria and Albert Museum is made of colorless cut glass[13] and a second one in the Corning Museum of Glass has a stain-painted decoration on greenish colourless glass.[14] The second category of rhyta includes

[5] C J Lamm, *Das Glas von Samarra. Die Ausgrabungen von Samarra*, vol. 4, Berlin, 1928.

[6] Letter dated August 16th, 1992. The T'ang statuette is published in E Knauer, 'Ex oriente vestimenta. Trachtgeschichtliche Beobachtungen zu Ärmelmantel und Ärmeljacke', *Aufstieg und Niedergang der Römischen Welt*, II, 12, 3, 1985, 578-741, pl. XVII: 27.

[7] Personal communication, August 1992.

[8] Memorandum dated 17 August 1992.

[9] Letter dated 25 August 1992.

[10] *Terres secrètes de Samarcande. Ceramiques du VIIIe au XIIIe siècle*, Paris, 1992, cat. no. 1, 75.

[11] See for example B Rowland, *Ancient Art from Afghanistan: Treasures from the Kabul Museum*, New York, 1966 and *Ancient Art in Afghanistan. Objects from the Kabul Museum*, London, 1971; J C Gardin, *Céramiques de Bactres*, Paris, 1957.

[12] A study on the two categories of rhyta (horn- and theriomorphic-shaped) is A S Melikian-Chirvani, 'Le rhyton selon les sources persanes. Essai sur la continuité culturelle iranienne de l'Antiquité à l'Islam', *Studia Iranica*, 11, 1982, 263-92. For the drinking horns see also M E Masson, G A Pugachenkova, *The Parthian Rhytons of Nisa*, Florence, 1982 (English ed.); V I Evison, 'Germanic glass drinking horns', in *Journal of Glass Studies*, XVII, 1975, 74-84.

[13] Inv. no. C75.1969; it can be attributed to the 8th or 9th century.

[14] Inv. no. 69.1.4, attributed to the 9th to 11th century. See *Journal of Glass Studies*, XII, 1970, 174, no. 23; R J Charleston, *Masterpieces of*

all theriomorphic objects (*takūk* in Persian) in the shape of various animals, especially bulls and lions, sometimes horses, rams, and others. Fragments of one of these theriomorphic rhyta in glass, probably bull-shaped, were excavated at Afrasiyab by archaeologists Pugachenkova and Rempel who dated the pieces to about the 8th or 9th century AD.[15]

The only complete extant zoomorphic glass rhyton is a colorless horse in the Toledo Museum of Art.[16] Like the Eretz Museum's anthropomorphic object, its details such as the saddle, reins, and head, and the funnel-shaped opening under its belly were created around a gourd-shaped bottle in the hot-worked technique. The technique of glass manipulation is so similar in the two objects that, notwithstanding the different subjects, they are likely to have been made in neighboring workshops in the same period. The horse has been assigned a 12th- or 13th-century date in the Syrian region by Bornstein and Soucek, an attribution that Carboni and Whitehouse revised in the light of the discovery of the anthropomorphic rhyton. Anthropomorphic rhyta, such as the present glass figure, are not mentioned in the literature as belonging to the *takūk*s, or theriomorphic, objects. Therefore, a new, third category of anthropomorphic rhyta should be created of which very little is known so far.

Turning our attention to the image represented by the small terracotta rhyton mentioned above, it is possible to notice that anthropomorphic terracotta statuettes with applied features like our glass object, have a long history in the Central Asian area. For example, they have been found by archaeologists in different sites in Afghanistan and some of them can be dated to the second millennium BC. The best known of these small anthropomorphic figurines belong to a group usually called 'the Margian goddesses' studied in particular by Pugachenkova and Grenet.[17] Their attributions range from the 2nd or 1st century BC to about the 3rd century AD and they have been found principally in Margiana but also in a larger area that includes Bactria. The goddesses are represented as female figures, sometimes naked, sometimes half-naked, more often fully dressed in tunics whose folds betray an obvious Hellenistic influence. The name—Margian goddesses—was assigned because they are thought to represent votive figures worshipped during cult rituals.

Glass. A World History from the Corning Museum of Glass, New York, 1990 (1st ed. 1980), 77; and Carboni and Whitehouse, *op. cit.*

15 G A Pugachenkova and L Rempel, *Istoriya Iskusstva Uzbekistana*, Moscow, 1965, 209-10, pl. 213.

16 Bornstein and Soucek, *op. cit.*, 34, no. 12; Carboni and Whitehouse, *op. cit.*

17 G A Pugachenkova, 'Margianskaya Boginya', in *Sovietskaya Arkheologia*, XXIX-XXX, 1959, 119-40; F Grenet, 'Trois documents religieux de Bactriane Afghane', in *Studia Iranica*, 11, 1982, 155-62.

A characteristic feature is the large headdress that most of these statuettes wear: it is tall, often extending above the head and, like a kind of hood, it envelops either side of the head. Grenet found an intact goddess statuette in Bactria: she holds a mirror in her right hand, in a Hellenistic fashion.[18] Pugachenkova found a large number of less artistic parallels to this statuette during her excavations, the headdress of one of which includes a pair of protruding snakes.[19] The glass rhyton under discussion may derive from a tradition similar to the above-mentioned Margian goddesses. Notwithstanding its rather crude execution and the unusual material it is made of, this rhyton manifests a distinctive classical quality and displays an archetypal aura that links it to ancient iconographies. Its headdress and the fact that it wears a robe are common features that aid in linking the glass rhyton to the Margian goddesses. If the suggestion is accepted that the rhyton may also be interpreted as a goddess holding a snake, then the parallel with the Margian figures becomes more evident.

Valentina Raspopova and Boris Marshak of the Hermitage, Saint Petersburg, mentioned that images of snake-holding goddesses are familiar in Central Asia, especially in Sogdiana.[20] They also showed me an unpublished photograph of a fragmentary terracotta figurine excavated at Panjikent, near the border between Uzbekistan and Tajikistan—datable to about the 8th century AD—which bears features, especially long plaits, that are strongly reminiscent of the technique of applied and pinched glass employed on the rhyton. Raspopova also surmised that fragments of glass with applied decoration found near Panjikent might come from objects similar to our rhyton. Gulsara Babajanova of the Hamza Institute, Tashkent, who attended the conference in Bukhara where I originally presented this paper, wrote that '... there exists an analogue to your glass rhyton that has been discovered during the excavations in Akhshket [in Ferghana, Uzbekistan] by the archaeologist Akhrarov. I was informed about it by Dr Abdurazakov who is associated with the Institute of Archaeology of the Academy of Sciences of the Republic of Uzbekistan in Samarqand.'[21] Unfortunately, I have not been able to obtain a photograph of this important—and to the best of my knowledge, unpublished—comparable glass rhyton.

18 Grenet, *op. cit.*, fig. 2.

19 Pugachenkova, *op. cit.*, fig. 10.2.

20 Personal communication, 1994.

21 Letter dated 23 December, 1993.

In conclusion, all related evidence suggests that this highly unusual glass rhyton was a ritual object utilized during a cult in which a goddess holding a snake was venerated. The presence of the snake points to an apotropaic intention for this statuette while its function as a rhyton may indicate that it contained some liquid with supposed healing properties. Its dimensions suggest that it could be comfortably held in one hand: the orifice above the head was closed with the thumb while the liquid was poured through the frontal, funnel-shaped spout from which one could also drink, provided this was part of the ritual.

The small terracotta rhyton found at Afrasiyab mentioned above (see note 10) offers evidence that anthropomorphic rhyta were produced in the 7th and 8th centuries. The glass rhyton, which is also linked to the earlier production of small terracotta votive statuettes like the Margian goddesses, for its somewhat classical appearance, should be attributed to the same period as the ceramic object from Afrasiyab. Its suggested date is also supported by the comparable zoomorphic rhyton in the Toledo Museum of Art, which clearly belongs to the Islamic period (see above, p. 60). Its place of production is difficult to establish but all evidence indicates Central Asia—in particular, modern Uzbekistan and Afghanistan—as the most likely area where this rhyton may have been created.

Pl. 4.1

5 TAKING A STAND

John Carswell

In the collection of Chinese porcelain at the British Museum is a blue and white porcelain stand, acquired when Basil Gray was the Keeper of Oriental Antiquities and Ralph Pinder-Wilson was his deputy. The circumstances under which it found its way to London from Syria are worth recording.

In the late 1960s a quantity of Chinese porcelain appeared on the market in Damascus, and I was intrigued enough by this phenomenon to start recording it. During my investigations as to its origin, I heard of a private collection of Chinese blue and white belonging to a well-known physician in Damascus, Dr Joseph Aractingi. I contacted him, and he showed me small but interesting private collection, mostly Ming, which he had bought over the years in various antique shops. One object in the vitrine immediately caught my eye, which was the stand in question (pl. 5.1). Undoubtedly of Chinese porcelain, the shape and decoration was most un-Chinese, and it appeared to carry an Arabic inscription. Further inspection revealed that it was actually based on an Islamic metal form, the prototype being an inlaid brass stand of the Mamluk dynasty (pl. 5.2). I photographed and drew it and promptly forgot about it.

Some months later I was in London, and went to visit Basil Gray. After chatting about various things, he said he wanted to show me something that they had just bought. He opening an imposing mahoghany case in his office, and inside was the stand from Damascus, which he said they had purchased for no great sum of money. Apparently Dr Aractingi had died, and his nephew (who had noted my special interest in the object) had flown with it to London and sold it to the museum. I was intrigued to see it once again, and it was at this point that Ralph Pinder-Wilson suggested I should do some further research on the object. This led to my first article in *Oriental Art*.[1]

During the course of writing the article, I found out a number of interesting things about the object. First, its use; in the context of the Islamic world, brass stands were used as supports for trays, so that a number of guests could be seated around and eat communally. The stands raised the trays at a convenient height from the ground, and were often elaborately embellished with engraved decoration and pious inscriptions, even dedications to Mamluk officials and bearing their blazons.[2] On a humbler level, glazed Mamluk pottery stands are recorded. But the Chinese stand could hardly have had a similar use, for no porcelain trays are known which they might have supported. At the time, the clue appeared to be the Arabic inscriptions, which were indecipherable, and obviously painted by a scribe who had no accurate knowledge of the language (pl. 5.1). More faithfully rendered were the interpretations of the engraved ornament, such as the roundels on the sides and radiating chevrons on the top. I concluded at the time that the fact that the stand had appeared in Damascus would suggest that it must have been a diplomatic present, sent by the Chinese to some dignitary in the Islamic world.

The date of the stand would appear to bear out that thesis, for the style of the painting (and particularly the only Chinese feature, the rosettes under the rim) was that of the early 15th century, exactly at the period when the emperor Yongle (1403-24) launched an extraordinary series of six maritime expeditions to the west between 1405 and 1421, with a seventh final mission dispatched in 1431 by his successor the emperor Xuande (1426-35). This was one of the very few instances when the Chinese were seriously interested in the rest of the world, reversing their normally isolationist approach. Added to this, all seven expeditions were under the command of a Muslim admiral, Zheng He, and his translator was another Chinese Muslim, Ma Huan, who had a working knowledge of Persian and Arabic, and whose chronicle of the expeditions is the chief source of information about them. Although most of the expeditions were to southeast Asia, India, the Persian Gulf and East Africa, seven emissaries on the last voyage (1431-

[1] John Carswell, 'An Early Ming Porcelain Stand from Damascus', *Oriental Art*, New series, Vol.XII, no. 3, Autumn 1966, 176-182.

[2] *Op. cit.*, 181-2.

33) left the main expedition at Calicut and actually got as far Jiddah via Dhufar, Aden and La'sa, then proceeding overland to Mecca. As we will see in a moment, it is important to note that this last expedition was the one that set forth under the reign of the emperor Xuande.[3]

When I first published the British Museum stand I made the classic mistake of assuming that it was an unique, one-off object. You can thus imagine my surprise when a second identical stand turned up in China itself, now in the Tianjin Municipal Museum, and I have since heard rumours of others.[4] However, the final link in the chain comes from Jingdezhen itself, the primary manufacturing site for blue and white porcelain. Here the recent excavations of Professor Liu Xinyuan at the Hutian kiln site in the city have produced a number of fragmentary Yuan and Ming vessels. Amongst these are Yongle plain white wares, many of them copying the shapes of Islamic metal vessels, including ewers, tankards, bowls, candlesticks, twin-handled flasks and a plain white stand of exactly the form under discussion. Moreover, many more vessels were recovered of the same Islamic shapes, but decorated in underglaze blue, some bearing Xuande reign marks. These include two fragments of a blue and white stand of precisely the same type as the subject of this article. The smaller fragment is from just below the rim, decorated with a rosette, and on the body part of an inscribed band, with the first four characters of a Xuande mark immediately above the roundel.[5]

These sherds conclusively link the British Museum stand to the period of the emperor Xuande (1426-35). As noted above, it was Xuande who ordered the seventh and last maritime expedition to the Western Ocean in 1431, of which part of the expedition split off when it reached Calicut and sailed for south Arabia and the Red Sea, landing at Jiddah and visiting Mecca. The chronicler Ma Huan gives a detailed description of the holy city and its monuments including the Ka'ba, which makes interesting reading when compared to Ibn Battuta's account of Mecca in 1326, just over a century earlier. Ma Huan states that the Mecca party included

> an interpreter [presumably Ma Huan himself] and others, seven men in all, and sent them with a load of musk, porcelain articles, and other such things. It took them one year to go and return. They bought all kinds of unusual commodities, and rare valuables, *ch'i-lin,* lions, 'camel-fowls' (ostriches) and other such things; in addition they painted an accurate representation of the 'Heavenly Hall' (the Ka'ba); [and] they returned to the capital (Beijing). The king of the country of Mo'ch'ieh (Mecca) also sent envoys who brought some local articles, accompanied the seven men – the interpreter [and others] who had originally gone there, and presented the articles to the court.[6]

The 'porcelain articles' may well have included the blue and white stand, and it is not difficult to imagine how it could have then travelled northwards overland at a later stage as far as Damascus. In any event, the political climate in China in the early 15th century with its unusual interest in the Islamic world provided just the right environment for the stand to begin its long voyage to the West.

---

3 Ma Huan, *Ying-yai Sheng-lan* ('The Overall Survey of the Ocean's Shores') [1433], trans. J.V.G.Mills, Hakluyt Soceity, Cambridge University Press, 1970. Mill's classic text is further discussed with regard to the maritime export of Chinese porcelain in the early fifteenth century in Carswell, *Blue & White, Chinese porcelain throughout the world,* British Museum Press, London, 2000, 82-91.

4 *Op. cit.,* 83, note 3.

5 *Op. cit.*, Plate 80, especially c, d.

6 Ma Huan, *loc. cit.,* 35-6, 173-8.

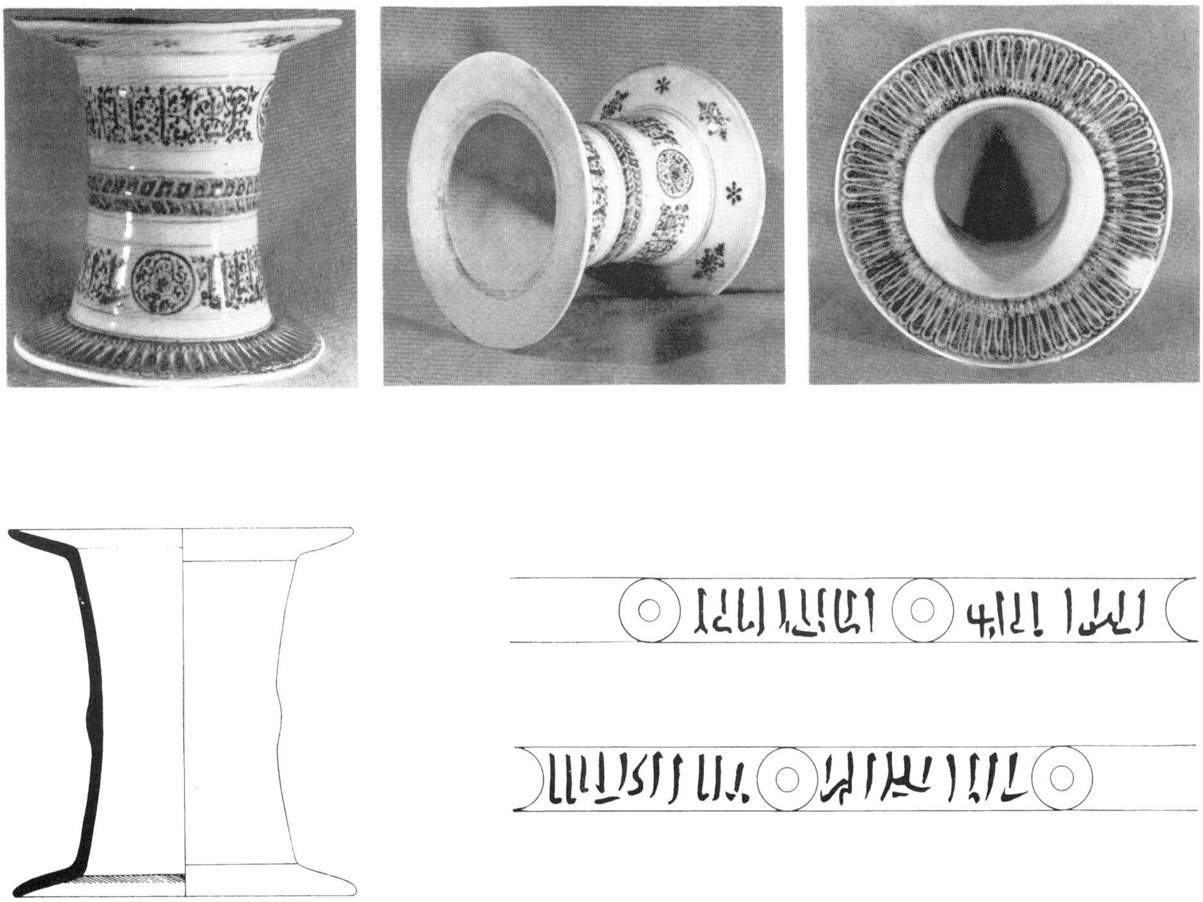

Pl. 5.1 Chinese blue and white porcelain stand, Jingdezhen, Xuande period (1426-35), H.17.2cm D.17cm. Found in Damascus. British Museum, London OA 1966. 12-15.1, Brooke Sewell Bequest.

Pl. 5.2 Islamic engraved brass stand, Mamluk dynasty, Egypt. 14th century H. 29cm D. 21cm. This stand is close in size to the Chinese porcelain stand, and also features roundels in the upper band which fall exactly half way between those on the lower register.

6 BEASTS THAT ROARED: THE PISA GRIFFIN AND THE NEW YORK LION

Anna Contadini, Richard Camber and Peter Northover

The Pisa Griffin

Anna Contadini

My interest in the Pisa Griffin (pl. 6.1) goes back to my childhood, when my parents took me to visit Pisa for the first time. I am still as impressed by the beast as I was then, but I am now equally intrigued by the mystery that surrounds it. As will be clear from this paper, although our knowledge of the Griffin has advanced somewhat, especially regarding the hypothesis of its function, there are still many questions that remain unanswered. Further, the discovery of a rather similar lion, sold at Christie's in 1993[1] and now on loan to the Metropolitan Museum of Art in New York, has opened up new avenues for research, especially technical, but also regarding style and provenance.

My research on the Griffin began ten years ago,[2] the findings being published in part in 1993, in the entry of the catalogue of the Venice exhibition *Eredità dell'Islam*,[3] where I was also able to publish the New York Lion (pl. 6.2) and to note, albeit briefly, its relationship to the Griffin. During a trip to Pisa in 1992 I had discovered something both puzzling and interesting. It was clear that the presumed function of the Griffin as a piece for a fountain needed further substantiation, and consequently that more needed to be learnt about its construction, so I conducted what one might call a gynæcological examination of the Griffin through the opening in the belly, and to my astonishment discovered that it had a womb! In other words, inside the Griffin and attached to the rear is a bowl-shaped vessel with slightly everted rims opening towards the front of the animal (pl. 6.3). It is fixed to the wall of the body by means of a short solid metal stem, and there is no opening to the outside. Further, it was possible to ascertain that the body is hollow, but that there is no trace of a hydraulic system. A year later, in 1993, I was able to establish that the New York Lion has the same internal characteristics: a bowl-shaped vessel with everted rim, opened towards the front (pl. 6.4) and attached to the rear of the body by a small piece of solid metal, a hollow body containing no trace of a hydraulic system, and hollowed legs, unfortunately damaged. We now can advance new arguments to support the likely hypothesis that these vessels were part of a noise-making mechanism (see *Function*).

After the Lion was sold at Christie's it remained in London for a long time, as its owner was keen to have it examined in order to discover more about its construction, metal composition and, ultimately, provenance and date. But it was evident that any study on the Lion had to go in tandem with that of the Griffin, and it was as a result of Ralph Pinder-Wilson's initial suggestion of a joint study that there emerged the collaboration between Richard Camber, Peter Northover and myself the provisional results of which are presented here. Even though Ralph has not contributed to this study in writing he has followed our research very closely, spending time discussing various aspects and providing useful suggestions. It is therefore only proper that this paper should be dedicated to him.

Description

The Griffin is 107cm high (to the top of the ear); 90cm long and a maximum of 46cm wide (measured at the base of the wings). It has a head slightly resembling that of a

---

1 Christie's 1993, 124-127, Lot 293.

2 Many people and institutions have helped over the many years of my research: I should like to thank first of all the President, Prof Ranieri Favilli and the Director of the Opera del Duomo di Pisa, Dr Antonio Lazzarini, for allowing me to study the Griffin and permission to take samples for analyses; Mr Andrea Cinacchi, of the Archivio dell'Opera del Duomo, who assisted in the study of the documents and facilitated the photography; Mons. Mario Beconcini of the Archivio Capitolare; and the staff of the Pisa National Archive. The owner of the New York Lion generously sponsored my second research trip to Pisa in 1994. Dr Brian Gilmour of the Royal Armouries of the Tower of London did much work on the technical construction of the Lion and spent time in discussion. My father, Attilio Contadini, has been of great assistance in translating the Latin passages in various documents. I should also like to thank Richard Camber, Peter Northover, and Ralph Pinder-Wilson for time for discussion, useful suggestions and for their generosity in sharing their superior knowledge with me.

3 Contadini 1993, 126-131, col. pls. 43 and 43b, and black and white fig. 43a.

cockerel, with two wattles and a slightly open beak. It has four legs with feline feet, and the wings are attached by rivets around the shoulders of the forelegs. There is an aperture in the beak and another at the rear within a rectangular block which measures H 8cm x W. 9.7cm. It was here, probably, that the base of the missing tail was inserted. There is a big, irregular aperture on the belly, inside which is the vessel described above (pl. 6.3). It occupies a considerable part of the belly, measuring *c.* 24cm in length, and has a rather uneven opening measuring *c.* 9.5cm in diameter.

The decoration of the Griffin is incised and organized in panels: there are semicircular plumes on the breast with, beneath, part of the inscription, and plumes with curls on the head, neck and wings. On the back there are scattered concentric circles with, between them, a decoration of crossed lines, and at the bottom of each flank are further parts of the inscription. At the shoulder joints between body and legs there are shield-like panels containing, on the forelegs, the figure of a rampant lion and, on the hindlegs, what appears to be a dove.

The Griffin was taken down from the Cathedral in 1828. It was placed first in the Camposanto and later in the Museum. The Griffin presently found on top of the Cathedral is a modern copy.

The Griffin in the early literature

During a second research visit to Pisa in 1994 I found iconographical evidence for the Griffin being placed on top of the Cathedral that dates back to the late 1400s. This is a representation of the leaning tower and part of the nave of the Cathedral towards the apse on top of which is a black bird with two legs and outspread wings. It appears in a marquetry panel on the underside of a chorus seat of the cathedral (pl. 6.5) which may be dated to the end of the fifteenth century.[4] It is interesting that at this early stage the animal is 'seen' as a bird and not as a Griffin.

In the literature we begin with an indirect mention of the Griffin (but with no illustration) from the early 1540s, when it was reported that a new column had been made to support it on top of the roof of the Cathedral.[5]

The Griffin is subsequently mentioned, but again not illustrated, by Raffaello Roncioni in his *Istorie Pisane*, a work datable to between the end of the sixteenth and beginning of the seventeenth century. It is there described as a hippogryph standing on top of the cathedral, and as a very beautiful bronze object with Egyptian characters inscribed on it.[6]

In *c.* 1643 Paolo Tronci made a watercolour of the cathedral with, on top,[7] the Griffin which is, however, still represented as a large, two-legged bird with spread wings resting on a column (pl. 6.6). He reports a rather fanciful account of the Griffin, saying that it was a very large and ferocious animal that lived in a wood (the 'Bosco detto Migliarino'), but that it was eventually captured and a bronze statue was made of it.[8] This account, together with Tronci's watercolour as it appears in the manuscript of *c.* 1643, was then published by Peleo Bacci in 1922.[9]

A further description was given in 1705 by Giuseppe Martini, accompanied by three engravings showing the Griffin, this time a clear four-legged griffin, on a short column on top of the roof of the Cathedral at the end of the nave, above the apse.[10] In these engravings it has outspread wings and no tail, and Martini is inclined to identify it as an eagle, one of the four symbols of the Apocalypse, on the grounds that the other three images are also found in the proximity of the apse.

The first representation from an examination at close quarters, even if a rather rapid one, is found in a work by Da Morrona dated 1787-93. He tells us that, pushed by an extreme curiosity to inspect the 'hippogryph', he went up the roof of the Cathedral, usually only accessible to builders, and saw with his own eyes that what Roncioni had thought to be characters engraved on the Griffin were instead decorative motifs. He took an impression of them and reproduced the Griffin in his work, with outspread wings but no tail. Like Roncioni, Da Morrona thinks that it is a work of antiquity, either Egyptian or Etruscan, as it was, so he relates, found during

4 For a discussion of the marquetry panels see Novello and Tongiorgi Tomasi 1986, especially 144, where the panels by Guido da Seravallino are discussed. Although the present panel is not mentioned, it seems that those of views of the town (possibly therefore including also ours) are to be attributed to Seravallino, who operated between 1488 and 1490. Also, for a brief discussion of those now in the Museum see Lucchesi 1993, 84-88. The panels that are still in the chorus can be dated to various periods of the late 15th century. A black and white representation of the panel under discussion is to be found in Burgalassi 1993, Fig. 9, where, however, the Griffin is not discussed.

5 Tanfani Centofanti 1897, 469.

6 The *Istorie Pisane* were compiled between the end of the 16th and the beginning of the 17th century: Roncioni 1844, vol. V, part I, 114.

7 Tronci *c.* 1643, fol. III.

8 Tronci *c.* 1643, fols. 6v-7r.

9 Tronci 1922.

10 Martini 1705, n. 10, 13, figs. 4, 5 and 7.

the excavations of the foundations of the Cathedral among the remains of Hadrian's palace.[11]

The Griffin continued to be mentioned and discussed throughout the 19th century, beginning in 1823 with Cicognara, the first to suggest that the object could be medieval rather than a work of antiquity, and possibly contemporary with the erection of the Cathedral itself.[12] But we have to wait for the well-known Arabist Michelangelo Lanci to have a correct interpretation of the inscription, which he read and translated in 1829, and in his *Trattato delle simboliche rappresentanze Arabiche* of 1846 where he also gives an engraving of the Griffin.[13]

Date and provenance

In 1839 Marcel, who published the inscription, if with some mistakes, and also an engraving of the Griffin, put forward the hypothesis of a southern Italian provenance, considering it an object produced by Muslims under the Normans.[14] For Rohault de Fleury, on the other hand, writing in 1866, it is the type of sculpture that Muslim merchants would order for a Christian or Jewish market, and is to be dated, according to the character of the letters of the inscription, to between the end of the 11th and the beginning of the 12th century.[15]

The hypothesis that starts to emerge in the second half of the 19th century is that the Griffin was booty captured during one of the battles won by the Pisans against the Muslims throughout the 11th and 12th centuries in Sicily, North Africa and Balearic Islands. However, even though the sources talk about fabulous booty, they are never specific about the objects captured. More recently, in 1978, Jenkins drew attention to an inscription on the façade of the cathedral dated 1063, which she considers to be its foundation date.[16] She associated the inscription, which is a report of the main victories of the Pisans in the 11th century, with a Pisan chronicle by Marangone, who, under the year 1088, gives an account of a naval expedition by the Pisans and Genoese against the African coast during the course of which they conquered Mahdiyya and Zawila in Tunisia, taking back rich booty including, according to Jenkins' translation, big bronze objects which were then used to enrich the Cathedral. Jenkins therefore suggests that the Griffin could have been among those objects, and that it was put on top of the cathedral, the construction of which had already started in 1063, as an ornament, and that, consequently, it is a Fatimid work of the 11th century, produced either in Egypt or Tunisia. But the source cited by Jenkins does not specify that the objects were large, and in any case *aeramentorum*, 'bronze objects', is just one of three possible readings, for other compilations of Marangone's text have *ornamentorum*, which can be translated as 'pieces of jewellery', and *ferrammentorum*, which can be translated as 'arms'.[17] Further, as far as the inscription dated 1063 is concerned, it may be pointed out that on the façade of the Cathedral there are six such inscriptions giving the *gesta* of the Pisans in the Mediterranean, with dates ranging from 1006 to 1114, and that they have been the cause of endless discussions among scholars as to which one is to be associated with the foundation of the church.[18] However, the date of the foundation is now accepted to be early in 1064 (and that of the consecration 1118).[19]

If one wants to associate the Griffin with Pisan booty, the sources report at much greater length the magnificence of the booty brought back from the Balearic conquest of 1114, which is also referred to on the façade of the Cathedral,[20] and in 1946 Monneret de Villard advanced the hypothesis that the Griffin, together with a 10th century marble capital from Spain set on the roof of the northern transept of the Cathedral, was Pisan booty either from the conquest of Almeria in 1089 or from that of the Balearic islands in 1114.[21] Monneret associated the Griffin with the deer found in Madinat al-Zahra' and the Monzón lion found in the ruins of an Islamic fortress near Palencia, emphasizing the similarity of decoration, especially

[11] Da Morrona 1787-93, I, 190-195.

[12] Cicognara 1823, 108-9.

[13] Lanci 1845-46, 54-58, fig. XXVII. For Lanci's translation of the inscription see Valeriani 1829.

[14] Marcel 1839.

[15] Rohault de Fleury 1866, 42 and 122-124, fig. XLVI.

[16] Jenkins 1978.

[17] The passage is found in Marangone 1845, vol. VI, part 2, 5-6. The whole Latin passage with an Italian translation is found in Contadini 1993, 130, note 8.

[18] Cicognara 1823, vol. II, 79-89, where the differences of opinions on the matter are discussed.

[19] Scalia 1993.

[20] For the passage in Marangone 1936, 94 on the 1114 Balearic conquest see Contadini 1993, 131, note 10.

[21] Monneret de Villard 1946, 21-3. The capital was subsequently moved to the Battistero, where, in the middle of the baptisimal font, it functioned as a support for the bronze statue of St. John. It is now in the Museum of the Opera del Duomo, sala 1, no. 30. For a discussion and a translation of the Arabic inscription see Contadini 1993, 122-3, no. 39. In this context it is interesting to point to the fact that there is another notable Islamic object in the Museo dell'Opera del Duomo in Pisa: a large brass tray, with a kufic inscription and various decorative motifs which has been preliminary dated to the 12th century. This, now in the Museum, was used in the Sacristy. See Baracchini 1986, where black and white reproductions of the tray, capital and griffin are found (figs. 71-73); also Lucchesi 1993, 20, nos. 29-31 and Fig. 15 (black and white detail of the inscription of the Griffin) and Pl. VI, colour reproduction of the Griffin.

that of the back, which is like a textile.[22] Arguing against Migeon who, in 1907, had classified the Griffin as a Fatimid work of the 11th century on the basis of generic stylistic affiliations,[23] Monneret considered it a Spanish piece of the late 11th-early 12th century. His hypothesis was to be followed in 1966 by Scerrato who, however, suggested an early 11th-century date, that is, during the caliphal period, and considered it a fountain piece.[24]

An 11th-century date was also preferred by Melikian-Chirvani. However, on the basis of the characteristics of static monumentality, the use of inscriptions in kufic script as if surrounding a textile, and the type of script, he argued in 1968 for an attribution to Iran (Khurasan),[25] although subsequently, in 1973, he proposed a Spanish attribution (but probably still at the hands of Iranian craftsmen),[26] thereby taking account of the observation by Fernández Puertas that the style of script in the Griffin is practically identical to that on a metal lamp now in the Archaeological Museum in Madrid.[27]

More recent scholarship has been marked by continuing hesitation over the date. The slightly earlier caliphal period of the late 10th-early 11th century is proposed by Almut von Gladis;[28] Cynthia Robinson, followed by Antonio Milone, opts for the Taifa period of the 11th century;[29] and the present writer cautiously prefers the 11th-12th century.[30] But there has been general agreement on provenance: earlier arguments for southern Italy or the Fatimid territories have been largely discounted, and the predominant view is that the Griffin is to be attributed to Spain. The Fatimid case, like the Spanish one, relies primarily on stylistic association, and given the paucity of comparative material is undeniably much weaker. If we move to Spain, however, there are stylistic affinities with pieces attributable to Spain with a good margin of security.

The most striking similarities are those exhibited by the Monzón lion. Found by Fortuny in an Islamic fortress near Palencia which fell in Christian hands in the 11th century,[31] it has much in common with the Griffin and the New York Lion: the organization of the decoration in sectors; the manner of representing hair/plumes on the chest; the way in which the joints of the legs are highlighted with a shield-like decoration; and the decoration of the back that is reminiscent of a textile edged with an inscription. Other animals attributed to Spain, such as the deer of Cordoba and Madinat al-Zahra', also have a decoration with circles that reminds us of a textile, but freely scattered over their backs,[32] and further such examples are the quadruped in the Bargello and the two aquamanile in the form of a peacock, one in Cagliari and the other in Paris.[33] There is a further aquamanile in the form of a lion in the Keir collection in London which has some similar decorative, incised, features, and has been attributed by Fehérvári to either Sicily or Spain and to the 11th or 12th century.[34]

In addition, Michael Rogers has observed that the decoration on the back of the Griffin, with its scattered circles bordered by a 'kufic' inscription, is extraordinarily similar to Spanish textiles of the beginning of the 13th century.[35] This form of decoration is common to all the animals assigned to Spain. Further, as pointed out above, Fernández Puertas has noted that the style of kufic used in the Griffin is basically identical to that on a metal lamp in Madrid assigned to the late 11th-early 12th century.[36]

Function

The Griffin and the New York Lion confront us with problems of function. Are the two animals pieces for a fountain, as has sometimes been supposed?[37] The fact that both have an opening in the belly and mouth and that the Lion has round lips almost as if to house a pipe, could

22 For the Monzón lion (Paris, Musée du Louvre, no. 7883) see Granada and New York 1992, 270, no. 54. Monneret also notes the similarity with the quadruped in the Bargello National Museum in Florence (inv. n. 63c), for which see Contadini 1993, 124-125, no. 41 and col. Pl., and with a lion in the Victoria and Albert Museum (M. 708-1910), which, however, is a modern, 19th century copy.

23 Migeon 1907, vol. I, 375, fig. 182.

24 Scerrato 1966, 78-80, and 83, fig. 33; also Gabrieli and Scerrato 1985, col. pls. on the flyleaf and on 489.

25 Melikian-Chirvani 1968.

26 Melikian-Chirvani 1973.

27 Published by Fernández Puertas in 1975.

28 Berlin 1989, n. 4/83, 592-3, fig. 195.

29 Granada and New York 1992, n. 15, 216-18. Milone 1993 provides a review of the literature on the Griffin within a book dedicated to the medieval and modern sculptures of the Pisa's Camposanto.

30 Contadini 1993. The above overview of the literature incorporates part of the Venice catalogue entry.

31 Amador de los Rios 1875. The piece is now in the Musée du Louvre, no. 7883. For a discussion of the piece and a bibliography on it see Contadini 1993, 125, note 6 and Contadini 2000, 58 and col. Pl. on 59. See also Granada and New York 1992, 270, no. 54.

32 Now in Cordoba, Museo Arqueológico Provincial, no. 500. See Granada and New York 1992, 210-211, no. 10.

33 Contadini 1993, 124-125, no. 41 (Bargello quadruped) and 125-126, no. 42 (Cagliari aquamanile). For the Paris aquamanile (Musée du Louvre, no. MR 1569) see Paris 1990, 148, no. 119.

34 Fehérvári 1976, no. 28, fig. 9b.

35 Rogers 1992, 552, no. 15.

36 Fernández Puertas 1975.

37 For the Griffin see, for example, Scerrato 1966, 78-80, and 83, fig. 33 and Cynthia Robinson in Granada and New York 1992, 218; and for the same suggestion for the Lion see Christie's 1993, 127.

be cited in support of such a hypothesis. Further, around the aperture on the belly of the Lion (but not the Griffin) is a square recess into which a plate of some sort had evidently been set, thus suggesting a function which required the aperture to be sealed, possibly therefore one involving the insertion of a pipe. What is certain is that any water would have to come through this route, since in both animals the legs are sealed at the top, so that water could not be channelled through them as, for example, in the Alhambra stone lions. Either, then, a pipe would have to be fed through from belly aperture to mouth or the belly would have to be sealed around an inlet pipe and function as a tank. But there is now no trace of a hydraulic system in either the Griffin or the Lion, and whichever method was used to convey water no discernible purpose would be served by the bowl-shaped vessels in the interior.

Could these have been receptacles of some sort? Nothing notable has come up from the samples taken from the interior of the two vessels, and the idea that they could be containers for fire is unlikely. The incense burners in the form of animals that we have from the medieval Islamic world are all of a much smaller scale and have pierced bodies to permit the smoke to come out.[38] Also, the angle at which the vessel is placed in both runs counter to it to be a receptacle, especially for anything liquid, as in both animals it is slightly downwards, towards the aperture of the belly (fig. 6.1).

Is it possible that the internal vessel was part of a mechanism to produce sound? We may take into consideration that the beasts are hollow, that the metal is resonant, and that the internal vessel could have functioned as a further resonator. On an anecdotal level I have always been fascinated by the accounts, found in the documents, which relate that when the original Griffin was still on top of the Cathedral, and the wind was blowing, it would emit eerie and fascinating sounds, channelling the wind through its hollowed body. It is also quite interesting to find that both al-Hamadani (early 10th century) and Yaqut (1179-1229/575-626) in describing the big and high Ghumdan palace in San'a' relate that '... on each of its corners a statue was set, of yellow brass(?), of the biggest size of lion there is. When the wind blew in the direction of one of these statues it would go in through its posterior and come out through the mouth and make the sound of a wild beast roaring.'[39]

[38] See examples in the form of small birds in Fehérvári 1976, pl. 37, nos. 109-111; and one in the form of a lion in Ward 1993, col. pl. 3 (Hermitage Museum, St. Petersburg, IR-1565).

[39] Yaqut 1866-73, vol. 3, 811; see also Serjeant and Lewcock 1983, 44, quoting al-Hamadani, *Iklil*, VIII, Baghdad, 1931, 24.

It is possible that both the Griffin and the Lion were designed to produce such effects, but if we recall the tenth century account by Liutprand of Cremona of the Byzantine throne having, around it, lions that roared, it may be preferable to consider them in the context of such contrivances.[40] The sound-producing mechanism, it may be hypothesized, resembled that of a bagpipe, with the bowl-shaped vessel in the interior acting as a rigid container for the air bag, both holding it in place and helping maintain pressure. Richard Camber consulted an organ builder,[41] who confirmed that this was feasible, and suggested that the Griffin and Lion were originally set on plinths containing bellows.[42] Air would be pumped through a tube set in the opening of the belly up to into the bag. When this was fully inflated and pressing against the vessel the air would be forced out through a reed-pipe leading towards the mouth. The bag would have to be sealed around both pipes and the reed(s) would have to be placed at the beginning of the sounding pipe to make the column of air vibrate. The longer the reed-pipe, the lower the sound, hence the position of the vessel at the back of the

[40] For Liutprand's account, see Liudprand 1930, *Antapodosis*, book VI, chapter 5, 207-8: '... Before the emperor's seat stood a tree, made of bronze gilded over, whose branches were filled with birds, also made of gilded bronze, which uttered different cries, each according to its varying species. The throne itself was so marvellously fashioned that at one moment it seemed a low structure, and at another it rose high in the air. It was of immense size and was guarded by lions, made either of bronze or of wood covered over with gold, who beat the ground with their tails and gave a dreadful roar with open mouth and quivering tongue ...'; also Hammerstein 1986, 45.

[41] Mr Murice Merrel, FRSA, of Bishop and Sons, Organ Manufacturers, London and Ipswich, to whom we are very grateful. Mr Merrel recreated the mechanism in his workshop.

[42] However, according to the various descriptions in both Western and Arab sources the driving mechanism could have been either pneumatic or hydraulic: see Brett 1954 for Byzantine sources. For both Byzantine and Arabic sources, see Hammerstein 1986, chapters 3 and 4 respectively. For a critical list of the Arabic sources, which go back to the eighth century, see Farmer 1965, which includes Yuhanna ibn al-Bitriq (d. *c.* 815/200), 1, no. 7, who briefly mentions a hydraulic organ used in warfare to create fear among the enemy; Banu Musa ibn Shakir (d. 873/259), 7, no. 43, who wrote a treatise on an automatic hydraulic organ, for which see Farmer 1931, 88-114 (Hill 1979 does not talk about the musical automaton); A'yrun (Hero), translated in the ninth century, 18, no. 110, who wrote a treatise on pneumatic machines; and Muristus (Moristos or Myrtos), translated in the ninth century, 18, no. 113, who wrote a treatise on the construction of the reed-pipe pneumatic organ 'the sound of which may be heard sixty miles.' For this, see also Farmer 1931, 60-73 and fig. 1, which is a diagram of the Muristus pneumatic organ. See also the treatise on Automata by Ibn al-Razzaz al-Jazari (early thirteenth century), *Kitab fi ma'rifat al-hiyal al-handasiyya*: Hill 1974, especially 170.

belly. This hypothesis would also account for the puzzling fact that in both the Griffin and the Lion the vessel is cracked: an imperfect casting would not be a problem, as the inner bag would not require a perfect seal around it.

The Griffin and the Lion

Anna Contadini and Richard Camber

The Pisa Griffin and the New York Lion have many characteristics in common. Both are constructed in a similar way, relying on the unusual technique of indirect lost wax casting, and both employed square-section wire or rod to support the internal core. In both there is a solid internal membrane at the top of the legs, a clear indication that the legs and body were cast separately. As already explained above, they have a large aperture on the belly and inside the belly is a very similar vessel which still bears traces of a ceramic mould.

Further, they have the same proportions and have similar incised decorations, including the feature of a 'saddle cloth' on the back with scattered incised circles beneath which is an Arabic inscription in angular script, and many other common decorative motifs, including the shields at the joints of the body with the legs. Indeed, on the foreleg shields of the Griffin a rampant lion is represented, corresponding to a griffin (with wings and tail) on those of the Lion, while on the hind leg shields of the Griffin we find a bird, possibly a dove, and in the Lion a rather more rapacious-looking bird, possibly an eagle.

Further, the style of the angular, floriated script, although not identical, is similar on both (pl. 6.7 and 8). The inscriptions, both made up of standard benedictory formulae, are as follows:

Griffin:

بركة كاملة ونعمة شاملة
غبطة كاملة وسلامة دائمة وعافية
كاملة وسعادة وعيدة (؟) لصاحبه

'perfect blessing and complete well being perfect joy and everlasting peace and perfect health and happiness and wishes to its owner'

Lion:

نعمة وبركة وعافية
وسلامة وسعادة ويمن
وكرامة وبقا لصاحبه

'God's favour and blessing and good health and peace and happiness and prosperity and honour and long life to its owner.'

Despite these similarities, however, it would be unwise to overlook the differences. It has, for example, been established that the bronze used for the Griffin is what is commonly known as gunmetal, with antimony as its most significant impurity, whereas that which was used for the Lion is an unleaded medium tin bronze, with silver as its most significant impurity. Additionally, although the legs in both cases were clearly separately cast, the membrane at the top of the legs of the Griffin is almost continuous with the body, whereas there is a slightly raised ledge around the membrane at the top of the legs of the Lion. Moreover, although the interior vessel of the Lion is cast from the same bronze as the body, in the case of the Griffin a high zinc brass entirely dissimilar to the gunmetal of the body has been employed.

Finally, although the presence in each of an inner vessel of similar structure is compelling, around the aperture on the belly of the Lion, as already noted, is a square recess into which a plate of some sort had evidently been set, while there is no such feature on the Griffin. However, the recess around the opening of the Lion, as Charles Little has observed, maybe due to later manipulation.

One may also add that while the general lack of repetition in the wish lists of the inscriptions might well be interpreted as suggesting complementarity, the style of script is not quite similar enough to indicate the same hand at work, and the inscription on the Griffin is also rather more clearly and accurately incised. These differences strongly suggest that, whatever the precise nature of the relationship between the Griffin and the Lion, they were not made in the same workshop.

Although a more detailed scientific examination of the Griffin is clearly desirable, it is by no means clear that this will cast further light on the nature of its relationship to the Lion. While it is tempting to think that one may have been the model for the other, it is equally conceivable that both derive from a common model. In either case, as the metallurgical evidence suggests, their respective places of origin could have been entirely different.

The New York Lion

Richard Camber [43]

When it first appeared on the London art market in 1993, the New York Lion was described as being Spanish, 11th-12th century.[44] One of the objectives of the present contribution is to draw the attention of students of Islamic art to a body of material from another part of the Mediterranean with which it might perhaps more usefully be compared.

Lacking its lower legs, the lion is 73cm in height; even in its original state, it would almost certainly have been slightly smaller than the Pisa Griffin, which has a maximum height of 107cm. The distinctive and powerful head has pointed oval eyes, the pupils of which are formed by semi-circular depressions. The slightly open mouth, enclosed within stylised lips, has a central aperture above which there is a naturalistically modelled nose. On one ear, there is a shield-like depression, which, like the eyes and the mouth, may once have been inset with a decorative inlay in a different material. The mane is engraved with stylised loops similar to those found on the head of the Pisa Griffin, while the back is decorated with a design of incised and pounced circles in the manner of a *tiraz* textile with a border comprising a dedicatory *kufic* inscription. The shoulders and haunches bear engraved ogival cartouches comprising a surrounding band decorated with small circles: on the shoulders these enclose a panel with the figure of a griffin within a scrolling vine, while, on the haunches, the figure represented is that of a bird, possibly an eagle. On the rear joints of the legs, immediately above the point where they have been broken off, there is an incised 'tear-drop' motif, to which further reference will be made below. It should also be noted that, at several points, the body has been pierced by what would appear to have been a series of projectiles, in much the same manner as the Pisa Griffin and the very much smaller figure of a deer in Munich.[45]

At the current stage of research, it cannot yet be determined whether the discovery that the raw copper used for casting the New York Lion came from an identifiable district in Cyprus is itself of particular significance as regards its place of origin. Not only was Cyprus known to Arab geographers as a source of copper, but, at least until the end of the 10th century, the island was what has been described as 'a demilitarised and neutral no-man's-land in which Christian and Muslim settlers lived side by side, under pledges of mutual toleration and protection'.[46] More significant, however, may be the finding that the alloy used for the figure was an unleaded medium tin bronze: this is an alloy which, while totally uncharacteristic of the Islamic world, does occur in the Latin West, in, for example, aquamaniles and bells. Quite how this is to be interpreted remains uncertain. It could be taken to imply that the Lion was made by an Islamic craftsman familiar with medieval European bronze casting technology; alternatively, it could be taken to mean that it was made by a European craftsman familiar with Islamic models. It is probably true to say that not enough is yet known about the techniques of monumental bronze casting in the Islamic world to rule out the former possibility, but the evidence regarding the familiarity of European craftsmen with Islamic models is so well-known as to suggest that the latter possibility is one that is worth exploring in more detail.

The inscribed *du'a* on the *tiraz* of the Lion, with its invocation of God's favour and divine grace, points to a closer acquaintance with Islam and the Arabic language than the pseudo-Kufic inscriptions found on many medieval European objects. While the crouching lion from Monzón de Campos, which may, because of its findspot, have been made for a Christian ruler, has an inscription in a similar style of kufic, no detailed metallurgical analysis appears to have been undertaken which would warrant the conclusion that it came from the same cultural background as the New York Lion.[47] Similarly, although genuine kufic inscriptions do appear alongside Christian iconography on the three large Middle Byzantine bronze candelabra in the Grand Lavra Monastery on Mount Athos and St Catherine's on Mount Sinai, current knowledge of monumental bronze casting of this period in the Byzantine world is largely confined to the series of bronze doors that were commissioned by Maurus of Amalfi and his family between 1060 and 1087 for presentation to churches

---

[43] For advice and assistance over a number of years, I should like to thank the late Dr Robert Bergman, Dr Tessa Garton, Dr Brian Gilmour, Dr Charles T Little and Mr Rainer Zietz.

[44] Christie's 1993, Lot 293. The lion was first brought to the attention of a wider public by Dr Anna Contadini. See Contadini 1993, 126-131 and figs.43a and 43b.

[45] Erdmann 1938, 252, who remarks of the Munich deer that 'offenbar hat es einmal als Zielscheibe gedient'. On the damage to the Pisa Griffin, Drescher 1985, 344 notes that that the holes in the body are 'durch Beschuss mit grosskalibrigen Gewehrkügeln in neurer Zeit entstanden'.

[46] Jenkins 1953, 1006-14. The late 10th century Persian *Hudud al-'Alam* notes that Cyprus was at that time renowned for its silver and copper mines (Vryonis 1962).

[47] Paris, Musée du Louvre, section islamique, in.no.7883. Kühnel 1924, 73, pl.121; Migeon 1927, I, 382, fig.191; Gomez-Moreno 1951, III, 336, fig.396a; Paris 1990, no.127, 154; Granada and New York 1992, no. 54.

in Amalfi, Monte Cassino, Rome, Monte Sant'Angelo and Atrani.[48] None of these throws any direct light on the techniques used for large-scale figurative bronzes of Constantinopolitan manufacture, although there is considerable documentary evidence that such existed in the 9th and 10th centuries: the case of the bronze lions noted by Liudprand of Cremona during his audience with the Emperor Constantine VII in 949 is well-known, but other descriptions have survived of palaces and churches whose courtyards were embellished with fountains around which there were placed bronze figures of animals from whose open mouths there flowed constant streams of water.[49]

All such evidence, it has to be admitted, is necessarily circumstantial and, in the present state of research, it would certainly be rash to draw hard and fast conclusions from the few fragmentary remains that have survived, whether in written form or otherwise. Scarcely less circumstantial, but certainly very much more abundant, is the evidence that has survived from Southern Italy and Sicily, where notwithstanding the gradual expansion of Norman rule from the second half of the 11th century onwards, local allegiance to Islamic and Byzantine cultural traditions remained widespread until late into the 12th century: from the period of the Norman occupation of Southern Italy, there have survived over seventy Arabic inscriptions, most occurring in a strictly Islamic context, but others in an indubitably Latin context.[50] Even after the Norman conquest of Southern Italy and Sicily, large Arab communities continued to live in the areas around Lucera and Messina, Arab craftsman were frequently employed on major building works and Arabic survived as one of the official languages of the kingdom. Arabic inscriptions, indeed, continued to be used on the coinage of the Emperor Frederick II in the early 13th century.[51]

The dependence of the Normans upon the cultural traditions of their Arab predecessors was not confined merely to matters of linguistic usage. Students of Early Romanesque sculpture in southern Italy have long been aware that much of what has survived in Apulia reveals the direct impact of Islamic models and that other centres, such as the coastline of Campania to the west, were home to a style which combined the influence of the Islamicizing Romanesque of Apulia with a more purely indigenous Lombard tradition.[52] In the present context, a detailed survey of the Apulian parallels for the dominant stylistic features of the New York Lion is clearly impossible, but the following partial list should at least serve to draw the attention of Islamic specialists to some of the relevant monuments: the marble oxen flanking the entrance to the church of S. Nicola at Bari, which display a similarly stylised treatment of the junction between the shoulders and the legs and which have, in addition, the same type of 'tear drop' motif on the rear joints of the legs (pl. 6.9), the capitals in the crypt of S. Nicola itself, a solitary unprovenanced capital with a winged lion in the Pinacoteca Provinciale at Bari, the carvings on the capitals and tympanum of S. Trinita, Venosa, the marble lion from the base of a lost episcopal throne at Siponto and the elephants and lions supporting the episcopal thrones at Canosa (pl. 6.10) and Monte Sant'Angelo respectively.[53] All of these are generally dated to the second half of the 11th century. Of the same period, but from further to the west in Campania, are the pair of marble lions from the episcopal

[48] Bouras 1991, 19-26; Bouras 1982, 480. On the Byzantine bronze doors of Italy: Matthiae 1971, pl. 1-4, 63-65 (Amalfi), pl. 5-15, 67-72 (Monte Cassino), pl. 16-48, 73-82 (Rome, San Paolo fuori le Mura), pl.49-66, 83-89 (Monte Sant'Angelo), pl. 67-70, 91-92 (Atrani); English Frazer 1973, 147-162; Bari 1975, no. 58; English Frazer in Salomi 1990, I, 271-277, II, pl.CCXIII-CCXXV; Bertelli in Salomi 1990 I, 293-305, II, pl.CCLIX-CCLXX. As English Frazer remarks in Salomi 1990, 275, the doors at Atrani, which are dated to 1076, may be a western copy of those at Amalfi, in which case they would be the earliest known bronze doors in southern Italy of local manufacture.

[49] Liudprand, *Antapodosis*, VI, 5, 8, in Mango 1972, 209-210 ('Now the Emperor's throne was of immense size ... and was, as it were, guarded by lions, made either of bronze or wood covered with gold, which struck the ground with their tails and roared with open mouth and quivering tongue'). Also 162, for Theophanes Continuatus' description of the construction by the Emperor Theophilus' (829-842) of the Mystic Fountain of the Triconch, adjacent to the peristyle of the Sigma in the Great Palace at Constantinople ('There, too, next to the long side of the Sigma have been erected two bronze lions with gaping mouths. These spouted water and flooded the entire hollow area of the Sigma ...'), and 194-195 for the description by the anonymous author of the *Vita Basilii* of the stone fountain commissioned by the Emperor Basil I (867-886) for the atrium of the Nea Ekklesia in the Great Palace ('... all round the upper rim of the fountain the artist has fashioned cocks, goats and rams of bronze, and these, by means of pipes, vomit forth jets of water onto the underlying floor').

[50] Gabrieli and Scerrato 1985, 282. For a recently studied example (by Jeremy Johns) occurring in a Latin context, see the comments by Tronzo 1997, 44-45, on the monumental kufic inscriptions from Roger II's palace at Messina which refer to the Norman monarch as *Rujjaru*.

[51] Curtis van Cleve 1972, 295, 303-306; Abulafia 1992, 15, 40-41; Matthew 1992, 169-170, 240-242 and 356; Gandolfo 1995, I, 46-47 and 54-55; Tronzo 1997, 101-105.

[52] Garton 1973, 100-116; Bari 1975; Pace 1977, 226-255; Garton 1984; Glass 1991; Garton 1996, 96-105; Gandolfo 1999.

[53] Dotoli and Fiorino 1987 (entrance porch, S.Nicola at Bari); Garton 1984, pl. XLVc and fig. 55 (crypt capitals, S. Nicola at Bari); Bari 1975, no.123 (unprovenanced capital, Pinacoteca Provinciale, Bari); Garton 1984, figs. 200, 204, 212c (S. Trinita, Venosa); Bari 1975, no. 74 (Siponto lion), no. 106 (Canosa elephants), no. 43 (Mont Sant'Angelo lions).

throne at Calvi Vecchia, capitals at Salerno and Aversa and the remarkable lion imposts on the façade of the church at Carinola.[54]

Limited as this list necessarily is, it should be sufficient to indicate that, in attempting to establish a possible place of origin for the New York Lion, the mainland of southern Italy in the late 11th century should not be overlooked. This is all the more true in that, as has frequently been remarked, much of this sculpture bears clear signs of having been derived directly from bronze prototypes, an observation which immediately raises the central issue of whether such prototypes were locally produced by Arab craftsmen or imported from elsewhere.[55] The present evidence is ambiguous. On the one hand, the fact that the series of silver-inlaid bronze doors commissioned by Maurus of Amalfi and his family between 1060 and 1087 were imported from Constantinople, as also were the two bronze Middle Byzantine candelabra now on Mount Athos, the so-called 'Amalfitan Candelabra', may suggest that there was no indigenous metalworking tradition in the area during the second half of the 11th century. On the other hand, several students of Early Romanesque sculpture in Apulia have noted that the fact that so much of this sculpture bears the imprint of metalwork prototypes may point to the existence in the region of a foundry with Arab craftsmen.[56] Still others have suggested that these prototypes may have been imported rather than made locally, as may have been the case with one of the bronze doors that was used between 1111 and 1118 for the tomb of Bohemond of Antioch at Canosa.[57] Placed at the entrance to a structure which is itself totally uncharacteristic of the region and may have been derived from Syrian models, the two doors to Bohemond's tomb are solid castings, unlike, for example, the earlier series of Byzantine doors in which singly cast plaques are attached to a wood core. As the inscription indicates, the right-hand door was made locally by a craftsman with the characteristically Norman name of '*Rogerius*', who identifies himself as a bell-founder and proudly states that he was also responsible for the Paschal candlestick in the adjoining cathedral.[58] Apart from its obvious indebtedness to the Byzantine doors in its use of a figurative silver inlay, it has long been recognised that this right-hand door is a loose copy of the left-hand door, which, with its applied *alif-lam* inscriptions around the lion's head masks, also repeated on the door of Rogerius, may either have been of local manufacture or a slightly earlier Near Eastern import. Even if it is a Near Eastern import, this does not necessarily imply that there was no indigenous tradition of monumental bronze casting before the end of the 11th century, since it could reasonably be argued that, both in this case as well as in that of the Byzantine doors, the recourse by the local Latin communities to Constantinopolitan or Near Eastern workshops is indicative of nothing more than the prestige that attached to such workshops and the admiration that these communities had for them. The whole matter, it must be said, remains very uncertain. All that is clear is that, at least from 1119 onwards, when the doors by Oderisius of Benevento were installed at Troia, all the other surviving sets of bronze doors in southern Italy are locally made.[59] The period of importation, spanning the last four decades of the 11th century and the opening years of the 12th century, had receded into history.

While none of the above necessarily implies that the New York Lion is unquestionably of south Italian origin, its use of a characteristically western alloy and its close stylistic relationship to the surviving Early Romanesque sculpture of the region does suggest that serious consideration should be given to the possibility that it was of local manufacture. Only further detailed

[54] Gabrieli and Scerrato 1985, figs. 451-453 (Calvi Vecchia lions); Pace 1977, fig. 23 (Salerno capital), nos. 48-50 ('capitello dell'organo' at Aversa) and no. 62 (Carinola imposts).

[55] Belli d'Elia and Garton have noted that, behind the lion at Siponto, there probably lay a long tradition of 'bronzetti arabi in forma di animali' and that this tradition also led to the 'celebri leoni della fontana di Granada, tardi, ma evidentemente esemplati, su più remoti modelli' (Bari 1975, 64). Valentino Pace in D'Onofrio 2001, 76-78, has recently remarked upon the closeness of the styistic relationship between the Granada lions and the sculptures at Aversa and Canosa. Nor does the copying in marble seem to have been confined to objects made within the Islamic cultural tradition, since it has been suggested that the celebrated pulpit of 1039-1041 at Canosa may have been derived from a lost prototype made probably of bronze and wood (Bari 1975, 80-86).

[56] Garton 1973, 104: 'The existence of a bronze foundry with Islamic or Islamic influenced craftsmen in Canosa in the 11th century would explain the apparent influence of oriental metalwork on the style of the 11th century stone sculpture of Canosa'. Garton is here specifically referring to the elephants of the Canosa throne, a capital with addorsed winged lions and the eagle and masks on the pulpit.

[57] Cadeimi in Salomi 1990, 360-366, II, pl. CCCXIII-CCCXXVI; Mende 1994, 41-47, 139-141, pl. 40-43, figs. 26-30.

[58] Roger describes himself as *Melfie campanarum*, which has been interpreted as meaning that he was a bell-founder from either Melfi in Apulia or Amalfi in Campania. Preference is now generally given to the former (see Mende 1994, 139-141). Francesco Aceto in D'Onofrio 2001, 56-58, has recently proposed that Rogerius is to be identified with the sculptor of the same name who, with his son Robertus, signed the ciborium and altar of shortly before 1150 at S. Clemente al Volmanno in the Abruzzi, a hypothesis which, as Pina Belli d'Elia remarks in D'Onofrio 2001, 260, gives rise to *non poche riserve*.

[59] Mende 1994, 141-143, pl. 44-49.

research, particularly in relation to the doors at Canosa, will reveal whether it should be regarded as an example of the type of either imported or locally made Islamic work upon which the Latin sculptors of the region based their own carvings or whether, by contrast, it should be thought of as an Islamicizing work made in the late 11th or early 12th century by a western bronze-caster familiar with Islamic models.

The Composition of the Lion and the Griffin

Peter Northover

The discussion of the compositions of the two sculptures will be made in the order in which the analyses were carried out, that is with the Lion first, followed by the Griffin. All the analyses have been made by electron probe microanalysis (EPMA) using wavelength dispersive spectrometry; this method has been well standardised against other current techniques so the results will be broadly comparable with those from other laboratories.[60]

In the Lion, basically the same alloy was found at all eight locations analysed (Table). The data will be to some extent affected by corrosion and segregation but the analyses generally tell the same story of a plain tin bronze with 11.0-12.5 percent tin, with arsenic, lead and silver as the principal impurities. The low tin contents in #R785/9 and the higher tin content in #R786 are the result of segregation in the casting and the small amount of metal analysed in each sample. There are also consistent traces of nickel and bismuth, while the other elements sought are at or very close to their limits of detection.

Because all the parts of the Lion were cast in the same plain tin bronze without any addition of lead it appeared probable that new metal had been used without any incorporation of scrap. As a result a lead isotope analysis was commissioned. The results showed convincingly that the copper in the alloy had come from either Skouriotissa or Apliki in Cyprus.[61] Archaeometallurgical interest in Cyprus has almost entirely been focussed on antiquity to the neglect of later periods so little is known about Byzantine, Arabic and Crusader exploitation of the island's resources. That copper production continued to be important in Cyprus is also shown by Cypriot copper being used in the manufacture of the 'Dardanelles Gun', a 16 tonne bronze cannon cast for the defence of the Dardanelles in 1464.

When originally considered these analyses were compared with the alloys typical of Islamic castings. Numerous analyses from the Islamic world are available in the literature[62] and all show that alloys based on the copper-lead-zinc system were the norm for this. This is true even of the western Islamic world; indeed in tenth century Spain zinc contents in cast metalwork were higher than in many other areas. The use of bronze is rather more reminiscent of the alloys used in the Roman world where it was standard for large sculpture. Both leaded and unleaded bronzes were used, the latter for statues that were going to be amalgam gilded because of the reaction of lead with gold amalgam produced a grey compound that could not be turned golden and which disfigured the gilding.[63]

As a first step the sculpture most closely related to the Lion, the Pisa Griffin, was analysed to determine whether the Lion was alone in being cast in bronze or was typical of a larger group of sculpture. With the cooperation of the authorities at the Cathedral Museum in Pisa five samples were taken from the Griffin as detailed in the table. It is immediately clear that both the alloy and copper source are very different. The alloy contains much less tin than in the lion but zinc and lead are now both part of the alloy. Again, the variation in composition is mainly the result of segregation but it would also appear from the results that the wings were made from a separate batch of metal, with less tin but more zinc and lead than in the body, and with more iron and less antimony than in the body.

The use of two different alloys for structurally very similar sculptures alters the question of the metallurgical traditions within which they were cast. The whole question of the main regional traditions in the demand for and the production of large castings in the period 1000-1250 AD—German, Italian, Islamic and Byzantine—into which we must fit the Lion and the Griffin would seem to be a profitable area for future research. We need to understand several aspects, among which are:

1. the origins of the casting technology in terms of moulding and also the melting of large quantities of metal;

2. the reasons for selecting specific alloys and the economic and political links portrayed by the sources of the metals used.

[60] Northover and Rychner 1998.

[61] S Stos, personal communication.

[62] Craddock, La Niece and Hook 1998.

[63] Anheuser 1996.

Analysis of the Lion and Griffin

sample	Object	Part	Fe	Co	Ni	Cu	Zn	As	Sb	Sn	Ag	Bi	Pb	Au	S
R485/1	Lion	belly	0.08	0.01	0.05	87.96	0.02	2.57	0.01	8.94	0.26	0.07	0.05	0.00	0.00
R485/2			0.03	0.00	0.06	83.70	0.08	0.00	0.00	14.99	0.78	0.03	0.28	0.04	0.00
R485/3			0.04	0.00	0.03	89.68	0.07	0.00	0.02	9.80	0.25	0.00	0.08	0.02	0.00
R486/1	Lion	right fore leg	0.00	0.00	0.04	87.41	0.07	0.00	0.02	11.71	0.51	0.00	0.20	0.00	0.03
R486/2			0.01	0.00	0.07	81.71	0.04	0.00	0.00	16.14	0.89	0.17	0.95	0.02	0.00
R486/3			0.01	0.00	0.00	89.30	0.06	0.00	0.00	10.01	0.40	0.04	0.18	0.00	0.02
R487/1	Lion	interior vessel	0.00	0.00	0.05	86.70	0.10	0.00	0.01	12.01	0.63	0.09	0.41	0.00	0.00
R487/2			0.02	0.00	0.04	88.71	0.04	0.00	0.00	10.37	0.51	0.02	0.29	0.00	0.00
R487/3			0.02	0.00	0.00	83.88	0.03	0.00	0.00	14.80	0.75	0.13	0.29	0.10	0.00
R785/1	Lion	right hind leg	0.00	0.00	0.00	88.35	0.00	2.40	0.05	8.71	0.46	0.02	0.00	0.00	0.01
R785/2			0.00	0.00	0.06	87.27	0.08	1.62	0.00	9.48	0.39	0.01	1.01	0.09	0.00
R785/3			0.00	0.01	0.04	87.52	0.11	0.00	0.02	11.08	0.63	0.00	0.43	0.16	0.00
R786/1	Lion	right fore leg	0.03	0.00	0.03	88.52	0.02	0.00	0.03	10.63	0.41	0.00	0.15	0.14	0.03
R786/2			0.02	0.02	0.05	75.23	0.00	0.48	0.06	19.92	1.60	0.47	2.05	0.00	0.11
R786/3			0.00	0.03	0.03	86.79	0.04	0.00	0.01	12.07	0.73	0.00	0.20	0.05	0.05
R786/4			0.00	0.00	0.00	84.43	0.04	0.00	0.09	13.87	1.12	0.00	0.41	0.03	0.01
R787/1	Lion	interior vessel	0.01	0.03	0.08	79.37	0.12	0.00	0.00	16.05	1.32	0.02	0.84	0.01	2.16
R787/2			0.04	0.00	0.00	86.25	0.11	0.38	0.00	12.47	0.58	0.03	0.12	0.01	0.00
R787/3			0.02	0.02	0.00	90.15	0.03	0.00	0.00	9.32	0.46	0.00	0.00	0.00	0.00
R788/1	Lion	finning in neck	0.01	0.00	0.01	86.36	0.00	1.64	0.00	11.04	0.53	0.06	0.00	0.32	0.02
R788/2			0.00	0.01	0.02	84.93	0.09	0.00	0.00	12.81	0.99	0.02	1.13	0.00	0.01
R788/3			0.03	0.03	0.01	86.63	0.00	0.00	0.00	12.49	0.64	0.00	0.08	0.09	0.00
R789/1	Lion	finning in body	0.02	0.01	0.00	91.91	0.00	0.00	0.07	7.57	0.33	0.07	0.00	0.03	0.00
R789/2			0.00	0.00	0.00	89.52	0.02	1.87	0.00	8.19	0.39	0.00	0.00	0.00	0.01
R789/3			0.01	0.00	0.00	90.69	0.09	0.33	0.03	7.81	0.71	0.07	0.20	0.03	0.04
R865/1	Griffin	left wing, drill hole	0.42	0.00	0.06	87.03	11.33	0.00	0.13	0.73	0.09	0.00	0.21	0.00	0.00
R865/2			0.39	0.00	0.06	83.95	11.43	0.00	0.15	1.08	0.11	0.04	2.79	0.00	0.01
R865/3			0.33	0.02	0.03	84.25	11.39	0.00	0.14	1.00	0.12	0.05	2.64	0.00	0.03
R865/4			0.28	0.01	0.03	80.15	10.61	0.00	0.46	2.17	0.23	0.06	5.92	0.00	0.08
R866/1	Griffin	right wing, drill hole	0.66	0.00	0.05	79.47	15.16	0.36	0.10	0.94	0.09	0.03	3.07	0.00	0.08
R867/1	Griffin	body, finning	0.10	0.01	0.04	90.21	6.44	0.00	0.22	2.51	0.11	0.00	0.27	0.09	0.00
R867/2			0.05	0.00	0.08	87.41	4.36	0.04	0.98	5.01	0.38	0.04	1.65	0.00	0.01
R867/3			0.11	0.00	0.04	89.76	6.96	0.00	0.28	2.31	0.09	0.00	0.45	0.00	0.00
R868/1	Griffin	vessel, upper	0.13	0.01	0.03	84.75	11.35	0.87	0.24	1.99	0.16	0.00	0.40	0.03	0.02
R869/1	Griffin	vessel, lower	0.15	0.04	0.05	85.23	9.09	0.00	0.37	2.90	0.19	0.00	1.87	0.07	0.05
R869/2	Griffin		0.20	0.00	0.04	85.51	10.18	0.91	0.25	2.34	0.15	0.00	0.35	0.00	0.08
R485	Lion	belly	0.05	0.00	0.05	87.11	0.06	0.86	0.01	11.24	0.43	0.03	0.14	0.02	0.00
R486	Lion	right fore leg	0.01	0.00	0.04	86.14	0.06	0.00	0.01	12.62	0.60	0.07	0.44	0.01	0.02
R487	Lion	interior vessel	0.03	0.00	0.04	86.63	0.06	0.43	0.01	11.93	0.52	0.05	0.29	0.01	0.01
R785	Lion	right hind leg	0.00	0.00	0.03	87.71	0.06	1.34	0.02	9.76	0.49	0.01	0.48	0.08	0.00
R786	Lion	right fore leg	0.01	0.01	0.03	83.74	0.03	0.12	0.05	14.12	0.96	0.12	0.70	0.06	0.05
R787	Lion	interior vessel	0.02	0.02	0.03	85.26	0.09	0.13	0.00	12.61	0.79	0.02	0.32	0.01	0.72
R788	Lion	finning in neck	0.01	0.01	0.01	85.97	0.03	0.55	0.00	12.12	0.72	0.03	0.40	0.14	0.01
R789	Lion	finning in body	0.01	0.00	0.00	90.70	0.04	0.73	0.03	7.86	0.48	0.05	0.07	0.02	0.02
R865	Griffin	left wing, drill hole	0.36	0.01	0.05	83.84	11.19	0.00	0.22	1.25	0.14	0.04	2.89	0.00	0.03
R866	Griffin	right wing, drill hole	0.66	0.00	0.05	79.47	15.16	0.36	0.10	0.94	0.09	0.03	3.07	0.00	0.08
R867	Griffin	body, finning	0.09	0.00	0.05	89.13	5.92	<0.20	0.49	3.28	0.19	0.01	0.79	0.03	0.00
R868	Griffin	vessel, upper	0.13	0.01	0.03	84.75	11.35	0.87	0.24	1.99	0.16	0.00	0.40	0.03	0.02
R869	Griffin	vessel, lower	0.17	0.02	0.05	85.37	9.63	0.45	0.31	2.62	0.17	0.00	1.11	0.03	0.07
R1075	Hind on stand	weld metal	0.05	0.01	0.04	89.01	3.66	0.56	0.01	5.55	0.95	0.00	0.13	0.00	0.03
R1076	Hind on stand	shaft	0.00	0.00	0.05	88.11	3.67	0.73	0.01	5.89	1.07	0.02	0.41	0.04	0.01
R1077	Hind on stand	left hind hoof	0.03	0.00	0.04	88.82	3.85	0.45	0.00	5.12	1.28	0.00	0.20	0.04	0.16

1. Inspection of the interior of both sculptures suggest that they were made by an indirect lost wax process with slabs of wax laid up inside a removable mould, the hollow wax filled with a clay core, and the exterior invested with a ceramic mould. The bodies were cast with projecting stubs for the legs which were then cast on separately. It was not possible to determine whether the heads had also been cast separately since severe finning inside the necks of both figures obscured any joins. The Griffin's wings were also separate castings which were then riveted in place. Chaplets were of square section wire; radiographic examination of the Lion has indicated the location of most and an endoscopic survey has shown that surviving chaplets are of iron wire. Moulding material is available for future study as much of the ceramic mould surrounds the vessel cast inside the Griffin. It is to be hoped that further large figures come to light for comparison.

2. References to the analysis of contemporary large copper alloy castings are very scattered. A useful survey of the compositions of a number of bronze doors is given by Forshell.[64] There was clearly knowledge of the behaviour of several alloy systems to call on:

a) High tin bronze and bell metal in, for example, the Vatican and in Orvieto cathedral, as well as part of the Hildesheim column.[65]

b) Plain low to medium tin bronze, as in the Lion, and in the lion and griffin from Perugia as well.[66] Later this became the preferred alloy for gun founding, as in the Dardanelles gun already referred to.

c) Leaded bronze.

d) Gunmetal, as in the body of the Griffin and in the doors at Montecassino.[67]

e) Brass, especially leaded brass; the Griffin's wings just about fall in this category (gilding metal and statuary bronze are more usual names for these alloys with relatively modest zinc contents. The brass can be free of bronze as in the work of Master II on the doors at Verona.[68] The use of brass may derive from both Islamic and Byzantine traditions.

With all these groups there appears to be a real division into unleaded and heavily leaded bronzes. It would be interesting to know whether this reflects the classical Roman tradition of using an unleaded alloy where, as mentioned above, amalgam gilding was to be used. Both the New York Lion and the body of the Pisa Griffin are cast in alloys which could be so gilded. The same possibly applies to the Griffin's wings, but the 3 percent lead that was measured could have caused problems.

As yet we have, at best, a limited technical context for the Lion and Griffin. However, recently, an interesting parallel for the impurity pattern in the Lion has come to light. This is a figure of a hind which is believed to have formed part of a composition with a stag on a fountain in Cordoba, Spain.[69]

Although the alloy is a gunmetal more like the body of the Griffin it has the same high silver content together with arsenic and lead impurities as the Lion. Given that coppers with high levels of silver are not particularly common it is very possible that much of the copper in the hind came from the same Cypriot source as already identified for the Lion. A *niello*-inlaid door knocker recently sold at Christie's may just fall into the same category although it contains only 0.3 percent silver.[70] Further comparisons are difficult because the published analyses of the bronze doors do not include impurities such as silver.

The metallurgical study of these sculptures has been very profitable but has potentially raised more questions than it has answered. The identification of Cyprus as source for the copper used is important for a period when Cyprus was accessible to both Arab and Byzantine worlds and in the eleventh and twelfth centuries to the Norman kingdom of Sicily. Much more work has to be done, though, on identifying the technological tradition in which they were designed and cast.

BIBLIOGRAPHY

Abulafia, D, 1992: *Frederick II: a Medieval Emperor,* London.

Amador de Los Rios, R, 1875: 'Léon de bronce encontrado en la tierra de Palencia', in *Museo español de antigüedades*, V, 1875, 139-162.

Angelucci, S, 1990: 'Primi risultati di indagini tecnico-scientifiche sul San Pietro di bronzo della basilica Vaticana', *Arte Medievale*, 2, 51-58.

Anheuser, K, 1996: *An investigation of amalgam gilding and silvering on metalwork*, unpublished PhD Thesis, Faculty of Physical Sciences, University of Oxford.

[64] Forshell 1992, 67-72.

[65] See respectively: Angelucci 1990; Gramaccini 1987; Drescher 1993.

[66] Marabelli 1973 and Cuccini 1994.

[67] Matthiae 1971, 71.

[68] Salomi 1990, I, 433.

[69] Christie's 1997, Lot 293.

[70] Christie's 2000, Lot 276.

Baracchini, C, 1986: 'Sculture del XII secolo pertinenti al Duomo', in De Angelis d'Ossat, G., (ed.), *Il Museo dell'Opera del Duomo a Pisa*, Silvana Editoriale, Cinisello Balsamo, 65-76.

Bari 1975: *Alle sorgenti del Romanico: Puglia XI secolo*, exh.cat., Bari, Pinacoteca Provinciale.

Berlin 1989: Sievernick, G., and Budde, H., (eds.), *Europa und der Orient—800-1900*, catalogue of the exhibition in Berlin, 28th May-27th August 1989, Berlin.

Bouras, L, 1982: 'Byzantine Lighting Devices', *Jahrbuch des Oesterreichischen Byzantinistik*, 32, 3, (= XVI.Internationaler Byzantinistenkongress, Vienna, October, 1981, Akten II/3).

Bouras, L, 1991: 'Three Byzantine Bronze Candelabra from the Grand Lavra Monastery and Saint Catherine's Monastery in Sinai', *Deltion tis Christianikis Archaiologikis Etaireias*, Athens, 1991, 19-26.

Brett, G, 1954: 'The Automata in the Byzantine "Throne of Solomon"', in *Speculum*, vol. XXIX, no. 3, July 1954, 477-487.

Burgalassi, S, 1993: 'Moduli e Tipologie Sociologiche nei Monumenti e nei Manufatti della Piazza del Duomo di Pisa: Analisi ed Indicazioni alla Ricerca delle Unità Culturali', in *Storia ed Arte nella Piazza del Duomo—Conferenze 1991*, Quaderno n. 1, Opera della Primaziale Pisana, Pacini Editore, Pisa, 215-246.

Christie's 1993: *Islamic Art and Indian Miniatures*, Christie's, London 19 October.

Christie's 1997: *Islamic Art and Indian Miniatures*, Christie's, London 25 April.

Christie's 2000: *Islamic Art and Manuscripts*, London 20 October.

Cicognara, L, 1823: *Storia della Scultura*, 2 vols., Prato (2nd edition).

Contadini, A, 1993: see Venice 1993, cat. entries 43 ('Il Grifone di Pisa'), 41 ('Quadrupede in bronzo') and 42 ('Acquamanile in forma di uccello').

Contadini, A, 2000: 'Le arti in Spagna e Marocco nei periodi almoravide e almoade', in Cassanelli, R, (ed.), *Il Mediterraneo e L'Arte nel Medioevo*, Jaca Book, Milan, 38-62.

Craddock, P T, La Niece, S C, and Hook, D R, 1998: 'Brass in the medieval Islamic world', in Craddock, P T (ed.), *2000 years of zinc and brass*, British Museum Occasional Papers, 50 (2nd edition), London, 73-114.

Cuccini, G, 1994: *Il grifo e il leone bronzei di Perugia*, Perugia.

Curtis van Cleve, T, 1972: *The Emperor Frederick II of Hohenstaufen: Immutator Mundi*, Oxford.

Da Morrona, A, 1787-93: *Pisa illustrata nelle arti del disegno*, 2 vols., Pisa (second edition Livorno 1812).

D'Onofrio, M, 2001: *La scultura d'età normanna tra Inghliterra e Terrasanta*, Rome-Bari.

Dotoli, G and Fiorino, F, 1987: *Storia e leggenda della Basilica di San Nicola a Bari*, Bari.

Drescher, H, 1985: 'Zur Giesstechnik der Braunschweiger Burglöwen', in Spies, G. (ed.), *Der Braunschweiger Löwe*, Brunswick (=*Braunschweiger Werkstücke, Reihe B, Veröffentlichungen aus dem Städtischen Museum*), 289-428.

Drescher, H, 1993: 'Zur Technik bernwardischer Silber-und Bronzegüsse', in *Bernward von Hildesheim und das Zeitalter der Ottonen*, exhibition catalogue, Hildesheim, Bd. I.

English Frazer, M, 1973: 'Church doors and the Gates of Paradise: Byzantine bronze doors in Italy', *Dumbarton Oaks Papers*, 27, 147-162.

Erdmann, K, 1938: 'Islamische Giessgefässe des 11. Jahrhunderts', *Pantheon*, 8, 251-254.

Farmer, H G, 1931: *The Organs of the Ancients from Eastern Sources*, London.

Farmer, H G, 1965: *The Sources of Arabian Music*, Leiden

Fehérvári, G, 1976: *Islamic Metalwork of the Eighth to Fifteenth Century in the Keir Collection*, London.

Fernández Puertas, A, 1975: 'Candiles epigrafiados de finales del siglo XI o comienzo del XII', in *Miscelanea de Estudios Arabes y Hebraicos*, XXIV, 107-114.

Forshell, H, 1992: *The inception of copper mining in Falun*, Theses and papers in Archaeology, Stockholm University Archaeological Research Laboratory, B:2, Stockholm.

Gabrieli, F, and Scerrato, U, 1985: *Gli Arabi in Italia*, Garzanti-Scheiwiller, Milan (1st edition Credito Italiano 1979).

Gandolfo, L, 1995: 'Le emissioni monetarie siciliane e pugliesi di Federico II', in Di Stefano, C A and Cadei, A (eds.), *Federico e la Sicilia: Dalla terra alla corona*, Palermo, I, 46-47 and 54-55.

Gandolfo, F, 1999: *La scultura normanno-sveva in Campania: Botteghe e modelli*, Rome.

Garton, T, 1973: 'Islamic Influences in Early Romanesque Sculpture in Apulia', *Art and Archaeology Research Papers*, 4, 100-116.

Garton, T, 1984: *Early Romanesque Sculpture in Apulia*, New York and London.

Garton, T, 1996: 'Some Apulian Romanesque Capitals in American Collections', *Studi in onore di Michele d'Elia*, Matera-Spoleto, 96-105.

Glass, D F, 1991: *Romanesque Sculpture in Campania: Patrons, Programs and Style*, University Park, Pennsylvania.

Gomez-Moreno, M, 1951: 'El arte arabe español hasta los Almohades, arte mozarabe', *Ars Hispaniae*, 3, Madrid.

Gramaccini, N, 1987: 'Zur Ideologie der Bronze im Mittelalter', in *Stadel-Jahrbuch*, 11, 1987, 147-170.

Granada and New York 1992: Dodds, J, (ed.), *Al-Andalus: the Art of Islamic Spain*, catalogue of the exhibition in Granada, Alhambra, 18 March-7 June 1992 and New York, Metropolitan Museum, 1st July-27th September 1992, New York.

Hammerstein, R, 1986: *Macht und Klang: Toenende Automaten als Realitaet und Fiktion in der alten und mittelalterlichen Welt*, Bern.

Hill D R, 1974: *The Book of Knowledge of Ingenious Mechanical Devices*, Dordrecht (Holland).

Hill, D R, 1979: *The Book of Ingenious Devices by the Banu (sons of) Musa bin Shakir*, Dordrecht (Holland).

Jenkins, M, 1978: 'New Evidence for the Possible Provenance and Fate of the So-Called Pisa Griffin', in *Islamic Archaeological Studies*, I, Cairo, 79-85.

Jenkins, R, 1953: 'Cyprus between Byzantium and Islam 688-965', *Studies Presented to D M Robinson*, Missouri, 1006-1014.

Kühnel, E, 1924: *Maurische Kunst: Die Kunst des Ostens*, 9, Berlin.

Lanci, M, 1845-6: *Trattato delle simboliche rappresentanze Arabiche*, 2 vols., Paris.

Lucchesi, G, 1993: *Museo dell'Opera del Duomo di Pisa*, Pacini Editore, Pisa.

Liudprand 1930: *The Works of Liudprand of Cremona*, translated by F A Wright, London.

Mango, C, 1972: *The Art of the Byzantine Empire 312-1453*, Sources and Documents in the History of Art Series (ed. H W Janson).

Marabelli, M, 1973: 'Esami chimici e fisici di bronzo esposto all'aperto', in Urbani, G, (ed.), *Problemi di Conservazione*, Bologna, 478-481.

Marangone, B, 1845: 'Vetus Chronicon Pisanum ex ms. Codice Bibliothecae Armamentarii Parisiensis', in Bonaini, F, (ed.) *Archivio Storico Italiano*, Firenze, vol. VI, part 2.

Marangone, B, 1936: *Gli Annales Pisani di Bernardo Marangone*, in Lupo Gentile, M., (ed.), vol. VI, part 2, Bologna.

Marcel, M J J, 1839: 'Notice sur un monument arabe conservé à Pise', *Journal Asiatique*, 3rd series, vol. VII, 81-88.

Martini, G, 1705: *Theatrum Basilicae Pisanae*, Rome.

Matthew, D, 1992: *The Norman Kingdom of Sicily*, Cambridge.

Matthiae, G, 1971: *Le porte bizantine in Italia*, Rome.

Melikian-Chirvani, A S, 1968: 'Le griffon iranien de Pise: materiaux pour un corpus de l'argenterie et du bronze iraniens, III', *Kunst des Orients*, 5, 68-86.

Melikian-Chirvani, A S, 1973: 'Greif', in Sourdel-Thomine, J and Spuler, B, (eds.), *Die Kunst des Islam*, Propyläen Kunstgeschichte, vol. IV, Berlin, 263.

Mende, U, 1994: *Die Bronzetüren des Mittelalters 800-1200*, Munich.

Migeon, G, 1907: *Manuel d'art musulman: arts plastiques et industrielles*, 2 vols., Paris.

Migeon, G, 1927: *Manuel d'art musulman: arts plastiques et industrielles*, 2 vols., Paris.

Milone, A, 1993: 'Grifone', in Baracchini, C., (ed.), *I Marmi di Lasinio—La collezione di sculture medievali e moderne nel Camposanto di Pisa*, Studio Per Edizioni Scelte, Firenze, 143-4.

Monneret de Villard, U, 1946: 'Le chapiteau arabe de la cathédrale de Pise', *Comptes Rendus de l'Académie des Inscriptions et Belles-Lettres*, January-March 1946, Paris, 17-23.

Northover, J P and Rychner, V, 1998: 'Bronze analysis, experience of a comparative programme', in Mordant, C, Pernot, M, and Rychner, V (eds.), *L'Atelier du bronzier en Europe du Xxe au VIIIe siècle avant Notre Ère*, I (Session de Neuchatel), Édition du CTHS, Paris, 19-40.

Novello, R P, and Tongiorgi Tomasi, L, 1986: 'Tarsie lignee', in De Angelis d'Ossat, G, (ed.), *Il Museo dell'Opera del Duomo a Pisa*, Silvana Editoriale, Cinisello Balsamo, 137-144.

Pace, V, 1977: 'Campania XI secolo: Tradizione e innovazione in una terra normanna', in *Romanico Padano Romanico Europeo,* Convegno internazionale di studi, Modena-Parma, 226-255.

Paris 1990: *Arabesques et jardins de paradis—collection françaises d'art islamique*, catalogue of the exhibition, Musée du Louvre, 16 October 1989-15 January 1990, Paris.

Rogers, J M, 1992: 'Granada and New York. The Art of Islamic Spain', review of the exhibition, in *The Burlington Magazine*, August 1992, 549-552.

Rohault de Fleury, G, 1866: *Les Monuments de Pise au Moyen Age*, Paris.

Roncioni, R, 1844: 'Delle istorie pisane', in Bonaini, F, (ed.), *Archivio Storico Italiano*, Firenze, vol. V, part 1.

Salomi, S, 1990: *Le porte di bronzo dall'antichità al secolo XIII*, Rome, 2 vols.

Scalia, G, 1993: 'La Consacrazione della Cattedrale Pisana', in *Storia ed Arte nella Piazza del Duomo—Conferenze 1991*, Quaderno n. 1, Opera della Primaziale Pisana, Pacini Editore, Pisa, 53-70.

Scerrato, U, 1966: *Metalli islamici*, Milano.

Serjeant, R B and Lewcock, R, 1983: 'The Church (al-Qalīs) of Ṣan'ā' and Ghumdān Castle', in Serjeant, R B and Lewcock, R (eds.), *Ṣan'ā', An Arabian Islamic City*, World of Islam Festival Trust, London, 44-48.

Tanfani Centofanti, L, 1897: *Notizie di Artisti tratte dai documenti pisani*, Enrico Spoerri Editore, Pisa.

Tronci, P, *c.* 1643: *Descrizione delle Chiese, Monasteri et Oratori della Città di Pisa*, Pisa, Archivio dell'Opera del Duomo—Archivio Capitolare, manoscritto cartaceo C152/153.

Tronci, P, 1922: *Il Duomo di Pisa, descritto dal Can. Paolo Tronci (1585-1648) con note e documenti inediti*, edited by Peleo Bacci, Pisa.

Tronzo, W, 1997: *The Cultures of his Kingdom: Roger II and the Cappella Palatina in Palermo*, Princeton.

Valeriani, D, 1829: 'Notizia d'una Iscrizione Araba', in *Antologia*, vol. 35, 129, no. 105.

Venice 1993: Curatola, G, (ed.), *Eredità dell'Islam—Arte Islamica in Italia*, catalogue of the exhibition in Venice, Doge's Palace, 30 October 1993-30 April 1994, Silvana Editoriale, Cinisello Balsamo.

Vryonis, S, 1962: 'The question of the Byzantine mines', *Speculum*, vol. XXXVII, 1-17.

Yaqut 1866-1873: *Yaqut ibn 'Abd Allah, al-Hamawi. Jacut Geographisches Wörterbuch*, ed. by Ferdinand Wüstenfeld, Leipzig, 6 vols.

Pl. 6.1 The Pisa Griffin, bronze. Museo dell'Opera del Duomo, Pisa. Spain (?), 11th-12th century. H. 107cm, L. 90cm, W. 46cm.

Pl. 6.2 The New York Lion, bronze. Metropolitan Museum of Art, New York, Mari-Cha Collection Ltd, L.2000.84. Southern Italy (?), 11th-12th century. H. 73cm (without lower legs), L. 82cm, W. 35cm.

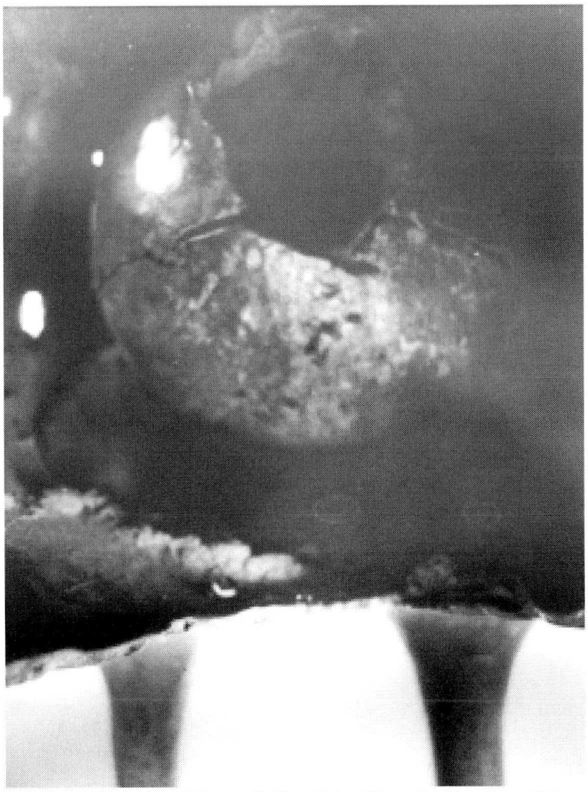

Pl. 6.3 Vessel inside the belly of the Pisa Griffin, L. c. 24 cm; diameter of the opening c. 9.5cm. Unlike the body, the vessel is not of bronze, but brass. The vessel was moulded in a ceramic mould, traces of which are still present. The cracks clearly visible on the vessel are not a result of later damage, but of the original, moulding process.

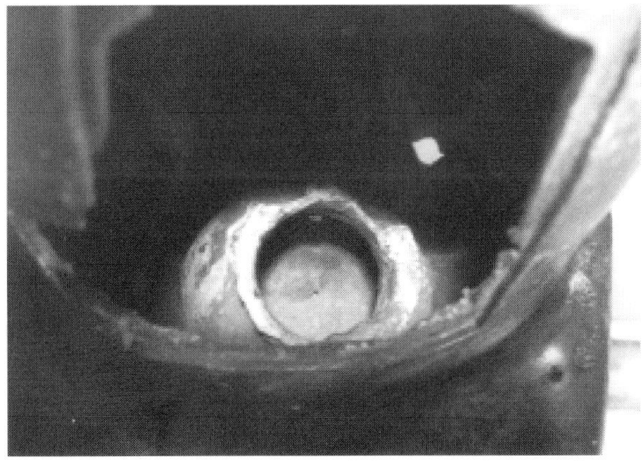

Pl. 6.4 Vessel inside the belly of the New York Lion. This vessel is, as the body, made of bronze. As in the case of the Pisa Griffin, the vessel was moulded in a ceramic mould, traces of which are still present. The everted rims are here more pronounced, and again the cracks visible are not a result of later damage, but of the original, moulding process.

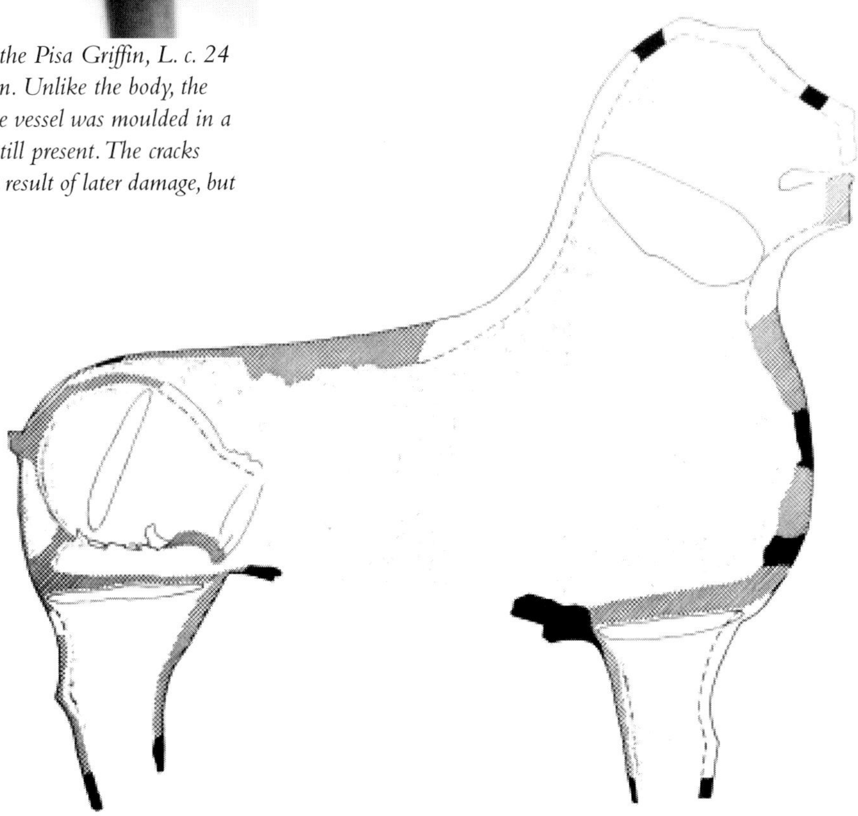

Fig. 6.1 Drawing showing the construction of the New York Lion, by Kikar Singh, Museum of London.

Pl. 6.5 Marquetry panel on the underside of a chorus seat of the Pisa cathedral. Late 15th century.

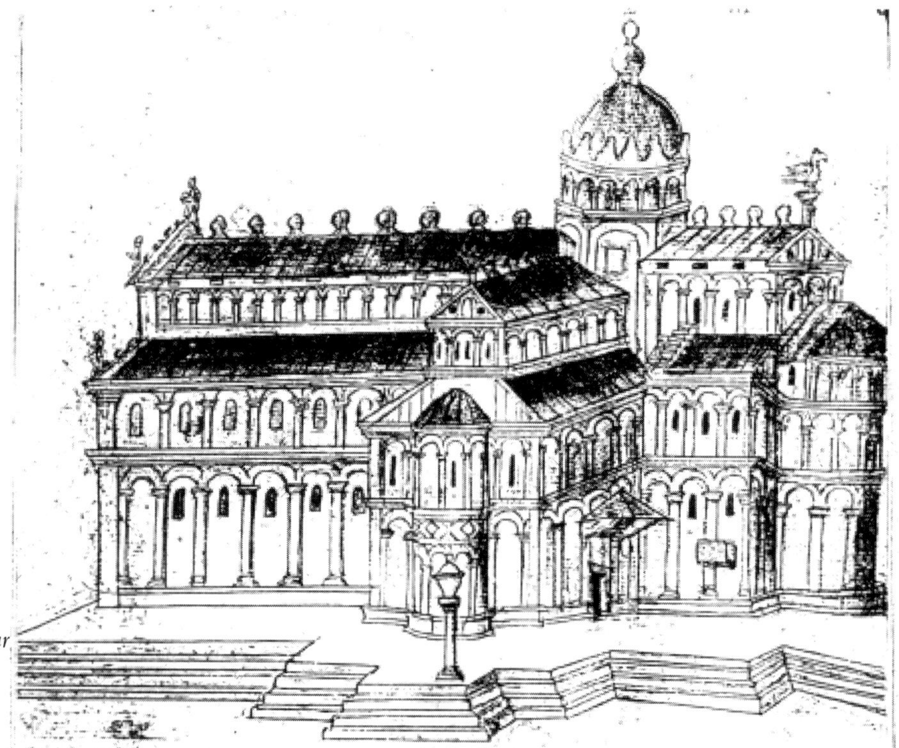

Pl.6.6 Watercolour by Paolo Tronci, c. 1643, fol. III (detail) (from Tronci, P, 1922).

Pl. 6.7 Detail of the inscription on the breast of the Pisa Griffin.

Pl. 6.8 Detail of the inscription on the right side of the body of the New York Lion.

Pl. 6.9 Marble figure of an ox flanking the entrance porch of S. Nicolò, Bari (Apulia), second half of the 11th century.

Pl. 6.10 Marble figure of an elephant supporting the episcopal throne. Canosa (Apulia), second half of the 11th century.

7 THE USE OF GREY IN CERAMICS OF THE WORLD OF ISLAM

Yolande Crowe

The colour grey or 'grisaille' appears at various times in different cultures. There are three periods in the world of Islam. The first one concerns the early production of tin glazing in Samarra and Susa in the 9th century. The second takes place under the Mongol rule in Persia with echoes in Egypt. The third period is concerned with the later stages of the Safavid rule with references to the excavations in Qandahar.

In a spring collection of the early 1950s the fashion designer Christian Dior created a dress which was simplicity itself. It had a rather wide three-quarter-length skirt and was made of plain grey denim. Immediately successful, it became a *must* for every woman. The colour grey acted as a perfect background for all kinds of jewellery and colourful scarves. Only later was it known that the textile manufacturer and racehorse owner Marcel Boussac, wanted to dispose of a large stock of grey denim. The story is worth recalling illustrating the whimsical ways of fashion.

Yet in Europe as early as the 13th century shades of grey, *grisaille*, as it is called in French, was used in monastic stained glass. In the 14th century Giotto painted illusionist figures and Taddeo Gaddi created *trompe l'oeil* of large allegories in fictitious openings on the Baroncelli Chapel ceiling of Santa Croce in Florence. *Grisaille* also appeared in the best French manuscript illuminations of the same period. And in the 15th and 16th centuries *grisaille* was used in some panels of Flemish and German altarpieces. The masters of the *seicento* often used it to recreate the illusion of stone architecture. By the 18th century *grisaille* panels on walls and above doorways enhanced staterooms of fashionable buildings: paintings of graceful deities and *putti* simulated more expensive work in stucco or wood. These are but a few examples to illustrate the general attitude towards the colour grey at certain stages of European art.

Need one then be surprised to find a similar attraction to the colour grey in ceramic decoration in the Islamic world at several stages of its development? There appear to be three particular periods when grey becomes accepted in the potter's workshop. The first occurs in Mesopotamia early in the 9th century, when grey is chosen as an alternative background to white for lustre, blue and green decoration. Then in the 14th century during the Mongol rule over Persia, grey occurs again either as a background or as a supplementary colour on bowls, dishes and tiles. Finally towards the latter part of the Safavid era when the influence of Chinese export porcelain appears to wane in favour of a new Persian type of decoration, shades of grey tending towards black are found on ceramic wares of different shapes and sizes.

The first dishes with a grey background could have been made in Mesopotamia at Samarra. Specialists greeted their appearance with suspicion. The colour was assumed to have been the result of some mistake in the composition of the newly invented tin-opacified lead glaze in imitation of Chinese early export porcelain. It was not until the early 1970s during French excavations in Susa, the winter capital of the Achaemenians, that this grey ground was recognised as a *bona fide* colour. The excavated sites confirmed an Abbasid level not fully studied by earlier excavators, eager to reach lower levels of greater significance to them.[1] At the same time the late Henry Hodges of the Institute of Archaeology in London, attempted to discover the nature of the grey colouring. He tested a grey shard in a kiln by heating it to a temperature of about 1000°. The grey glaze matured into pale pink droplets which revealed the presence of manganese oxide. Apparently black specks of manganese oxide had been used in the glaze to create the colour grey, a colour made possible by the low firing of kilns.[2] At first sight it might have appeared to be accidental, but judging by the finds in Susa,[3] it had to be considered a style in its own right.

---

1 See J M Rogers's review article *Bibliotheca Orientalis* XXXIII No.5/6 1976, 370-4. M Rosen-Ayalon, *Ville Royale de Suse IV*. La poterie islamique, Paris 1974.

2 Y Crowe, 'Early Islamic pottery and China', *Transactions of the Oriental Ceramic Society*, vol. 41, 1975-7, 263-78.

3 M Kevran, 'Les niveaux islamiques du secteur oriental du tépé de l'Apadana, II Le matériel céramique', *Cahiers de la Délégation Archéologique Française en Iran*, VII 1977, 75-161.

Most of the grey finds were rather miserable shards with a compact yellow body, although it was possible to recognise that the shapes they belonged to were similar to those of dishes with a white ground. The rims could be straight or lobed, in fact no different from Samarra dishes. The wide and narrow base rings imitated Chinese models. It was obvious that the grey surface could not be left plain and required some ornament. Geometric patterns with stylised elongated leaves, rosettes, imitation Kufic, all in blue, recalled similar decoration on white dishes and bowls. Broad geometric patterns were also selected to decorate later T-rim and straight rim bowls of a coarser nature (pl. 7.1). Groups of green runs starting from the inner rim seem to have been a regular feature. A more unusual use of colour was a green broad line running towards the bowl centre almost covered by a large black line edged in white (pl. 7.2). None of these motifs contribute to a startling catalogue of designs. Yet a complete lustre dish (pl. 7.3 and 4) was found in Susa during the 1974 campaign. It had a straight rim, a narrow base ring; the glazed inner ring was marked with a dark red stroke. Outer roundels and leaves were painted in the same dark red and recalled similar designs in Samarra. Inside the bowl a monochrome lustre palmette with various fillers showed great affinity with designs on lustre tiles in the mosque of Kairouan.

In the late 1970s John Carswell brought to the Ashmolean Museum a collection of shards which he had gathered during his research on the West Coast of India, Sri Lanka and the Maldives. Most of them were Chinese but among a few Mesopotamian glazed shards, there was a small grey fragment[4] found in Mantai, an ancient town on the Northwest coast of Sri Lanka. Trade links across the Indian Ocean did of course work in both directions.

Fashions come and go and the next appearance of the colour grey in the potter's workshop occurs during the *Pax Mongolica* under Mongol rule in Persia over a century from approximately 1250 to 1350. In an earlier paper I showed how Chinese textiles influenced the decorative arts of Western Asia after studying a group of line drawings based on details of rich clothing from a tomb dated 1243. Some of these Chinese motifs became the new designs, which were used on tilework of the Takht-i Sulaiman in north-west Iran before 1282, the year of the death of the Il-khan ruler Abaqa Khan.[5] Thereafter, the site appears to have been abandoned. Yet these new textile motifs became standard designs for bowls, dishes and tiles early in the 14th century across the Mongol world. At first bowls have T-rims (pl. 7.5), then straight or scalloped rims. The base rings are usually narrower than in earlier times thus imitating contemporary Chinese porcelain bowls. The lotus, the dianthus, the phoenix and the deer are all painted in a new colour scheme where grey and white seem to dominate with an occasional blue outline. Some pseudo-calligraphy, geometric patterns and elegant figures are local contributions to the new style (pl. 7.6). Dealers gave these well-known ceramics the name of Sultanabad wares although there is no evidence as yet of knowing where they were made. They soon appeared in most collections of Islamic art before the second World War.[6] There is little need to dwell on them but for the fact that tiles such as those in the tomb of Pir-i Baqran (1312) near Isfahan are also an interesting example of the use of grey in monumental decoration.

If Christian Dior could find a suitable use for an occasional grey textile, could one not imagine a similar possibility in 14th century China? Unfortunately little evidence has survived except for some details in paintings such as those of the *Jamic al-Tawarikh* of Rashid al-Din in Edinburgh dated 706/1306-7. On several miniatures the conquering ruler and his warriors wear a kind of tunic over their armour. The material is grey and patterned with lotus and dianthus in blue or pale red. Furthermore, although slightly beside the point, these textile patterns are also seen on the dark blue ground of drapes in scenes of the Demotte *Shah Namah* (*c.* 1335). Could this be the origin of the *lajvardina* colour scheme with gold leaf recalling gold painting on dark blue silk? The latter textiles were part of the clothing listed in the 1243 Chinese tomb.

As tiles on the cenotaph of Ala al-Din in Khiva would suggest, it is likely that by the mid 1350s underglaze painting had become a more effective technique for enhancing not only tiles but also dishes and pouring vessels. It was already used in Persia by the end of the 13th century. The 1350s happened to coincide with increasing production and export of Chinese blue and white porcelain which continued in the Ming dynasty beyond the fall of the Yuan rule in 1368. These ceramics represented the most efficient use of cobalt painting under a transparent colourless glaze. In the world of Islam potters could do no better than proceed along the same lines. Grey was soon to be discarded.

[4] J Carswell, 'China and Islam in the Maldive islands', *Transactions of the Oriental Ceramic Society*, 41, 1975-7, 121-97. Pl.67d no. 614.

[5] Y Crowe, Late thirteenth century Persian tilework and Chinese textiles, *Bulletin of the Asia Institute*, New Series, vol. 5, 1991, 153-61.

[6] P Morgan, 'Some Far Eastern. Elements in coloured-ground Sultanabad wares', J W Allan ed., *Islamic Art in the Ashmolean*, Oxford Studies in Islamic Art, vol. 10, part 2, 1996, 19-44.

It would take over three centuries for the colour grey to come back into fashion. A constant handling of cobalt blue in the potter's workshop with occasional chromite black for outlines may have prompted the potter to explore further possible shades of blues and greys. The time coincided with the retreat of Chinese ceramic influence over Persian workshops due to two factors: the decline of state production towards the end of the Ming dynasty around the 1650s, and the appearance of a more decorative and less dramatic style under the Xing dynasty. As a result, the style of Persian ceramics ceased to respond slavishly to Chinese influence. Except for Arthur Lane's pioneering work in his *Later Islamic pottery* of 1957 little research has been done on these rather unexpected wares.[7] One suspects that most collections have set these wares aside for a lack of understanding either technique or motif. Fortunately, excavations in Qandahar have brought to light a number of relevant grey examples predating the total destruction of the town by Nadir Shah in 1738.[8]

A lion with or without brocaded ball has been a favourite design since the tiles in the Takht-i Sulaiman, yet when it is made to prance in the centre of a late Safavid dish, it has become a crazy beast surrounded by leafy sprigs. Its bushy tail is transformed into a strange leaf attached to its back (pl. 7.10). The most bizarre of all animals is perhaps a reserved-painted hare crouching amidst dense scrolling and half-palmettes inside a dish with a plain blue outside (pl. 7.11). It is difficult to trace the origin of this composition.

Strange mutations also occur when *transitional* Chinese motifs take on a new lease of life on larger dishes. Groups of two or three figures as well as a lion are here enclosed in loose frames on the flange and in the centre. Their surprisingly small size leaves room for gnarled trees, leafy rocks, further figures and birds. Balustrades and horizontal stripes add to the whimsical composition (pl. 7.12). A bizarre world has come into being with no master plan to give it real meaning. A similar effect can be noticed in a deep bowl with a large flange (pl. 7.13). Here again *transitional* elements have been distorted. On the flange dark dotted bands create four spaces with gathered filaments or roots and small trees and leafy branches. The same components make up the decoration in the centre. Both bands and roots appear to be a distortion of the underlining blue wash in Chinese *transitional* painting chiefly used on dishes.

None of these designs seem to have lasted for long. They make up a small group in the late Safavid period possibly lasting into the early days of the Zand dynasty. Mapping Persian ceramic production beyond 1738 is still a difficult task. At this stage it is not easy to visualise which types of ceramics fit into the gap before the appearance of dated Qajar pieces. All that can be said with certainty is that grey ceramic decoration disappears fairly soon after the fall of the Safavid dynasty. There is still a question to be asked: are there *grisaille* ceramics in the world of Islam beyond those of Persia? The tight black scrolling in late 16th century Iznik dishes hardly qualifies for the word *grisaille*.

[7] G Fehérvári, Safavid Pottery', *Persian and Mughal Art*, Colnaghi, London 1976, 259-300. 'A hoard of blue and white sherds from the Dasht-e Kavir', *Ars Decorativa,* Budapest 1977, 107-22.

[8] Y Crowe, 'The glazed ceramics', *Excavations at Kandahar 1974 and 1975*, A McNicoll and W Ball, BAR International series 641, 1995.

Pl. 7.1 Susa 1974: bowl, w: 25cm. (Photo Y Crowe)

Pl. 7.2 Susa 1974: shard. (Photo Y Crowe)

Pl. 7.3 Susa 1973: lustre bowl, w: 21.5cm, in. (Photo Y Crowe)

Pl. 7.4 Susa 1973: lustre bowl, out. (Photo Y Crowe)

Pl. 7.5 British Museum: Sultanabad T-rim bowl, w: 41.2cm. (Photo Y Crowe, courtesy of the Trustees of the British Museum)

Pl. 7.6 British Museum: Sultanabad bowl, w: 24.3cm. (Photo Y Crowe, courtesy of the Trustees of the British Museum)

Pl. 7.7 Victoria and Albert Museum: Bowl, w: 18.6cm. 480-74. (Photo Y Crowe, courtesy of the Trustees of the Victoria and Albert Museum)

Pl. 7.8 Victoria and Albert Museum: Dish, w: 7.8cm. 167-1884. (Photo Y Crowe, courtesy of the Trustees of the Victoria and Albert Museum)

Pl. 7.9 Victoria and Albert Museum: Dish, w: 14.8cm. 461-74. (Photo Y Crowe, courtesy of the Trustees of the Victoria and Albert Museum)

Pl. 7.10 Victoria and Albert Museum: Dish, w: 21.3cm. 1115-76. (Photo Y Crowe, courtesy of the Trustees of the Victoria and Albert Museum)

Pl. 7.11 Victoria and Albert Museum: Dish, w: 16.8cm. 1322-76. (Photo Y Crowe, courtesy of the Trustees of the Victoria and Albert Museum)

Pl. 7.12 Victoria and Albert Museum: Dish, w: 44.8cm. 460-78. (Photo Y Crowe, courtesy of the Trustees of the Victoria and Albert Museum)

Pl. 7.13 Victoria and Albert Museum: Bowl, w: 23.3cm. 2864-76. (Photo Y Crowe, courtesy of the Trustees of the Victoria and Albert Museum)

8 FRAGMENTS OF DRAWINGS AND PAINTINGS FROM FUSTAT

Edmund de Unger

The art of Fatimid Egypt is of crucial importance for the development of later Islamic Art. Figurative representation was fairly scarce in Islamic art before the Fatimid period. It is under the Fatimids that every object of art begins to be decorated with figures and it is not an exaggeration to state that the result became an 'explosion' of figurative art.

The ravages of time have not spared the monuments and artefacts of the Fatimid period. More then 800 years have elapsed since the rule of the last Fatimid caliph came to an end. Nevertheless, we should still be grateful to be able to admire such splendid monuments as the Mosques of al-Azhar and al-Hakim or the perfect masonry of the Bab al-Nasr and the Bab Zawila, to mention just a few. The development in the decoration of stone carving during the period is astonishingly delicate and beautiful. In ceramics, the extraordinary 'golden glass' of lustre-ware is without a parallel in Islamic Art. In rock crystal, it was the Fatimid artists who carved the most magnificent objects. The few surviving rock crystal ewers are the pride of the Louvre, the Victoria and Albert Museum and the Treasury of St Marco, Venice. Nothing else created since in this material surpassed these in quality. Overall, despite the scarcity of remaining material, Fatimid art is one of the most splendid and exciting of Islamic art. Perhaps it is because so little has survived that our curiosity is aroused, demanding to know more about this period and explore it more fully.

This particularly applies to the art of painting. Fatimid art was very much a 'figurative' art, and the development of the representation of the human figure makes it an important area of study. Unfortunately, apart from the evidence of some sherds from a few bowls (mostly repaired), our knowledge of Fatimid figurative art in Egypt is limited. The only surviving mural from a bath in Cairo prompts us to search for more material. One of the greatest tragedies of Islamic art—and particularly of Fatimid painting—was the plundering of the Treasury and Library of Caliph Mustansir by rebellious Turkish troops in 1068. The library is said to have contained over 100,000 books on every branch of learning and *belles lettres*.[1] It also had 1400 Qur'ans and innumerable works of art of incomparable value. Rare manuscripts went to light fires, their leather binding was used to mend the shoes of the Turkish officers' slaves.[2] Nothing remained, and in order to gain some more information in an attempt to reconstruct the art of painting of this period one is compelled to resort to sherds and even to small fragments of paper which were found in Fustat.

The Keir Collection, Ham, contains five fragments of drawings and paintings from Fustat which is 'the largest number of fragments preserved anywhere'.[3] The majority of these fragments would seem to date from the 12th century, although some may be later. It would appear that most of them originate from the Fatimid period. They depict a variety of subjects: human faces, animals, warriors' amulets and decorative drawings, mostly in sketch form. Looking at them, the obvious question arises as to the purpose or use of these drawings. I have selected at random a few drawings and propose to compare them here with sherds of the Fatimid period found in Fustat, as well as some other objects, to see whether they relate to each other.

Pl. 8.1 shows a horseman. The rider is wearing a decorated dress with gold and pearl necklace and his horse appears to be richly caparisoned. Grube attributes the drawing to the early Fatimid period. [4] A similar subject can be seen on a sherd illustrated in pl. 8.2.[5] The rider on this sherd turns in the opposite direction to that on the drawing. The design on the sherd is not as fine as that on the drawing. Another horseman on a caparisoned horse is seen on an ornamental garment in the Brooklyn Museum

1 Stanley Lane Poole, *History of Egypt, Middle Ages*, London 1901, 149.

2 *Ibid.*, 150.

3 Ernst J Grube, 'Fustat fragments', in B. W. Robinson, *Art of the Book*, London 1976, 63, Henceforth cited as 'Robinson', B W Robinson's book is in effect the catalogue of Islamic paintings and manuscripts in the Keir Collection. Grube's study on Fustat fragments, p. 25-66, is an invaluable introduction to the subject. See also Grube, this volume.

4 Robinson Ill. 8 on pl. 3.

5 Ali Bey Baghat and Felix Massoui, *Le Céramique Musulmane de l'Egypt*, Cairo 1930, pl. LI.

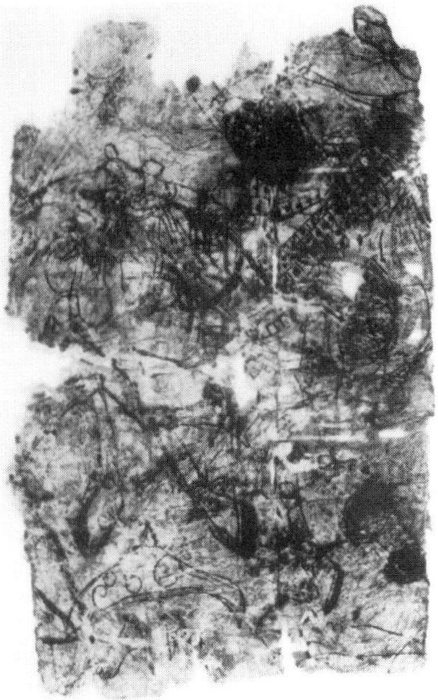

Pl. 8.1

(Pl. 3).[6] There is more movement on this truly splendid fragment than on the previous illustration. It would seem that mounted warriors were a popular subject as they consistently recur on Fatimid artefacts.

In pl. 8.4[7] we see the drawing of a male face. The portrait has enormous eyes which seem to dominate the drawing. Broadly speaking, the sources of Fatimid paintings seem to be either Central Asia—via Samarra—or Hellenistic Art. The latter seems to have lingered on in Egypt since the Classical period. The drawing illustrated relates more the 'Samarra' style. Another face is illustrated on pl. 8.5.[8] Pl. 8.6[9] also shows a similar face and pl. 8.7[10] shows a drawing of a dancing figure. This drawing is of excellent quality: it is very freely sketched and remarkably fluid and naturalistic for the 11th century.[11] A similar dancing figure, perhaps less freely drawn and naturalistic, can be seen on the superb piece of ceramic preserved in the Freer Gallery, Washington DC, and illustrated in pl. 8.8.[12]

Pl. 8.2

Pl. 8.9 figures a 'Lions hunt' on parchment.[13] The horseman pursuing a lion is again very freely drawn: one can almost feel the speed of his horse chasing the lion! Another lion chase is preserved on a woodcutting in the Islamic Art Museum of Cairo (pl. 8.10). This piece was originally displayed in the Maristan of the Qalawun Mosque and is dated from the 11th century.[14]

On pl. 8.11[15] a mounted falconer can be seen. An almost identical falconer figures on pl. 8.12.[16] Another version—perhaps in a more elaborate style—is in pl. 8.13.[17]

Lastly, on pl. 8.14 [18] we find a sketch of a galley. A fragment of a bowl in pl. 8.15 [19] shows the same subject. It is interesting to note that both on the drawing and sherd the galley is shown with flags and a mast.

The above are just a few examples to demonstrate the connection between these fragments with ceramics and woodcarving. Many more examples could be shown. The solution to the purpose of these drawings can be arrived at perhaps by a process of elimination. Clearly, these sketches were unlikely to be meant for court manuscripts. It seems equally unlikely that they were made simply without any purpose, to be thrown away at a time when paper and parchment was not cheap. Having seen the same subject figuring more than once on ceramics and woodcarvings perhaps it is not unreasonable to assume that these drawings were made for the use of artisans such as potters and woodcarvers: they must have been part of an artisan's 'pattern book'. Indeed, as we have seen, their

6 In: Brooklyn Museum, '*The Collectors Eye*'. *The Ernest Ericson collection in the Brooklyn Museum. Exhibition Catalogue*, New York, 1987, pl.139, 157.

7 Robinson pl. 4, 9.

8 *Le Céramique Egyptienne de l'epoque Musulmane*, Musée de l'Art Arabe, Cairo and Basle, 1922, pl. 83.

9 Helen Philon, *Early Islamic Ceramics*, Benaki Museum, Athens 1980, 224, pl. 474.

10 Robinson pl. 5.

11 As attributed by Grube.

12 E Attil, *Ceramics from the World of Islam*, Washington, 1971, pl. 58.

13 Robinson pl. 5.

14 Wilfrid Seipel, *Schätze der Kalifen, Islamische Kunst zur Fatimidenzeit*, Exhibition Catalogue, Kunsthistorisches Museum, Vienna, 1998, 74, plate.

15 Robinson pl. 9.

16 *Céramique Egyptienne de l'epoche Musulmane*, pl. 52

17 Attil, *op, cit.*, pl. 57.

18 Robinson pl. 10, I.34.

19 *Céramique Egyptienne de l'epoche Musulmane*, 12.

Pl. 8.3

Pl. 8.5

Pl. 8.4

Pl. 8.6

subjects recur frequently. Their quality varies. Some are good, freely drawn and naturalistic. It is tantalising to hazard a guess as to the quality of manuscripts prepared for the Court Library if the quality of simple artisans' sketchbooks were of the quality of some of these drawings. Unfortunately, the Court manuscripts all disappeared during the fateful looting in 1068 and we shall never know what they really looked like.

In any event, very little early Islamic painting survives before the 12th century. Apart from the Umayyad murals in the ruins of Khirbat al-Mafjar, Qusayr ᶜAmra and Qasr al-Hayr (all of the 8th century) there is not much left. For this reason alone the Fustat fragments are—regardless as to their aesthetic quality—unique and important. These small pieces of papers and parchments—often in not very good condition—give us some insight as the state of paintings in the Muslim world and particularly in Egypt between the 11th and 13th centuries.

Pl. 8.7

Pl. 8.8

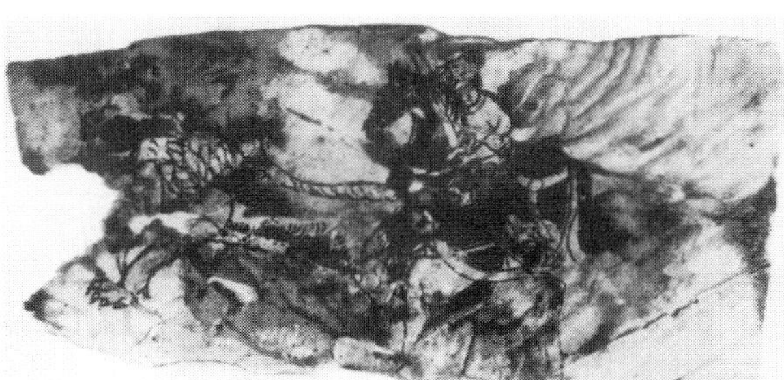

Pl. 8.9

Pl. 8.10

Pl. 8.11

Pl. 8.12

Pl. 8.13

Pl. 8.14

Pl. 8.15

9 ACHAEMENID INDIAN GOLD

David Fleming

To Ralph, whose own explorations showed us the way.

In his Histories, *when discussing the Achaemenid empire's taxation districts, Herodotus recorded that 'India' paid 360 talents of gold dust each year. This amount has prompted little discussion. However, when one realizes that it is equivalent to more than nine tonnes, or 300,000 troy ounces, of gold, the question of whether this amount of gold could have been produced each year, and then transported to the Persian capital, suddenly becomes very interesting. This paper discusses whether this total was even plausible, given the formidable difficulties that would have attended its production, collection and transportation.*

Introduction

When Alexander of Macedon's troops sacked the Achaemenid capital of Persepolis in 330 BC, they found gold and silver bullion in the Treasury amounting to the enormous (to them) sum of 120,000 talents, when reckoned in terms of silver.[1] This must have seemed living proof of the tales of Herodotus, whose listing of the annual tribute assessments of the Persian dominions in the mid-5th century BC had revealed to the Greeks, for the first time, the wealth of the empire. Yet we know very little about this wealth, and even less about the processes by which it was assessed, accumulated, transported, stored, and disbursed in an economy that remained very largely rural and land-based. What follows is a discussion of one part of this wealth, the tribute reportedly assessed in gold dust and sent from 'India' as part of the annual payments by the taxation districts to the central government.

The 'Indian' tribute

In Herodotus' *Histories* there is a lengthy discussion[2] of the tribute that was assessed each year from twenty separate parts of the Achaemenid empire. It is specifically noted that nineteen of these areas were taxed in terms of silver, for a total of 7,740 Babylonian talents,[3] but that the twentieth, that of 'India',[4] was each year required to pay 360 Euboic talents of gold dust.[5] This gold was recovered, it is further stated by Herodotus, who carefully qualified his remarks with the phrase 'according to the Persians',[6] by harvesting the dirt thrown up by huge ants burrowing into gold-bearing sands. This highly implausible account is almost certainly a tale spun at the time in an effort to conceal the true sources of the gold, whatever they were, and has rightly been dismissed by those studying the question of the possible origin of the Indian tribute.[7]

---

1 Diodorus 17.71.1., who stated that the amount recovered in this one place was δωδεκα μυριάδες ταλάντων, or twelve myriad (i.e., 12 *x* 10,000) talents. According to Callataÿ (1989: 261 nn. 4 and 6), this was expressed in Attic (or Euboic) talents of 25.98 kilograms. This is slightly smaller than the measurement of 26.1 kilograms for Attic or Euboic talents noted by Descat (1985:105) for the period in which Herodotus was writing. Using Callataÿ's figures, this means that the total reported holdings of the Persepolis Treasury alone (which is an essentially unverifiable number) were some 3,118 tonnes of bullion, or about 100.2 million Troy ounces. We do not know how much of this was gold and how much was silver, nor its purity. For comparison, the primary gold reserves of the United States, held in Fort Knox in Kentucky and reported by the US Department of the Treasury in its Treasury Bulletin for June 2000, were equivalent to 261.6 million Troy ounces, or about 8,136 tonnes, of fine gold.

2 Herodotus, *Histories* 3.89-95.

3 That is, about 234 tonnes or 7.53 million Troy ounces of silver, at the equivalents of 1 Babylonian talent = 30.24 kg (Descat 1989: 17) and 1 Troy ounce = 31.103 grams.

4 The location of which is still not absolutely certain; see Fleming (1993) and references therein. The most probable location is the middle Indus valley and the land to the west of this. That Achaemenid India existed, at least as an official concept, is clear from its frequent mention in the Persepolis Fortification Tablets (Hallock 1969: *passim*, especially 'Q' texts) as a destination for parties of travellers setting out from Persepolis.

5 The Euboic, or Attic, talent was lighter than the Babylonian, and as mentioned above, Note 1, was equivalent to 26.1 kilograms at the time Herodotus was writing. The annual Indian tribute was therefore equal to about 9.40 tonnes or 302,000 Troy ounces of gold dust.

6 Herodotus 3.95.

7 As pointed out by Vogelsang (1988: 257), gold-digging ants are recorded in the Indian epic the *Mahabharata*, which antedated the Persian presence in the Indian subcontinent by many centuries.

However, what has been less fully examined are the related questions of whether the amount of gold being assessed each year was even remotely recoverable, given the technology available at the time, and how such a mass of bullion was transported from its point of origin to the imperial treasury in Persepolis, some thousands of kilometres from the nearest possible assembly point. We will consider whether the recovery means available in the 5th century BC could have yielded the annual totals specified by Herodotus, and what logistical problems would have been faced by the administrators whose duty it was to ship the tribute to the capital.

The amount of the tribute

As mentioned, Herodotus reported that the Indian satrapy was required to pay an annual tribute of 360 Attic or Euboic talents, in modern terms some 302,000 Troy ounces, of gold dust. Once in Persepolis, the gold dust, and the silver bullion, was reportedly melted down into ingots and stored in the imperial Treasury,[8] to be used as and when required.[9] Neither Herodotus, nor any other ancient writer, says anything about how the tribute was brought to Persepolis.[10]

The description of the form of the gold is important, because it shows that the gold was *placer gold*, that is, gold recovered in powdered form from alluvial deposits that were originally created through erosion from gold-bearing matrices by glaciation or other natural forces. It was not gold found either as nuggets (in any case, both very rare and very unpredictable), or as gold that had been smelted from ores dug out of relatively shallow deposits, the other two means of recovery known to the ancient world.[11] Modern gold recovery methods that are based on a combination of mechanised processing of huge quantities of gold-bearing rock and extraction of the metal by the use of powerful solvents were totally unknown in the mid-first millennium BC. Even the first chemical extraction method, the 'patio process' that used a (highly toxic) combination of mercury, copper sulphate and salt to refine gold and silver from their ores, was not developed until the mid-16th century AD, and was used mostly in Mexico and Peru. Therefore, gold that was being recovered for inclusion in any tribute being paid to Persepolis would almost certainly have been collected from alluvial deposits by hand, an immensely laborious and not especially productive process.

Quite why the gold was required in the form of dust is not known. Gold dust is very inconvenient to handle, because it is simultaneously valuable, easy to lose, and difficult to transport in fixed amounts. Its purity is completely unpredictable, and variable, depending on what other metals were present in the original matrix from which it was eroded. To the best of my knowledge, no other pre-industrial society transported or stored gold bullion in this fashion, preferring either some form of ingot, or minted coins of known weight and purity. For example, in mid-19th century California, gold dust was converted to ingots at government-run assay offices at the miners' first opportunity.

Could manual methods have produced the immense totals required, decade after decade, by the Persian Treasury? After all, the entire official annual gold output of the modern Republic of India for the ten-year period 1989-1998 was an average of only 2.3 tonnes, or about 74,000 Troy ounces, each year,[12] or less than one-quarter of the annual tribute demanded from 'India' by the Achaemenid kings. Furthermore, most modern Indian production is from deep mines in central and southern India, in the regions of Karnataka and Andhra Pradesh, thousands of kilometres from wherever Achaemenid India was in the north-western part of the subcontinent and not sources of placer gold. As for modern Pakistan, the certain location of Achaemenid India and the ancient region of Dardistan (modern Gilgit, in the Karakorams), known for its relatively pure alluvial gold[13] that was still collected in the 19th[14] and early 20th[15] centuries, modern gold production is so minimal that it does not even register in

---

[8] Herodotus 3.96.2.

[9] The discussion by Lewis (1989) of the Persian empire's essential 'gift-giving' nature, in which gold and silver were both offered and accepted as a sign of reciprocal social obligation, is an extremely perceptive review of the probable reality of the Persians' need for precious metals.

[10] No modern writer known to me has wondered this, either, and no one seems to doubt the essential accuracy of the amounts mentioned by Herodotus. In fact, Descat (1989:16) has argued that the totals recorded by Herodotus were taken from satrapal records in Sardis, the capital of Lydia in Asia Minor, and are therefore quite probably correct.

[11] Wilford (2000).

[12] Data are from Klapwijck *et al.* (1999: Table 3).

[13] Bernard (1987:179), with references to Megasthenes in Strabo 15.11.44 (706) and 15.1.57 (711).

[14] Biddulph (1880:22), who stated '... many of the streams are rich in gold, especially those flowing from the great Rakiposh mountain'.

[15] Schomberg (1935:100-1), mentions that in the Hunza region, villages on gold-bearing streams each had eight *khuraput* or gold washers who were excused all other riverine labours, but that their work was not very rewarding.

standard industry sources,[16] and Pakistan is now discussed almost entirely in terms of a country that imports gold, rather than as a source of new production.[17, 18]

Here we must argue by analogy, because we have no information whatsoever on the 'Indian' gold industry in the time of Herodotus. We will use as an example of manual gold recovery the greatest 'gold rush' of the mid-19th century, the California gold rush of 1848-49.[19] We have chosen this event because it was the most significant of the 19th-century 'pre-industrial' gold rushes, in which, initially at least, gold was recovered by methods that had not changed in millennia. The California gold rush is also a relatively well-documented event, for which we have extensive records of amounts of gold recovered, and in what forms. We will also examine the Spanish records of the amounts of bullion recovered from Mexico and Peru, and will consider the economic implications of how these masses of precious metal were mined, refined and transported.

The most famous, although not the first, gold rush in California began in early 1848 near Sacramento in the central part of the state. By the end of 1849, according to the most careful estimate,[20] and using only hand recovery of placer (alluvial) deposits, the total amount of gold recovered by highly motivated men working in a very productive area was 502,936 ounces, of which most (491,072 ounces) was recovered in 1849. However, the gold washings that yielded the alluvial placer gold were already being worked out within a decade of their discovery, and deep mines soon took their place. By 1850, the discovery of the Grass Valley lodes of gold-bearing quartz led to the development of shaft mining, and by 1854 the lucrative but destructive technique of hydraulic mining (that is, washing away the gold-bearing soil with high-pressure water hoses) had brought the annual total produced to 3.4 million ounces. The total of gold produced in the period 1848-1996 is set at 116.12 million ounces, with the greatest production early in the period.[21] It is probable that if no new sources had been discovered in 1850, the rush would have petered out, with dwindling totals of gold produced from washings by men who, however powerful their motivation, expended ever-greater efforts to recover ever-smaller amounts of gold dust.

To 16th-century Europe, the avalanches of gold and then silver that poured into Spain from Mexico and Peru seemed unbelievable. From being a poor, arid land on the edge of the continent, Spain went to being the richest country in the world, and all in the space of a few years. The quantities of bullion that were sent back to Spain were immense,[22] and the early greed for easy finds was notorious.[23] However, the initial seizures of gold in Mexico, Peru and elsewhere represented the scouring of accumulations built up over centuries, and are not representative of the annual capacity of the land to produce. Their very ease probably misled the Spanish (and everyone else in Europe) into thinking that much more

[16] Klapwijk *et al.* (1999).

[17] As pointed out by the World Gold Council (1999), by 1998 Pakistan consumed roughly 100 tonnes of gold a year, which was satisfied by a mixture of internal trading (10 tonnes), legal imports of bullion (35 tonnes) and worked jewellery (30 tonnes), and smuggling (25 tonnes, at least in estimate). Modern industry sources make no mention of any production of any quantity in Pakistan.

[18] One may reasonably point out that perhaps a very productive ancient gold source was completely worked out, to the point that no economic trace of the source remained, and that this could account for the apparent lack of any modern trace of a source that in antiquity satisfied the demands of a distant imperial treasury. While this argument is initially plausible, it cannot survive in the face of modern mining technology, which can detect recoverable amounts of precious metals in far lower concentrations than could ever have been identified in antiquity using the methods then available. In some cases, known pre-industrial sources are being reworked by modern mining companies, who quite reasonably identify a cost advantage in going through the tailings left by previous miners, as opposed to starting fresh excavations. An example of this is seen at the huge silver source at Potosí in Bolivia, where the US mining firm Asarco recently announced its intention of exploring some of the loose earth around the base of the mountain, left from the sixteenth-century mining operations (reported on Cable News Network, February 22, 1999).

[19] For reasons of space, we cannot discuss the Australian gold rush of 1851 and the Yukon gold rush of 1898, nor the more industrial beginnings of the gold industry in South Africa in the 1880s.

[20] Discussed in Hill (1999: 65).

[21] Hill (1999: 117; 133; and 263, Table A4 'California gold production').

[22] Hamilton (1934) remains the standard statistical source, although his conclusions have generated enormous arguments. In the period 1503-1520 there were no silver imports, and 14.12 tonnes of gold (nearly 454,000 Troy ounces, all from Mexico, the Caribbean, and Central America, because the Spanish did not enter Peru until 1532) were registered as imports (data from Hamilton 1934:42, Table 3). By 1540 the dominant metal was silver, and for the period 1503-1660 Hamilton determined that 16,886.8 tonnes (543 million Troy ounces) of silver and 181.3 tonnes (5.8 million Troy ounces) of gold had been extracted in the New World and sent to Spain (Hamilton 1934: *loc. cit.*). The total gold officially recovered in the entire Spanish New World in over a century and a half was therefore equal to twenty years' worth of tribute from one small part of the Achaemenid empire, as recorded by Herodotus.

[23] The story of how Francisco Pizarro demanded a ransom for the Inca Atahualpa, who offered to fill a room 22 feet long and 17 feet wide with gold up to a line about eight feet off the ground, is found in many of the conquest narratives (Hemming 1970:48). Even nearly a century later, the indigenous chronicler Felipe Guaman Poma de Ayala was to depict the Spaniards of the conquest being so greedy for gold that they were viewed as saying *este oro comemos* ('we eat this gold') (Poma de Ayala 1980 [1615]: 369 [371]).

gold lay there simply for the taking.[24] It quickly became apparent that to loot the work of others was easy and could have a high yield, but was a process that could only happen once. The sustained production of riches took years of work and the investment of enormous capital.

Far more indicative of just how productive, or not, indigenous communities operating in a pre-industrial milieu really were, are the records of annual tribute paid in Peru by indigenous communities, as established by the Viceroy Francisco de Toledo and in force by 1582. Unlike the huge industrial silver centres in Zacatecas in Mexico and Potosí in Bolivia, where silver was mined and processed on an enormous scale, most of Peru and Mexico was relatively poor. By about 1580, or less than half a century after the Spanish conquest of the Inca empire, the annual taxes being assessed on Indian communities in Peru were being measured in thousands, rather than millions, of pesos of silver,[25] each peso (or 'piece of eight') being about 29 grams, or slightly less than one Troy ounce, of silver.[26] That is, the land so rich that it gave rise to the saying 'eso vale un Perú' ('it is worth a Peru') was rich only because of Spanish Colonial silver mining technology. It was not producing, and never did produce, vast amounts of alluvial gold.

The logistical requirements

Transport by land

The physical mass of the 'Indian' gold would have been an important consideration in arranging its transportation.[27] Gold in the form of dust is less economical to transport than gold in the form of smelted bricks, because gold dust takes up more space than cast bricks and is virtually never as pure. Research in the 19th century into the carrying capacities of various Old World cargo animals established that mules and horses can carry 200 lbs (91 kilograms) for extended periods, while camels can carry 300 lbs (136 kilograms) for extended periods[28] (these totals do not include the weight of the animals' pack saddles and bridles). By this reckoning, the minimum number of animals that would have been required to carry the annual tribute would have been 104 horses or mules, or 69 camels, or obviously some combination. Furthermore, packhorses working in arid regions require an average of at least 20-24 lbs (9-11 kilograms) of provisions and an average of 8 imperial gallons (36 litres) of water each day, requirements that rise sharply when the animals are working in arid regions.[29] Camels can carry more, but require a minimum of 10 lbs (4.5 kilograms) of grain and 25 lbs (11 kilograms) of straw each day, along with 10 imperial gallons (45 litres) of water.[30]

These totals ensure that the minimum daily water and fodder needs for the transport animals alone (saying nothing of the needs of the animals carrying the attendants

[24] Permit this writer one personal anecdote. In a small village in the mountains of south-central Peru, in 1981, I was told by the local chief of police that a day or so away by horse, there was a site that had been a gold mine (in fact, it was a small settlement at 4,100 metres above sea level marked on the topographical maps as 'abandoned gold washings'), where gold lay on the ground, he whispered confidentially, 'like sand.' Unfortunately, I have yet to visit this site, so the veracity of the police chief's remarks remains untested.

[25] Cook (1975: *passim*).

[26] Swiss Bank Corporation (1988).

[27] The US gold depository at Fort Knox stores its gold in bars of 400 Troy ounces (28.5 lbs avoirdupois or 12.9 kilograms), each bar measuring approximately 7 x 3.625 x 1.75 inches and occupying 44.4 cubic inches or 727.7 cubic centimetres. On this standard, the annual tribute from India would have consisted of approximately 730 gold bars, each weighing nearly 30 lbs. Data are from the US Treasury, *Office of Public Correspondence Fact Sheet OPC-79*, available at www.ustreas.gov/opc/opc0079.html.

[28] Engels (1978:14 and n.11). Note that these data on animal carrying capacity, carefully worked out by the British and Indian Armies in the later nineteenth century and essentially confirmed by the US Army's own research at the time, are far more credible than the much higher carrying capacities of up to 300 kilograms per camel proposed by Callataÿ (1989: 263), although heavier loads can be carried for shorter distances (Engels 1978: 14, note 11). It must be remembered that until the Second World War, many armies relied to an enormous degree on animals for transporting stores, munitions and equipment, and therefore had to know within very tight limits what each animal could do. Plutarch (*Alexander* 37.4) mentions that 10,000 mules and 5,000 camels were needed to take the accumulated booty from Persepolis to Ecbatana. The booty reportedly consisted either of 180,000 (according to Diodorus, 17.80.3., ταλάντων ʼοκτωκαίδεκα μυριαδες) or 190,000 (according to Justin, 12.1.1, *pecunia omnis, cxc milia talentum Ecbatana congestis*) talents of bullion, a total accepted by Callataÿ (1989: 263), who does not consider the logistical problems that would have accompanied the creation and management of such a colossal caravan. In any case, either the booty totals are too high, or the numbers of animals are too low. Using the known carrying capacities of camels and mules given above, 10,000 mules and 5,000 camels could have carried a total of 1,590 tonnes, or about 61,000 Attic talents, or only one-third of the purported booty. If all the booty were carried in one caravan, there would have been required 30,000 mules and 15,000 camels, each needing to be fed and watered at the rates given above, and most attended by men who also had to be fed, watered and protected. Even if three trips were made (something for which we have no evidence), transporting this mass of treasure would have been a huge undertaking. The economic consequences of such a vast horde of animals and men passing through the local countryside would have been catastrophic.

[29] Engels (1978: 126-127).

[30] Engels (1978: 129-130).

and guards, and these persons themselves) would have been almost 4,000 litres of water and well over 1,000 kilograms of fodder. We have no idea at all of how many men would have accompanied the annual shipments, but one must assume that such an important, and enticing, shipment would have been heavily escorted by men whose primary duty would have been armed defence and who would themselves have required feeding at the basic rate of about 1.5 kilograms of grain and 10 litres of water each day.[31] For a journey that probably covered no more than 35 kilometres a day, the 2,000-kilometer-plus overland trip from somewhere in the Indus valley to Fars would have required a minimum of ten weeks, assuming no rest stops, which would have been very unlikely. The logistics of such a trip would have been formidable and the risks enormous.[32]

Transport by sea

An alternative would have been to move the tribute by sea, down the Indus river and along the route to Susa purportedly pioneered by Skylax of Caryanda in the late 6th century BC.[33] By the 1st century AD, this route was well known to Mediterranean pilots, as is clear from the *Periplus of the Erythraean Sea*,[34] and was probably the route followed by Nearchos when he brought the Macedonian fleet back to the Persian Gulf while Alexander crossed the Gedrosian desert.[35] It is also very probable that the route would have been known from much earlier by pilots whose regular journeys were between the mouths of the Tigris and Euphrates and the Indus. In fact, it is very likely that the route was known by the fourth millennium BC, on the basis of the archaeological evidence from Bahrain (ancient Dilmun) and the ancient mentions of Magan and Meluhha. It is certainly known that there was some contact between the head of the Persian Gulf and the Indus valley by the mid-third millennium BC, although it is not known if this contact was by sea.[36]

The logistics of this mode of transport would have been much easier, because a cargo of 9.4 tonnes can be carried in one small sea-going vessel crewed by a few men instead of on a huge herd of camels managed by hundreds of attendants, guards, and camp followers, and even a very modest daily voyage of 100 kilometres is vastly more rapid than a land voyage on foot or horseback. However, we know almost nothing of what would now be called merchant shipping in the Achaemenid period. As with any land transport of the tribute, this cargo would have required heavy guard, both to protect against pirates, and to prevent the crews from absconding with the cargo, and would probably have been divided between a number of vessels. The loss of vessels to bad weather, uncharted reefs, or human action must have been a regular occurrence that would also have remained a constant concern to the imperial administration.

Far more important than the number or size of the vessels would have been the wind. In the Arabian Sea, in the north-western portion of the Indian Ocean, the winds tend to blow from the north-east from September to April (the north-east monsoon), before reversing direction and blowing from the south-west from April to September (the south-west monsoon), when they reverse once more and blow from the north-east.[37] If we assume that the annual tribute would have been due at the New Year festival in March, it should have been possible to sail down the Indus in December or January, and sail along the northern shore of the Arabian Sea with a favourable wind, returning to the Indus with the south-west monsoon between June and August. Unfortunately, we have no way to determine whether this mode of transporting the annual tribute would have been preferred, and it will have to remain an interesting hypothesis.

Conclusion

I believe I have shown that in terms of the known productivity of gold-producing regions that could have been in 'India,' there is not one single territory that could

[31] Engels (1978:125).

[32] We must also remember that all other eastern taxation districts would have been sending their tribute to Persepolis at the same time; if all tribute caravans had travelled together it would have been safer, but the demands on local resources would have been even greater.

[33] Herodotus, *Histories* 4.44, where the journey is said to have taken thirty months, ending at an Egyptian port on the Red Sea. A thirty-month journey would have been useless for the purposes of transporting annual tribute, as well as most unusual, even in an era of modest seamanship; the first voyage of Columbus across the Atlantic and back, in waters that were completely unknown to European navigators and over a much greater distance, took 6½ months in all (Fernandez-Armestro 1991:67 *et seq.*).

[34] Casson (1989).

[35] Arrian, *Indica*; Tarn (1950:481-5).

[36] Rawlinson in Durand (1880) was an early proponent of the location of Dilmun in Bahrain. Magan and Meluhha are generally thought to have been the region of either Oman or the Makran coast of Iran, and the Indus valley region, respectively (see, for example, Hansman 1973), although Michaux-Colombot (1998) suggests that they were both somewhere on the Red Sea.

[37] Lavery (1989:267).

have yielded anything remotely like the amounts listed by Herodotus, especially when one considers that the gold was alluvial gold from superficial deposits. Furthermore, the incidental logistical problems that would have accompanied the gold's production, collection, and transport would have been overwhelming. Only if the gold had come by sea would the annual shipment have been manageable, and we know nothing of this side of Achaemenid history. In addition, if this track down the Indus and along the Iranian coast had been the only route, it was probably not a very safe one. It is clear from the records left by the Alexander historians that by the mid-4th century, the Indus valley had long since ceased even thinking of itself as 'Persian,' if ever it had. There is little archaeological evidence to suggest that even in the 6th and 5th centuries BC, the local cultures were in any way under Persian control, however ephemeral.[38]

So what was happening? Did Herodotus record something that was true, or once true, or true only in the official mind, or completely fantastic? In writing of the Indian tribute, did Herodotus bear in mind the problems we have alluded to, while compiling his figures? I believe that what probably happened was something similar to what occurred two millennia later, when the Spanish entered Mexico and Peru. The initial discoveries of accumulations of gold produced completely unrealistic expectations about the potential of the regions to produce similar quantities of the precious metal indefinitely. However, by the time it was clear that the golden productivity of the region (be it 'India' or Peru) could not hope to match the demands being put on it, the region had either slid away from under central control (as seems to have happened with 'India'), or other sources of riches had been found (as happened in Peru, with the development of new silver mines). Therefore, the sums in Herodotus may indeed have been the official totals, recorded in satrapal archives and established at the height of the empire's dominion at the end of the 6th century BC, but I doubt very strongly that the amounts listed in the official documents were attained in the annual tribute payments, even by the mid-5th century when Herodotus was writing.[39] That the sums were still being listed in official documents long after they ceased to be paid is not surprising, because there are repeated examples throughout history of official refusals to recognise unwanted changes in circumstances. This, I believe, is what lies at the heart of the tribute list; the list is a compilation of the official, the statutory, indeed the hoped-for, yield from the empire's component parts, and is not an accounting document. It is, in other words, propaganda, and the satrapal secretaries must have been thrilled that Herodotus included it in his text.

BIBLIOGRAPHY

Bernard, Paul (1987): 'Les indiens dans la liste des tributs d'Hérodote', *Studia Iranica* 16, 177-191.

Biddulph, John (1977 [1880]): *Tribes of the Hindoo Koosh*. Karachi: Indus Publications.

Callataÿ, François de (1989): 'Les trésors achéménides et les monnayages d'Alexandre: espèces immobilisées et espèces circulantes?', *Revue des etudes anciennes* 91, 259-274.

Casson, Lionel (1989): *The Periplus maris Erythreai: text with introduction, translation and commentary.* Princeton: Princeton University Press.

Cook, Noble David (1975): *Tasa de la Visita General de Francisco de Toledo.* Lima: Universidad Nacional Mayor de San Marcos, Dirección Universitaria de Biblioteca y Publicaciones.

Descat, Raymond (1985): 'Mnésimachos, Hérodote et le système tributaire achéménide', *Revue des etudes anciennes* 87, 97-112.

Descat, Raymond (1989): 'Notes sur l'histoire du monnayage achéménide sous le régne de Darius Ier', *Revue des etudes anciennes* 91, 15-29.

Engels, Donald W (1978): *Alexander the Great and the logistics of the Macedonian Army*. Berkeley/London: University of California Press.

Fernandez-Armestro, Felipe (1991): *Columbus*. Oxford: Oxford University Press.

Fleming, David (1993): 'Where was Achaemenid India?', *Bulletin of the Asia Institute* 7, 67-72.

Hallock, Richard T (1969): *Persepolis Fortification Tablets*. Chicago: University of Chicago Press.

[38] Fleming (1993: 70).

[39] Two alternative suggestions can be advanced for the nature of any annual tribute. The first would be that the amounts listed represented the equivalent value of goods and/or services, rather than a mass of bullion. That is, each year, India had to supply 360 gold talents' worth of grain, or wool, or labour to either the local satrapal capital, or the imperial capital in Persis. This idea can be dismissed with two separate arguments. In the first place, 360 talents' worth of grain or wool would have been such a huge mass that one would have needed transportation facilities far in excess of anything discussed above, and the logistics would have been a nightmare. In the second place, we have no records of any such equivalences in any other part of the empire, and no notes that discuss the accounting complexities of any such system. The second alternative would be that the tribute simply went to the satrapal capital, and not to the imperial capital. From what we know of the centralisation of the Achaemenid empire, and the watchfulness of the officials known as the 'King's Eyes', this would have been unthinkable, especially in India's case. Of course, were we ever to identify the capital of Achaemenid India archaeologically, and locate and excavate the satrapal archive, this notion might have to be revisited.

Hamilton, Earl J (1934): *American treasure and the price revolution in Spain, 1501-1650.* Cambridge, Massachusetts: Harvard University Press.

Hansman, John (1973): 'A periplus of Magan and Meluhha', *Bulletin of the School of Oriental and African Studies* 36, 554-587.

Hemming, John (1970): *The conquest of the Incas.* London: Macmillan.

Hill, Mary (1999): *Gold: the California story.* Berkeley/London: University of California Press.

Klapwijck, Philip *et al.* (1999): *Gold Survey 1999.* London: Gold Field Mineral Services Ltd.

Lavery, Brian (1989): *Nelson's navy: the ships, men and organization.* London: Conway Maritime Press.

Lewis, David M. (1989): 'Persian gold in Greek international relations', *Revue des etudes anciennes* 91, 227-234.

Michaux-Colombot, Danielle (1998): 'Magan and Meluhha: a re-appraisal through the historiography of thalassocratic powers. Abstract of paper submitted to the 45th Rencontre Assyriologique Internationale', Cambridge, Massachusetts, July 5-8, 1998.

Poma de Ayala, Felipe Guaman (1980 [1615]): *El Primer Nueva Corónica y Buen Gobierno. Edición crítica de John V. Murra y Rolena Adorno. Traducciones y análisis textual del quechua por Jorge L. Urioste.* Mexico City: Siglo Veintiuno Editores, S.A.

Rawlinson, Henry C (1880): Notes. In Captain Durand (1880) 'Extracts from report on the islands and antiquities of Bahrain', with notes by Major-General Sir H C Rawlinson. *Journal of the Royal Asiatic Society (NS)* 12, 189-227.

Schomberg, R C F (1935): *Between the Oxus and Indus.* London: Martin Hopkinson Ltd.

Swiss Bank Corporation (1988): *Coins of Peru. Auction 20, September 14 and 15, 1988.* Basel/Zürich: Numistmatic Department, Swiss Bank Corporation.

Tarn, W W (1951): 'Ormuz: a lost kingdom', Appendix 12 of *The Greeks in Bactria and India.* Cambridge, England: Cambridge University Press.

Vogelsang, Willem (1988): 'Indian antics. A reply to P Bernard (1987)', *Studia Iranica* 17, 253-258.

Wilford, John Noble (2000): 'The Secrets of Croesus' Gold: Archaeologists Learn How Ancient King Made His Money, Literally', *The New York Times,* Tuesday, August 15, 2000, pages F1, F5.

World Gold Council (1999): 'Window on Pakistan', *Gold demand trends.* Issue N° 26, February 1999, Web edition. Available at www.gold.org/Gedt/Gdt26/W_pak.htm.

10 BETWEEN GHAZNA AND DELHI: LAHORE AND ITS LOST *MANĀRA*

Finbarr B Flood

Many a palace built Mahmud,
which in height rivalled the moon.
Now not one of their bricks remains in
place,
but the eulogies of ᶜUnsuri have stood
firm.[1]

The paper highlights an important literary reference to a minaret constructed in Lahore fort by Mahmud of Ghazna. Drawing together the literary and archaeological evidence for Ghaznavid architecture and architectural patronage in Lahore, it suggests that the importance of this city for our understanding of Ghaznavid and Ghurid architecture in South Asia has been greatly underestimated. It argues that while the ultimate prototypes of Ghurid monuments such as the Qutb Minar might lie in Afghanistan, the Ghaznavid architecture of the Indus Valley offered models closer to home. Finally, the context of Mahmud's minaret in Lahore is discussed in connection with the theme of military victory and its suggested relevance to the construction of Ghaznavid and Ghurid minarets.

Our knowledge of Ghaznavid architecture is largely derived from a relatively small corpus of Afghan buildings, many of which were brought to light by fieldwork undertaken in the second half of the 20th century. Preëminent among the surviving monuments are the palaces at Lashkar-i Bazar[2] and the minarets at Ghazna,[3] but various smaller mosques and shrines of the same period are scattered throughout Afghanistan.[4] Despite the undoubted importance of these monuments, and their ability to clarify aspects of the chronology and stylistic affinities of Ghaznavid art, our dependence upon them means that the parameters of our knowledge of Ghaznavid architecture have largely been set by the vagaries of chance. Most of the Panjab came under the sway of the Ghurids in the first quarter of the 11th century, and while we know from literary sources that the architectural patronage of the Ghaznavid rulers extended to India, little of that architectural legacy survives. Until recently, the sole material remains of the period in South Asia were some random fragments brought to light during excavations in Lahore fort in 1959.[5] Subsequent fieldwork in Pakistan has highlighted the existence of several structures datable to the Ghaznavid period. These include a small mosque excavated at Raja Gira in Swat,[6] and another, less extensively published, hilltop mosque at Giri, near Taxila.[7] To these two mosques may be added a small domed mausoleum at Zairan in the North-West Frontier Province

---

1 Niẓāmī 'Aruḍī, cited in Jerome W Clinton, *The Divan of Manūchihrī Dāmghānī*, Bibliotheca Islamica, Minneapolis, 1972, 17. On the rapid decay of the Ghaznavid monuments see Clifford Edmund Bosworth, *The Ghaznavids: their Empire in Afghanistan and Eastern Iran 994-1040*, Edinburgh University Press, Edinburgh, 1963, 139.

2 Daniel Schlumberger, *Lashkari Bazar: une résidence royale ghaznévide et ghoride*, 1A Architecture, MDAFA 18, Boccard, Paris, 1978; Janine Sourdel-Thomine, *Lashkari Bazar: une résidence royale ghaznévide et ghoride*, 1B Le décor non figuratif et les inscriptions, MDAFA 18, Boccard, Paris, 1978.

3 Y A Godard, 'L'inscription du minaret de Masᶜūd III a Ghazna', *Āthār-e Iran*, 1, 1936, 367-69; Janine Sourdel-Thomine, 'Deux minarets d'époque Seljoukide en Afghanistan', *Syria*, 30, 1953, 110-21; Ralph Pinder-Wilson, 'The Minaret of Masᶜūd at Ghazni', *Studies in Islamic Art*, The Pindar Press, London, 1985, 89-102.

4 The available information on the Ghaznavid monuments known to western scholarship is now conveniently summarised by Robert Hillenbrand, 'The Architecture of the Ghaznavids and Ghurids', in Carole Hillenbrand, ed., *The Sultan's Turret: Studies in Honour of Clifford Edmund Bosworth, Volume 2: Studies in Persian and Turkish Culture*, Brill, Leiden, 2000, 124-206. See also Bosworth, *op. cit.*, 139-41.

5 Anon., 'Lahore Fort Excavations', *Pakistan Archaeology*, 5, 1968, 159, pl. LVIIIb; Gulzar Muhammad Khan, 'Pre-Mughal Mosques in Lahore', in *Architectural Heritage of Pakistan II: Sultanate Period Architecture*, Proceedings of the Seminar on Sultanate Period Architecture in Pakistan held in Lahore in November 1990, Lahore, 1991, 127.

6 Muhammad Nazir Khan, 'A Ghaznavid Historical Inscription from Uḍegrām, Swāt', *East and West*, new series, 35, 1985, 153-66; Umberto Scerrato, 'Research on the Archaeology and History of Islamic art in Pakistan: Excavation of the Ghaznavid Mosque on Mt Raja Gira, Swat', *East and West*, new series, 35, 1985, 439-50.

7 Khan, *op. cit.*, 127-28; Abdul Rehman, 'Sultanate Period Architecture in Panjab (1000 AD–1500 AD)', in *Architectural Heritage of Pakistan II: Sultanate Period Architecture*, Proceedings of the Seminar on Sultanate Period Architecture in Pakistan held in Lahore in November 1990, Lahore, 1991, 40, figs. 2-3. For Giri in the Ghaznavid period see Abdur Rahman, 'Taxila under the Ghaznavids', *Journal of Central Asia*, 6, 1983, 173-77.

which, it has been argued, is of similar date; if so, it would probably be the earliest surviving Muslim funerary monument in South Asia.[8]

While the monuments unearthed in Swat and the Salt Range form a very welcome addition to the corpus of surviving monuments, they are unpretentious structures located at a remove from the urban centres of the Panjab. They thus provide an insight into the type of monuments being built to serve the Muslim populations of small and relatively remote settlements in the foothills of the Himalayas. They are all executed in a stone rubble medium, which was standard in this region, sometimes with a brick superstructure (as at Taxila). The mode of construction stands in marked contrast to the brick idiom that was the norm throughout the lowland regions of the Indus Valley. While perhaps reflecting aspects of eastern Iranian architecture, in their present state, they reveal no great formal or decorative innovations. If one seeks to identify any such innovations, it is to the newly conquered urban centres of the Panjab and to the monuments erected there at the behest of the Ghaznavid sultans and their vassals that one should probably look. Here one is, of course, hampered by the lack of surviving monuments, for the continued growth of such urban centres as Lahore and Peshawar, together with their repeated destruction and rebuilding over the past eight or nine centuries, has served to erase all trace of pre-Mughal architectural glories.

There are nevertheless tantalising glimpses of contemporary architectural patronage to be found in various passing references to the Ghaznavids and their activities in South Asia contained in the medieval Arabic and Persian sources. Among these is a report of a *manbra* built by Mahmud of Ghazna (*r.* 388-441/998-1030) in the fort of Lahore. While the significance of this reference was long ago recognised by Pakistani scholars writing on the history of that city, it has been largely overlooked by western scholars, and its wider implications ignored.[9] This neglect is, to say the least, surprising, since the report raises significant questions about the development and meaning of the minaret in eastern Iran and South Asia. In the light of Ralph Pinder-Wilson's work on the Ghaznavid and Ghurid minarets of Afghanistan, it seemed appropriate to offer this reconsideration of the lost *manbra* in a volume intended to honour his pioneering scholarship.

The reference to the vanished structure occurs in a source, which, although rich in incidental detail for Ghaznavid and Ghurid history (and art history), has not received the attention that it clearly deserves. The *Ādāb al-Ḥarb wa'l-Shujā'a* of Fakhr-i Mudabbir Mubarakshah is a treatise on the arts of war dedicated to Shams al-Din Iltutmish, the sultan of Delhi (r. 607-33/1211-36). The manuscript contains numerous references to the personalities and events of Ghaznavid history, which are perhaps drawn from earlier works by authors such as Bayhaqi; some of the material may also reflect oral lore, for one of the author's maternal ancestors was the father-in-law of Sultan Mahmud.[10] The relative neglect of the *Ādāb al-Ḥarb* is no doubt due to its limited availability; a printed recension of the Persian text was first published in 1967, and only excerpts are available in translation.[11]

The relevant passage of the work describes the victory of Mahmud of Ghazna over the raja of Qanauj, an important dynastic urban centre in northern India:

> The sultan pursued them and conquered Qanauj and found such quantities of gold and silver that no one took anything but gold and silver vessels. When he returned from that battle, he ordered a Friday mosque to be built in Ch.n.d (?) and a

---

[8] Abdur Rahman, 'Saif ad-Dawla Mahmud and his Tomb in Zairan', *Journal of Central Asia*, 12, 1989, 79-88; Rehman, *op. cit.*, 38-39, fig. 1.

[9] Abdulla Chaghtai, 'Pre-Mughal Architecture of Lahore (Ghaznavide Period)', *The Proceedings of the Pakistan History Conference (Second Session) held at Lahore, 1952*, Karachi, 1952, 231-32; Abdulla Chaghtai, 'The oldest extant Muslim architectural relic at Lahore', *Journal of the Pakistan Historical Society*, 12, no. 1, 1964, 61; Khan, *op. cit.*, 128. In the first of his articles, Chaghtai erroneously connects the reference with Mahmud's victory in the Panjab rather than Qanauj, as specified in the text. A rare mention of this reference in a work published outside Pakistan occurs in Peter Alford Andrews, 'Lāhawr: 2. Monuments', *Encyclopedia of Islam*, new edition, Volume 5, Leiden, 1986, 599.

[10] Charles Rieu, *Catalogue of the Persian Manuscripts in the British Museum*, Volume 2, Trustees of the British Museum, London, 1881, 488; (Miss) Iqbal Shafi, 'Fresh Light on the Ghaznavîds,' *Islamic Culture*, 12, No. 2, 1938, 195; Muhammad Nazim, *The Life and Times of Sultān Maḥmūd of Ghazna*, Munshiram Manoharlal, New Delhi, 1971, 9.

[11] Extracts from the Persian text of the *Ādāb al-Ḥarb* were made available in 1938 as a supplement to *the Lahore Oriental College Magazine*, 14, 1938. An English translation of selected excerpts was published in the same year: Shafi, *op. cit.*, 189-234. Further translated extracts relating to armoury were published by Claude Cahen as an appendix to 'Un traité d'armurerie composé pour Saladin', *Bulletin d'Études Orientales*, 12, 1947-48, 160-6. A complete printed version of the Persian text was published only in 1967: Fakhr-i Mudabbir, *Ādāb al-Ḥarb wa'l-Shujā'a*, ed. Ahmad Suhailī Khwānsarī, Tehran, 1346 (solar). A facsimile of the British Library copy of the work is also available: Ananiasz Zajeczkowski, *Le Traité Iranien de l'art militaire Ādāb al-Ḥarb wa-š-Šaǧāʿa du XIIIe siècle*, Warsaw, 1969.

Pl. 10.1 Minaret of Masʿud III at Ghazna (photo: W Ball).

manāra in the fort of Lahore as a memorial (*yādkār*).[12]

Not the least remarkable aspect of this account is the date of 422/1030 ascribed to Maḥmūd's Qanauj expedition, for the sultan had expired one year earlier, in 421, while the Qanauj expedition had in fact taken place over a decade previously, in Shaʿbān 409 (December-January 1018-19).[13]

This is one of a number of anachronisms and historical inaccuracies in the *Ādāb al-Ḥarb* that might cause one to question the veracity of this anecdote. Given the confusion over the dates, one might for example surmise that the intended reference is to Masʿud III (r. 492-508/1099-1115) who also led an expedition (or expeditions) against Qanauj, and who built the earlier of the two surviving minarets at Ghazna (pl. 10.1).[14]

The expedition of Masʿud is not in question, however, for the name of the ruler of Qanauj given in the *Ādāb al-Ḥarb* corresponds with Jaipal, the Rāṣṭrakūṭa raja mentioned in al-ʿUtbi's account of the same expedition, while the ruler at the time of the later raid on Qanauj was M.h.l.y or M.l.h.y, possible to be identified with the Gāhaḍavāla raja Madanachandra or Madanapala.[15] That the anecdote refers to Mahmud's expedition to Qanauj is therefore not in doubt, even if the date given by Fakhr-i Mudabbir is incorrect; thus, the basic information which he conveys may well be right, even if his precise chronology is not. Moreover, the commemoration of the expedition through the construction of a *manāra*, a term frequently used for the minarets of mosques, would fit with what we know of Mahmud's architectural patronage; it was upon his return from this very expedition that the material fruits of Mahmud's Indian victories were sunk into the construction of Ghazna's celebrated Friday Mosque, 'the Bride of Heaven,' and its associated *madrasa*.[16] The balance of probability therefore supports Fakhr-i Mudabbir's assertion that Mahmud commemorated his sack of Qanauj by the construction of a mosque in an unknown place and a *manāra* in Lahore fort.

It is impossible to resolve the matter conclusively, but with this caveat in mind I would like to draw attention to some of the implications of this important reference. Presuming that the term *manāra* refers to a minaret, as seems likely, the first point to be made is that the Lahore minaret, constructed in 409/1019, would have pre-dated the surviving royal minarets of Ghazna (pl. 10.1) by eighty years; in fact it would be among the earliest securely dated minarets of the eastern Islamic world. It is highly likely that the minaret was only one of a number of structures

[12] Fakhr-i Mudabbir, *op. cit.*, 475; *Lahore Oriental College Magazine*, 14, 1938, supplement, 55; Shafi, *op. cit.*, 233; Zajeczkowski, *op. cit.*, fol. 185 recto. Although Shafi also suggests that, reading *chand* for ch.n.d, the text might refer to the construction of several Friday mosques with minarets in Lahore fort, the British Musuem manuscript reads quite clearly *'dar Ch.n.d (?) masjid-i ādīna wa dar qalaʿ-i Lāhawr manāra ...'* In other words, these are indicated as monuments erected in two distinct places. Although present in the Lahore version, the *wa* and second *dar* are omitted in the printed version of the Persian text, producing the impression that the two structures were one and the same. For the use of the term *manāra*, see Jonathan Bloom, *Minaret Symbol of Islam*, Oxford Studies in Islamic Art, Vol. 7, 1989, 36-54. I am grateful to Dr Massumeh Farhad for her suggestions as to the possible meanings of this passage.

[13] According to al-ʿUtbi, Mahmud reached Qanauj on the eighth of Shaʿbān 409: H M Elliott and John Dowson, *The History of India as told by its own Historians*, Volume 2, Delhi, 1990, 45. See also N A Baloch, 'The Ghaznawid dominions and establishment of the Kingdom of Lahore', *Erdem*, 7, 1991, 544-45.

[14] M. Longworth Dames-[J Burton-Page], 'Kanawdj', *Encyclopedia of Islam*, new edition, Volume 4, 1973, 533.

[15] There is some uncertainty as to whether it was Jaipāl or his son Trilochapāla who faced Mahmud: Shafi, *op. cit.*, 231 n.10; D C Ganguly, 'The historical value of Dīwān-i-Salmān', *Islamic Culture*, 16, 1942, 426; R C Majumdar, ed., *The Struggle for Empire*, The History and Culture of the Indian People, Bombay, 1957, 95; Alessio Bombaci, *The Kūfic inscriptions in Persian verses in the court of the royal palace of Masʿūd III at Ghazni*, IsMEO, Rome, 1966, 31; Nazim, *op. cit.*, 110-11, 204-6; H C Day, *The Dynastic History of Medieval India (Early Medieval Period)*, Munshiram Manohralal, New Delhi, 1973, 554; Clifford Edmund Bosworth, *The Later Ghaznavids: Splendour and Decay*, Edinburgh University Press, Edinburgh, 1977, 85.

[16] Alessio Bombaci, 'La "sposa del cielo",' in *A Francesco Gabrieli. Studi Orientalistici offerti nel sessantesimo compleanno da suoi colleghi e discepoli*, Università di Roma, Rome, 1964, 21-34. See also note 61 below.

built by Mahmud or his governors in the northern Panjab after its incorporation into the Ghaznavid domains. References in contemporary histories to the construction of mosques in the region following its conquest have been confirmed by recent archaeological finds.[17]

Among the lost mosques known from such literary works, the *Khistī* (Brick) or *Habashī* (Abyssinian) mosque in Lahore may also have been built by Mahmud after that city was captured.[18] More germane still are reports of a minaret that stood at Sodhra, about 50 kilometres north of Lahore, until 1864.[19] The minaret consisted of an octagonal shaft set on a square base; although shorter than the surviving Ghaznavid and Ghurid minarets, rising over 30 metres and with a diameter of roughly 7.2 metres in its octagonal section, the minaret must have been a substantial structure, taller than many of the Seljuq minarets still preserved in Khurasan.[20] The alternation of square and octagonal sections is a formula used for minarets in the eastern Islamic world in the 11th and 12th centuries, but relatively rare in Indian minarets of the Sultanate and Mughal periods. The use of square baked bricks measuring 27.5 x 27.5 x 5.5 centimetres would also appear to relate the minaret to Seljuq and Ghaznavid monuments in eastern Iran.[21] It is therefore possible that the minaret was another Ghaznavid or Ghurid survival; local tradition held that it had been built by Malik Ayaz, Mahmud's favourite and the governor of Lahore.[22] The construction of a minaret here presumably reflects the importance of the town in medieval times, standing as it did at a point where the Chinab river could be forded.[23]

Like the destroyed minaret at Sodhra, we may be fairly certain that Mahmud's minaret in Lahore was built of brick for, without the mountainous regions of the Himalayan foothills and the Salt Range, this had been the exclusive medium of Indus Valley architecture for several millennia. The function of Mahmud's minaret is no less relevant than its form or date, for the author of the *Ādāb al-Ḥarb* quite clearly relates its construction to the commemoration of the sultan's victory over the raja of Qanauj in 409/1018-19. In a remarkable passage in the *Tārīkh al-Yamīnī,* al-ᶜUtbi suggests that the very name of the place connoted victory, for opening the Qur'ān and seeing the word 'victories' *(futūḥ)*, Mahmud is said to have taken as a favorable omen the similarities between the Arabic spelling of that word (فتوح) and of 'Qanauj' (قنوج).[24] While no doubt apocryphal, the story does suggest a close association between the Indian city and the theme of military victory in the contemporary imagination. It is surely relevant that the 'King of Qanauj' is something of a stock figure in the *Shāhnāma*, and later appears in Indo-Persian literature as one of the pre-Islamic rulers of the world.[25] Given the universal status of its ruler, it seems significant that of all Mahmud's Indian encounters, the

---

17 Muhammad Nazim, ed., *Kitab Zainu'l-Akhbar composed by Abu Sa'id 'Abdu'l-Ḥayy b. aḍ-Ḍahhak b. Maḥmud Gardizi,* Luzac and Co., London, 1928, 75; notes 6-8 above.

18 In the published text of the *Ādāb al-Ḥarb* the mosque is referred to quite clearly as Habashi Mosque rather than the Khistī Mosque: *Ādāb al-Ḥarb*, 307. There is some confusion over this in other published references to the mosque: Muhammad Nazim, 'The Hindu Sháhiya Kingdom of Ohind', *Journal of the Royal Asiatic Society*, 1927, 486, n.3. Contrary to what is often asserted (for example, Khan, *op. cit.*, 130), I could find no explicit attribution of this mosque to Mahmud og Ghazna. This attribution seems to be based solely on the fact that the mosque reportedly stood on the site of a former Hindu temple.

19 Alexander Cunningham, *Report of a Tour in the Punjab in 1878-79*, Archaeological Survey of India Reports, 14, republished in Varanasi, 1970, 43-44; A.B.M. Hussain, *The Manara in Indo-Muslim Architecture*, The Asiatic Society of Pakistan, Dacca, 1970, 26-27.

20 The minarets at Sangbast and Khusrawgird, for example, stand 22 and 22.5 metres high respectively: Antony M Hutt, *The Development of the Minaret in Iran under the Saljūqs*, unpublished MPhil. thesis, London University, 1974, 208, 249. It is possible that the octagonal section of the Sodhra minaret served in its turn as a base for a cylindrical tower: this was the case with the minaret of Masᶜud at Ghazna and with an 11th- or 12th-century minaret at Sirwan near Herat: Nicolai Khanikov, *Mémoire sur la partie méridionale de l'Asie centrale*, Paris, 1861, 134. In this case the minaret would have attained a much greater height than the 30 metres that survived in the 19th century.

21 Square bricks were standard in Seljuq and Ghaznavid architecture, but rectangular bricks were preferred in the Ghurid monuments of the Indus Valley: Finbarr B Flood, 'Ghurid Architecture in the Indus Valley: the Tomb of Shaikh Sadan Shahid', forthcoming in *Ars Orientalis*, 2001. The sizes of the bricks used in eastern Iranian monuments of the 11th and 12th centuries are comparable to those found at Sodhra: for example, the preferred size of the baked bricks used in the caravanserai at Ribat-i Mahi was 25 centimetres square, by 4.5 centimetres thick. Square bricks ranging in width between 22 and 40 centimetres were excavated at Ghazna: Umberto Scerrato, 'Summary report on the Italian Archaeological Mission in Afghanistan II. The two excavation campaigns at Ghazni 1957-8', *East and West*, new series, 10, 1959, 33.

22 According to later Indian historians, Ayaz built the fort of Lahore: Cunningham, *op. cit.*, 44; Muhammad B*ā*qir, 'Lahore (being an account complied from original sources)', *Islamic Culture*, 18, 1944, 33.

23 The minaret might conceivably have marked a territorial boundary, for Firishta tells us that Mahmud pursued the Hindu Shahi ruler Anandpal to Sodhra, but no further: G Roos-Keppel and Mahmud Khan, *Translation of the Tarikh-i-Sultan Mahmud-i-Ghaznawi*, Lahore, 1908, 12

24 Elliott and Dowson, *op. cit.*, 45.

25 Peter Hardy, 'Growth of authority over a conquered political élite: early Delhi Sultanate as a possible case study', in J F Richards, ed., *Kingship and Authority in South Asia*, Oxford University Press, Delhi, 1998, 237; Carl W Ernst, *Eternal Garden: Mysticism, History, and Politics at a South Asian Sufi Center*, State University of New York Press, Albany, 1992, 43.

Pl. 10.2 Qutb Minar and a reused pre-Islamic iron pillar, Ghurid Friday Mosque of Delhi.

expedition to Qanauj is alone deemed worthy of explicit mention in Farrukhī's elegy on the sultan.[26]

In a recent study of victory monuments in the medieval Islamic world, Thomas Leisten concludes that in order to connect the literary topos of victory towers with the surviving Ghaznavid and Ghurid minarets,

> ... the missing link is an inscription or a literary description that tells us we should perceive such a minaret as a tower of victory. As long as no such evidence is forthcoming, there is no reason to believe that minarets were ever used on specific occasions to signify an important event in Islamic history.[27]

While the minaret itself no longer stands, the historical context and reported function of the Lahore minaret offer strong support for Ralph's interpretation of the later Ghazna and Delhi minarets (on which quotations from sura 48, the Sura of Victory, are prominent) as commemorative towers related to the various Indian victories of the Ghaznavids and Ghurids.[28] That Mahmud's *manāra* is said to have been built in Lahore Fort brings to mind the siting of the Qutb Minar (pl. 10.2) in the Chauhan fort of Dehli, a fact commemorated in the inscriptions above the eastern entrance to the adjoining mosque.[29] In both cases it seems likely that the meaning of the minaret derived not just from the contemporary historical context, but from its physical association with a fortified stronghold.

The mode in which Mahmud's victory over the raja of Qanauj was commemorated inevitably recalls the suggestion, first made by Fergusson and later repeated by various scholars, that the Ghaznavid and Ghurid minarets owe something to the pillars (*stambhas* or *lats*) erected to advertise the great deeds and military exploits of medieval Indian rulers;[30] one is invariably reminded of Ralph's characterisation of the Ghazna towers (pl. 10.1) as 'a visible realization of the faṭh-nāma' issued to advertise and memorialise a victorious military campaign.[31] Regardless of whether these minarets were ever associated with mosques,[32] the evidence from the *Ādāb al-Ḥarb* supports

[26] Clifford Edmund Bosworth, 'Farrukhi's Elegy on Mahmud of Ghazna', *Īṣan*, 29, 1991, 45, 47.

[27] Thomas Leisten, 'Mashhad al-Nasr: Monuments of War and Victory in Medieval Islamic Art', *Muqarnas*, 13, 1996, 14.

[28] Pinder-Wilson, *op. cit.*, 100. The association between the Ghazna towers and the theme of military victory was first suggested by Ernst Diez in connection with his rather dubious suggestion of an Indian origin for the minaret itself: Ernst Diez, 'Manāra,' *Encyclopedia of Islam*, Vol. 3, 1936, 228. It should be noted that while the Lahore minaret was intended to commemorate a particularly successful campaign against a Hindu kingdom, in other monuments the theme of victory may be associated with Ghaznavid and Ghurid compaigns against the heterodox Muslims of southern Panjab and Sindh. See Flood, *op. cit.*

[29] The inscription refers to the construction of the mosque within a *hiṣār*: S K Banerji, 'The Qūwat-ul-Islām or the oldest mosque in Delhi', *Journal of the Royal Asiatic Society of Bengal*, 4, 1938, 291. This text is unique among the foundation inscriptions of all the surviving Indo-Ghurid mosques and shrines in being written in Persian rather than Arabic. It is possible that, as Ralph suggested (*op. cit.*, 102, n. 23), it is a later replacement for a lost Arabic original. However, foundation inscriptions in Persian are known from Central Asia as early as the late 11th century: Bombaci, *Kūfic Inscriptions*, 36-37.

[30] See notes 28 above, 54 below.

[31] Pinder-Wilson, *op. cit.*, 101.

[32] It is now known that certain isolated minarets, such as that at Qasimabad in Iranian Sistan, were once associated with mud brick mosques: Bernard O'Kane, 'Salǧūq Minarets: some new data', *Annales Islamologiques*, 20, 1984, 85. It has been suggested that aerial photographs show the remains of such structures around the Ghazna minarets: Alessio Bombaci, 'Ghaznevid Art,' *Encyclopedia of World Art*, Volume 6, New York/Toronto/London, 1962, 306. Whether or not this is so, an association with a mosque would not of itself be sufficient to preclude a commemorative function. The function of many of these eastern Iranian minarets is still uncertain (Robert Hillenbrand, 'Manāra, manār,'

such an interpretation. However, it also begs the question of where such a mode of victory memorial originated.[33] To the best of my knowledge, outside the Ghaznavid realm there is no evidence for the construction of towers or minarets as victory monuments.[34] In India by contrast, the memorialisation of military victories by the erection of pillars inscribed with bombastic accounts of a victorious king's exploits had been standard practice for several centuries.[35] Although different in form, the later assimilation of these homologous modes of memorialising victory, in popular perception at least, is witnessed by the description of the Qutb Minar as a *kirtistambha* (pillar of fame) and *jayastambha* (pillar of victory), in the *devanagari* inscriptions left by those who worked on it.[36] The function of the minaret and its form clearly enabled it to be identified with a known quantity; this was a process which came to work both ways, for later Arabic and Persian sources refer to the pre-Islamic pillars re-erected in Delhi (pl. 10.2) and elsewhere (often in association with mosques, as they had once been with temples) as *manārs*.[37]

One does not have to look far for potential sources of information concerning the commemorative practices of Indian kings. In addition to the likelihood that participants in Mahmud's various Indian expeditions had themselves seen *jayastambhas* and *kirtistambhas*, it should

Pl. 10.3 Ghurid minaret at Jam (photo: W Ball).

be borne in mind that there was an Indian community resident in Ghazna at this period.[38] Whatever their meaning, the practice of erecting pillars may also have been familiar from the antiquities which survived in Afghanistan itself, most obviously the enigmatic pillars (known as *minars*) which still survive in the region around Kabul.[39] Although, unlike the Indian pillars, the surviving

---

Encyclopedia of Islam, new edition, Volume 6, 1991, 365) and as Ralph himself notes (*op. cit.*, 100-1), both piety and propaganda may have been equally relevant to the semiotics of the Ghazna minarets.

33 Note the tendency to conflate the question of whether the Ghazna towers commemorate the Indian campaigns of the Ghaznavids with the issue of a possible relationship to Indian victory columns: Alessio Bombaci, 'Introduction to the excavations at Ghazni', *East and West*, new series, 10, 1959, 7. Both questions are addressed separately here, although the relationship between them is considered in the final part of my paper.

34 The use of quotations from the Sura of Victory might, however, suggest that certain 11th- and 12th-century minarets were associated with this theme. See, for example, the minaret at Barsian in the Isfahan Oasis, which carries verse 5: Erica Cruikshank Dodd and Shereen Khairallah, *The Image of the Word: a Study of Quranic Verses in Islamic Architecture*, Volume 2, American University in Beirut Press, Beirut, 1981, 120.

35 For an early 9th-century example see Michael D Willis, 'Religious and Royal Patronage in North India,' in Vishakha N Desai and Darielle Mason, eds., *Gods, Guardians, and Lovers. Temple Sculptures from North India AD 700-1200*, Mapin Publishing Pvt. Ltd., Ahmedabad, 1993, 54, fig. 17.

36 J A Page, *An Historical Memoir on the Qutb: Delhi*, Memoirs of the Archaeological Survey of India, No. 2, reprinted New Delhi, 1970, 39-41; M C Joshi, 'Some nagari inscriptions on the Qutb Minar', *Medieval India: a Miscellany*, 2, 1972, 3, 5; Pushpa Prasad, *Sanskrit Inscriptions of Delhi Sultanate*, Oxford University Press, Delhi, 1990, 2-3.

37 William Jeffrey McKibben, 'The Monumental Pillars of Fīrūz Shāh Tughluq', *Ars Orientalis*, 24, 1994, 112-13

38 See notes 57-58 below.

39 Richard N Frye, 'Notes on the History of Architecture in Afghanistan', *Ars Islamica*, 11-12, 1946, 201; Warwick Ball, 'The so-called "minars" of Kabul', *Studia Iranica*, 13, 1988, 117-27; Klaus Fischer, 'Citations and copies of Islamic towers and Buddhist columns', in John Guy, ed., *Indian Art and Connoisseurship, Essays in Honour of Douglas Barrett*, Mapin Publishing Pvt. Ltd., Ahmedabad, 1995, 270-71. At least one scholar has interpreted the reference to the Lahore *manāra* in the *Ādāb al-Ḥarb* as indicating that Mahmud erected a victory pillar (rather than a minaret) in Lahore fort: Ghulam Mustafa Khan, 'The Ghaznawid Heritage in Pakistan', *Journal of the Research Society of Pakistan*, 14, 1977, 31. Based on contemporary usage of the term, this seems unlikely. See note 12 above.

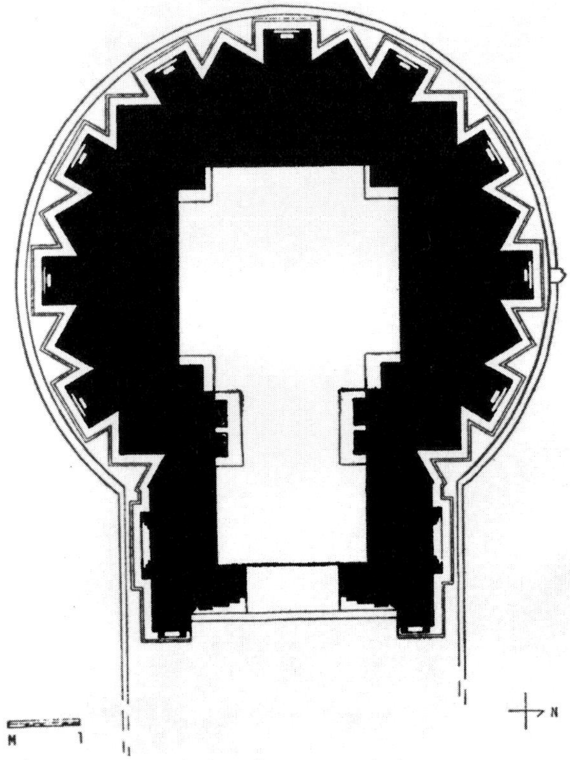

Pl. 10.4 Ground plan of Gargaj Mahadeva Temple, Indor (after Meister, 'The Udayeśvara Temple Plan').

Ghaznavid and Ghurid minarets are not inscribed with historical texts commemorating specific victories, the prominence afforded quotations from the Sura of Victory in their decoration has frequently been noted,[40] and the Lahore minaret may well have been similarly inscribed. While the *Ādāb al-Ḥarb* indicates that historical minarets were indeed erected to commemorate specific events, the epigraphic memorialisation of such events was clearly seen as less important than locating them within a general (and largely ahistorical) cultural context provided by Qur'anic precedent.[41]

As the earliest in the series of Ghaznavid and Ghurid minarets known to us, the lost minaret could well have set the tone for subsequent patrons and builders, a fact which might cause us to reconsider the genealogy of the Indo-Muslim minaret *par excellence*, the Qutb Minar in Delhi. Although the surviving Ghazna minarets (pl. 10.1) have been cited as the prototypes for the Qutb Minar (pl. 10.2),[42] the resemblances between the Indian and Afghan minarets are outweighed by their dissimiliarities. While the use of a local stone idiom in Delhi may explain some of the aesthetic differences, formal and structural distinctions are less easily dismissed; it is true that a stellate section is included in each case, but the alternation of stellate and cylindrical sections is not found in Delhi, while the pronounced taper of the Qutb Minar further differentiates its profile from that of its earlier counterparts in Ghazna. It has frequently been noted that the Delhi minaret is in fact much closer in form to the fragmentary brick minarets at Nad-i ^{c}Ali and Khwaja Siyah Posh in Afghan Sistan, or to a minaret in the Great Mosque of Kirman that shows a similar alternation of rounded and angular flutes.[43] The Khwaja Siyah Posh minaret, with its convex cusps set in the interstices of sharp stellar projections is particularly close, and is often cited as the prototype for the Qutb Minar.[44] Nevertheless, it is surely significant that what was undoubtedly the *pièce de résistance* of Ghurid minarets, the minaret erected at Jam (pl. 10.3), in or near the Ghurid capital of Firuzkoh, bears only a passing resemblance to the minaret erected almost contemporaneously for the same dynasty in Delhi (pl. 10.2).[45]

Built over one hundred and seventy years before construction of the Delhi minaret began, the Ghaznavid *manāra* of Lahore (or other Panjabi minarets) would have offered a potential source of inspiration closer to home than any of the Afghan minarets which survive today. It might well be therefore that Mahmud's lost minaret in Lahore, or another Panjabi minaret, acted as a 'missing

---

[40] Pinder-Wilson, *op. cit.*, 91; Hillenbrand, *op. cit.*, 173.

[41] As Thomas Leisten notes (*op. cit.*, 22), 'we must assume that the type of ephemeral victory monument was given preference deliberately, since it does not appear as if Islamic victory monuments were erected with form and decorative as well as inscriptional material that was geared to guarantee a kind of commemoration which was permanent.' See however, note 53 below.

[42] Pinder-Wilson, *op. cit.*, 100; Bloom, 174.

[43] For an extensive, if now slightly outdated, bibliography on these minarets see Warwick Ball, *Archaeological Gazetteer of Afghanistan*, Volume 1, Paris, 1982, 162, 189-90. See also Antony Hutt, 'Three Minarets in the Kirman Region', *JRAS*, 1970, 91-107; O'Kane, *op. cit.*, 97-101; Hillenbrand, *op. cit.*, 152-5.

[44] Klaus Fischer, 'Interrelations of Islamic Architecture in Afghanistan', *Marg*, 24/1, 1970, 56; Z A Desai, 'Cultural relations between Afghanistan and India during the medieval period', *Afghanistan*, 28/3, 1975, 12; J. Burton-Page, 'Manāra, manār,' *Encyclopedia of Islam*, new edition, Volume 6, 1991, 368; Koch, *op. cit.*, 95, n. 74. Although it is true that Sistan was politically important in the 12th century (Clifford Edmund Bosworth, 'Sīstān', *Encyclopedia of Islam*, new edition, 9, 1997, 683), and was sometimes praised for its architecture (O'Kane, *op. cit.*, 92), methodologically, one needs to consider the possibility of a prototype closer to Delhi, even if it no longer survives.

[45] On the relationship between the two see André Maricq, 'La signification du monument son rapport avec le Qutb-Minar de Delhi', in André Maricq and Gaston Wiet, eds., *Le Minaret de Djam*, Librairie C Klincksieck, Paris, 1959, 65-67.

link' between the Afghan and Indian minarets. It is not known when the minaret in Lahore fort disappeared, but Lahore came under Ghurid suzerainty in 1186, several years before the conquest of Delhi.[46] Just as the form of the Qutb Minar itself was sometimes cited in later victory monuments erected by regional potentates,[47] so the Lahore minaret may have provided an obvious source of inspiration for the memorialisation of Ghurid victory in Delhi.

The possibility of an Indian inspiration for the stellate form of the Qutb Minar has sometimes been raised, usually in connection with the idea that the erection of the latter was inspired by Indian victory columns.[48] It is, however, important to distinguish between function and form; while it seems likely that the manner in which Ghaznavid (and probably Ghurid) victories were memorialised owed something to practices associated with Indian kings, this is not of itself sufficient to establish that Ghaznavid and Ghurid minarets owed a formal debt to Indian architectural traditions. Although assimilated conceptually, the formal differences between medieval Indian victory pillars and Afghan minarets are striking. This is not to dismiss the idea that the stellate minaret owes something to Indian architecture. The distribution of surviving minarets making use of such pronounced stellate forms is confined to the eastern fringes of the Islamic world in the late 11th and 12th centuries. In terms of its general aesthetic, it is of course possible that the stellate plan may owe something to the 'corrugated' appearance of certain earlier Central Asian monuments, such as the caravanserai of Ribat-i Malik and the minaret at Yar Kurgan, or to a vanished minaret at Sirwan, near Herat.[49] However, seen from another perspective, the eastern extreme of the *dar al-Islam* was the western edge of India; if, therefore, the stellate plan of these minarets was inspired by the architecture of western India, its distribution might be explicable by reference to the proximity of that region.

It may be no more than coincidence, but the exteriors of certain medieval north Indian temples in which sharp flanges repeat or alternate with rectangular projections to form a circular plan (pl. 10.4) produce an effect remarkably similar to that of stellate minarets such as those in Delhi (pl. 10.2) and Sistan. Temples of this plan are most plentiful in central India, especially Malwa and the surrounding regions (roughly corresponding to parts of Madhya Pradesh, and the adjoining fringes of eastern Gujarat and Rajasthan), where they were particularly common from the 11th to the 14th centuries.[50] There are no surviving medieval temples of this type in the north-west of the subcontinent, and Mahmud, unlike his successors, did not campaign in Malwa; stellate plans are, however, described in medieval texts explaining how to lay out a temple.[51]

It is, of course, impossible to say anything about the form of the Lahore *manāra*, but it was built in a region which had recently formed part of a Hindu kingdom, and which was clearly an important (if frequently underestimated) arena for a vibrant cultural exchange at this period. The possibility of an influence from contemporary temple architecture cannot therefore be ruled out. The adoption of a stellate plan capable of recalling the exteriors of certain temples, might conceivably have been intended as a visual mnemonic related to the nature of the victory commemorated;[52] this would not have been the first time in the Islamic world that the specific form or style of a victory monument

[46] André Wink, *Al-Hind: the Making of the Indo-Muslim World*, Volume 2, Oxford University Press, Delhi, 1999, 144.

[47] Ebba Koch, 'The Copies of the Quṭb Mīnār', *Iran* 29, 1991, 103.

[48] James Fergusson, *History of Indian and Eastern Architecture*, Volume 2, John Murray, London, 1910, 205-6; Diez, *op. cit.*, 228; Page, *op. cit.*, pl. 18a; Syed Hasan Barani, 'History of Delhi to the time of Timur's invasion', *Islamic Culture*, 12, 1938, 310. On more general aspects of Indian influence on the Ghazna minarets see Ernst Diez, 'Die Siegestürme in Ghazna als Weltbilder', *Kunst des Orients*, 1, 1950, 37-44, especially 42-44. For the unlikely suggestion that the Ghaznavid and Ghurid minarets owe something to Tibetan architectural traditions, see Hutt, *op. cit.*, 102-3, 195-96.

[49] De Khanikov, *op. cit.*, 134; Henry Field and Eugene Prostov, 'Archaeological Investigations in Central Asia, 1917-37', *Ars Islamica*, 5, 1938, 252-53, fig. 13; Eric Schroeder, 'Islamic Architecture: Seljūq Period', *Survey of Persian Art*, Volume 2, Oxford University Press, London/Oxford, 1939, 1025.

[50] Krishna Deva, 'Bhumija Temples,' in Pramod Chandra, ed., *Studies in Indian Temple Architecture*, American Institute of Indian Studies, Varanasi, 1975, 98-102, 106; Donald M Stadtner, 'Ancient Kosala and the Stellate Plan,' in Joanna G. Williams, ed., *Kalādarśana: American Studies in the Art of India*, Brill, Leiden, 1981, 137-45; Michael W Meister, 'Analysis of Temple Plans: Indor,' *Artibus Asiae*, 43/4, 1981-82, 302-28; Michael W. Meister, 'The Udayeśvara Temple Plan,' *Śrīnidhiḥ: Perspectives in Indian Archaeology, Art and Culture, Shri K.R. Srinivasan Festschrift*, New Era Publishing, Madras, 1983, 85-93.

[51] Stadtner, *op. cit.*, 143-44. For later Ghaznavid incursions in the region see Ganguly, *op. cit.*, 424; T W Haig-[Riazul Islam], 'Mālwa', *Encyclopedia of Islam*, new edition, 6, 1991, 309-10.

[52] Note the intriguing suggestion that the stellate form of the central Indian temples may have been intended to suggest a protected or fortified place: Michael W Meister, 'Śiva's Forts in Central India: Temples in Dakṣina Kosala and their "Daemonic" Plans', in Michael W Meister, ed., *Discourses on Śiva. Proceedings of a Symposium on the Nature of Religious Imagery*, University of Philadelphia Press, Philadelphia, 1984, 119-41.

Pl. 10.5 Stone window-grille from the palace of Mas'ud III at Ghazna (after Bombaci, Kūfic Inscriptions*).*

Pl. 10.6 Ghaznavid relief with capital of Indian inspiration (after Kalter, Linden-Museum Stuttgart, Abteilungsführer Islamischer Orient*).*

proclaimed the nature of the victory which it commemorated.[53] Although the lack of a convincing single Indian prototype for Ghaznavid and Ghurid minarets renders such a scenario unlikely, we should be open to the possibility of a relationship between these disparate structures, while being wary of the diffusionist phylogenetic schemes so characteristic of much early scholarship on South Asian architecture. At the very least one may conclude that neither the aesthetic nor the function of the Qutb Minar would have been as alien to medieval Indian observers as has sometimes been assumed.

Whether any relationship existed between temple and minaret, it is in any case clear that the practice of commemorating military victories through the erection of pillars and towers was common to the rulers of both eastern Iran and the Indian subcontinent in the 11th and 12th centuries, regardless of their religious or cultural affiliations.[54] The latter clearly determined the precise form which the commemoration took, but even here the visual similarities between *qutb* and column enabled these two homologous modes of memorialising victory to be conflated in the eyes of medieval Indians. As I hope to show elsewhere, Mahmud's construction of a minaret to commemorate a military victory may have been one of a number of practices inspired by the visual rhetoric of contemporary Indian rulers.[55]

Although the notion that ideas flow from west to east is often implicit in much writing on the medieval architecture of the eastern Islamic world, this is clearly not the case. Elsewhere, I have drawn attention to the degree of transculturation in the Ghurid architecture of Afghanistan;[56] it may be that in this, as in much else, Ghurid patrons were following a precedent already established by their Ghaznavid predecessors. It may seem anomalous to raise the possibility of Indian influence on Ghaznavid architecture, when the ubiquitous trope of temple desecration has come to colour so much historical and art historical writing on the relationship between the Ghaznavids and the subcontinent, but the degree and nature of cross-cultural interaction was clearly much greater and much more complex than the medieval sources suggest.[57] Not only did Mahmud make use of Indian modes of warfare (notably elephants), or have Hindu soldiers and generals in his employ, but it should also be borne in mind that a community of Indians was resident in Ghazna itself.[58] A chance reference in an 11th-century

[53] See the suggestion that the Byzantine style of an 'Abbasid victory monument at Hiraqla in northern Syria was designed to commemorate a Muslim victory over the Byzantines: Michael Meinecke, *Patterns of Stylistic Changes in Islamic Architecture: Local Trends versus Migrating Artists*, New York University Press, New York, 1996, 23.

[54] The idea of a *manāra* in the form of a tower was well-established in the Islamic world by the 11th century, but the construction of victory monuments in the form of free-standing towers was also known in western India, to judge from the 12th-century victory monument at Chittor in southern Rajasthan: Fergusson, *op. cit.*, 59, fig. 295.

[55] See my forthcoming paper, 'Looking at Loot: Spolia, Insignia and the Visual Rhetoric of the Ghurid Sultans'.

[56] Flood, 'Ghurid Architecture'.

[57] For a recent re-examination of this topos which has far-reaching implications see Richard Eaton, 'Temple Desecration and Indo-Muslim States', in David Gilmartin and Bruce Lawrence, eds., *Beyond Hindu and Turk: Rethinking Religious Identities in Islamicate South Asia*, University of Florida Press, Gainsville, 2000, pp. 246-81.

[58] Elliott and Dowson, *op. cit.*, 125-29; Nazim., *op. cit.*, 163.

Syrian text to instances of *sati* within this community suggests that it enjoyed a remarkable degree of freedom with respect to cultural practices; the presence of temples serving it in Ghazna may perhaps be inferred, even if this fact was omitted from the contemporary histories celebrating Mahmud as the 'idol-destroyer'.[59]

When accounts of such activities are read against an intriguing citation from a *fatḥ-nāma* purportedly sent to Ghazna to tell its inhabitants of Mahmud's success during the campaign of 409/1018-19 (that is, the campaign which the Lahore minaret commemorated) a more ambivalent attitude to Indian art and architecture emerges. Describing the city of Mathura, the sultan notes:

> There are here a thousand edifices as firm as the faith of the faithful; most of these of marble, besides innumerable temples; nor is it likely that this city has attained its present condition but at the expense of many millions of dinars, nor could such another be constructed under a period of two centuries.[60]

The practical consequences of Mahmud's aesthetic admiration for Indian monuments may be reflected in various Indian borrowings in Ghaznavid architecture, for it should be noted that the campaign to Mathura and Qanauj in 409/1018-19 coincides with the transformation of Ghazna through Mahmud's architectural patronage.[61] The mention of marble is particularly interesting, since several scholars have suggested that the overwhelming use of that stone in Ghaznavid architecture was inspired, or at least intensified, by the experience of contemporary Indian monuments.[62]

Some of the uses made of marble in later Ghaznavid architecture were clearly based on Indian prototypes; the most obvious examples are the marble window embrasures and pierced geometric transennae (pl. 10.5), the distant ancestors of the *jalis* so familiar from the Mughal architecture of the subcontinent.[63] Such Indian borrowings were not just aesthetic or formal, but also iconographic; a remarkable Ghaznavid relief now in the Linden Museum in Stuttgart depicts a scene which owes something to the *jataka* episodes common on reliefs from the Gandhara region, and which may illustrate an episode from a literary text such as *Kalila wa Dimna* (pl. 10.6).[64] The column and capital which frames the image is of a type unknown in Iran and Central Asia, but very common in western India; capitals of this type were later to become standard in the Ghurid architecture of Afghanistan, and were to become standard in Indo-Ghurid architecture.[65] Thus the appearance of the column is itself good evidence for an Indian influence on the arts of Ghazna during the 11th century that has frequently been denied. [66]

Situated between the Ghaznavid heartlands and the Hindu polities of northern India, and until recently the centre of the Hindu Shahi kingdom, it is an a priori probability that the northern Panjab provided a crucible for the mediation and melding of different artistic traditions, and a conduit for artistic influences from elsewhere in northern India. In drawing attention to its lost Ghaznavid monuments here, I have attempted to highlight the fact that the degree of cultural interaction between the eastern Islamic world and India was probably greater than either the fragmentary remains or surviving texts suggest. The increasing importance of India to the Ghaznavid sultanate is demonstrated by a letter written

---

59 Vincent Mansour Monteil, tr., *L'Epître du pardon par Abû-l-cAlâ' al-Macarrî*, Paris, 1984, 224-25. The importance of this reference lies both in the fact that it is a contemporary account based the observations of a scholar or traveller from Ghazna, and that it occurs in a work that bears no relation to the courtly narratives on which we are usually dependent for mention of the Indians in Ghaznavid employ. For the presence of scholars from Ghazna in Syria at this time see Finbarr B Flood, *The Great Mosque of Damascus: Studies on the Makings of an Umayyad Visual Culture*, Brill, Leiden, 2000, 6.

60 Elliott and Dowson, *op. cit.*, 44-45. See also Roos-Keppel and Khan, *op. cit.*, 29; Gardizi, *op. cit.*, 75; John Briggs, *History of the Rise of the Mahomedan Power in India till the year AD 1612*, Volume 1, New Delhi, 1981, 34.

61 *Ibid.*, 36. The Ghazna mosque was apparently ordered before the sultan's departure, but only its basic structure was established by the time of his return: James Reynolds, tr., *The Kitab-i-Yamini*, London, 1858, 463; Nazim, *op. cit.*, 166; Bombaci, 'Sposa del cielo', 30-31. Some of the spoils from the expedition to Mathura and Qanauj were undoubtedly sunk into the mosque. The remainder are usually described as trophies, but note the suggestion that they may also have had some aesthetic and/or antiquarian value: Scerrato, *op. cit.*, 39-40; Bombaci, 'Ghaznevid Art', 302.

62 Bombaci, 'Ghaznevid Art', 304; Hillenbrand, *op. cit.*, 199. Note that Bombaci contradicts his earlier assertion that it is unnecessary toascribe the use of marble in Ghaznavid architecture to Indian influence: Alessio Bombaci, 'Introduction to the Excavations at Ghazni', *East and West*, new series, 10, 1959, 8. See also Scerrato, *op. cit.*, 37.

63 Bombaci, *Kūfic Inscriptions*, pl. XXXVIII.

64 Johannes Kalter, *Linden-Museum Stuttgart, Abteilungsführer Islamischer Orient*, Stuttgart, 1987, 64. The scene appears to correspond to no known study in this book of animal fables, however.

65 A slightly more stylised version of the same type of capital appears on a tombstone from Bust dated 591/1195: Hillenbrand, *op. cit.*, pl. 11. For Indian influence in other Ghurid monuments, see Flood, 'Ghurid Architecture'.

66 Bombaci, 'Introduction', 8; Scerrato *op. cit.*, 37, n. 34.

by Ḥurra-yi Khuttalī, the aunt of Mahmud, upon his death: in it she describes Ghazna and Khurasan as the centres of an empire that has its face turned towards India.[67] There can be little doubt that this openness towards the subcontinent included more than a desire for the revenues that flowed from it to underwrite the cost of splendid public monuments such as the Ghazna mosque or the Lahore minaret.

Of course, the chronological, cultural, and iconographic speculations offered here all hinge on an incidental reference in the *Ādāb al-Ḥarb* being accurate. Nevertheless, the potential of such an incidental reference for opening up new perspectives on Ghaznavid (and Ghurid) architecture serves to underline our dependence on what is, regardless of its intrinsic aesthetic or historical value, the flotsam of history. As the verses from Niẓāmī 'Arūḍī cited at the outset intimate, in making any overall assessment of Ghaznavid architecture, we are as dependent on passing literary references as on randomly preserved ruins.[68]

[67] Cited in Bosworth, *The Ghaznavids*, 235.

[68] For an attempt to sift through such literary material for the architectural information that it contains see Bombaci, 'Sposa del cielo'; Julie Scott Meisami, 'Palaces and Paradises: Palace Descriptions in Medieval Persian Poetry', *Princeton Papers*, forthcoming. I am very grateful to Dr Meisami for supplying me with a copy of her unpublished paper.

Colour plate I (11. 1) Painted wooden lid of a lost circular box. Kuwait, the al-Sabah Collection. inv. no. LNS 36W, diameter 120 mm

[facing p. 113]

11 A PAINTED WOODEN LID IN THE AL-SABAH COLLECTION IN KUWAIT

Ernst J Grube

Very little Fatimid painting has survived and so far no complete Fatimid illustrated manuscript has been recorded, although a few folios and some fragments of such manuscripts have been found among the so-called Fustat fragments.[1] The few fragments of wall paintings in the *muqarnas* zone of a small bath hall near the sanctuary of Abu'l-Suᶜud in Old Cairo (Fustat) have almost invariably been attributed to the Fatimid period, although they have recently been reassigned, together with the building they decorate, to the ᶜAbbasid/Tulunid period.[2] Of the cycles of paintings documented for both public and private places, only their reflections on lustre-painted ceramics of the period convey even an approximate idea. And the only major document of monumental painting, the wooden ceiling of the Cappella Palatina in Palermo, part of the palace of the Norman kings of Sicily and datable around 1140 AD, has generally been identified as a work of Fatimid artists and is thought to give an idea of what Fatimid painting on a grand scale must have been like, although the Fatimid attribution of the paintings has recently been seriously questioned.[3]

For this reason, a small wooden lid in the al-Sabah Collection in Kuwait, only half of which survives, takes on special significance (Colour plate I, 11.1).[4] The lid originally belonged to a small circular box which has been lost. It is painted with the bust of a beardless turbaned youth who would appear to be playing a musical instrument, probably a lute. The painting is executed in black and dark purple (which has turned a deep brown) on an amber-red background; it is not painted directly onto the wooden lid but is supported by a thin layer of white gesso, clearly visible along the cracks of the painted surface or where the paint has been worn off, especially at the lower left-hand side. The bust of the musician is framed by double lines, at the outer edge of which is a band of small golden pearls set into a black band. It is this pearl band that immediately brings to mind the paintings in the *muqarnas* of the bath hall in Fustat (pl. 11.2), and also the paintings on the wooden ceiling of the Cappella Palatina, equally painted on a gesso base (pl. 11.3). The motif of pearl-banding is, of course, far older and appears both in Samarra wall painting (pl. 11.4) and on other paintings in the eastern Iranian, Sasanian manner, most notably on a wooden box from 7th-century Kucha (pl. 11.5).[5] The quality of the al-Sabah painting itself—rather more a quick sketch carried out in a series of assured brush strokes and somewhat carelessly filled in with colour—recalls nothing so much as the representations of musicians on Fatimid lustre-painted ceramic vessels (pl. 11.14). The facial features of the young man appear clearly derived from the Central Asian tradition, the basis of the

---

[1] See Ernst J Grube, *Studies in Islamic Painting*, Pindar Press, London, 1995, which republishes a number of the author's studies on Fatimid painting; see especially the 1985 'A Drawing of Wrestlers', which not only offers some corrections and new material, but also has an appendix with an almost fully illustrated catalogue of the so-called 'Fustat-Fragments'. See also de Unger, this volume.

[2] See Grube, as in note 1 with all pertinent references. See now also Laila ᶜAli Ibrahim and ᶜAdil Yasin, 'A Tulunid Hammam in Old Cairo', *Islamic Archaeological Studies*, 3, Cairo 1988, 34-78.

[3] Giovanni M[aria] D'Erme, 'Contesto archittettonico e aspetti culturali del soffitto della Cappella Palatina di Palermo', *Bollettino d'Arte*, 92, 1997, 1-32. For the painted ceiling of the Cappella Palatina, see Ugo Monneret de Villard, *Le pitture musulmane al soffitto della Cappella Palatina in Palermo*, Rome, 1950; see now also the author's 'La pittura islamica nella Sicilia normanna del XII secolo', in *La pittura in Italia: L'Altomedioevo*, edited by Carlo Bertelli, Milan, 1994, 416-431, and his forthcoming 'The Painted Ceiling of the Cappella Palatina in Palermo and its Relation to the Artistic Traditions of the Muslim World and the Art of the Middle Ages', in *Islamic Art*, VI, 1994-1995 (2002), with all pertinent literature. The same volume will also include Jeremy Johns' important study on 'The Date of the Cappella Palatina'.

[4] Inv. No. LNS 36 W, diameter 120mm; I am grateful to Shaikh Nasser and Shaikha Hussa al-Sabah for having allowed me, on a recent visit to Kuwait, to study and photograph the object and for having given me permission to publish it here. I am equally grateful to Sue Kaoukji, Deputy Keeper of the al-Sabah Collection, for her kind assistance in many ways during that study period.

[5] Tokyo, Terizo Kimura Collection, see Nobuo Kumagai, 'A Painted Casket from Kucha, East Turkestan', *The Bijutsu Kenkyu, The Journal of Art Studies*, No.191, The Institute of Art Research, Tokyo, March 1957, 239-265, and pls. I-IV; for colour illustrations of two details of this box, see Mario Bussagli, *Painting of Central Asia*, Geneva, 1963, 86-87.

physical appearance of the majority of male figures in Fatimid, and Fatimid-derived, painting (pls. 15-17). Very similar figures appear on painted ivory boxes that have been attributed to 12th-century Sicily by Kühnel as early as 1914,[6] an attribution which has been generally accepted and, most recently, reconfirmed by the *festeggiato* of this volume, Ralph Pinder-Wilson[7] (pls. 11.6-11).[8] Only one other similarly attributed object that includes human figures is known to me, a long, narrow wooden panel with painted decoration. This piece is now in the Berlin collections but its origin does not appear to have been established (pl. 11.31).[9] It shows two small seated figures, one holding a drum (?) or tambourine, the other raising a glass; the figures flank what would appear to be a cross, a somewhat curious iconographical combination. They are even sketchier than that of the al-Sabah lute player. The Berlin panel may well have decorated a piece of furniture or, perhaps, even a ceiling, in a Coptic church in Egypt. Which leads us back to the painted ceiling of the Cappella Palatina, partaking of the same general tradition of painted wood and ivory that is undoubtedly one of the possible sources for the small wooden lid in the al-Sabah Collection.

This continuous tradition, from late-Classical Central Asian wall-painting through Umayyad, Abbasid (pls. 11.2 and 4), and Fatimid painting (pls. 11.13-16) to the paintings on Sicilian ivories (pls. 11.6-11) and the Cappella Palatina ceiling (pls. 11.3 and 17) has long been recognised.[10] What still remains unclear is the precise attribution both in place and time of any of the individual objects decorated with painting in this style. In most cases, attributions are possible because the paintings appear in an architectural context, albeit the date of the Abu'l-Suᶜud paintings (pl. 11.2) is still a subject of discussion.[11] And even though the painted ivories are fairly securely dated and their assignment to Sicily well established—thanks to the fundamental work of Ralph Pinder-Wilson—the attribution of the small wooden lid is still problematic. Perhaps certain peculiarities in the facial features of the young man there represented may help in refining it.

The great variety of renderings of the human physiognomy, especially of male figures, in Fatimid art has been widely noticed. While most adhere closely to the Central Asian manner, it is equally evident that the 'classical' form of this physiognomy (best represented by the Samarra wall paintings) (pl. 11.4 and 11.21) freely intermingles with, and often replaces, the imported 'Central Asian' type, especially in Egypt, where local 'Hellenistic' manners remained strong. This is nowhere more evident than in the figures of older bearded men seen on a variety of Fatimid lustre-painted vessels, of which the two in the Keir Collection (pl. 11.18), and the Cairo wrestler bowl, are perhaps the best examples.[12]

The facial features of the young man on the lid in the al-Sabah Collection are basically of the 'Central Asian' type but of a specific variation. The typical face, in this tradition, has large almond-shaped eyes with large pupils hanging from the upper lid but often filling the entire centre of the eye (pls. 11.15-16); here the pupils of the young musician are smaller and attached to the upper lid. The eyes are not set under the usual arch-shaped brows, and the eyebrows are practically reduced to two straight lines. The nose, which in the classical form in profile appears bent, often ending in a hook or even a broad tip (pl.

6 Ernst Kühnel, 'Sizilien und die islamische Elfenbeinmalerei', *Zeitschrift für bildende Kunst*, XLIX, 1914, 162-170.

7 See Ralph Pinder-Wilson and C N L Brooke, 'The Reliquary of St. Petroc and the Ivories of Norman Sicily', *Archaeologia*, CIV, 1973, 261-305; reprinted in his *Studies in Islamic Art*, The Pindar Press, London, 1985, 168-243.

8 For these ivories see pl. 11.6: Perry Blythe Cott, *Siculo-Arabic Ivories*, Princeton, 1939, 36-37, no. 38, pl. 19; pl. 11.7: *ibid.*, 42-43, no. 79, pl. 34; pl. 11.8: *ibid.*, p. 35, no. 33, pl. 16: pl. 11.9; pl. 11.9, *ibid.*, 37, no. 39, pl. 20: pl. 11.10, *ibid.*, 37-38, no. 42, pls. 22-23; pl. 11.11: *ibid.*, p. 43, no. 38, pl. 23.

9 Berlin, Museum für islamische Kunst, inv.no.I.1963, 130 x 720mm, identified as being probably from a wooden ceiling, Syria or Egypt, Fatimid period, 10th-11th century(?). It was first shown in the exhibition *Das Staunen der Welt; Das Morgenland und Friedrich II (1194-1250)*, Berlin, 1995, no. 87, and has now been illustrated in colour in Monique Rey-Delqué (ed.), *Le Crociate, l'Oriente e l'Occidente da Urbano II a San Luigi, 1096-1270* (catalogue of an exhibition, Rome, Palazzo Venezia, 14 February-30 April, 1997), Milan, 1997, p. 324 (cat. no. 194), where it is identified as Egypt, 12th century.

10 See Ernst J Grube, *The Classical Style in Islamic Painting*, Edizioni Oriens (Lausanne) 1968, 12-15, figs. 1-9.

11 In my article quoted in note 1, the building and its decoration are attributed to the ᶜAbbasid/Tulunid period, an attribution to which my friend and colleague Jonathan Bloom has taken exception. He attributes the building, because of its development of muqarnas elements in the intermediary zone which carried the figurative paintings in question, to the Fatimid period. See his 'The Introduction of the Muqarnas into Egypt', *Muqarnas*, 5, 1988, 21-28. For the controversy, see the quotation from Bloom's letter which he kindly wrote me after my questioning his attribution, in my forthcoming study on the painted ceiling of the Cappella Palatina quoted in note 3.

12 The famous bowl with an old and a young man preparing their fighting cocks for an engagement (inv. no. 88, see Ernst J Grube, *Islamic Pottery of the Eighth to the Fifteenth Century in the Keir Collection*, London, 1976, p. 138-142, and colour plate facing p. 136), and the fragment of a bowl with a man carrying a basket (inv. no. C.7, see Oliver Watson, in *Islamic Art in the Keir Collection*, edited by B W Robinson, London, 1988, 149-150, and colour plate 38). For the Cairo wrestler bowl, Museum of Islamic Art, inv. no. 9689, see Richard Ettinghausen, *Arab Painting*, Geneva, 1962, p. 55, and the author's article quoted in note 1.

11.13), is here depicted by a straight line ending in a point, with an upward-curling nostril clearly in evidence. And the nose-line would appear to be attached to the right eyebrow, a feature again not always seen in Fatimid painting but almost always present in the rendering of facial features in the Cappella Palatina paintings (pls. 11.3 and 17), and on Sicilian painted ivories (pls. 11.6-9). It is also present in an important al-Sufi manuscript produced in North Africa (Ceuta) at the beginning of the 13th century AD. (pl. 11.12), where it almost certainly harks back to a much earlier local tradition. The mouth, as the eyebrows, is equally reduced to a short straight line. Some of these features can also be found in the facial rendering of young men on Fatimid lustre-painted pottery (pl. 11.20, 22), and in a few of the surviving Fustat sketches (pls. 11.23-24),[13] and they are even foreshadowed by some of the Samarra faces (pl. 11.21); nonetheless they are somewhat unusual, for it is the more curvilinear design of eyebrows, nostrils and mouth that prevails.

On the other hand, the rectilinear articulation of eyebrows, nose, and mouth is frequently found on Syrian lustre-painted pottery of the Tell Minis type (pls. 11.25-28),[14] to which two fragments (pls. 11.29-30)[15] may be added, since they show faces of a remarkably similar kind. Similar faces can also be seen in the unique painted panel in Berlin (pl. 11.31), and they reappear in the majority of facial renderings of Sicilian painted ivories. Whether the peculiarities in the rendering of the young man's face on the al-Sabah lid are specific enough to allow a more precise dating, or even perhaps to attribute this piece to a specific place, remains to be seen. At this moment, the available comparative material inadequately supports such an attempt, but the series of faces of young men on a variety of contemporary objects offered in this article may at least begin the task.

Such a comparison would link the al-Sabah lid more closely to Syrian and—to a degree, by derivation—Sicilian paintings of the type, than to Egyptian Fatimid examples. It may also indicate a somewhat earlier phase in the development of the classical Fatimid male type. These are clearly rather tenuous considerations and only the hope of further discoveries of objects like the al-Sabah lid, virtually unique at this moment, will permit the more secure attribution, and precise interpretation, of this fascinating small object.

Pl. 11.2 *Turbaned youth with a beaker. Painting in a* muqarnas *niche, in the bath hall near the Sanctuary of Abu'l-Sucud, Old Cairo (Fustat).*
Cairo, Museum of Islamic Art.

[13] For these pieces see Ernst J Grube, in *The Keir Collection, Islamic Painting and the Arts of the Book*, London, 1976, 40-43, No. I.11, and 39-40, No. I.10a & b.

[14] For Tell Minis pottery, see Venetia Porter and Oliver Watson, in *Oxford Studies in Islamic Art*, IV, 1987, 175-248.

[15] For the piece in pl. 11.29, see Edmund de Unger in *Islamic Art in the Keir Collection*, London, 1988, p. 144, No. 143, No. C3iii, ill. on p. 143, where he comments on the fact that 'No exact parallels to Fatimid faces seem to have survived.' The piece should perhaps be attributed to Syria rather than Egypt.

Pl. 11.3 A female dancer. Painting in the muqarnas zone of the central ceiling of the Cappella Palatina (A12.13), Palermo, about 1140 AD.

Pl. 11.5 Detail of painted wooden box from Kucha, 7th century AD.
Tokyo, Terizo Kimura Collection.

Pl. 11.4 Man wrestling with a ram. Reconstruction by Ernst Herzfeld of a wall painting from Samarra, 9th century AD.

Pl. 11.6 Detail of painted lid of ivory box, Sicilian, 12th century AD.
Palermo, Cappella Palatina, Treasury.

Pl. 11.7 Falconer with his falcon and the falcon's prey. Detail of a ivory pyxis, Sicilian, 12th century AD. Halberstadt, Cathedral Treasury, inv. no. 55.

Pl. 11.8 Musician. Detail of painted ivory pyxis. Sicilian, 12th century AD. Berlin, Museum of Islamic Art, inv. no. KFMV 9b.

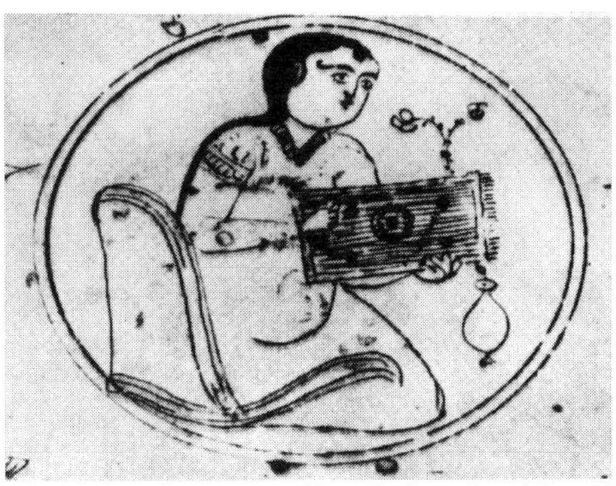

Pl. 11.9 A musician. Detail of a painted ivory box. Sicilian, 12th century AD. London, The Victoria and Albert Museum, inv .no. 603-1902.

Pl. 11.10 A princely figure in a circular medallion, below hunters. Detail of a painted ivory box. Sicilian, 12th century AD. Florence, Museo Nazionale del Bargello.

Pl. 11.11 Falconers. Detail of the front of a painted ivory box. Sicilian, 12th century AD. Trento, Museo del Duomo.

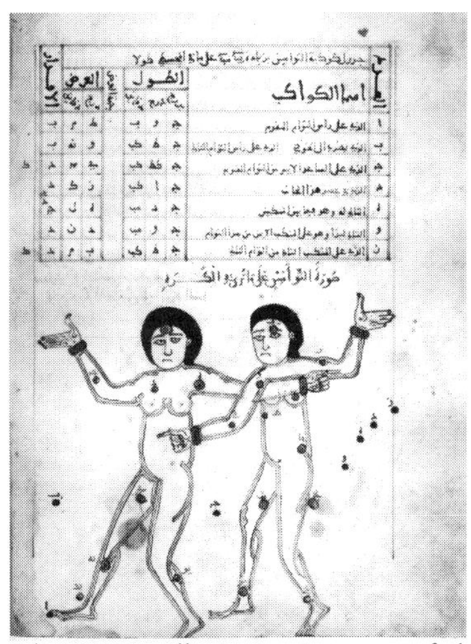

Pl. 11.12 Illustration in a copy of al-Sufi's Kitab suwar al-kawakib al-thabitah *('Book of Fixed Stars'). Ceuta (Morocco), 621/1224. Città del Vaticano, Biblioteca Apostolica Vaticana, MS Ross. 1033, fol. 49rv:* surat al-taw'amayn *('picture of the twins')—Gemini.*

Pl. 11.13 A youthful drinker. Lustre-painted ceramic bowl, Egypt, 10th-12th century AD.
Cairo, Museum of Islamic Art, inv. no. 15501.

Pl. 11.15 Dancer. Lustre-painted ceramic bowl. Egypt, 10th-12th century AD.
Cairo, Museum of Islamic Art, inv. no. 15950.

Pl. 11.14 Musician. Lustre-painted ceramic bowl. Egypt, 10th-12th century AD.
Cairo, Museum of Islamic Art, inv. no. 14923.

Pl. 11.16 Dancer. Lustre-painted ceramic bowl, Egypt, 10th-12th century AD.
Washington, Freer Gallery of Art, acc. no. 46.30.

Pl. 11.17 Dancer. Painting in the muqarnas zone of the central ceiling of the Cappella Palatina (A12.10), Palermo, about 1140 AD.

Pl. 11.19 Detail of object ill. in Colour pl.I (11.1).

Pl. 11.20 A sphinx. Fragment of a lustre-painted ceramic vessel. Egypt, 10th-12th century AD.
Athens, Benaki Museum, inv. no. 11722.

Pl. 11.18 Preparation for a cock-fight. Lustre-painted ceramic bowl. Egypt, 10th-12th century AD.
The Keir Collection, inv. no. 88.

Pl. 11.21 Face of a young man. Fragment of a wall painting from Samarra, 9th century AD. Berlin, Museum of Islamic Art, inv. Sam. no.

Pl. 11.23 A bearded man. Fragment of a painting on paper, Egypt, 10th-12th century AD. The Keir Collection, inv. no. I.11.

Pl. 11.22 Groom with a giraffe. Lustre-painted ceramic bowl, Egypt, 10th-12th century AD. Athens, Benaki Museum, inv. no. 749.

Pl. 11.24 A young woman and a young man. Coloured drawings on paper. Egypt or Syria, 12th century AD (?). The Keir Collection, inv. no. I.10a&b.

Pl. 11.25 A prince holding a beaker. Lustre-painted ceramic bowl, from Tell Minis, Syria, 12th century AD. Copenhagen, The David Collection, inv. no. Is195.

Pl. 11.27 A youth holding a beaker. Lustre-painted ceramic bowl, from Tell Minis, Syria, 12th century AD. Toronto, The Royal Ontario Museum, acc. no. 960.219.1.

Pl. 11.26 A sphinx. Lustre-painted ceramic bowl, from Tell Minis, Syria, 12th century AD. Toronto, The Royal Ontario Museum, acc. no. 960.219.2.

Pl. 11.28 A youth holding a flower (?) and a beaker. Lustre-painted ceramic bowl, from Tell Minis, Syria, 12th century AD. London, The Victoria and Albert Museum, inv. no. C48-1960.

Pl. 11.29 Face of a young woman (?). Fragment of a lustre-painted ceramic vessel, probably from Tell Minis, Syria, 12th century AD.
The Keir Collection, inv. no. C3iii.

Pl. 11.30 Face of a youth, and a bowl of fruit. Fragment of a lustre-painted ceramic vessel, Egypt or Syria, 12th century AD.
New York, Private Collection.

Pl. 11.31 Two seated figures, a musician and a drinker flanking a cross.
Painted wooden panel, Syria or Egypt, 12th century AD.
Berlin, Museum of Islamic Art, inv. no. I.1963.

12 THE GHURID TOMB AT HERAT

Robert Hillenbrand

Introduction and earlier work

The so-called tomb of Ghiyath al-Din Muhammad b. Sam, demolished in the 1950s, was formerly one of the glories of the Friday Mosque of Herat.* Its significance was manifold—the location on the north side of a Friday mosque was unusual; its architecture was striking, with a zone of transition not readily paralleled in pre-Mongol buildings; and the dominance of epigraphy in its interior decoration set new standards of complexity and virtuosity. Happily, the building was photographed by Oskar von Niedermayer during the First World War,[1] and carefully recorded by Donald Wilber in 1937, with the results published (including two excellent photographs by Arthur Upham Pope) in his book on Ilkhanid architecture,[2] while supplementary photographs of it, though with minimal accompanying text on the building, were published by Richard Frye in 1948.[3] Finally, Bernt Glatzer published a trove of pictures taken by the Swiss architect Rudi Stuckert, who had worked on the mosque in 1942-3, and provided a detailed commentary and analysis of the mausoleum in particular.[4] The special strength of Glatzer's study lies in its detailed treatment of the epigraphy of the mosque and mausoleum, and in the hitherto unpublished views he was able to include. Still further and hitherto unpublished documentation is also available and that, together with a fuller discussion of the architecture and epigraphy of this lost monument, is the prime justification for the present study. Robert Byron made four excellent photographs of the mausoleum in 1935;[5] these have passed to the Courtauld Institute of Art in London, as have two by Eric Schroeder,[6] while the Department of Art History at Ann Arbor, Michigan, has several further views taken by Wilber.[7] The publication of much of this further material here provides an opportunity to look at this lost masterpiece in the detail that it deserves. In particular, the clarity of these images has made it possible to add to the epigraphic material already available.

Function and antecedents

Funerary *madrasas* were the norm in the Iranian world in the pre-Mongol period,[8] but funerary mosques were not, for all that other parts of the Islamic world knew them. Thus, according to Yaqut, Sultan Sanjar's mausoleum was sited next to a mosque, though the discrepancy in height would have been far greater than it was at Herat.[9] This trend was taken still further at Sultaniyya, where a small oratory is placed alongside a towering mausoleum, like a pilot fish beside a whale.[10] The implied downgrading of

* It is a pleasure to dedicate this study to Ralph Pinder-Wilson, who has done so much to encourage younger generations of specialists in Islamic art, and whose own work has so significantly furthered the study of medieval Islamic architecture in Afghanistan.

1 O von Niedermayer, *Afghanistan*, Leipzig, 1924, 54-7, pls. 154-6.

2 D N Wilber, *The Architecture of Islamic Iran. The Il Khanid Period*, Princeton, 1955, 136-7, fig. 24, pls. 63-4; cf. *idem*, 'The Institute's Survey of Persian Architecture. Preliminary Report of the Sixth Season of the Survey. Part III', *Bulletin of the American Institute for Iranian Art and Archaeology* V, 1937, 121.

3 R N Frye, 'Two Timurid Monuments in Herat', *Artibus Asiae* XI, 1948, 206-12.

4 B Glatzer, 'Die Grosse Moschee und das Mausoleum des Ghiyat ud-Din in Herat', *Afghanistan Journal* 7/1, 1980, 3-22. I am much obliged to my old friend Bernard O'Kane for the extended loan of this rare issue.

5 Cf. R Byron, 'Timurid Monuments in Afghanistan', *IIIe Congrès International d'Art et d'Archéologie Iraniens*, Leningrad, 1935, *Mémoires*, Moscow and Leningrad, 1939, 35.

6 Cf. E Schroeder, 'Preliminary note on work in Persia and Afghanistan', *Bulletin of the American Institute for Persian Art and Archaeology* IV, 1935, 135. I should like to thank Dr Lindy Grant for her help in tracking down these images.

7 I should like to express my gratitude to Sheila Blair and Jonathan Bloom for their help in securing these prints for me.

8 For example, see R Hillenbrand, *The Tomb Towers of Iran from 1000 to 1550* (unpublished D.Phil. thesis, University of Oxford, 1974), I, 228-30.

9 See his *Mu'jam al-Buldan*, ed. F Wüstenfeld, Leipzig, 1866-73, IV, 509, tr. Barbier de Meynard as *Dictionnaire géographique, historique et littéraire dela Perse etudes contrées adjacentes*, Paris, 1861, 529. A Russian *sondage* in 1937 confirmed that the tomb of Sultan Sanjar adjoined the Great Mosque and indeed opened into it, just as Yaqut reports (J M Rogers, *Patronage in Seljuk Anatolia 1200-1300*, unpublished D.Phil. thesis, University of Oxford, 1972, 203.

10 See the ground plan published by A Godard in A U Pope and P

Pl. 12.1 Friday Mosque, Herat: qibla *façade (photograph Stuckert; after Glatzer).*

Pl. 12.2 Friday Mosque, Herat: north iwan (photograph Stuckert; after Glatzer).

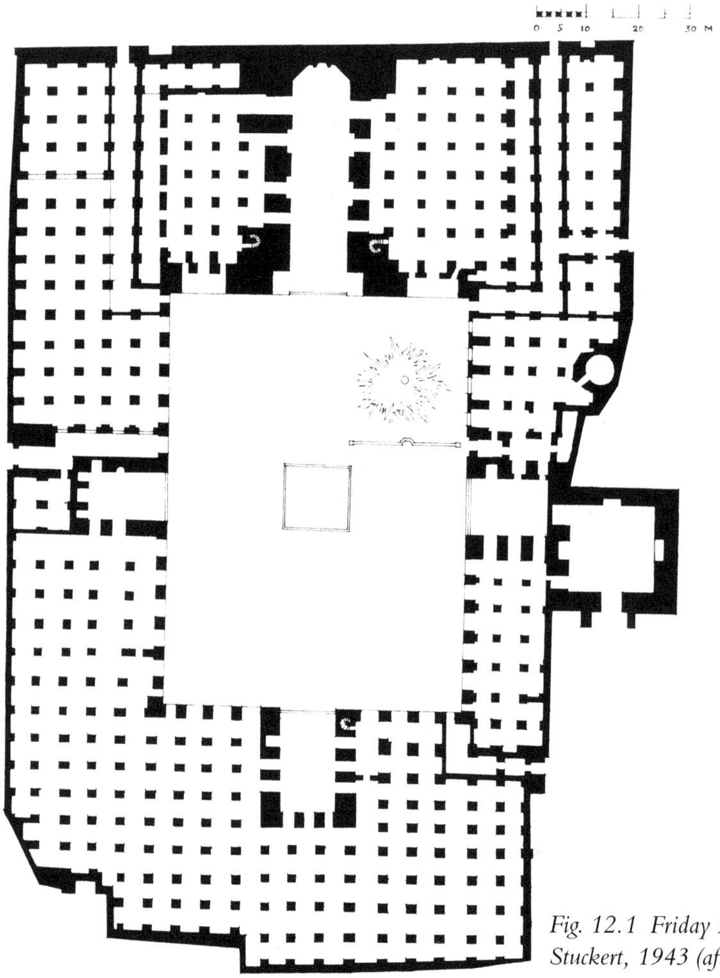

Fig. 12.1 Friday Mosque, Herat: plan by Stuckert, 1943 (after Glatzer).

Pl. 12.3 Mausoleum of Ghiyath al-Din: east portal (photograph Schroeder).

the mosque in this type of formula may be enough to explain why the idea did not find favour in later times. In this functional respect, therefore, the building is out of the ordinary, though the exact degree to which it is actually innovative in this respect in the Iranian context remains to be seen. Given that the mosque in question is the Friday mosque of a major city (pls. 12.1 and 2), it is not surprising that the tomb is that of a ruler. As for its location in Herat, at the western periphery of the Ghurid empire, one may see in the entire rebuilding of the mosque, as in the construction of the mausoleum at the same time, a desire on the part of Ghiyath al-Din to underline the importance of the major city in the western part of the Ghurid dominions, perhaps as a counter-balance to the aggressive expansionism of the dynasty on its eastern frontier under the leadership of his brother Mu^{c}izz al-Din Muhammad.[11] Nevertheless, the proximate cause of the rebuilding was the destruction of the mosque by fire.[12]

In type, this dome chamber is indistinguishable from the great *maqsura* domes of Saljuq mosques in Iran.[13] Nevertheless, there is no doubt that its function is very different. Its location makes this plain, for the chamber is situated in the middle of the north-western flank of the mosque rather than on its *qibla* side (fig. 12.1). Indeed, there is now no dome chamber at all on the *qibla*, which instead is marked by a preternaturally long *iwan* (pl. 12.1). Moreover, no attempt has been made to integrate the dome chamber into the body of the mosque; it is an obvious excrescence. Even its alignment with the northern *iwan* is skewed, as if to drive home the point that the building is removed from the liturgical function of the mosque.

Ackerman (eds.), *A Survey of Persian Art from Prehistoric Times to the Present*, London and New York, 1938, 1117, fig. 401.

11 Bosworth, *The New Islamic Dynasties*, Edinburgh, 1996, 299.

12 Juzjani, *Tabakat-i-Nasiri*, tr. H G Raverty, Calcutta, 1881, I, 404, n. 1.

13 Though it was probably much smaller; J Sauvaget has already drawn attention to a mistake in the drawing made by Niedermayer (*Afghanistan,* 55, fig. 5) in the proportions of the tomb, the result of which would be to create a diameter of 40 metres ('Glanes Epigraphiques', *Revue des Etudes Islamiques*, 1941-6, 28, n. 2). The true figure is some 17 metres (Wilber, *Architecture,* 136).

Pl. 12.4 *Mausoleum of Ghiyath al-Din: east portal, detail (photograph Wilber).*

Exterior

It is a great pity that the photographic documentation available for this lost building does not include more views of the exterior. The images available are confined to the east[14] façade of that exterior (pls. 12.3 and 4), including, it seems, the ENE side (pl. 12.5), which may perhaps suggest that the two remaining sides that were free-standing, namely the south and the west (for the north side was joined to the mosque) were left blank and were therefore not of interest to the few Westerners who photographed the building. An even greater degree of blankness is found on a monument which is typologically if not functionally similar, namely the north dome of the Isfahan Jami^c, which also stands proud of the perimeter walls of the mosque and is also on the north side.[15] It is interesting that this dome chamber too is attached to a mosque, though with the difference that its function has yet to be established; the Ghurid monument may thus be seen as evidence pointing to a funerary purpose for the Isfahan dome chamber. The parallel can indeed be taken further, for the absolute simplicity of the exterior of the Isfahan dome belies the decorative and structural complexity within.

[14] Actually north-east—see the orientation given in Wilber's drawing (*Architecture*, fig. 24), whereas Stuckert's plan has no north point—but for the sake of simplicity the main cardinal points will be used in what follows.

[15] For a ground plan, see *Survey*, fig. 328 opposite 954.

Pl. 12.5 *Mausoleum of Ghiyath al-Din: ENE side, detail (photograph Wilber).*

But there is one crucial distinction between the two structures: the Herat mausoleum possesses a splendid entrance portal to the east (pls. 12.3 and 4) which yields nothing to the contemporary south-east portal of the adjoining mosque (pl. 12.6). Indeed, the two portals display the same set of visual idioms, and even their epigraphy is well-nigh indistinguishable in form and content alike. This very close similarity suggests that the two portals were part of the same building campaign, which would imply very strongly that the same patron—Ghiyath al-Din Muhammad b. Sam, the Ghurid sultan who erected the minaret of Jam in 590/1194[16]—was responsible not only for the restoration of the mosque (whose south-east portal is dated Ramadan 597/June-July 1201)[17] but also for his own mausoleum, in which he was buried in Jumada I 599/February 1203.[18] One should nonetheless mention here the assumption by Sauvaget[19] that the mausoleum was built by the son of Muhammad b. Sam, Mahmud. This prince, who according to Bosworth ruled from 602/1206 to 609/1212-13,[20] is credited by Khwandamir[21] with completing the rebuilding of the mosque, a task left unfinished at the death of his father. But there is no mention of the mausoleum in Khwandamir's account. Parallels for the practice of building a tomb in one's own lifetime are not hard to find in pre-Mongol Iran, beginning with the Gunbad-i Qabus.[22] It is also possible that the mausoleum was begun by Muhammad but, like the adjoining mosque, completed by his son. The issue must be left open pending further information, but it does not seriously affect issues which depend on dating, since there is likely to be no more than fourteen years' difference between the two possibilities.

The eastern portal of the mausoleum did not undergo a Timurid transformation, as did the south-eastern portal of the *jami*ʿ itself.[23] This was later blocked and in

Pl. 12.6 Friday Mosque, Herat: south-east portal (after Glatzer).

any case was ill placed to act as the principal entrance to the mosque. That function was probably discharged by the portal *iwan* in the middle of the south side, which gave onto an open corridor leading directly to the courtyard. The portal to the mausoleum itself was perhaps left unchanged because it was recognised as the personal mausoleum of a long-dead ruler rather than as an integral part of a Friday mosque in which the whole community had a stake, and which was therefore worth repairing. At all events, the fact that its original structure was respected makes it easier to reconstruct its original layout. Like the south-eastern portal, only more so, it projected strongly from the perimeter wall of the mosque (pl. 12.3), with broad flanking walls enclosing a narrow arched entrance. But the area around the portal to the mausoleum strikes out in a direction not paralleled in what remains of the area surrounding the mosque portal. The lower part of the wall to the north had lost its decoration at the time that Schroeder, Wilber and Stuckert photographed it, but the degraded plaster coating and the remains of stepped niches indicate that it once bore some kind of ornamental scheme. Moreover, its upper portion still had sufficient of the original layout left to allow a reconstruction (pl. 12.7). This decorative scheme was executed not in brickwork but in carved terracotta, a diagnostic feature of Ghurid architecture, and stood proud of the wall surface. The basic idea was one that is known in other Ghurid

[16] This date has been read by R H Pinder-Wilson in his forthcoming 'Ghaznavid and Ghurid Minarets', *Iran* XXXIX, 2001.

[17] See the discussion by A S Melikian-Chirvani, 'Eastern Iranian architecture: apropos of the Ghurid parts of the Great Mosque of Herat', *Bulletin of the School of Oriental and African Studies* XXXIII/2 1970, 322-5.

[18] L Golombek, 'The Resilience of the Friday Mosque: the case of Herat', *Muqarnas* I 1983, 95; but her footnote for this statement does not unambiguously cite the source of her information. For the date, see C E Bosworth, 'Ghurids', *Encyclopaedia of Islam,* 2nd ed., 1101.

[19] J Sauvaget, *op. cit.*, (1941-6), 28.

[20] Bosworth, *NID*, 298. For a discussion of 609 as the likely date of his death, see Raverty, *op. cit.*, I. 407, n. 5 and 410-12, n. 6.

[21] Cited by Raverty, *op. cit.,* I, 404, n. 1.

[22] Another example is the tomb tower of Radkan West; see M van Berchem in E Diez, *Churasanishe Baudenkmäler,* Vienna, 1918, 103.

[23] Melikian-Chirvani, *op. cit.*, pls. XIII-XV.

Pl. 12.7 Mausoleum of Ghiyath al-Din: NNE exterior façade (photograph Schroeder).

monuments such as the minaret of Jam,[24] the mosque-cum-*madrasa* of Zuzan[25] and the recently destroyed *madrasa* of Shah-i Mashhad.[26] It can in fact be found as far west as the portal *iwan* of the Friday mosque of Firdaus.[27] It involves a succession of panels linked by knotted frames, often (as in this mausoleum) with further ornament inside these knots (pls. 12.3, 5 and 7).[28] The best-preserved of these panels bore a Kufic inscription of which only the opening words survive (see below). It seems permissible to assume that this was the prelude to the full name and lengthy titles of the intended occupant of the mausoleum, and that this epigraphic band would have framed the entire eastern portal. Taken together with the evidence cited above to the effect that the east façade below this band formerly bore a decorative scheme, this suggests that the main façade of the mausoleum was elaborately decorated, as was indeed the contemporary norm for mausolea. What is noteworthy here is that the mausoleum was not, as it were, modestly and seamlessly integrated into a subsidiary façade of the mosque, but was allowed to make its own striking and individual statement.

When the mausoleum was first photographed in the early 20th century by Niedermayer, it had already lost all its superstructure above the zone of transition, and it is therefore impossible to reconstruct this part of the building. It is not even possible to determine whether it had a hexadecagon above the squinch zone, and thus whether there was an intermediate drum on the exterior. The basic domed square type as it had developed by the late 12th century, however, especially in buildings of this scale, favoured a strongly marked external zone of

24 A Maricq and G Wiet, *Le Minaret de Djam. La Découverte de la capitale des sultans ghorides (XIIe-XIIIe siècles)*, Paris, 1959, pls. I-II, IV-V.

25 A Godard, 'Les mosquées de Forumad et de Zawzan', *Athar-é Iran* IV/1, 1949, 119, fig. 100.

26 M J Casimir and B Glatzer, 'Šah-i Mašhad, a Recently Discovered Madrasa of the Ghurid Period in Ġarǧistan (Afghanistan)', *East and West* 21, 1971, figs. 23, 25 and 27.

27 R Hillenbrand, 'Islamic Monuments in Northern Iran', *Iran* VIII, 1970, 206.

28 The evidence of the contemporary Ghurid portal of this same mosque, and of the Firdaus mosque just mentioned, suggests that there may have been glazed ornament here.

transition, whether marked by a gallery as at Sangbast or the mausoleum of Sultan Sanjar at Merv[29] or by stepping, from square to octagon to hexadecagon to dome, as in the Jabal-i Sang at Kirman.[30]

The ground plan made by Wilber shows that the external walls bore no secondary articulation, for example niches, reveals or engaged columns, and this preference for simplicity and unadorned mass in the lower part of the building makes it likely enough, though by no means certain, that a similar austerity reigned in the upper part of the structure.

Interior

It is worth noting in the context outlined above that the lower walls of the interior reveal a continuation of this somewhat severe aesthetic, in that three-dimensional articulation is strikingly absent. As a result, the hectic, dynamic energy of the squinch zone, conceived as it is primarily in sculptural terms, draws the eye like a magnet (pl. 12.8). Much of the power of this zone depends on the contrast which it offers to the flat surfaces which predominate in the rest of this interior. Its muscular expansions and contractions are carefully calculated to create a steadily rising and then falling rhythm, with the focus of attention resting not on the squinches themselves (fig. 12.2), as had been normal in the tri-lobed squinch zones of the Isfahan area, from which the Herat example ultimately derives, but on the arches which mark the cardinal axes (pl. 12.9). These have a greater width and depth than any other arched form in the squinch zone. Moreover, a secondary arch, substantially narrower and shallower, mediates between the axial arch and the squinch (fig. 12.3). This solution is far more innovative than the one adopted for the squinch zone at Shah-i Mashhad, which dates to a generation earlier (fig. 12.4). Here the squinches, not the axial arches, dominate the zone by virtue of their greater width, which encroaches on the space which notionally 'belongs' to the axial arches (pl. 12.10). At Herat that relationship is exactly reversed.

Both of these solutions differ from the classical balance achieved in the squinch zones of the Isfahan school earlier in the 12th century, where squinches and axial arches divided the transition zone equally. Indeed, the Ghurid structures build on that model, even if their efforts involved trying to improve on perfection. These late Ghurid transition zones, as illustrated by the examples at Herat and Shah-i Mashhad, may perhaps be seen as the apotheosis of the trilobed motif, a form encountered as early as the Arab-ata mausoleum at Tim[31] (Rabi' I 367/October-November 977)[32] and the Davazdah Imam mausoleum at Yazd (429/1037).[33] In a sense, perhaps, these forms, as interpreted in Afghanistan in the late 12th and early 13th centuries, could be regarded as conservative; but a similarly focused development of the zone of transition is to be found nowhere else in the Iranian world in the half-century preceding the Mongol invasions. This drives home the fact that the eastern provinces had definitively supplanted western and central Iran as the centre of excellence in structural innovation as in architectural ornament.[34] The alternative collateral tradition, as illustrated by the transition zones of north-western Iran, was substantially less complex.[35]

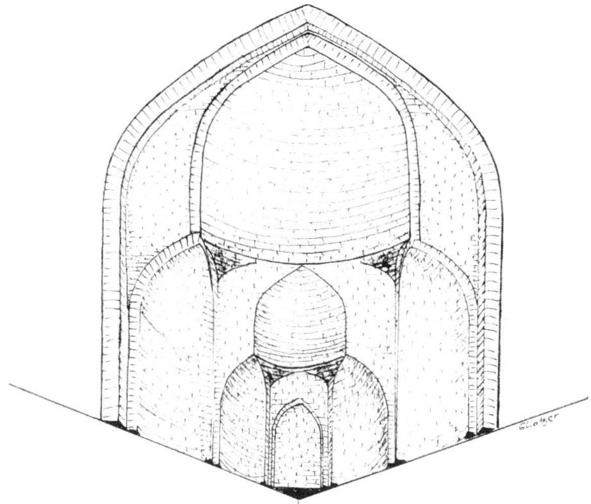

Fig. 12.2 Mausoleum of Ghiyath al-Din: reconstruction of squinch (after Glatzer).

The next stage of evolution tells the same story. Only some two decades after the Herat tomb, at Zuzan,

[29] A U Pope, *Persian Architecture*, London and New York, 1965, figs. 104 and 149 respectively; the idea goes back at least to the tomb of the Samanids in Bukhara—see G Stock, 'Samanidenmausoleum', *Archaeologische Mitteilungen aus Iran* 23, 1990.

[30] *Survey*, pl. 281; the same solution is found in the south dome of the Friday Mosque of Isfahan, *ibid.*, pl. 279.

[31] O Grabar, 'The Visual Arts', in R N Frye (ed.), *The Cambridge History of Iran. Volume 4. The period from the Arab invasion to the Saljuqs*, Cambridge, 1975, pl. 9.

[32] S S Blair, *The monumental inscriptions from early Islamic Iran and Transoxiana*, Leiden, New York, Kobenhavn and Köln, 47; she voices a lingering suspicion that the date on the building might be that of the tenant's death, which would leave open the date of the mausoleum itself (*ibid.*, 47-8).

[33] *Survey*, pl. 273A.

[34] R Hillenbrand, 'The Architecture of the Ghaznavids and Ghurids', in C Hillenbrand (ed.), *Studies in Honour of Clifford Edmund Bosworth Volume II—The Sultan's Turret: Studies in Persian and Turkish Culture*, Leiden, Boston and Köln, 1991, 167.

[35] R Hillenbrand, 'Saljuq dome chambers in North-west Iran', *Iran* XIV, 1976, 97-8 and pls. IIa-b and IIIb-d.

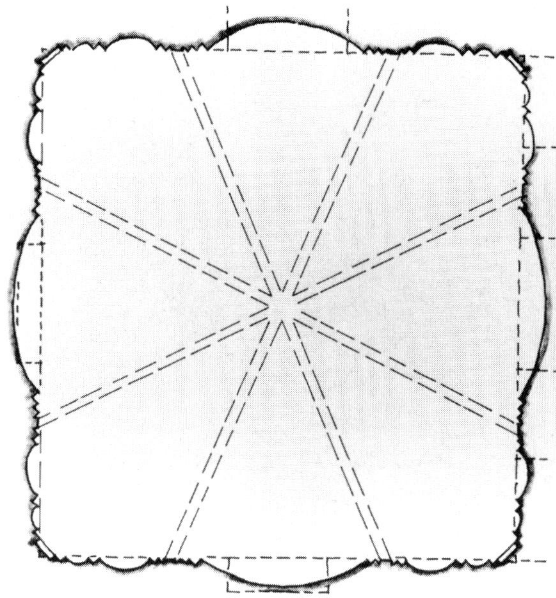

Fig. 12.3 Mausoleum of Ghiyath al-Din: plan of zone of transition (after Glatzer).

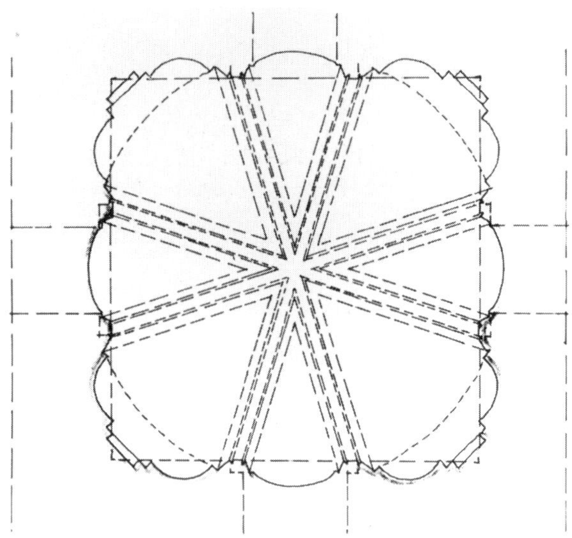

Fig. 12.4 Shah-i Mashhad madrasa: *plan of zone of transition (after Glatzer).*

the arch of the *iwan* contains a developed *muqarnas,*[36] and this was of course to be the standard solution in future centuries; once again, the obvious parallel is to be found in the Isfahan oasis, in the stalactite cupola of the mosque at Sin, dated 529/1134-5.[37] Here again, the eastern Iranian solution, though closely related to, and later than, that of the Isfahan school, differs from it significantly in points of detail and can thus be seen as a logical continuation of the ideas developed in that school.

[36] A Godard, 'Mosquées', 123, fig. 105.

[37] M B Smith, 'Material for a corpus of early Iranian Islamic architecture. III. Two dated Seljuk monuments at Sin (Isfahan)', *Ars Islamica* VI/1, 1939, figs. 4, 19 and 21-2.

Later work

The ground plan of the Herat mausoleum published by Wilber (fig. 12.5) betrays certain inconsistencies which suggest either that it was no straightforward matter to graft the mausoleum onto the mosque, or that the mausoleum underwent later alterations. Certain photographs of the interior elevation tell the same story. The most revealing detail in this connection is the arch[38] whose profile breaks into the major inscription band at the base of the zone of transition (pl. 12.11). It is hard to believe that the original architect planned that this should happen, and thereby destroyed the symmetry of the inscription band. One of the arches in this interior has a flat-topped shouldered segmental profile (pl. 12.12), and while this is not in itself unusual in Saljuq times, it is indeed odd in view of the fact that the others are of the four-centred type standard in this period. Finally, the arches in the lower wall of the interior elevation are of differing height and breadth, and are not placed symmetrically—for example, at the centre of each side, as one would expect. The deep niche within the *mihrab* is also markedly off-centre, and there is no attempt to correlate the articulation of the north and south sides. The cumulative weight of all this evidence suggests that such irregularities point to a later refashioning of the interior. Several possible dates for this present themselves, and the two most likely occasions for intervention occurred in the 14th century, under the Kart rulers Ghiyath al-Din Muhammad in 720/1320-1 and Muᶜizz al-Din Husain between 765/1364 and 771/1369-70; indeed, the latter was buried in this very mausoleum in 775/1373-4.[39] A Timurid refurbishment, less thorough than that applied to the south-east portal of the mosque, is a further possibility.[40]

[38] It is not clear on which side of the mausoleum this occurs, since the captions of the published photographs are silent on this matter.

[39] Golombek, *op. cit.*, 96. The Timurid chronicler of Herat, Mu'in al-Din Muhammad Zamchi Isfizari says that a member of the Kart ruling house was buried at the Herat Jamiᶜ (*Raudat al-Jannat fi Ausaf Madina Harat*, tr. C A C Barbier de Maynard ['Extraits de la chronique persane d'Herat, tranduits et annotés', *Journal Asiatique*, 1861], 514). His father, as well as a Ghurid ruler, were likewise buried 'under the north dome' of the mosque, and this orientation can only indicate the Ghurid mausoleum.

[40] For this portal, see Lézine, 'Hérat, Notes de voyage', *Bulletin d'Etudes Orientales* XVIII, 1964, 137, 142-4, pl. IXb.

Pl. 12.8 Mausoleum of Ghiyath al-Din: interior, zone of transition (photograph Pope; after Wilber).

It is hard to propose a convincing explanation for these changes now that the building is no longer in existence. Perhaps, however, the most likely solution is that the mosque itself underwent some fundamental changes, in the course of which the relationship between it and the mausoleum changed. The most obvious candidate for such a change is the north *iwan* of the mosque (pl. 12.2). Its skewed location *vis-à-vis* the mausoleum is all too noticeable (fig. 12.1) and it is hard to believe that matters were always so. The north *iwan*, moreover, was not placed where it was as an isolated element of the design; its placing was interdependent with that of the other three *iwans*.

Date

The key question of date has long been settled, at least in general terms. After the exhaustive analysis by Glatzer,[41]

[41] Glatzer, *op. cit.*, 15-18.

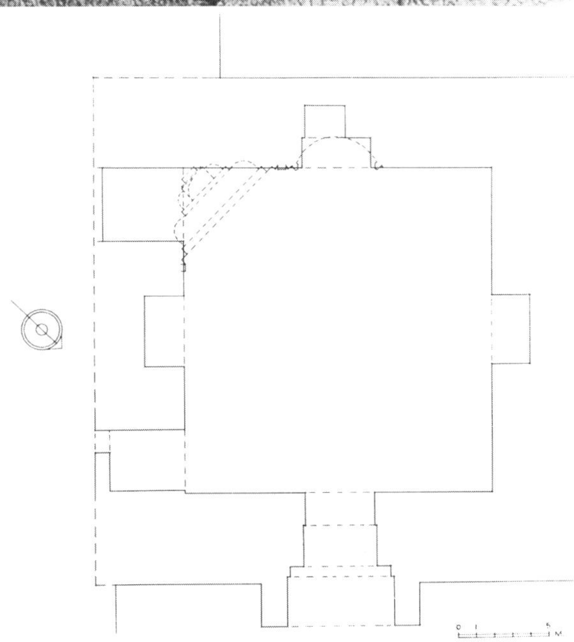

Fig. 12.5 Mausoleum of Ghiyath al-Din: ground plan (after Wilber).

Pl. 12.9 Mausoleum of Ghiyath al-Din: east side, showing zone of transition and alleged grave of Ghiyath al-Din (photograph Stuckert; after Glatzer).

Pl. 12.10 Madrasa of Shah-i Mashhad, zone of transition (after Glatzer).

which contains a thorough and discriminating evaluation of all earlier scholarship on the matter, there can be no doubt that the oldest visible parts of the mosque are to be dated around the year 597/1201; and all of the mausoleum, as recorded in the first half of this century, to the same year or at the latest to the following decade. Thus the view of Donald Wilber that the building contains work from two distinct periods, *c.* 1200 and *c.* 1300-*c.* 1330, is mistaken.[42] He places the core structure in the earlier period and most of its decoration in the later one. Is this indeed the case? Happily several ways of approaching this problem present themselves. They are: the range of decorative techniques involved; the style of the inscriptions; their content; and the relationship between the dome chamber and the mosque itself.

Issues of epigraphy will be dealt with in the following section, and thus for the time being the discussion will limit itself to decoration and to the location of the mausoleum *vis-à-vis* the mosque. So far as decoration is concerned, the division between the preferred modes for interior and exterior—stucco for one, including the interior of the east portal, and carved terracotta for the other—suggests that clear distinctions were applied by the craftsmen concerned on the basis of what they considered appropriate for these different contexts. It must be conceded that the overall grid of square Kufic inscriptions incised in stucco, which is the principal decorative element in the interior of the funerary chamber

[42] Indeed, several of his attributions, such as the date of the south-east portal, are demonstrably mistaken; see *Architecture*, 136-7.

Pl. 12.11 Mausoleum of Ghiyath al-Din: arched niche intruding into main inscription band (photograph Wilber).

Pl. 12.12 Mausoleum of Ghiyath al-Din: segmental arch below zone of transition (photograph Wilber).

Pl. 12.13 Mausoleum of Ghiyath al-Din: NNE exterior façade, detail (photograph Schroeder).

itself, could—in the matter of technique alone—almost equally well date from any period between the 12th and 15th centuries.[43] But two other types of decoration clearly belong to the 12th century. The first is the repertoire of carved terracotta and decorative brickwork used on the exterior of the portal. The motifs are varied. They include, for example, doubled stretchers of standard Khurasani type with narrow rising joints filled with terracotta spindle shapes or rings and broad rising joints filled with addorsed motifs in the form of a figure 3 (pl. 12.7). A whole series of Saljuq buildings in Turkmenistan attests similar motifs.[44] The same goes for the saltire crosses in a *girikh* network (pl. 12.7).[45] Of more locally Iranian type is the narrow vertical panel filled with free and delicate floral terracotta (pl. 12.13), and the knotted frame (pls. 12.5 and 7)—both of these features are found at Zuzan.[46] Similar floral terracotta motifs fill the upper parts of the main portal inscription (pl. 12.6).

The second major dating control is to be found within the portal of the mausoleum, namely the lightly incised interlocked swastika designs spangled with triangular, pentagonal or rhomboidal insets (pl. 12.14). Very

[43] For the possibility of a date as late as the Timurid period, see B O'Kane, 'Timurid Stucco Decoration', *Annales Islamologiques* XX, 1984, pls. IIb-d and IIIa.

[44] G A Pugachenkova, *Puti Razvitiya Arkhitekturi Yuzhnogo Turkmenistana pori Rabovladeniya i Feodalizma*, Moscow, 1958, 245, 252-5, 313 and 333.

[45] Cf. *ibid.*, 309 for a version of this theme. Cf. too the south portal at Shah-i Mashhad (Glatzer, *op. cit.*, Abb.18, reproduced in the present article as pl. 12.24).

[46] Godard, 'Mosquées', 119, fig. 100.

Pl. 12.14 Mausoleum of Ghiyath al-Din: interior of portal, decorative ensemble (photograph Byron).

Pl. 12.15 Mausoleum of Ghiyath al-Din: interior of portal, decorative ensemble (photograph Byron).

similar work can be seen on the soffit of the Saljuq north-east *iwan* of the Friday Mosque of Qazwin.[47] Taken together, these pieces of evidence point unambiguously to a late 12th-early 13th century date. Attention should also be drawn to the wonderfully complex stucco design of radiating stellar polygons flanked by meander borders within the east portal of the mausoleum (pls. 12.14 and 15). Its outer border was yet another epigraphic band in cursive script, of which only a tiny portion remained (pl. 12.14, lower right; pl. 12.15, left).

What of the position of the mausoleum in relation to the mosque itself? Excavation would be required to fix the exact sequence of events. Nevertheless, there are sufficient clues in the ground plan of the mosque and mausoleum to indicate that Stuckert's plan of 1943 (fig. 12.1) depicted not the essential Ghurid mosque but a much-mangled version of it. The asymmetrical opposition of the north and south *iwans* is a case in point; so is the

[47] R. Hillenbrand, 'Saljuq Monuments in Iran: I', *Oriental Art* N.S. XVIII/1, 1972, 14, n. 47. Cf. too the closely related work in the Saljuq part of the Friday Mosque of Qurva (Hillenbrand, 'Saljuq dome chambers', pl. IVd).

Pl. 12.16 Mausoleum of Ghiyath al-Din: NNE exterior façade, detail of inscription (photograph Schroeder).

south portal, with its curious dogleg and its lack of access to the south *iwan*. Equally aberrant is the present context of the south-east portal (pl. 12.6). But the fact that the mausoleum is blocked off from the back of the north *iwan*, (pl. 12.2) and is off-centre from it, clearly points to major post-Ghurid alterations to the mosque. That the mausoleum continued in use is confirmed both by the literary sources, which indicate that it served as a dynastic mausoleum,[48] and by the quantity of cenotaphs within its interior (see for example pl. 12.9). Equally hard to explain is the flattened U-shaped excrescence attached to the southern inner wall of the mausoleum.

Epigraphy

Such Ghurid epigraphy as the mosque and mausoleum still possessed in the first half of the 20th century has to be assembled from a variety of sources. The major one is Melikian-Chirvani's account of the inscriptions associated with the mosque itself;[49] this incorporates the information from Saljooqi[50] and from the *Répertoire Chronologique de l'Epigraphie Arabe*, no. 3213, which is wrongly placed in that volume under the year 550 AH, indicating that in the opinion of the editors this undated inscription is to be placed between 500 and 550 AH.[51]

Pl. 12.17 Mausoleum of Ghiyath al-Din: portal inscription (photograph Stuckert; after Glatzer).

(a) Exterior

The largely destroyed panel to the NNE of the exterior portal (pl. 12.11) bore a Kufic inscription whose opening words were read by Glatzer[52] as *hadha al-mashhad al-*('this

[48] Golombek, *op. cit.*, 96.

[49] A S Melikian-Chirvani, *op. cit.*, 322-4 and pls. IV-VIII.

[50] F Saljooqi, 'The Complete Copy of the Ancient Inscription of the Ghiassuddin Grand Mosque in Herat', *Afghanistan* XX/3, 1967, 80.

[51] E Combe *et al.*, *Répertoire Chronologique d'Epigraphie Arabe*, IX, Cairo, 1937, 8.

[52] Glatzer, *op. cit.*, 17.

Pl. 12.18 Mausoleum of Ghiyath al-Din: interior, east bay, showing two types of square Kufic (photograph Byron).

mausoleum ...'); in fact the letter *mim* and the beginning of the letter *ba* can be read after this fragment, which suggests that the next word was *mubarak* ('blessed') as is so often the case in such a formula. Thus the fragment can be reconstituted as *hadha al-mashhad al-mubarak* ('this blessed mausoleum'). That opening clearly indicates a historical inscription, presumably identifying the tenant of the mausoleum.

The lacunary main inscription (pl. 12.17), as deciphered by Glatzer[53] reads:

> *... [al-um]am, maula muluk al-ʿarab wa'l-ʿajam, mughith al-ʿibad, zull Allah fi'l-[ard].*

Comparison with other inscriptions from the mosque suggest that this titulature, which fits with that of Ghiyath al-Din Muhammad b. Sam, read in part '[master of the necks of the na]tions, lord of the kings of the Arabs and Persians, succour of the slaves [of God], shadow of God on [earth]'. The parallels with the text of the south-east portal of the mosque are very close indeed, and this closeness extends to the style of the inscription.

[53] Glatzer, *loc cit.*

Pl. 12.19 Mausoleum of Ghiyath al-Din: showing historical inscription in square Kufic (photograph Pope, after Wilber).

There is no way of telling whether either of these exterior inscriptions were executed in blue glaze, as was the comparable inscription in the south-east portal of the mosque.

(b) Interior

On either side of the inner walls of the east portal to the mausoleum is a wide band with an elegant cursive inscription notable for the mannered precision and delicacy of its letters, its preternaturally long shafts and the hooked tips which crown them (pl. 12.14-15). It is not complete on either side, thanks to the later walls abutting onto it. Sauvaget[54] read it as follows:

> A. *[Al-sultan] al-muʿazzam shahanshah al-aʿzam malik riqab al-umam*
> B. *Maula muluk al-ʿarab wa'l-ʿajam mughith al-ʿibad zull Allah fi ['l-ard]*
>
> ('the mighty sultan, the supreme king of kings, master of the necks of the nations, lord of the kings of the Arabs and Persians, succour of the slaves [of God], shadow of God on [earth]').

The background to this inscription comprises tight scrolls from which issue leaves of various shapes, often bifurcated, with their surfaces further animated by punching and hatching.

Above it, sandwiched between torus, foliate and meander borders of varying width, is a narrow inscription band in Kufic which repeats the words *al-hukm li'llah* (though with slightly incorrect orthography) many times (pl. 12.14). This message, which may be translated 'judgment belongs to God', has a long Islamic history, for it was the motto which the Kharijites inscribed on their standards at the battle of Siffin. Similar mottoes, similarly repeated, are not rare in Iranian architecture at this time.

Below this is a fragmentary stucco Kufic inscription on a much larger scale (pl. 12.14). It features block-like letters vouchsafed only a minimum of ornamental shaping but enriched by redundant and varied knotting in the middle tier and by internal knotting in the bottom register within the words themselves. Where the words do not yield a regular series of uprights, these are added, alongside U-shaped motifs, so as to create a regular rhythm in the topmost tier of the band. This area is further singled out by an unbroken row of trilobed punched designs. The inscription has certain parallels with that of the Khwaja Atabek tomb in Kirman.[55] So far this inscription has resisted complete decipherment, though the odd sequence (e.g. ... *Allah qahir* ...) can be made out.

The ornament on the interior walls marks a distinct stage in the evolution of a style based on monochrome brickwork. It shows the transfer to a plaster surface of modes first developed for the interplay of actual bricks. In that sense it may, perhaps, be related to the fake brickwork executed in plaster in the Sultaniya vaults. But it also foreshadows the networks of square Kufic names first encountered *en masse* in Ghaznavid minarets and destined to end say in the sanctuary of Pir-i Bakran[56] or in the *qibla* wall of the Yazd *jamiʿ*.[57] And the brickwork at Sujas[58] shows that in other parts of the Iranian world too the idea of carrying brick patterns into plasterwork had found favour. What is new at Herat is, first, that such huge expanses of the interior walls have been covered in this ornament derived from brickwork; and, second, that the theme of this ornament is epigraphic—and not just Qur'anic or the repetition of holy names, but secular and political inscriptions too. This seems to be a first in Iranian architectural ornament.

There is little doubt that this fashion is a distinctively Ghurid one. As such it can be paralleled in a whole series of monuments in Afghanistan, but perhaps above all in India. For the nearest lineal descendant of the Herat tomb is the mausoleum of Iltutmish in Delhi.[59] The major difference between the two monuments, which are only a generation apart in time, lies in the content of the two epigraphic programmes: that of the Ghurid mausoleum is overwhelmingly royal and secular, while that of the mausoleum of Iltutmish is overwhelmingly Qur'anic. This may of course have much to do with the very different religious environments in which the two buildings were erected; Herat had been solidly Muslim for centuries, while Delhi was still in the throes of conversion. The mausoleum of Iltutmish and other Muslim North Indian buildings of the late 12th and early 13th centuries were destined to

[54] Sauvaget, *op. cit.*, 27-8.

[55] D Hill and O Grabar, *Islamic Architecture and its Decoration*, 2nd ed., London, 1967, pls. 533 and 535.

[56] S P Seherr-Thoss, *Design and Colour in Islamic Architecture*, Washington, 1978, p. 50.

[57] *Survey*, pls. 442-3.

[58] R Hillenbrand, 'Salǧuq Monuments in Iran. III. The Domed Masgid-i Ǧamiʿ at Suǧas', *Kunst des Orients*, X/1-2, 1975, figs. 9, 11-13.

[59] For an accessible illustration, see J D Hoag, *Islamic Architecture*, New York, 1977, 289; for its inscriptions, see E C Dodd and S Khairallah, *The Image of the Word*, II Beirut, 1981, 190-1.

Pl. 12.20 Mausoleum of Ghiyath al-Din: naskhi *inscription beneath zone of transition (photograph Byron).*

Pl. 12.21 Mausoleum of Ghiyath al-Din: naskhi *inscription beneath zone of transition (photograph Stuckert; after Glatzer).*

establish a lasting fashion in the sub-continent for inordinately lengthy quotations from the Qur'an in religious and funerary architecture—so lengthy that the building in effect becomes the Holy Book itself. But it is worth remembering the Ghurid source of this fashion.

The most innovative feature of this epigraphy is without doubt the incised plaster which serves as a decorative skin for most of the lower portion of the interior—that is, for the area below the squinch zone. It consists entirely of 'square' or 'seal' Kufic. The motif in itself is not new; its first dated occurrence is on the minaret of Gar, near Isfahan, which is dated 515/1121-2[60]—almost a century earlier than the Herat tomb. The novelty lies rather in the sheer scale of its use in the later building, where it is employed with the utmost confidence and panache. It might be argued that this represents the next stage in the development of decorative brickwork, but the areas where this ornament has disappeared show that the inscriptions are only incised into a plaster skin[61] and are not mirrored in the underlying surface, which appears to be of mud brick. Sometimes the script mimics brickwork in that it has a serrated outline, but sometimes it has a straight outline and is much more compressed (pl. 12.18).

As early as the minaret of Masᶜud II at Ghazna, as Ralph Pinder-Wilson has shown,[62] interlocking Kufic script (known as 'square' in the West, *muᶜaqqali* locally) which was used still earlier in Iran to spell out sacred names, was employed for the names and titles of first the Ghaznavid and then the Ghurid sultans. The Ghurid mausoleum at Herat represents the climax of this fashion. Here at least one inscription is in boustrophedon[63] and—most significantly—gives a portion of the titlature of Ghiyath al-Din Muhammad b. Sam:[64] *muᶜizz al-islam wa'l-*

[60] M B Smith, 'The Manars of Isfahan', *Athar-é Iran* I/2 1936, 323 and fig. 213; Y Godard, 'Notes épigraphiques sur les minarets d'Isfahan', *ibid.*, 363.

[61] Cf. the parallel but less developed case of Sujas (Hillenbrand, 'Sugas', fig. 11).

[62] R Pinder-Wilson, 'The Minaret of Masᶜud III at Ghazni', in R Pinder-Wilson, *Studies in Islamic Art*, London 1985, 89-102.

[63] This is a relatively rare device in Islamic epigraphy; other examples include the *mihrab* of the Imamzada Nur at Gurgan (R Hillenbrand, 'Saljuq Monuments in Iran. V. The Imamzada Nur, Gurgan', *Iran*, XXV, 1987, 72 and 74 and pls. XIa-XIIb) and the late 14th-century inscription above the entrance of the *minbar* in the Ulu Cami at Manisa.

[64] Maricq and Wiet, *op. cit.*, 52.

Pl. 12.22 Shah-i Mashhad, naskhi *inscription in northern section (after Glatzer).*

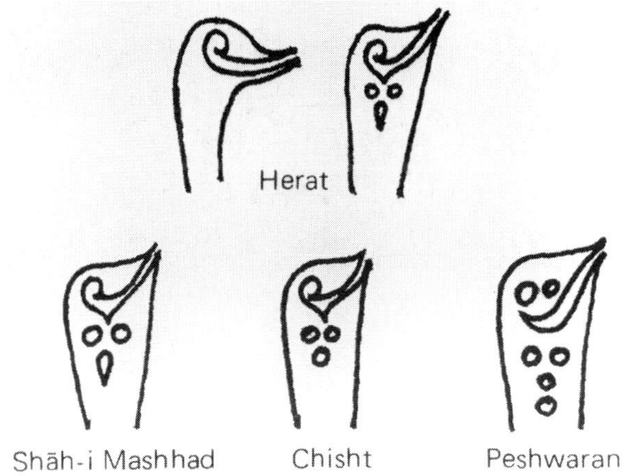

Fig. 12.6 Zoomorphic hastae *tips in Afghan buildings (after Glatzer).*

muslimin, sultan salatin al-sharq wa'l-gharb.[65] In the centre of the east bay is the word 'Muhammad' repeated in blocks. On the outer face of the arch, to the left[66] can be read: ... *allah/illah ibn al-m...*, while below the major inscription in the bay can be read: *yalid wa lam* ... (this sequence is written upside down). Below that major inscription, to the right of that bay, can be seen 'Muhammad' repeated at least twice, perhaps three times; while above the major inscription, in the centre of the bay, the word 'Muhammad' is written repeatedly at various angles. Elsewhere[67] one can decipher: ...*lad Allah/ mulk li'llah*; while below that, the word 'Allah' is written at various angles and separated from the area above by a band. Higher up, at the south corner, immediately below the *naskhi* inscription, is a quotation from Sura 112: ... *qul huwa Allahu ahad Allahu al-samad lam yalid wa lam yulad wa lam yakun lahu* ('Say: He is God, The One and Only; God, the Eternal, Absolute; He begetteth not, Nor is He begotten; And there is none [like unto Him]'). The main inscription in the bay is Qur'an 3:18, 'Allah (Himself) is witness that there is no God save him. And the angels and the men of learning (too are witnesses).'[68] The sheer pervasiveness of these square Kufic inscriptions makes for a potent combination of religious and political messages within the chamber, and this is achieved alongside (and without diminishing) the role of these messages as sheer ornament.

Another notable feature of the epigraphy is the *naskhi* inscription in the band below the transition zone. This band had been plastered over at some stage, and very little of it remained in the 1930s, though enough to indicate that it was not of Qur'anic content. Against an extraordinarily complex scrolling background which echoes the lush, curvaceous, even baroque mobility of the letters themselves with decorative arabesques floating in the upper register there unfolds an inscription of quite outstanding rhythmic verve. Exaggerated contrasts between tall and short, thick and thin letters lie at the heart of its unpredictable, discontinuous but urgent tempo. The reason for its powerful impact lies not only in its intrinsic energy and visual éclat but also in the juxtaposition of its riotous curvilinearity with the rectilinear grid of the interlocking square Kufic inscriptions which cover the lower surfaces of the chamber like wallpaper, and which Byron dismisses as 'ye olde bryckeworke'.[69] Byron confidently dates this inscription to the 14th century but gives no detailed reasons for his opinion. Yet similarly extravagant cursive inscriptions are known from Dandanaqan in Turkmenistan, datable to the 12th century.[70] Moreover, the treatment of the tips of the *hastae*, whose punctuations lend these shafts a witty zoomorphic character, even an element of caricature, is itself a dating control. Not only is it especially popular in Ghurid territory at this period (pl. 12.22 and fig. 12.6),[71] but it is also clearly related to the animated script which

[65] Bay in east wall: Wilber, *Architecture*, 63, right.

[66] Wilber, *Architecture*, pl. 63.

[67] *Ibid.*, pl. 64.

[68] The phrase *wa ulu'l-ʿilm* ('and the men of learning') lacks the second of its three *waws*.

[69] R Byron, *The Road to Oxiana*, London, 1950, 104.

[70] S Khmel'nitski, *Medzhdu Samanidami i Mongolami. Arkhitektura Srednei Azii XI—nachala XIII vv. Chast' 1*, Berlin and Riga, 1996, 80, fig. 43; the best surviving pieces of this inscription are on display in the National Museum in Ashkabad.

[71] Glatzer, *op. cit.*, 18 and 21.

Pl. 12.23 Friday Mosque, Herat: interior, arch flanked by inscriptions (photograph Byron).

was fashionable in Iranian metalwork of the late 12th and early 13th centuries and whose origins seem to lie precisely in Herat—at all events, the earliest well-developed use of such motifs which can be precisely dated is on the so-called Bobrinski bucket, made in Herat in Muharram 559/ December 1163.[72] It is perhaps not surprising to see these flirtations with the depiction of living creatures in a religious monument at this time, given the emphasis on figural art at the court of the Ghaznavids.

Finally, among Robert Byron's photographs of the mosque is one with a hitherto unpublished view of a keyhole arch—a type much favoured by the Ghaznavids—set above an intricate terracotta frame for a four-centred arch, and flanked to the far right by a narrow panel of knotted designs (pl. 12.23). The arch itself has a thick profile decorated with various terracotta insets—triangles, lozenges, stars and elongated buckles—and is set against a continuous network of terracotta stars and lozenges framed by alternating rings and billets. At either side of this composition, and flanked by a vertical knotted design of alternating ovals and lozenges, are the remains of a Kufic inscription broadly comparable to those of the south-east portal of the mosque and the east portal of the mausoleum. It reads:

> *al-sultan al-muʿazzam, shahanshah al-ʿ[arab…] … [al-]mu'minin khallada Allah sultanahu wa aʿala sha'nahu*

which may be translated

> 'the mighty sultan, king of kings of the [Arabs] ... [the] believers, may God prolong his authority and elevate his dignity'.

Conclusion

The foregoing discussion shows clearly enough that the Ghurid tomb attached to the Friday Mosque of Herat was a masterpiece on many counts. In its terracotta as in its stucco decoration, especially the square Kufic ensembles which drape the lower walls of its interior like textiles,[73] it yielded nothing to the best work of its time. The architecture of its zone of transition tells the same story. Yet it is principally in the domain of epigraphy that the mausoleum breaks new ground, for while it cannot match, say, the virtuoso knotting of the main inscription at the Shah-i Mashhad *madrasa* (pl. 12.24), it is unrivalled in its own time or earlier in its full-scale use of square Kufic for wall decoration, and the sure mastery it displays in several quite distinct epigraphic modes.

Pl. 12.24 Shah-i Mashhad madrasa, *inscription on south portal (after Glatzer).*

[72] R Ettinghausen, *Islamic Art and Archaeology. Collected Papers*, ed. M Rosen-Ayalon, Berlin, 1984, 317, fig. 1. These vividly punctuated tips of certain letters are also known in Western Iran, for example at Sujas; see Hillenbrand, 'Suğas', fig. 8.

[73] One may compare the walls of the mausoleum of Sangbast (Seherr-Thoss, *op. cit.*, pl. 3.)

13 THE SCULPTURES OF THE PRE-ISLAMIC *HARAM* AT MAKKA

G R D King

Makka under its pre-Islamic Quraish rulers appears to have been unique in western Arabia as a great shrine,[1] if we follow the construction of western Arabian history that emerges from the Islamic tradition, effectively our only source for Makka's ancient past.[2] Yet with the material evidence of pre-Islamic Makkan idolatry lost, our only record of the sculptures, stones and paintings that were eradicated from the *Haram* by the Prophet Muhammad is that which can be gleaned from the Islamic textual sources. The Islamic tradition has such a deep antipathy to paganism that its dismissiveness of the *jāhilīya* has had the effect of leaving us with hardly any record of the appearance of the statues, paintings and stones that were worshipped as idols at Makka. Only the results of excavations at pre-Islamic Arabian sites like Dedan (al-ᶜUlā') in Saudi Arabia, at Khirbat al-Tannūr in Jordan, Qaryat al-Fau in Saudi Arabia, Ma'rib in Yemen, Palmyra in Syria, al-Dūr (ed-Door) in the United Arab Emirates and other sites can provide us with any comparative material that may show us the nature of the arts at pre-Islamic Makka, for at present it seems unlikely that Makka itself can produce much in the way of material cultural evidence. But while comparison is a way of recreating that which is lost, it is no substitute for direct evidence from the *Haram*.[3]

We are left with the literary tradition provided by the Islamic historians and they are far from precise: indeed, the Islamic sources' descriptions of the lost idols of Makka border on the semaphoric. We know the names of certain deities at Makka—Hubal, al-ᶜUzza, Manāt, al-Lāt, Isāf, Na'ila and al-Khalasa—but we know little or nothing of their appearance, whether as sculptures or as standing stones. Nor do we know their antiquity with any certainty. It is generally accepted that c. 608 AD marks the rebuilding of the Kaᶜba by the Quraish, brought about because its predecessor had been destroyed when a woman worshipper caused an accidental fire. This rebuilding marks the earliest possible date for the Kaᶜba's internal wall paintings and the decorations (*hilya*) inside the building. However, it does not follow that the same date applies to the 360 sculptures and stones that were said to be in the Kaᶜba or around the *Haram* when the town fell to Islam and the Prophet in 8/630.[4] There is every reason to assume that they were older.

At the time of the conquest, the Prophet ordered every sign of idolatry to be removed from the Kaᶜba before

[1] It is a great pleasure to dedicate this paper to Ralph Pinder-Wilson who twice honoured me by being my external examiner. He may conclude that this subject suggests a retreat on my part from the relative certainties of the Umayyads in Spain and Syria to a period devoid of much at all in the way of concrete fact. Only excavation is likely to bring forward some new material on the art of Arabia in the last centuries of the *jāhilīya*, and on that little work has so far appeared.

[2] The possibility should be considered that Makka was not unique as a *haram* but, rather that it was but one of a number of significant pagan shrines in Arabia. The long resistance of al-Tā'if to Islam may have been related to its own importance as an independent and autonomous *haram* of scale. Another major shrine was *al-Qalīs* which Abraha tried to establish *al-Qalīs* at Sanᶜā' to serve as an all-Arabian centre of pilgrimage, a Christian *haram*. On *harams*, see R B Serjeant, 'Haram and hawtah, the Sacred Enclave in Arabia', *Mélanges Taha Husain*, Cairo, 1962, pp. 41-58; reprinted in *Studies in Arabian History and Civilisation*, London, 1981; R B Serjeant, *South Arabian Hunt*, Luzac, London, 1976; M Gawlikowski, 'The Sacred Space in Ancient Arab Religion', and A Hadidi, *Studies in the History and Archaeology of Jordan*, Department of Antiquities, Amman, 1982, pp. 301-303. In a challenge to the conventional view, P Crone (*The Meccan Trade*, Blackwell, Oxford, 1987), with good justification has questioned the concept of a significantly wealthy Makka with a great volume of rich trade passing through the hands of the Quraysh. G R Hawting (*The Idea of Idolatry and the Emergence of Islam From Polemic to History*, CUP, Cambridge, 1999) has recently reconsidered the nature of faith at pre-Islamic Makka.

[3] There are rumours of the discovery in the last 20-30 years or so of pre-Islamic sculptures found smashed and buried at Makka, presumably on the Prophet's orders at the conversion of the Holy City to Islam. However, these reports have never been substantiated and so this sole tangible source of information which, if it exists, would bring us close to the *jāhilīya*, is unavailable to scholarship.

[4] The main sources are Hishām b. al-Kalbī, *The Book of Idols (Kitāb al-Asnām)*, trans. into English from the Arabic by N A Faris, University Microfilms International, Princeton, NJ, 1952; al-Azraqī's *Akhbār Makka*, ed. R S Malhas, 4th printing, Makka, 1983/1403, and Yāqūt al-Hamawī, *Muᶜjam al-Buldān*, ed. F Wüstenfeld, as *Jacuts geographisches Wörterbuch*, Leipzig, 1866-1869 (largely drawing on Ibn al-Kalbī). For modern accounts of the deities of Makka and the Kaᶜba before Islam, see J Wellhausen, *Reste arabischen Heidentums*, Berlin, 1897; and H Lammens, 'Le culte des bétyles et les processions religieuses chez les Arabes préislamites', *Bulletin de l'Institut français d'archéologie*

he would even enter it and all signs of paganism were consigned to a bonfire in the *Haram*. However, a pair of ram's horns were retained: they were said to have belonged to the beast sacrificed by the Prophet Ibrāhīm in place of his son, the Prophet Ismāᶜīl.[5] Paintings covering the interior of the Kaᶜba were wiped from the walls of the shrine, with the sole exception of a picture of Jesus (ᶜĪsā b. Maryam) with his mother. This was spared at the Prophet's behest, surviving until 64/683 when the Umayyads used catapults to bombard Makka during their rivalry for the Caliphate with ᶜAbd Allāh b. al-Zubair. As a result, the Kaᶜba was destroyed by fire and this last painting vanished. It is at this point that all physical historical connection with the pre-Islamic Kaᶜba of c. 608 AD is broken. The ram's horns also were lost, crumbling to dust when they were touched by ᶜAbd Allāh b. al-Zubair. This may suggest that they were already extremely old, or perhaps had been severely fire damaged.

The *Haram* sculptures

Ibn al-Kalbī says that simple stones that were worshipped by the pre-Islamic Arabs were termed *ansāb* (baetyls) but where a stone had the appearance of a living form, it was termed a *sanam* (pl. *asnām*), an idol, or a *wathan* (pl. *awthān*), an image. Elsewhere, he cites another tradition, stating that a *sanam* was a statue in wood, gold, or silver, but if of stone, it would be termed a *wathan*.[6] Just how many of the idols at the *Haram* were in the form of figurative sculptures is quite unknown to us. According to Ibn al-Kalbī, when the Prophet entered Makka at the Islamic conquest of the Holy City, 'he found the idols arrayed around it. Thereupon he started to pierce their eyes with the point of his arrow saying, "Truth is come and falsehood is vanished. Verily, falsehood is a thing that vanisheth" [*Qur'ān* xvii, 83]. He then ordered that the idols be knocked down, after which they were taken out and burned'.[7] This reference to the idols' eyes suggests that at least some were figurative representations[8] and the reference to burning may suggest that at least some were of wood. As to the deities that took the form of *ansāb*, these are reflected in the rough hewn stones that were worshipped as al-Lāt, al-ᶜUzza and Hubal at al-Tā'if and which were still there when Charles Doughty visited the town and sketched them in 1878.[9]

Apart from the *asnām*, *awthān* and *ansāb* at the *Haram*, every household in Makka had its own idol[10] and the demolition of the idols that the Prophet initiated at the *Haram* extended to those at private houses. But if we know little of the appearance of the *Haram* idols, we know nothing whatsoever of those in private houses.

The group of figurative sculptures at the *Haram* appear to have included Isāf, Nā'ila, Hubal and possibly al-Khalasa. Isāf and Nā'ila were a man and a woman from Yemen who had been punished for adultery in the Kaᶜba by undergoing metamorphosis into two stones, apparently retaining their human forms.[11] Ibn al-Kalbī calls them *miskh*, a term that reflects the process of metamorphosis. In time, he says, people forgot that Isāf and Nā'ila had been turned into stone as a punishment and they came to be worshipped instead by the people at Makka. One stood at Safā and the other at Marwa, the two low hills on the east side of the Kaᶜba between which the pilgrims still run to complete the *masayy'* during the Islamic *hājj*.[12] Under the Quraish, Isāf and Nā'ila were placed beside the well of Zamzam, and this is where they stood at the coming of Islam.[13] Although apparently anthropomorphic, we have no idea of the appearance of Isāf and Nā'ila, and it does not seem legitimate on the little we know of them to assume that their Yemeni origins had any affect on their forms as figurative sculptures.

As to al-Khalasa, ᶜAmr b. Luhayy is said to have set up this female deity in the low part of Makka

orientale, t. xvii, 39-101; G Ryckmans, *Les Religions arabes préislamiques*, Louvain, 1951; J Chelhod, *Le Sacrifice chez les Arabes*, Paris, 1955; A I Sharīf, *Makka wa'l-Madina fi'l-jāhilīya wa'l-ᶜahd al-rasūl, Dār al-fikr al-ᶜarabī*, 1965; Toufic Fahd, *Le Panthéon de l'Arabie Centrale à la Vieille de l'Hégire*, Paris, 1968; K A C Creswell, *Early Muslim Architecture*, Clarendon Press, Oxford, 1969, I, part 1, 1-5; O Grabar, *The Formation of Islamic Art*, Yale University Press, New Haven and London, 1973, 60; 80-81; Jawad ᶜAlī, *Al-mufassal fi ta'rīkh al-ᶜarab qabl Islām*, Baghdād, 1980, vol. 6; and U Rubin, 'The Kaᶜba. Aspects of its ritual functions and position in pre-Islamic and early Islamic times', *Jerusalem Studies in Arabic and Islam* 8, 1986, 97-131.

5 Al-Azraqī, i, 166.

6 Ibn al-Kalbī, 28, 46.

7 Ibn al-Kalbī, 27.

8 Al-Azraqī says much the same (i, 121): 'When the Prophet (S.) prayed the midday prayer on the day of the conquest he ordered that all of the idols (*asnām*) that were around the Kaᶜba were to be gathered together then they were burned with fire and were smashed ...' While not conclusive, the use of fire may suggest that some of the idols were of wood rather than stone.

9 C M Doughty, *Travels in Arabia Deserta*, CUP, Cambridge, 1888, ii, 515-517.

10 Al-Wāqidī, *Kitāb al-Maghāzī*, ed. M Jones, OUP, London and Cairo, 1966, ii, 870.

11 Al-Azraqī, i, 122; Ibn al-Kalbī, 8.

12 Al-Azraqī, i, 119.

13 Al-Azraqī, i, 88, 120; Ibn al-Kalbī, 8; 24-5.

(presumably at the *Haram*, the lowest part of the city which flooded after rain).[14] Al-Azraqī takes his information from Ibn Ishāq according to whom the Quraish would dress al-Khalasa with necklaces (*yalbisūna-hā al-qalā'id*), and they would make offerings of barley and wheat and pour *laban* over her. They would also make sacrifices and hang ostrich eggs on her.[15] Although not explicitly stated, this account may be construed as meaning that the al-Khalasa idol had some figurative characteristics, if necklaces were hung around her neck.

While doubt must persist with regard to whether Isāf, Nā'ila and al-Khalasa were figurative sculptures, of Hubal there is no uncertainty. It is the Makkan *sanam* of whose appearance we know most as the principle Makkan deity, taking the form of a red agate sculpture and it was housed in the Kaᶜba over a well-pit (*jibb*). Al-Azraqī says:

> Hubal was the greatest of the idols (*asnām*) of the Quraysh and it was set up at the well in the interior (*batn*) of the Kaᶜba.[16]

Elsewhere, al-Azraqī says:

> According to Muhammad b. Ishāq: Hubal was of agate (*kharaz al-caqīq*) in the form of a person (*insān*) and its right hand was broken and the Quraysh repaired it and they put on it a gold hand and there was a tank for sacrifices ...[17]

Hubal's cult was associated with divination with arrows. Ibn al-Kalbī and al-Azraqī (the latter following Muhammad b. Ishāq), report that, associated with the Hubal statue in the Kaᶜba, were seven divining arrows, each inscribed with their specific oracular conclusions for purposes of divination. The divination arrows would be shuffled and thrown by the lord of the arrows (*sāhib al-qidāh*) and those who enquired of their fate would give the sum of 100 *dirhams* to the *sāhib* for Hubal. Money was also thrown into the well beside Hubal.

There is no suggestion that the Hubal idol actually held arrows or representations of arrows: the divining arrows by definition were separate from the sculpture. Nor is there any evidence to allow us to compare the Hubal figure with that of the sculpture of the deity Wadd at Dūmat al-Jandal discussed below, which does indeed seem to have included sculpted arrows as an intrinsic part of the sculpture rather than as separate divining instruments.

The Hubal sculpture at Makka had been brought from the north, from either Jordan or Hīt in al-ᶜIrāq (*ard al-Jazīra*)[18] and its right hand had been lost,before it was carried to Makka, for Ibn al-Kalbī says 'It came into the possession of the Quraish in this condition, and they, therefore, made for it a hand of gold'.[19] The idol is said to have been introduced to Makka by Khuzaima b. Mudrika, and hence it was known as Khuzaima's Hubal.

The Quraish were of north Arabian ancestry, descended from Khuzaima b. Mudrika through the line of Qusayy who is thought to have lived in the first half of the 6th century AD. The genealogy is recorded as follows:[20] Qusayy b. Kilāb b. Murra b. Kaᶜb b. Lu'ayy b. Fihr (or Quraysh) b. Ghālib b. Mālik b. al-Nasr b. Kināna b. Khuzaima b. Mudrika b. Ilyās (or al-Yās) b. Mudar b. Nizār b. Maᶜadd b. Adnān. Khuzaima thus lived eleven generations before Qusayy. Allowing 25-30 years per generation over the eleven generations between Khuzaima and Qusayy, Khuzaima, if he existed, would have lived some time in the later 3rd-early 4th century AD, with which approximate date we should then associate the import of the Hubal statue to Makka. However, the value of this observation depends entirely on the genealogy being complete and on the authenticity of the Makkan tradition that al-Azraqī preserves.

The sources of the *Haram* sculptures

There is far too little information extant to allow us to estimate the style of the sculptures at Makka of Isāf, Nā'ila or al-Khalasa: indeed, it is not even certain that they were figurative statues. Nor does our vague knowledge of the place of origin and the rough *terminus ante quem* that is proposed here for the Hubal sculpture really help us to estimate its character: rather, it leaves us with an incoherently

[14] Although (Dhu)'l-Khalasa was worshipped at Makka, the main shrine of the deity was at Tabāla in modern Bilād Zahrān to the south of al-Tā'if. See Ibn al-Kalbī, 31; Ibn Saᶜd, *Biographie Muhammads (Kitāb al-Tabaqāt al-Kabīr)*, ed. E Mittwoch and E Sachau, Leiden, 1917, I, ii, 78. Malhas refers to the final destruction of Dhū'l-Khalasa in the 18th century., at the hands of either the Āl Suᶜūd *Imām*, Muhammad b. Suᶜūd al-Kabīr or his son, ᶜAbd al-ᶜAzīz (Malhas, in al-Azraqī, *op. cit.*, I, 388).

[15] Al-Azraqī, i, 124.

[16] Al-Azraqī, i, 117.

[17] Al-Azraqī, i, 119.

[18] Al-Azraqī, i, 100, 117.

[19] Ibn al-Kalbī, 23; al-Azraqī, ed. R S Malhas, i, 119.

[20] G Levi Della Vida, 'Kusayy', *Encyclopaedia of Islam*, new ed., hereafter *EI*². W Montgomery Watt, 'Ḳuraysh', *EI*².

vast choice of sculptural styles as potential sources and parallels. In these circumstances, no suggestion can be proposed legitimately as to the appearance of the statue of Khuzaima's Hubal.

The alleged northern origin of the Hubal figure, whether from Jordan or al-ᶜIrāq, corresponds to another tradition preserved by Hishām b. al-Kalbī who attributes the import of pagan practices from the north into Makka to ᶜAmr b. Luhayy.[21] ᶜAmr b. Luhayy is said to have imported idols to the Hijāz from the Balqā' in northern Jordan. This account is a part of the complex construct whereby the Islamic tradition sees idolatry introduced to Makka as a corruption and a pollution of the older monotheism that derived from the association of the Prophet Ibrāhīm (Abraham) with the *Haram* and with the Holy City.

ᶜAmr is said to have encountered idols when he went to al-Shā'm to be cured of sickness at a hot spring and found the people worshipping idols in order to bring rain and to bring victory. He acquired some and carried them back to the Hijāz where he set them up at Makka around the Kaᶜba. Another version recorded by Ibn al-Kalbī has ᶜAmr b. Luhayy finding idols on the Tihāma at or near Jidda where they had been washed up after floating down there from Mt Nawdh during the Great Flood of Noah.[22] ᶜAmr sent some of the idols with ᶜAwf b. ᶜUdhrah of the north Arabian tribe of al-Qudaᶜa to be distributed to the Arabs after the pagan Makkan *hajj*. They were sent to Wādī 'l-Qūra to the north of al-Madīna and to Dūmat al-Jandal at the southern end of the Wādī 'l-Sirhān. This account personalises the origins of idolatry in Arabia before Islam, placing responsibility for Arabian paganism on ᶜAmr b. Luhayy. However, J W Fück questions whether ᶜAmr b. Luhayy even existed, and instead, he suggests that he was created as a convenient scapegoat to carry the blame for Makka's pagan customs. Yet Ibn al-Kalbī's account, like the others recorded of the acts of ᶜAmr b. Luhayy, shows a persistent tendency to associate pagan statues in Makka ultimately with a northern origin, whether the Balqā', al-Hīt, or the landscape of Noah and the Flood.

If the reports from any of these sources possess a grain of hard fact, it would appear that the Makkans knew something of the sculptures of the north, of Syria or of al-ᶜIrāq. The ᶜAmr b. Luhayy episode and his visit to the hot-springs, as presented by Ibn al-Kalbī, occurs in a pagan *milieu* of idol-worship in the Balqā' of Jordan, and ostensibly it should therefore have occurred before the establishment of Christianity and the eradication of paganism in the Byzantine world in the late 4th/5th century AD. By the 5th century AD, the Balqā' appears to have been Christianised like the Hawrān to the north and Palestine to the west, but it was not necessarily a profound and complete Christianisation. Until well into the 5th century, as Trimingham has observed, the desert Arabs of north Syrian remained for the most part pagan and indeed, he argues that the spread of Monophysite Christianity among the nomads occurred only after the expulsion to the desert of anti-Chalcedonian monks in 521 AD.[23] This slow decline of the nomads' paganism in the north was probably matched elsewhere in the desert frontier regions and could mean that the Quraish encountered idolatry in *Bilād al-Shā'm* even later than the putative late 3rd-4th century AD date that is suggested here for Khuzaima's introduction of the Hubal sculpture to Makka.

* * *

There is evidence of the import of sculptures into Arabia from early times as well as exposure to external influences that led to the formulation of an indigenous sculpture tradition. An early example of such an import is provided by an Archaic Greek sculpture of c. 530 BC which reached south Arabia at some point.[24] A group of extremely fine bronze sculptures from the museums of Aden and Sanᶜā', and the British Museum reflects the impact of Hellenistic and Roman sculpture on southern Arabia[25] while a bronze of Maᶜādī Karib,[26] now in the National Museum at Sanᶜā', has echoes of external sources. At Dedan (al-Khuraiba), to the north of al-ᶜUlā' in the Hijāz, there is a group of sculptures which is associated with the Lihyānite kingdom.[27] Stylistically, some of these sculptures betray influences that lie somewhere between late Pharaonic sculpture and Greek *kouroi* of the 7th century BC. Parr and Caskel have dated the destruction of Dedan to no later than the 1st century BC/1st AD. As far as we are

[21] Ibn al-Kalbī, 7, 46-7. J W Fück, 'ᶜAmr b. Luhayy', *EI*[2].

[22] Ibn al-Kalbī, 45-46.

[23] J S Trimingham, *Christianity among the Arabs in Pre-Islamic Times*, Longman and Librairie du Liban, London and New York, 1979, 85, 103.

[24] W Daum ed., *Yemen. 3000 Years of Art and Civilization in Arabia Felix*, Pinguin, Innsbruck and Frankfurt/Main, 1988, 91.

[25] B Doe, *Southern Arabia*, London, 1971, pl. 38; pl. 40-43.

[26] W Daum, *Yemen* ..., 75.

[27] A Jaussen and F Savignac, *Mission Archéologique en Arabie*, II, *El-ᶜEla, d'Hégra à Teima, Harrah de Tebouk*, Le Roux, Paris, 1914, II, 57-58, and *Atlas*, plates XXVIII-XXXII. W. Caskel provides a list of the sculptures found at al-Khuraiba by 1953 (W Caskel, *Lihyan und Lihyanisch. Arbeitsgemeinschaft für Forschung des Landes Nordrhein-Westfalen*, heft 4, Cologne, 1953, 56 and Abb. 3; P J Parr, G L Harding and J E Dayton, 'Preliminary Survey in N.W. Arabia, 1968', *Bulletin of the Institute of Archaeology*, 1968-9, 8-9, 214.

aware, these sculptures were produced at Dedan but under the impact of outside influences. Other sculptures which were recorded by Jaussen and Savignac and which they saw at Damascus were said to be from Dedan. These were quite different and stylistically, they derived from the same traditions as the sculptures and reliefs from Palmyra and Hatra of the early centuries AD. Judging by the published illustrations, these appear to have been imports to the Hijāz from Syria or al-ᶜIrāq and it is something of an irony that they should have found their way north again to Damascus from al-ᶜUlā' where Jaussen and Savignac found them. These sculptures, if indeed they are from al-ᶜUlā', provide evidence of the import of sculpture from the north to the Hijāz shrine of Dedan in exactly the manner that is meant to have happened in the case of al-Khuzaima's Hubal at Makka.

In the same area of north-west Arabia, by the 1st century BC-1st century AD, the Nabataeans had also developed a tradition of sculpture, suggesting yet another possible source for the Quraish sculptures. While the Romans terminated the Nabataean kingdom in 106 AD, the sculptures of the great days of Nabataea remained at their rock cut tombs and at some of the temples, especially at Khirbat al-Tannūr.[28] Madā'in Sālih, the southern centre of the Nabataean kingdom, lay on the caravan route from Yathrib/al-Madīna to Syria and it must have been well known to the Quraish. It was certainly known to the Qur'ān where Madā'in Sālih is called al-Hijr and its rock-cut facades are explicitly, if briefly, described (*Sūrat al-Hijr*, xv). The Prophet passed by the place with his forces on his march to Tabūk in 9/630 but he avoided stopping to water there because of its polytheistic associations.

Whatever became of the Nabataeans as a tribal confederation, their cultural (and religious?) impact persisted. At a temple put up by Thamūd Arabs at Ruwwāfa in the northern Hijāz in the 160s AD to the Roman emperors Marcus Aurelius and Lucius Verus, a Nabataean version of the dedicatory inscription exists alongside a Greek one, underlining the persisting strength of Nabataean cultural impact among Arab confederations like that of the Thamūd.[29] A century later, a certain Kaᶜb b. Hāritha built a tomb at Madā'in Sālih for his mother, Raqūsh bint ᶜAbd Manāt, in 276 AD.[30] The writer used classical Arabic for the inscription, but written in Nabataean script, and like the Qur'ān, Kaᶜb b. Hāritha also knew the site as al-Hijra. This Arabo-Nabataean inscription suggests the continuation of life at Madā'in Sālih in some manner, in a Nabataean cultural context rather than a political *milieu* into the later 3rd century AD. This opens up the possibility that the caravan drovers of western Arabia would have been familiar with whatever remained of the temples and sculptures as well as the tombs of the Nabataeans.[31] Even if the use of Nabataean script may have faded by the 6th century AD when the Quraish flourished, with their caravans to Syria, they may well have been familiar with the sculptures of the landscape of the lost Nabataean kingdom and its centres in NW Arabia.

Further afield, there seems to be evidence of the import of sculpture to Qaryat al-Faw, on the western edge of the Empty Quarter, between Najrān on the Saudi Arabian/Yemen border and Yamāma. At Qaryat al-Faw, A R al-Ansary has excavated numerous sculptures that range from diminutive cast bronzes to fragments of hollow-cast, over life-size sculptures, the latter of a scale and quality that recalls the large hollow cast figurative sculptures in the museum at Sanᶜā'.[32] It seems likely that many of these were imported on camel-back to Qaryat al-Fau from somewhere in Yemen, for it is hard to imagine such large works being made at Qaryat al-Fau itself.

Most striking for the context of the present paper is a male sculpture in stone from Qaryat al-Fau which is taken by al-Ansary to represent Muᶜāwiya b. Rabīᶜa al-Qahtānī, described in an epigraphic south Arabian (*musnad*) inscription at al-Faw as king of the tribes of Qahtān and Mudhhij. The sculpture was reduced to a torso which al-Ansary compares to works from Petra, Palmyra and Hatra. His parallel with sculptures from the north dated to the

[28] See, for example, N Glueck, *Deities and Dolphins*, Cassell, London, 1966, *passim*.

[29] G W Bowersock, *Roman Arabia*, Harvard University Press, Cambridge, Mass. and London, 1983, 96-98. M C A Macdonald notes an inscription in Thamudic D (JS Tham 1) beside the Arabo-Nabataean dedicatory inscription mentioning the name and patronymic of a deceased indivual. It may be contemporary to the Arabo-Nabataean inscription (Nab 17) but this is said with diffidence and Macdonald certainly does not go so far (M C A Macdonald, 'Thamudic', *EI*^{2}).

[30] A Jaussen and F Savignac, *Mission Archéologique en Arabie*, Paris, 1914, II, pp. 172-176 (Nab. 17). A R al-Ansary, A H Ghazāl and G R D King, *Muwāqiᶜ athariya wa suwar min hadārat al-ᶜarabīya fī'l-mamlikat al-ᶜarabīyat al-suᶜūdīya. Al-ᶜUlā (Dīdān), al-Hijr(Madā'in Sālih)*, King Saud University, Riyadh, 1984/1404, 32-33.

[31] The potency of Nabataean imagery may have affected Christian ecclesiastical decoration in the Hawrān in northern Jordan. I have suggested elsewhere that snakes on a Madā'in Sālih rock-cut façade of 35-36 AD had some impact on stylised ribbons on the lintel of the West Church at Umm al-Surab in the Hawrān, of c. 5th century AD (G R D. King, J L King and J D Deemer, 'Some Churches of the Byzantine Period in the Jordanian Hawrān', *Damaszener Mitteilungen* 3, 1988, 44).

[32] A R al-Ansary, *Qaryat al-Fau. A Portrait of Pre-Islamic Civilisation in Saudi Arabia*, Croom Helm, London, 1982, 103-117.

early centuries AD works well with Qaryat al-Fau's *terminus ante quem* of the early 4th century AD.[33]

It is unfortunate that, as far as I am aware, the sculpture of king Muᶜāwiya b. Rabīᶜa has not been published. However, the present author saw the Muᶜāwiya statue *in situ* in 1973 and memory suggests that the stylistic association that al-Ansary makes with the world of Palmyra and Hatra is quite justified. Whether the sculpture itself was an import is less clear but the point should be considered. Al-Fau is a site of great eclecticism and as a caravan town with contacts with Syria and with al-ᶜIrāq as well as Yemen, it is conceivable that the Muᶜāwiya b. Rabīᶜa sculpture could have been carried to the site on a camel: alternatively, it was made by someone with a good knowledge of contemporary imagery in the north.

* * *

From Dūmat al-Jandal in the oasis of al-Jauf in northern Arabia there is another possible example of the import of a sacred sculpture. Ibn al-Kalbī records a sculpture there representing the deity Wadd.[34] Wadd was 'as big as the largest of human beings' and wore two robes, the one forming his inner clothing, the second his cloak. The figure carried a bow on his shoulder and a sword at his waist. In one hand he held a spear with a standard and in the other hand was a quiver for his arrows. The Wadd statue sounds like a military figure but we have no idea of its date nor its origin. Only the date of destruction is known to us, 9/630. There are any number of hunter or military sculptural traditions in Syria, al-ᶜIrāq and Iran, and there is no way that we can know if Wadd was indeed an import. If it was, it could have been associated stylistically with figurative art from the any of the margins of Arabia, from Nabataea, Palmyra, Dura Europos or Hatra, or with the Roman, Parthian or Sassanian traditions.[35]

It is worth finally considering whether any redundant pagan sculptures were imported into Arabia from the many overthrown in the late 4th/early 5th century AD in the Byzantine empire. In this period, the Byzantine emperor Theodosius II allowed free range to ferocious gangs of monks to eradicate the surviving temples of the near east, overturning the idolatrous statues of the old deities and destroying the street sculptures, redolent of the paganism that they so abhorred.[36] Did any of the toppled and broken sculptures that suddenly were unwanted in the towns of Byzantine Syria and Palestine make their way into Arabia where paganism was to survive intact and relatively unchallenged until the coming of the Prophet Muhammad and Islam? A slightly damaged statue, carried down to Makka on the back of a camel in a Quraish summer caravan, the Qur'ān's *rihlat al-sayf*, can be imagined being set up, repaired in gold and venerated as Hubal in the *Haram*. It is a tangible consequence of the Makkan trade that rings true.

BIBLIOGRAPHY

J ᶜAlī, *Al-mufassal fī ta'rīkh al-ᶜarab qabl Islām*, Baghdād, 1980, vol. 6.

A R al-Ansary, *Qaryat al-Fau. A Portrait of Pre-Islamic Civilisation in Saudi Arabia*, Croom Helm Ltd., London, 1982.

al-Azraqī's *Akhbār Makka*, ed. R S Malhas, 4th printing, *Matābiᶜ dār al-thaqāfa*, Makka, 1983/1403.

W Caskel, *Lihyan und Lihyanisch. Arbeitsgemeinschaft für Forschung des Landes Nordrhein-Westfalen*, Heft 4, Cologne, 1953.

J Chelhod, *Le Sacrifice chez les Arabes*, Paris, 1955.

K A C Creswell, *Early Muslim Architecture*, Clarendon Press, Oxford, 1969.

P Crone, *The Meccan Trade*, Blackwell, Oxford, 1987.

W Daum ed., *Yemen. 3000 Years of Art and Civilization in Arabia Felix*, Pinguin, Innsbruck and Frankfurt/Main, 1988.

B Doe, *Southern Arabia*, Thames and Hudson, London, 1971.

C M Doughty, *Travels in Arabia Deserta*, CUP, Cambridge, 1888.

T Fahd, *Le Panthéon de l'Arabie Centrale à la Veille de l'Hégire*, Paris, 1968.

O Grabar, *The Formation of Islamic Art*, Yale University Press, New Haven and London, 1973.

G R Hawting, *The Idea of Idolatry and the Emergence of Islam From Polemic to History*, CUP, Cambridge, 1999.

Ibn Saᶜd, *Biographie Muhammads (Kitāb al-Tabaqāt al-Kabīr)*, ed. E Mittwoch and E Sachau, Leiden, 1917.

33 Al-Ansary, *Qaryat al-Fau*, 29; communication, Dr Asem Barghouthi, al-Riyād, 29 May, 1987.

34 Ibn al-Kalbī, 49.

35 Examples of military deity figures are numerous and were widespread in Syria and al-ᶜIrāq in the Parthian and the Sasanian period. Examples are represented by Shadrafa of 55 AD in the British Museum; the Palmyrene gods in relief, like Aglibōl, Baalshamin and Malakbel in the Louvre, 1st century AD, R Ghirshman, *Iran. Parthes et Sassanides*, Librairie Gallimard, 1962, pl. 84; the figures in relief at the entrance to the temple of Bel/Baal at Palmyra, 1st century AD; a figure of Nergel from Hatra of the 2nd century AD in the Baghdād Museum (R Ghirshman, *Iran. Parthes et Sassanides*, pl. 98); and a Parthian figure of a prince from the Irān Bastān museum in Tehran of the 2nd century BC. Many others examples could be cited.

36 For the effects of the end of paganism on a specific urban context, see Yoram Tsafrir and Gideon Foerster, 'From Scythopolis to Baysān—Changing Concepts of Urbanism', in *The Byzantine and Early Islamic Near East II Land Use and Settlement Patterns*, ed. G R D King and A Cameron, Darwin Press, Princeton, 1994, 108-109.

A Jaussen and F Savignac, *Mission Archéologique en Arabie*, II, *El-ʿEla, d'Hégra à Teima, Harrah de Tebouk*, Le Roux, Paris, 1914.

Hishām b. al-Kalbī, *The Book of Idols (Kitāb al-Asnām)*, trans. into English from the Arabic by N A Faris, University Microfilms International, Princeton, NJ, 1952.

H Lammens, 'Le culte des bétyles et les processions religieuses chez les Arabes préislamites', *Bulletin de l'Institut français d'archéologie orientale*, t. xvii, 39-101.

G Levi Della Vida, 'Kusayy', *Encyclopaedia of Islam*, new ed. (EI^2).

U Monneret de Villard, 'L'arte degli Arabi in Syria avanti l'Islam', *Introduzione allo studio dell'archeoligia islamica*, San Giorgio Maggiore, Venice and Rome, 1966, 23-88.

W Montgomery Watt, 'Ḳuraysh', EI^2.

P J Parr, G L Harding and J E Dayton, 'Preliminary Survey in N.W. Arabia, 1968', *Bulletin of the Institute of Archaeology*, 1968-9, 8-9, 163-242.

U Rubin, 'The Kaʿba. Aspects of its ritual functions and position in pre-Islamic and early Islamic times', *Jerusalem Studies in Arabic and Islam* 8 (1986), 97-131.

G Ryckmans, *Les Religions arabes préislamiques*, Louvain (1951).

A I Sharīf, *Makka wa'l-Madina fi'l-jāhilīya wa'l-ʿahd al-rasūl, Dār al-fikr al-ʿarabī*, 1965.

Yoram Tsafrir and Gideon Foerster, 'From Scythopolis to Baysān—Changing Concepts of Urbanism', *The Byzantine and Early Islamic Near East II Land Use and Settlement Patterns*, ed. G R D King and A Cameron, Darwin Press, Princeton, 1994, 108-109.

J S Trimingham, *Christianity among the Arabs in Pre-Islamic Times*, Longman and Librairie du Liban, London and New York, 1979.

Al-Wāqidī, *Kitāb al-Maghāzī*, ed. M Jones, OUP, London and Cairo, 1966.

J Wellhausen, *Reste arabischen Heidentums*, Berlin, 1897.

Yāqūt al-Hamawī's *Muʿjam al-Buldān*, ed. F Wüstenfeld, as *Jacuts geographisches Wörterbuch*, Leipzig, 1866-1869.

14 THE SAMARRA BOWL WITH THE HALF-PALMETTE ANIMALS RECONSIDERED

Jens Kröger

This paper will deal with one of the finest glass fragments excavated in Samarra and published by C J Lamm, Das Glas von Samarra. *Berlin 1928, p. 77, fig. 50. The following is a new drawing and a discussion to try to place the dish within its context and analyse the iconography, as a tribute to Ralph Pinder-Wilson for his important contributions to our knowledge of Islamic glass and rock crystal.*

During the excavations undertaken by Ernst Herzfeld in the Jausaq palace of Samarra in 1912-13 seven fragments of a colourless glass bowl were excavated within the cupola hall of the harem. The decoration of the bowl consists of an animal running from left to right. It is repeated three times. One detail is very typical for this creature as a scroll-stem grows out of its mouth, describes a spiral and ends in a half-palmette (figs.14.1-2. pls.14.1-3).

The find was first published by Carl Johan Lamm in his catalogue of the Samarra glass. It was accompanied by a drawing by Ernst Herzfeld, who integrated six of the seven fragments. An additional plate shows five of the fragments.[1] Nearly a century after the excavation, these fragments still belong to one of the outstanding glass vessels of the ninth century. Therefore it seems worthwhile to reconsider this object of luxury in detail.

When Lamm published the bowl in 1928 he called it a *Prachtglas*[2] which shows that he recognised the extraordinary quality of this bowl. As most authors following him, he recognised the importance in connection with the Fatimid rock crystal vessels. Remarks by later authors show that all shared the view of the uniqueness of this bowl. Charleston in 1942 recognised the importance not only in the design and the fine cutting but also due to its being a datable work.[3] Honey in 1946 used words of highest praise 'The most admirable cut glass found at Samarra, however, consists of fragments, chiefly bowls, bearing strongly stylised decoration, often of animals and arabesque foliage ... This 9th century work is of extraordinary vitality and refinement, unsurpassed in the history of art ...'[4] Erdmann in 1953 mentioned the fragments of the bowl as belonging to the most beautiful glass fragment among the finds from the caliphal palace.[5] Pinder-Wilson equally saw these fragments as the most important relief-cut finds with figural design.[6] For Oliver they were a basis of her chronology of early Islamic cut glass.[7] Only recently, Contadini saw the fragments of the bowl in the tradition of pre-Islamic glass and rock crystal carving centres in Iraq.[8]

The seven fragments seen in the drawing (fig.14.1)[9] belonged to a bowl whose low side slopes inwards to a flat base (fig. 14.2). The fragments nos. 1 and 2 fit together. The height of their wall measures 60mm.[10] The rim was cut to a thinness of less than 1mm at the top of the rim. The inside of the upper wall has been ground down 15mm to produce a thin lip. This feature is typical for early Islamic relief-cut glass.[11] It may be an indication that the vessel was used as a drinking bowl. The diameter of the bowl can be reconstructed to 205mm. The thickness of the wall measures 1-2mm. A low foot-ring is found just at the place where the sides and the flat base meet. This foot-ring has a pattern of herringbone notches which already reminded Lamm of the

1 Lamm 1928, 77 nos. 243-4 (Inv.-no. 606) fig. 50 pl.VI. The fragments belong to the Samarra excavation finds within the Museum für Islamische Kunst, Staatliche Museen zu Berlin-Preußischer Kulturbesitz.

2 Lamm 1928, 62.

3 Charleston 1942, 215 fig. 3 and 5.

4 Honey 1946, 41.

5 Erdmann1953, 194-5 fig. 53.

6 Pinder-Wilson1963, 39 note 24.

7 Oliver 1961, 10. 28.

8 Contadini 1999, 324 fig. 4.

9 The fragments (fig.1) are counted from left to right, no. 7 being the piece set below the frieze.

10 No. 1 Height 31mm Width 38mm. Thickness of the wall 2mm. Thickness of the wall at the rim 15mm. Thickness of the relief 2mm. No. 2 Height 35mm Width 56mm. Thickness of the wall 2mm. Thickness of the base 15-2mm. No. 3 Height 36mm Width 34mm. No. 4 Height 47mm Width 33mm. No. 5 Height 34mm Width 57mm. No. 6 Length 24mm.

11 Lamm 1928, 68-9 no. 187 pl.V (the rim is cut 0.3-0.4cm but this detail is not mentioned by Lamm). cf. also Pinder-Wilson1963, 37 pl. XVIII. Kröger 1995, no. 182.

laurel wreath pattern used in the Samarra stuccoes.[12] The smallest fragment, no. 7, which is drawn below the frieze (fig. 14.1), belongs to this bowl due to the glass, and the pattern of the foot-ring.[13] Initially it seemed probable that it could have come from a second foot-ring somewhat nearer to the centre of the base (fig. 14.2). However, it now appears doubtful whether this is correct due to its slight concavity. Lamm's initial idea that it may not have belonged to this bowl could be correct.[14]

The shape of this bowl is very typical for a group of early Islamic relief-cut glass vessels. A similar shaped bowl datable to the 9th century was excavated in Fustat and published by Ralph Pinder-Wilson and George T Scanlon.[15] It too has a low side and a decoration of birds in roundels. A second cut glass bowl to be mentioned has an ornamental pattern. It was excavated in Dvin in Armenia and given an 8th-9th-century date. It was one of those glasses that were seen as an import to Dvin from the ʿAbbasid caliphate.[16] Both bowls show straight sides and have a foot-ring. They thus belong to a somewhat similar tradition and form a distinctive group. Among the pottery excavated in Samarra a related vessel form with a much higher wall is typical for lustre decorated dishes.[17]

The relief-cut decoration of the Samarra Bowl consists of a horizontal frieze between an upper ridge and the foot-ring of the vessel. The subject shown is an animal running from left to right. The creature has a scroll-stem growing out of its mouth which then describes a spiral and ends in a half-palmette. This subject is repeated three times. The animal cannot be precisely identified. It has a sort of mane with parallel notches but a horse is not meant. One fragment shows a leaf below a ridge. This must have been a part of the upper zone of the vessel and thus may have been meant as part of the ear of the animal. However, this detail is not very clear. The eye stands out as a flat circle. The tail is given with the same notches as the foot-ring. Only one foreleg and one hind leg are shown. The foreleg is characterized with a circle hollowed out and an additional line.[18] Both the outlines of the animal and the scroll have vertical notches (pl. 14.2).

The differences in details which result from the difficult process of cutting the subject out of the glass are obvious. As Charleston already wrote, 'the design is left in the relief by grinding away the surface of the vessel, while the fields of the figures so left are countersunk, and enlivened by hatching ...'[19]

Before the process of the relief-cut decoration began, the vessel had to be blown into a mold or was cast. The walls of the vessel are of an even thickness, remarkably regular and smooth on the inside. On all fragments except no. 7 numerous very thin horizontal lines in two bands (width 5mm) are noticeable on the inner surface. To grind down the wall of the bowl to such a thinness can only have been achieved in a glass workshop with master craftsmen. Numerous vessels must have broken in the process of grinding down parts of the surface of the glass in order to leave the patterned areas standing in relief. One can clearly see the marks of taking away the ground and cutting on the outer walls. At places longish grinding marks or flutes are to be seen. Measurements show a height of the relief of only 15-20mm.

The glass is colourless and nearly flawless. There is not a single impurity but a few tiny bubbles can be seen. An analysis has shown that the vessel is of glass and not of rock crystal.[20] Lamm used the incorrect term of *Kristallglas* or crystal clear glass for this and other colourless glass fragments.[21] Among the Samarra finds only a very limited number of fragments of cut glass has a similar colourless glass quality.[22] Although at least six of the seven fragments belong to one bowl, their state of preservation is very different. The two larger fragments, nos. 1 and 2, show a brownish patina, doubtless due to soil conditions. Such a patina is absent on the other pieces which stand out due to their clarity.

The purity of the colourless glass of these fragments gives the vessel a very special place in the discussion of the relationship between glass and rock crystal. Lamm and Erdmann[23] saw the fragments of the Samarra

12 Herzfeld 1923, 125 (Orn. 177a) and 217-222 (Orn. 276).

13 No. 7 Length 37mm Width 15mm. Thickness of the wall 2mm. Thickness at the foot-ring 3mm. Width of the foot-ring 2.5-3mm.

14 Lamm 1928, no. 244.

15 Pinder-Wilson and Scanlon 1973, 26-7 no. 20 (Diam. 21cm).

16 Janpoladian 1974, 53 pl. 9. Lamm 1928, nos. 243-246 are given as close parallels.

17 Sarre 1925, no. 155 pl. XVI.

18 The eye of an animal on another Samarra relief-cut fragment is shown in this way cf. Lamm 1928, no. 245 pl. VI. Kröger1995, 143 fig. 10.

19 Charleston 1942, 215.

20 The glass was analyized by the Rathgen-Forschungslabor of the Staatliche Museen zu Berlin-Preußischer Kulturbesitz on March 10, 2000. The result in German was the following: 'Ein Kali-Kalk-Glas, ein kalziumhaltiges Glas mit Pottasche als Flußmittel'. I would like to thank J Riederer for his kind help in this matter.

21 Lamm 1928, 51. According to him this glass dominated the groups D and H of the cut and engraved glass. The term Kristallglas was taken up by Erdmann1953, 194-5.

22 Lamm 1928, nos. 234 and 242. A further fragment with remains of an animal running to the right is without number. The stylistically related fragments nos. 245 and 246 (pl. VI) have a greenish tinge. Identical in glass and fine cut is the handle Lamm 1928, no. 189.

23 Erdmann 1953, 194.

Bowl as a predecessor of Fatimid rock crystal vessels. For Contadini the fragments of the bowl served as an indication of 'a survival of a late pre-Islamic tradition of rock crystal and glass carving in Iraq into the early Islamic period'.[24] All scholars seem to agree that the Samarra Bowl sets the highest standards of an Islamic glass production. We still know relatively little about the relationship of sophisticated glass and rock crystal in Iraq during the 9th century but the Samarra Bowl with the half-palmette animals must have been an outstanding work of art at its time. There is no reason to believe that bowls of rock crystal should have had a higher estimation.[25] Indeed, it is possible that most admirers looking at the Samarra Bowl would not have seen a difference from rock crystal. While one should not think of purposeful deceit it certainly is obvious that the workmanship was on the same lines as if had been rock crystal.[26]

A stylistic comparison with some other fragments of cut glass excavated in Samarra shows a number of similarities. Those fragments that have ornamental subjects seem to come closer than those with figural depictions. The half-palmette leaf is found in a similar stylised form on fragments which belong to a vessel of greenish glass.[27] The animals[28] on a further Samarra fragment are stylistically different from the half-palmette animals.

Lamm, Charleston and Erdmann all saw the Samarra Bowl as a precursor of the Buckley Ewer[29] due to the glass quality and the animals. Apart from a general relationship of finely engraved vessels, there are precise differences of style. The Buckley Ewer and the Samarra Bowl were cut in different ateliers. Perhaps the stylistic differences are those between Mesopotamian and Iranian ateliers. Both the notches, the mane of the animals and the dot-like protruding eyes on the Samarra Bowl can be found on vessels said to be from Iran and datable to the 9th-10th centuries.[30] It was Erdmann who mentioned the fact that the art of the ᶜAbbasid period in Iraq had closer links with Iran and that certain objects such as the Buckley glass bowl can be seen in a continuity of Sasanian silver plates.[31]

The motif of animals which have plants growing from their mouth is familiar in Sasanian and early Islamic art. Both the *senmurv* and the griffin are two fantastic animals which are characterised in such a fashion.[32] On the late Umayyad facade of the palace of Mshatta both animals appear affronting a vase, but only the *senmurv* has a plant growing out of its mouth.[33] A later and possibly ᶜAbbasid example is the silver gilded plate in the British Museum with a *senmurv*.[34] The half-palmette animals are thus a continuation of this theme.

The more complex iconography of the Buckley Ewer[35] is of special importance for the Samarra Bowl, as the palmette tree in the centre of the vessel sends its branches toward the mouth of the birds and towards the ibexes. A somewhat enigmatic feature is the connection of the branches to the eyes of the ibexes. However, it is obvious that the general motif is a variant of the tree of life theme.[36] Due to this example the half-palmette animals on the Samarra Bowl can be understood as a short version of the tree of life subject. Such an abbreviation of a more complex motif is also found on early Islamic stucco plaques in Sasanian tradition[37] and thus seems to be a feature typical for early Islamic art.

Whether and to what extent the Sasanian connotation of fertility and the growth of plants was still present in the early Islamic period is difficult to decide. It may also be valid for the Islamic period that ' a design that signifies abundance and life is appropriate for an object of luxury that may have been used at banquets'.[38]

The fragments of the Samarra Bowl with half-palmette animals were excavated in the cupola hall of the harem of the Jausaq Palace. This palace was built in 836 for the ᶜAbbasid caliph al-Muᶜtasim and was a ruin in the time of the caliph al-Muktafi in 903. The conclusions reached by Sarre and Herzfeld on dating the finds to the 9th century are still valid.[39]

The Jausaq Palace was of great importance for the glass finds. Among them are also the fragments of the *millefiori* glass-tiles.[40] As Northedge has recently shown, the largest quantities of pottery also came from this palace.[41] Lamm already mentioned that the glass finds from the

[24] Contadini 1999, 324 fig. 4.

[25] Cf. Stern 1997, 192-206 on the matter of estimation in antiquity. For the Islamic period cf. Shalem 1996, 58-60.

[26] This was already noted by Pinder-Wilson, Some rock crystals 84.

[27] Lamm 1928, no. 246 pl.VI.

[28] Lamm 1928, no. 245 pl.VI. Kröger1995, 143 fig. 10.

[29] Lamm, 1939, 2597 pl. 1441. Erdmann 1953, 191-2 fig.50. Contadini 1999, 323 pl. 44.

[30] Kröger 1995, 141 fig.9. 140-142 no. 193.

[31] Erdmann 1953, 194-198.

[32] Kröger 1999, 201-202 pl. xxviii,2.

[33] Kröger 1999, pl. xxviii,2.

[34] *Splendeur des Sassanides* 1993, no. 71. Kröger 1999, 201-202 pl. xxviii.

[35] Lamm 1939, 2597 pl.1441. Contadini 1999, pl.44.

[36] For the late Sasanian stucco version of this theme cf. *Splendeurs des Sassanides* 1993, no. 7.

[37] Kröger 1998, 333.

[38] Harper 1978, 46 no. 10.

[39] Northedge 1996, 241.

[40] Lamm 1928, 109 nos. 304-312.

[41] Northedge 1996, 236.

Balkuwara palace built in 851-859 and the private houses were less important [42].

Within the Jausaq palace the cupola hall of the harem was a place were a number of other glass finds were made, though not all of them are of the same quality as the bowl with the running animals.[43] Because a more exact location of the findspot and stratigraphic considerations are absent, the find-spot can only be taken as a general indication that the vessels were used within the caliphal residences. As has been shown, this certainly applies to the bowl with the half-palmette animals which we may justly consider as a work worthy of the ᶜAbbasid empire in its zenith.

BIBLIOGRAPHY

Charleston, R J (1942): 'A Group of Near Eastern Glasses', in *The Burlington Magazine* September, 212-218.

Contadini, A (1999): 'The Cutting Edge', in *L'Egypte Fatimide. Son art et son histoire* (M. Barrucand ed.), Paris, 319-329.

Erdmann, K (1953): 'Die fatimidischen Bergkristallkannen', in *Forschungen zur Kunstgeschichte und christlichen Archäologie*, vol. 2, Baden-Baden, 189-205.

Harper, P. O. (1978): The Royal Hunter. Art of the Sasanian empire. New York.

Herzfeld, E (1923): *Der Wandschmuck der Bauten von Samarra und seine Ornamentik*. Berlin.

Honey, W B (1946): *A Handbook for the study of glass vessels of all periods and countries & a guide to the Museum collection*. London.

Janpoladian, H M (1974): *The Medieval Glassware of Dvin*. (The Archaeological Monuments and Specimens of Armenia No. 7) Yerevan.

Kröger, J (1995): *Nishapur. Glass of the Early Islamic Period*. New York.

Kröger, J (1998): 'Die Reliefplatten aus Chal Tarkhan-Eshqabad mit Enten und Weinblättern im sasanidischen Stil in der Abegg-Stiftung', *Riggisberger Berichte* 6, 323-334.

Kröger, J (1999): 'Vom Flügelpaar zur Flügelpalmette. Sasanidische Motive in der islamischen Kunst', in *Rezeption in der islamischen Kunst, B. Finster-Chr.* Fragner-H Hafenrichter eds., Beirut (Beiruter Texte und Studien), 193-204.

Lamm, C J (1928): *Das Glas von Samarra*. Die Ausgrabungen von Samarra Bd. 4. Berlin.

Lamm, C J (1939): 'Glass and Hard Stone Vessels', in: *A Survey of Persian Art* (A U Pope ed.), London and New York. vol. 3, 2592-2606, vol. 6 pl. 1439-54.

Northedge, A (1996): 'Friedrich Sarre's *Die Keramik von Samarra* in Persepective' in *Continuity and Change in Northern Mesopotamia from the Hellenistic to the early Islamic period*, K Bartl-S R Hauser (eds.), Berlin, 229-258.

Oliver, P (1961): 'Islamic Relief Cut Glass: A Suggested Chronology', *Journal of Glass Studies* 3, 9-29.

Pinder-Wilson, R H (1954): 'Some rock crystals of the Islamic period', *British Museum Quarterly* 9, 84-7.

Pinder-Wilson, R H (1963): 'Cut-Glass Vessels from Persia and Mesopotamia', *British Museum Quarterly* 27, 33-9.

Pinder-Wilson, R H and Scanlon, G T (1973): 'Glass finds from Fustat: 1964-71', *Journal of Glass Studies* 15, 12-30.

Sarre, F (1925): *Die Keramik von Samarra*. Berlin.

Shalem, A (1996): *Islam christianized: Islamic portable objects in the medieval church treasuries of the Latin West*. Frankfurt am Main.

Splendeurs des Sassanides. L'empire perse entre Rome et la Chine 224-642 (1993). Musées royaux d'Art et d'Histoire, Bruxelles.

Stern, E M (1997): 'Glass and rock crystal: A multifaceted relationship', *Journal of Roman Archaeology* 10, 192-206.

[42] Lamm 1928, 4-5 'An allen Plätzen, wo im Jausaq genauere Ausgrabungen stattfanden, aber ganz besonders in dem südlich von den Vor- und Thronsälen gelegenen Harem, wurde Glas gefunden. Ein Vergleich mit den in Privathäusern gefundenen Gläsern zeigt deutlich, daß die feineren Gattungen ganz besonders im Khalifenschloß gebraucht wurden.'

[43] Lamm 1928, nos. 123. 129. 141. 182. 208. 209. 234. 241. 259. 277.

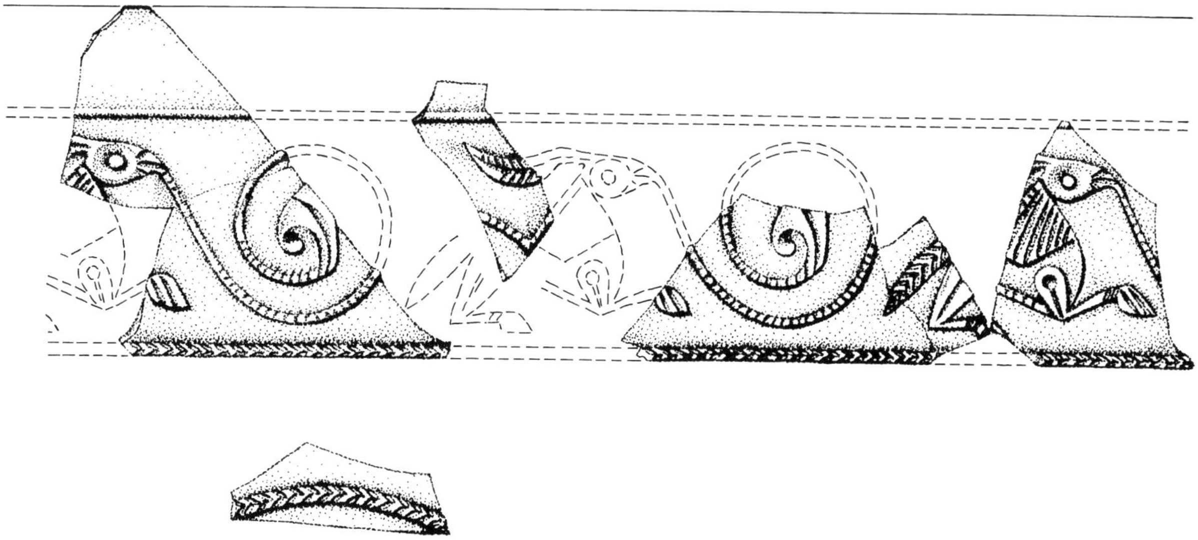

Fig. 14.1 Glass bowl with relief-cut decoration. Reconstruction of decorated frieze. Samarra, Iraq. First half 9th century (Drawing by K Kitt)

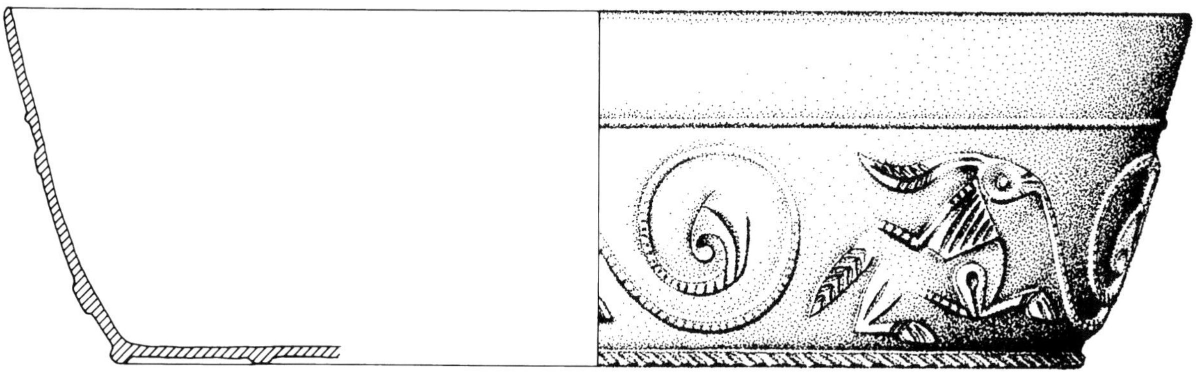

Fig. 14.2 Glass bowl with relief-cut decoration. Reconstruction of shape. Samarra, Iraq. First half 9th century. (Drawing by K Kitt)

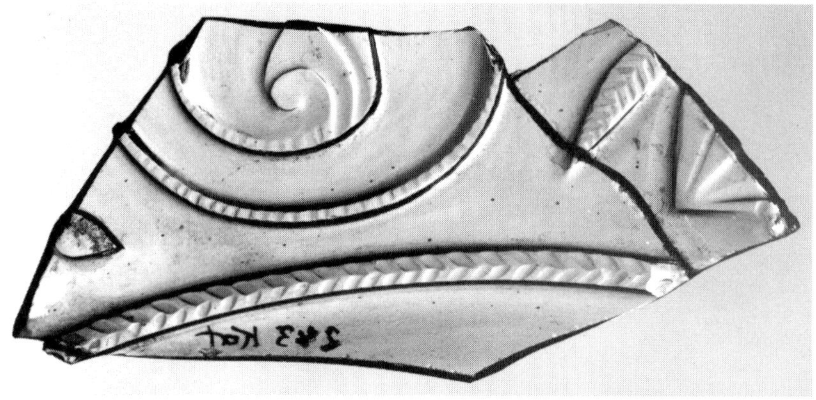

Plate 14.1 Fragment of glass bowl with relief-cut decoration. Samarra, Iraq. First half 9th century. Staatliche Museen zu Berlin-Preußischer Kulturbesitz Museum für Islamische Kunst Photograph by P Grunwald)

Plate 14.2 Fragment of glass bowl with relief-cut decoration. Samarra, Iraq. First half 9th century. Staatliche Museen zu Berlin-Preußischer Kulturbesitz Museum für Islamische Kunst (Photograph by P Grunwald)

Plate 14.3 Fragments of glass bowl with relief-cut decoration.Samarra, Iraq. First half 9th century. Staatliche Museen zu Berlin Preußischer Kulturbesitz Museum für Islamische Kunst (Photograph by G Niedermeiser)

15 THE ARMENIANS OF KABUL AND AFGHANISTAN

Jonathan L Lee

Afghanistan, whilst predominantly a Muslim country, has been for many centuries the home for four[1] religious minorities; Jews, Hindus, Sikhs and Armenian Christians.[2] As far as the Armenians are concerned, though they appear occasionally in the annals of European travellers there has been very little attempt to write a systematic history of this remote Christian community.[3]

The Afghan Armenians acted as brokers for the overland trade between Europe, Central Asia and India for, as non-Muslims, they were permitted to take and receive interest on loans from Muslims. As active merchants themselves, they played a major role in the overland trade, having close links with fellow-countrymen in India, Bukhara, Iran (in particular, Julfa, the Armenian suburb of Isfahan) and the Ottoman empire.[4] However, with the rise of European imperialism in the 17th century, and the expansion of the East India Company, the overland trade routes declined with the opening up of faster sea routes.[5]

It is not known exactly when the first Armenians settled in what is today Afghanistan. 19th century sources state that the colony in Kabul, which was by far the largest Armenian community in Afghanistan, was settled there by Nadir Shah Afshar (d. 1747) following his wars with Turkey in c. 1735[6] in order to stimulate trade in the empire.[7] Others say they came later, being brought to Kabul by Ahmad Shah Durrani (d. 1773) from either Mashhad[8] or Lahore.[9]

In fact Armenians had settled in Afghanistan decades before the conquests of Nadir Shah. In *c.* 1670 Jesuit missionaries in Agra learnt from Armenian merchants from Kabul that certain tribes of Kafiristan (now Nuristan) at one time professed the Christian faith. As a consequence, Benedict de Goës travelled through Afghanistan and from thence to China to ascertain the truth of these reports.[10] At the time the Armenian colony in Kabul was 'thriving',[11] which suggests that the community was already well established. By 1707 the Kabuli Armenians had obtained special privileges from the Mughal authorities, including 'complete freedom of movement, freedom from restrictions on dress, and reductions of various taxes'.[12]

In or around 1737 Nadir Shah resettled some 200-300 Armenian merchants in Afghanistan,[13] whilst Ahmad Shah (ruled 1747-1773) brought a further fifty

1 V Gregorian, 1969, *The Emergence of Modern Afghanistan*, Stanford, 61 refers to only three religious minorities and omits the Sikhs.

2 A number of other Christians lived in Afghanistan prior to the 20th century. During the 17th century some 12,000 Georgian cavalrymen garrisoned Qandahar for the Safawids, Gregorian, 431, n. 67. In the following century, the Georgian Prince, Giorgi XI of Katli, with a garrison of Georgian troops, also governed Qandahar for the Safawids. In Kabul in the 1790s, there was at least one Georgian called 'Bagdasir', G A Forster, 1808 (2nd ed.), *A Journey from Bengal to England*, London, ii, 92, 115. There was also the grave of a Georgian bishop, who died sometime in 15th/16th century on Kabul's Koh-i Asmayi, C. Masson, 1842 (reprint Delhi, 1997), *Narrative of various Journeys in Balochistan, Afghanistan, and the Panjab*, London, ii, 275. In *c.* 1808, there was a native of Constantinople, who 'professed the Catholic religion' who had lived in Kabul for 'ten or twenty years' and a Catholic priest of Greek descent in the same city, M Elphinstone, 1815, *An Account of the Kingdom of Caubul*, London, i, 266-7. The grave of an Englishman, Henry Khan, who had married an Armenian woman from Kabul, was located in the Armenian cemetery in Kabul, C Masson, *Journal*, 1 July 1832-14 July 1833, entry under 18 May 1833, British Library, Oriental and India Collection [hence, OIC], Mss. Eur. E163.11 fol. 19B.

3 Gregorian, 61-5, has a short section; the best account is M J Seth, 1937 (reprint, New Delhi, 1992), *Armenians in India*, Calcutta, 207-24.

4 Gregorian, 61-2; M J Seth, 1926, *Armenians and the East India Company*, Calcutta.

5 Seth, *Armenians and the East India Company*. There were, though, other factors. Political unrest, following the break up of the Saffawid Empire, led to increased insecurity of the roads, in particular, Turkman raids on trading caravan in Iranian Khurasan.

6 See L Lockhart, 1938, *Nadir Shah*, London, 75, 87.

7 Cf. Forster, ii, 87; I N Allen, 1843, *Diary of a march through Sinde and Afghanistan*, London, 312-3; A Burnes, 1834, *Travels into Bukhara*, London, i, 148; J A Grey, 1895, *At the Court of the Amir*, London, 209.

8 J Wolff, 1835, *Researches and Missionary Labours*, London, 225-6.

9 Forster, ii, 67; Seth, *Armenians in India*, 207; Masson, *Journal*, 1 July 1832-14 July 1833, entry under 5 June 1883.

10 Seth, *Armenians in India*, 207; Col. Sir H Yule, 1916, *Cathay and the Way Thither*, vol. 4, Hakluyt Society, series II, no. XLI, , 226.

11 Gregorian, 65; Seth, *Armenians in India*, 222.

12 Gregorian, 65.

13 Allen, 312-3; Gregorian, 66.

families from Mashhad.[14] By the end of the 18th century, Armenians were living in Kabul, Qandahar and Herat[15] with trade connections with the Caucasus, the Central Asian Khanates and northern India.[16] In 1755, Ahmad Shah engaged Armenian gunners from Lahore, some of whom were skilled in the art of cannon casting.[17] These Lahori Armenians served as *Janissaries* in Ahmad Shah's bodyguard, accompanying him on military expeditions.[18] They continued to be employed in the same capacity by his son, Timur Shah (d. 1793), though by the time of his death they had lost much of their influence and fallen into penury[19] or drunkenness.[20] The position of these Armenian soldiers declined further in the following two decades as power in Afghanistan shifted from the Sadozai to the Barakzais.[21] Those Armenians still martially inclined, either returned to the Caucasus or found work as mercenaries—one Kabuli Armenian being employed as such by Ranjit Singh.[22]

The Armenian quarter (*mahalla*) of Kabul was located inside Kabul's Bala Hissar.[23] It consisted of a single street of shops, with at least one *sarai* situated on the north side of the main street behind the Jalalabad Gate.[24] In an alley to the left, in a *sarai*-style courtyard, was the Armenians' church, probably established in the latter half of the 18th century.[25] This 'small, dark building', which did not hold even one hundred persons,[26] was carpeted and kept spotlessly clean.[27] The altar, near the east wall, was located on a raised dais and separated from the congregation by a railing. On the altar were six candlesticks,[28] two small crosses and two copies of the gospels.[29] On the east wall was an icon of the Holy Family, whilst on a small lectern outside of the altar rails, lay a book of daily prayers in Armenian.[30] In May 1832, Revd Dr Joseph Wolff preached in the church during his visit to the Afghan capital.[31]

Under the Sadozai Amirs, the Armenians enjoyed the protection of powerful individuals such as Wazir Fatteh Khan and were accorded full rights as citizens of Afghanistan and religious toleration.[32] Later, under the Barakzais, however, they suffered periodic harassment and persecution.[33] After the middle of the 1820s the community did not have the services of a priest[34] but retained their Christian identity. The Armenians, however, adopted Afghan names, spoke Persian rather than Armenian,[35] and observed local customs by removing shoes and weapons before entering their church.[36] Their Muslim neighbours accorded them great respect and Armenians accompanied the bodies of Muslims to the cemetery, gave gifts at Nauroz and ʿId and received them during Easter and Christmas.[37] At Easter one of the local Armenian customs was to visit their burial ground and say prayers over the graves.[38] In May, the Thursday before

[14] Burnes, *Travels*, i, 148; Forster, ii, 87; Wolff, 225-6.

[15] Forster, ii, 115, 132-3; Masson is wrong to claim that: 'In Khandahar there are no Armenians or Jews,' *Private Notes of Mr Masson as drawn up from Memory*, OIC, Mss. Eur. B218, fol. 44.

[16] Gregorian, 66.

[17] Seth, *Armenians in India*, 207. The famous Zamzam gun, which featured in Kipling's, *Kim*, was cast by an Armenian, Seth, *Armenians in India,* 115-8, 128.

[18] Forster, ii, 87; Seth, *Armenians in India*, 115-8, 128.

[19] Cf. Burnes, i, 149; Forster, ii, 87; Ganda Singh, 1959, *Ahmad Shah Durrani,* Bombay, 340; Wolff, 225-6; Masson, *Journal, 1832-1833,* entry under 5 June 1833.

[20] Elphinstone, i, 266-7.

[21] Burnes, i, 148-50.

[22] Wolff, 226.

[23] Masson, ii, 255.

[24] *Ibid.,* Allen, 312, Masson, *Private Notes*, fol. 32.

[25] Forster, ii, 186-7; Gregorian, 66; Grey, 209. It is not possible to state exactly when the church was built, but the influx of Armenians in the reigns of Nadir Shah and Ahmad Shah would seem to be the logical point when the community was granted its own place of worship.

[26] Burnes, i, 150.

[27] Allen, 311-2.

[28] When the Armenian community was expelled in 1896 (see below), they brought some of the sacred vessels from their church to Peshawar and manuscripts 'of rare antiquity', Seth, *Armenians in India*, 218-20, quoting from the *Englishman*, 11 Feb. 1907 (however, this date is wrong as no such notice appears in this edition of the newspaper). Until recently, two of the silver candlesticks were displayed near the altar of the Peshawar Mission Hospital church. In *c.* 1977, Revd Dr D Woodberry, then minister of the Community Christian Church of Kabul (an expatriate Protestant church) asked the Peshawar Mission Hospital Church to donate the candlesticks to the newly-built Protestant Church in Kabul. Fortunately they were not handed over, for the church was later demolished by the Afghan government, Revd Dr D Woodberry, *personal communication*, October 2000.

[29] In 1849, an elderly Kabuli Armenian, Yusuf Khan, arrived in Calcutta with some manuscripts for sale, including a rare copy of the Armenian New Testament. His asking price was too high and he returned to Kabul with the volume unsold, Seth, *Armenians in India*, 220.

[30] Allen, 311-2, they also had a copy of the Oxford English pocket Bible in the church and claimed to possess a prophetic book written by 'Meiden Nerses, Patriarch of Ech-Miazin', see, Wolff, 227.

[31] Wolff, 226-8.

[32] Cf. Burnes, ii, 124; Elphinstone, ii, 266-7; J. Harlan, 1939, *Central Asia; a personal narrative of General Josiah Harlan, 1823-41*, ed., F E Ross, London, 66; Masson, ii, 244, 247; Wolff, 227.

[33] Allen, 313.

[34] Allen, 314; Seth, *Armenians in India*, 208.

[35] At the marriage of Dr Grey, his Armenian servant signed his name in the register in Persian, not Armenian, Grey, 44, 452.

[36] Allen, 316; Burnes, i, 150.

[37] Masson, ii, 246.

[38] Masson, *Journal*, 1832-1833, fol. 163, entry under 13, 14 April 1833, though Masson wrongly claims they were celebrating Ascension Day, which actually falls in mid-end May, or 40 days after Easter (see n. 40 below).

the Feast of the Ascension, the Armenian women also celebrated the ancient festival of 'Mother of Flowers' (*Calkamor ton*).[39] Masson, records how:

> ... the females place rings or other trinkets in a vessel filled with roses and flowers, they sing hymns over it, and then as it were draw lots, by which they prognosticate good or bad fortune for the succeeding year—This is in imitation of the apostles who as they say drew lots to ascertain in what countries each should circulate the tidings of the Gospel.[40]

The Armenians of Kabul had their own graveyard, located, according to Masson, 'directly opposite the 'takia' or shrine of Shir Ali Lapchak'[41] near the shrine of Khwaja Khizr. Surrounded by Muslim burial grounds, this cemetery was encompassed by a low, dry stone wall.[42] Burnes noted several inscriptions, presumably in Persian, which confirm that Armenians lived in Kabul before the reign of Ahmad Shah Durrani.[43] One headstone, in the form of a mitre, indicated that at least one priest was buried there.[44] Unfortunately, though Masson sketched the 'Ziyarat of Kheddar',[45] he made no drawings of the graveyard or its inscriptions. In the portfolio of the war photographer, John Burke, taken in 1879, there is an image entitled 'Armenian burying place, tomb near Bala Hissar',[46] which shows a low, walled enclosure encompassing some ancient trees and one or two unreadable headstones. Behind the graveyard is a burnt brick, domed shrine which is completely different architecturally to Masson's sketch of the shrine of Khwaja Khizr.[47] Furthermore, neither Masson's drawing, nor Burke's photograph, bears much resemblance to the present-day shrine of Khwaja Khizr. Thus, so far, it has not been possible to locate the Armenian cemetery in Kabul.[48]

By the early 1830s, the Armenian community of Kabul, which in its heyday comprised some 500 people,[49] had dwindled to some twenty to twenty-five individuals; four male heads of households and their wives and children.[50] Due to economic circumstances, the Armenians relied increasingly on the distillation and sale of wines and spirits,[51] which were enjoyed by Muslim and Christian alike.[52] Thus when, in 1826 Dost Muhammad Khan became Amir of Kabul and banned the drinking of alcohol by the Muslim population, this was another body blow to a community already in decline.[53] The increased political involvement of the British and other European powers in the affairs of Afghanistan, however, meant that the Armenians were able to supplement their income by hosting visiting foreign Christians[54] and acting as translators for them.[55] This involvement with European imperialism expanded when, in 1839, the 'Army of the Indus' entered Kabul and placed Shah Shuja^c al-Mulk[56] on the Afghan throne. During the period of the occupation of Afghanistan

39 For the traditions of this festival see, J R Russell, 1987, *Zoroastrianism in Armenia*, Harvard Iranian Series, V, 375-8. In another place I have argued for a link between 'Mother of Flowers', another ancient Armenian festival, that of Vardavar, and the New Year festival of Gul-i Surkh, celebrated in Balkh during March-April, see J L Lee, *The New Year's Festivals and the Shrine of cAli ibn Abi Talib at Mazar-i Sharif, Afghanistan*, unpublished PhD. thesis, Dept. of Theology and Religious Studies, University of Leeds, September 1998, 168-79.

40 In 1833 'Mother of Flowers' was celebrated by the Armenians on 22 May, Masson, again, mistakenly refers to this as the Feast of Ascension, Masson, *Journal,* fol. 20b, entry under 23 May 1833.

41 Masson, ii, 274, but no such shrine is known to the present *mutawalis* of Khwaja Khizr or Panja-yi Shah-i Mardan, but in the autograph the reading 'takia' is doubtful, see Masson, *Journal,* 1832-1833, fol. 12b, entry under 2 June 1833. In the autograph journal, Masson gives a different location for the graveyard, to the right of the road leading to the shrine of Panj-i Shah-i Mardan on the way to 'Killa Aga Yaqut', (a place which also appears to no longer be known), Masson, *Journal,* fol. 17b, entry under 3 May 1833.

42 Burnes, i, 248-9; Masson, ii, 274-5.

43 Burnes, i, 248-9.

44 Masson, ii, 275.

45 Masson, *Sketches and Drawings*, OIC, Eur. Mss F.64, no. 120 [IOR Neg. 20861].

46 *John Day Photographic Collection*, OIC, Photo 98/16; but another copy in the OIC merely reads, 'Tomb near Bala Hissar' *Curzon Photographic Collection* 'Afghan War 1878-79', OIC, Photo 430/2.

47 Burke's photograph bears more resemblance to one or other of the *gunbad*-style Timurid shrines which lie further down the Sher Darwaza hills, north and west of the present road to Panja-yi Shah-i Mardan. Given Burke's lack of local knowledge, it is possible he mistook one of these buildings for the shrine of Khwaja Khizr and hence his photograph is not of the Armenian graveyard at all.

48 The shrine of Khwaja Khizr today consists of a single storied, mud roof building dating, at the earliest, from the 1920s, when the present *mutawali's* family took charge.

49 Gregorian, 430, n. 62; Seth, *Armenians in India*, 208, quoting from a letter of Amir ^{c}Abd al-Rahman Khan to the Armenians of Calcutta, 1896.

50 Wolff, 226; Burnes, i, 149 has 21 persons. A decade or so later, the community had increased to 35 persons, Allen, 312-3.

51 Allen, 313; Burnes, i, 148-50.

52 Masson, ii, 246. Fatteh Khan (d. 1803), Wazir to Shah Mahmud Sadozai (reigned in Kabul 1800-1803 and 1809-1817), was more than a little partial to the Armenian wines, Masson, *Journal*, fol. 19A, entries under 17 and 18 May 1833.

53 Burnes, i, 148-50; Masson, ii, 246-7; Wolff, 226.

54 Burnes, i, 150; Masson, ii, 245; Wolff, 226.

55 Masson, *Journal,* fol. 12B, entry for 13 July 1832.

56 Seth, *Armenians in India*, 224, on the basis of a coin inscription attributed to Shah Shuja^c al-Mulk which is mentioned in the *Tarikh-i Sultani* of Sultan Muhammad Khan, transl. J Rodgers, 1888, *Journal of the Royal Asiatic Society of Bengal*, LVII/I, claims that Shah Shuja^c had an

by the British-Sikh army, two Armenian merchants 'were instrumental in procuring provisions' for the force.[57] The community, who had not had a priest for many years,[58] asked the British army chaplains to conduct baptismal services and on two separate occasions Revd G Piggott and Revd I N Allen, performed this sacrament in their church, using the Anglican rite.[59]

Following the British withdrawal in 1842, the Armenians' fortunes continued to decline. By 1847 another of their families had left and the community was reduced to twelve individuals.[60] In this same year, Dost Muhammad Khan's second son, Sardar Muhammad A^c^zam Khan, fell in love with one of the daughters of Timur, a Kabuli Armenian. Timur, however, opposed the union and, fearing the girl would be taken by force, the community appealed to Major Lawrence, British Political Agent in Peshawar, to intervene.[61] In response, Lawrence wrote 'privately and friendly to the Amir ... to request his interference on their behalf'.[62] Dost Muhammad Khan too, initially opposed the marriage, but by the summer of 1848 he had given his consent to the marriage, after having 'satisfied himself that the girl was willing.'[63]

Following the death of Dost Muhammad Khan in 1862, Afghanistan plunged into a bitter civil war. In 1867, A^c^zam Khan assumed the Amirship in Kabul after the death of his elder brother, Afzal Khan. He ruled less than a year, being deposed by another brother, Sher ^c^Ali Khan and fled to India, where he died shortly afterwards. In 1868, A^c^zam's son by Timur's daughter, Sardar Ishaq Khan, fled to Samarkand where he supported the claims of his half cousin, ^c^Abd al-Rahman Khan.[64] During the reign of Sher ^c^Ali Khan (1868-1879) the Armenians again found themselves on the wrong side of the political divide. Their association, by marriage, with Ishaq Khan appears to have led to occasional harsh treatment. Seth even claims the Amir tried to forcibly convert them and turn their church into a mosque.[65] More certainly, we know that in *c.* 1870 several Armenians[66] were imprisoned and were subsequently released 'through the intercession of the missionary at Peshawar'.[67] It is likely, however, that this persecution was political rather than religious, for in this year the Amir imprisoned Ishaq Khan's mother, accusing her of fomenting disturbances in Kabul.[68]

The Armenians' association with the CMS missionaries in Peshawar, implied by their intervention in the case of Ishaq Khan's mother, was well established by the 1870s. The Peshawar Mission Report for 1870-71 states that one Kabuli Armenian had been educated in the Mission school and had a 'fair knowledge of English'.[69] It was probably this individual who later acted as translator for Dr Grey during his residence in Kabul.[70] The report continues that whilst the Armenians 'have not been able to make much effect towards the spread of Christianity,' on two occasions they had referred Muslim 'enquirers' to Peshawar and records how a certain robber, after an unsuccessful attempt to steal the church plate, had 'delivered himself up to the Armenians and begged for Christian baptism'.[71]

Following the fall of Sher ^c^Ai Khan in 1879 and the occupation of Kabul and Southern Afghanistan by British troops, Kabul's Armenians could be forgiven for thinking that their fortunes had turned. However, the reverse was the case. On 16 October 1879, the magazine in the Upper Bala Hissar exploded and all but destroyed the fortress' ancient bazaar,[72] its royal residences,[73] the

Armenian mother. However, the inscription, which declares the Amir to be the 'light of the eyes of Lord Burnes and the dust of the feet of the Company' (*nur-i chashm-i lard burnz, khak-i pai-yi kampany*) is a manifest forgery and doubtless struck by Shah Shuja^c^'s enemies.

57 Lady F Sale, 1843, *A Journal of the Disasters in Afghanistan*, London, 58.

58 Their priests were appointed by the Archbishop of Julfa, Seth, *Armenians in India*, 208. It may be that the mitred tomb in the Armenian cemetery was that of the last Armenian priest to minister to this community, see Masson, ii, 275.

59 Allen, 311-5; Seth, *Armenians in India*, 222-3. Allen baptised by full immersion.

60 Political Diary of Maj. G. Lawrence, 1-7 Aug. 1847, *Punjab Government Records, Lahore Political Diaries, 1846-1849*, vol. IV, 378.

61 *Ibid*; Political Diary of Maj. G. Lawrence, 8-14 Aug. 1847, 4-10 June 1848, *PGR, LPD, 1846-1849,* vol. IV, 380, 498.

62 *Id*.

63 *Id*; Political Diary of Maj. G Lawrence, 30 July-5 Aug. 1848, *PGR, LPD, 1846-1849*, IV, 528. Two more sons of Dost Muhammad Khan expressed an interest in marrying two other of Timur's daughters, though nothing seems to have come of this, Political Diary of Maj. G Lawrence, 13-19 Aug. 1848, *PGR, LPD, 1846-1849*, IV 537.

64 J L Lee, 1992, *The 'Ancient Supremacy', Bukhara, Afghanistan and the Battle for Balkh, 1732-1901*, Leiden, 317-8, 340-1.

65 Seth, *Armenians in India*, 223.

66 'Some Account of the Armenian Christians in the City of Cabul', Appendix to, *CMS Peshawar Mission Report,* 1870-71, extracts(?) of which are published in Seth, *Armenians in India*, 208, which says the Kabul Armenians consisted of 6 males and 12 females. However, under the census organised by Sher ^c^Ali Khan, the total number of Armenians in Afghanistan was put at 100 persons, see Government of India, 1895, *Gazetteer of Afghanistan*, part IV, 'Kabul', Calcutta, 360.

67 Seth, *Armenians in India*, 209, from CMS, *Account*, 1870-71.

68 *Ibid*., 208, 224, One Kabuli Armenian did provide occasional intelligence to the British Political Officer in Peshawar, see *Peshawar Confidential Diary*, 12 Feb. 1881, OIC, L/PandS/7/27, fol. 1401-3.

69 Seth, *Armenians in India*, 208.

70 Grey, 44. A photograph of Grey with this Armenian in native dress appears in his book facing p. 230. This Armenian accompanied Grey to England and acted as a witness at Grey's marriage. It appears he had relatives in London, Grey, 433, 449-52, 460.

71 Seth, *Armenians in India*, 209.

72 In the early 1830s there were some 1,000 houses and shops in the Bala Hissar-i Payin, Masson, ii, 255.

73 With the exception, ironically, of Shah Shuja^c^ al-Mulk's *Diwan Khana*, traces of which can still be seen today.

armourers' shops,[74] the Armenian church and most, if not all, of the Armenians' private residences.[75] As one ninety-year old Armenian woman from Kabul remarked, the church 'built by a Mahomedan king for their use' had been 'destroyed by Christians'.[76] A few months after the explosion, *mujahidin* under Musk-i ᶜAlam took the Bala Hissar and plundered its bazaars.[77] On its recapture, the British dismantled what was left of the private houses, gardens and bazaars in the Lower Bala Hissar to make way for a new parade ground and a 'fine road'.[78] And so, within a matter of a year, this famous and reputedly impregnable fortress, lay derelict and abandoned.[79]

In 1880 the British forces withdrew, ᶜAbd al-Rahman Khan became Amir of Afghanistan and appointed Ishaq Khan as governor of Balkh. It seems that on his appointment some Kabuli Armenians, made homeless by the British, decided to seek their fortunes in Afghan Turkistan, for by the end of 1885 there were more Armenians living in Mazar-i Sharif than in Kabul. When the remaining Kabuli Armenians petitioned the Amir for permission to join their fellow-Christians in Afghan Turkistan, he ordered them all to move north and nearly 40 families sold up and left for Mazar.[80] At the same time, they wrote to the Government of India complaining about the Amir's rule, for he had threatened to confiscate all their goods and to expel them completely from Afghanistan.[81]

In the autumn of 1888 Ishaq Khan rebelled, but was swiftly defeated and he and members of his family living in Turkistan, fled to Samarkand, never to return.[82] In the aftermath of the uprising, ᶜAbd al-Rahman Khan inaugurated a 'Reign of Terror' unprecedented even in Afghanistan's blood-spattered history.[83] Amongst others, the Amir's wrath fell on members of Ishaq's family still in the country.[84] Ishaq's maternal aunt, and at least two of her brothers, were living in Kabul at the time of the uprising. A third brother, Lucas A Joseph, or Sarwar al-Din Khan,[85] was in charge of the gunpowder factory in Jalalabad. Joseph was ordered to Kabul and put under house arrest. Shortly afterwards he, his brother, Badr al-Din, and another brother, were imprisoned.[86] Their mother, meanwhile, was confined 'in a very narrow place', and the rest of Joseph's extended family placed under house arrest.[87] A month later, the Amir expelled the whole clan to Peshawar and auctioned all their property.[88]

Sometime during the next eight years Lucas Joseph and his family, consisting of some twenty-one persons,[89] returned to Afghanistan, where he was reinstated as manager of the Jalalabad gunpowder factory.[90] In the same period, Lucas' first wife died, for in early 1896, Joseph, described as a 'widower with three motherless children, two boys and a girl',[91] left Kabul for Calcutta to find a new wife. He took with him a letter from the Amir addressed to the Armenians of that city, urging them to send 'ten or twelve families, men of education and some profession, to live in the Dominions of Afghanistan'.[92] Doubtless Joseph briefed the leaders of the Calcutta Armenians about the way in which the Amir had treated his family and tried to deter any of them from undertaking such a dangerous enterprise.[93] The Amir's iron rule also deterred any eligible woman from agreeing to become Lucas Joseph's wife.

In rejecting ᶜAbd al-Rahman Khan's appeal, the leaders of the Calcutta community couched their reply in carefully worded phrases. Whilst acknowledging, 'the high honour conferred on us' and promising to encourage Armenians to move to Afghanistan, they informed the Amir that regrettably, 'no families are likely to remove from

[74] J Duke, 1883, *Recollections of the Kabul Campaign, 1879 and 1880*, London, 176.

[75] Duke, 176, 314; *Gazetteer of Afghanistan*, IV, Appendix C, cxliv; C M MacGregor, 1985, *War in Afghanistan, 1879-80*, ed. W Trousdale, Detroit, 108-10.

[76] Grey, 209.

[77] *Gazetteer of Afghanistan*, iv, 371.

[78] Duke, 168.

[79] *Ibid*; *Gazetteer of Afghanistan*, iv, 386 and Appendix C.

[80] *Kabul Newsletter*, 1 Jan. 1886, OIC, L/P&S/7/46, fol. 1190; *Trans-Frontier Journal*, March 1886, OIC, L/P&S/7/47, fol. 1428.

[81] *Peshawar Confidential Diary*, 13 Feb. 1886, OIC, L/P&S/7/47, fol. 1548.

[82] Lee, 507ff. In his autobiography, the Amir unjustly calls Ishaq Khan 'illegitimate' and his mother 'one of the women of the harem, and not one of my uncle's wives', Sultan Muhammad Khan, 1900, *The Life of Abdul Rahman Khan*, London, ii, 262-3.

[83] For an account of the 'Reign of Terror' see Lee, Chap. IX.

[84] Cf. The fate of Ishaq Khan's father-in-law, Najm al-Din, *Kabul Newsletter*, 14 Sept. 1888, OIC, L/P&S/7/55, fol. 480; C L Griesbach, *Memorandum on the Disposal of the Turkistan Prisoners*, 13 Aug. 1889, OIC: L/P&S/7/58, fols 147-9.

[85] Seth, *Armenians in India*, 212-3.

[86] Cf. *Kabul Newsletter*, 24 and 28 Aug., 4 and 7 Sept., 1888, OIC, L/P&S/7/55, fols. 19, 21-24, 189, 193; *Peshawar Confidential Diary*, 12 Sept. 1888, OIC, L/P&S/7/55, fol. 499.

[87] *Kabul Newsletter*, 25 Sept. 1888, OIC, L/P&S/7/55, fol. 619.

[88] *Ibid.*; *Kabul Newsletter*, 3 and 9 Oct. 1888, OIC, L/P&S/7/55, fols. 691, 707.

[89] This would indicate that perhaps Dr Grey's Armenian interpreter was a member of the Joseph family.

[90] Seth, *Armenians in India*, 212-4.

[91] *Ibid.*

[92] *Ibid.*, quoting from an English translation of the Amir's letter.

[93] *Ibid.*, 217. In the end, the only persons who return with Lucas were two 'superannuated Armenians of the never-do-well class'.

here, for the reason that they are established in business and in the practice of their several professions, having also all their connections of kinship ... which they would be loath to sever.'[94] They then appealed for the Amir to allow the Kabul Armenians to visit Peshawar to meet with an Orthodox priest and to permit the children of the Kabul community to study in the Armenian school in Calcutta.[95]

The Amir appears to have taken this snub badly, for less than a year later Joseph and his family were again expelled from Afghanistan. Stripped of all their assets, the impoverished Armenians arrived in Peshawar bearing the sacred vessels and manuscripts they had managed to salvage from the wreck of their church.[96] Abandoning all hope of returning to their homeland, many settled in Calcutta or Dhaka.[97] Some, though, settled in Peshawar and in 1907, Archbishop Sahak Ayvadian paid them a pastoral visit and, finding that their children had already been baptised in the Anglican Church, he confirmed them according to the rites of the Armenian Orthodox Church.[98]

The Peshawar Armenians attended All Saints Church where they sat together in one section of the transept and were distinguishable from the Punjabi Christians and Muslim population, by their distinctive clothing.[99] Amongst those who settled in Peshawar was, Sarwar al-Din, or Lucas A Joseph. One of his daughters, Kathleen Arathoon, or Arathuniyan,[100] studied medicine at the Medical Missionary College in Ludhiana. Known as 'auntie Kitty' to the Christian community, she lived near the Mission Hospital with her sister,[101] Kinosie Hyripiet, or 'auntie Kinnie', who was a trained nurse-midwife. The passports of the 'two aunties' stated that they were born in Kabul of Armenian descent.[102] The two sisters are now dead, 'auntie Kitty' dying in 1999 at over one hundred years of age.[103] Lucas Joseph's son, Paul Joseph, now also deceased, was Medical Superintendent of the Peshawar Mission Hospital from 1945-1958.[104] Dr Joseph's daughter, Mary Joseph, by his first (American) wife, now lives in England. His son, Dr Dennis Joseph, born to him by his second (Panjabi) wife, currently teaches at Edwardes College, Peshawar.

It appear, though, that at least one family of Kabuli Armenians either survived the expulsions of 1896, or returned to Afghanistan, and remained in the country until the late 1990s. In the spring of 2000, an Afghan refugee, Abil Armaniyan, son of Araj Manukiyan[105] and Mariyam, claimed to be of Armenian descent and that he had fled Afghanistan in 1999, following the persecution of his family. Abil's father, who died when he was four years old, originated from the Shor Bazaar area of the old city of Kabul, but later moved to Kot-i Sangi on the north-west side of the city. Abil states he is the last member of his family to leave Afghanistan, and claims that up to some fifty years ago as many as one hundred persons of Armenian extraction, were living in Kabul.[106] Given that his name and that of his family are Armenian, his claim appears to be genuine. If so, Arbil and his daughters by his first, Armenian, wife, are some of the last representative of one of the most unusual Christian communities in Central Asia.

Acknowledgement

This article is a summary of continuing research supported by the British Academy's Small Personal Grant, whose financial assistance is gratefully acknowledged.

94 *Ibid*, 214-5.

95 *Ibid*, 215-6.

96 *Ibid.*, 217-8. Seth blames this expulsion on the machinations of the Ottoman Sultan, ʿAbd al-Hamid.

97 Mr D Rowley and Revd Dr D Woodberry, *personal communications*.

98 Seth, *Armenians in India*, 217, 219.

99 Revd W Jukes, 1925 (reprint, Peshawar 2000), *Reminiscences of Missionary Work in Amritsar, 1872-1873, and on the Afghan Frontier in Peshawar, 1873-1890*, CMS, London, 8; Revd S Azgar, *personal communication*, April 2000.

100 Possibly this was what the 'A' in Lucas A Joseph stood for.

101 Or maybe half-sister, as in 1895 Lucas Joseph was said to have had two sons and one daughter by his first marriage. It may be that he did, after all, find another Armenian wife, once he had settled in Peshawar.

102 Mr D Rowley, *personal communication*. Mr Rowley used to handle some of the aunties' affairs, including renewal of passports etc. According to him, 'auntie Kitty's' passport stated that she was born in Kabul in 1888.

103 D Rowley, *personal communication*.

104 Dr Catherine Ujager, *History of the Mission Hospital, Peshawar*, n.d. (photocopied publication in possession of Mission Hospital, Peshawar); D Rowley, Miss Mary Joseph, Miss Joy Arathoon, Dr J Shaw, *personal communications*, September 2000.

105 Son of Safdariyan. Abil had three brothers (Azim Armaniyan, Safi Armaniyan) and two sisters (Rahima, Murmina). His first wife, who died in Herat in *c*. 1995, was called Maduna, her mother, Mayikurds, her sister (Abil's maternal aunt), Jamal Mayikhurd.

106 Abil Armaniyan, *interview*, 8 May 2000.

16 THE RABATAK INSCRIPTION AND THE NAMELESS KUSHAN KING[1]

David W Mac Dowall

The recently discovered inscription from Rabatak in Northern Afghanistan provides us for the first time the genealogy of the main Kushan dynasty. Kujula was father of a Vima Takto, grandfather of Vima Kadphises and great grandfather of Kanishka. Without full consideration of the circumstances it has been suggested that the coins of the Nameless King were issued by Vima Takto but it seems more likely that they were issued by Kujula himself, after he had unified the five Yabghu of the Yueh-chi.

The Rabatak inscription

In March 1993 a new Bactrian inscription of the early Kushan period was discovered from the Kushan site at Rabatak, Kafir Qalᶜa (36.09 N, 68.24 E), about 40 km. east of Haibak on the road to Pul-i Khumri in northern Afghanistan.[2] The inscription belongs to the time of Kanishka who is said to have obtained the kingship 'from Nana and all the gods'. It records that the King Kanishka gave orders to Shafar the Karalang to make a sanctuary and images of a range of gods for King Kujula Kadphises his great grandfather (line 12), for King (Vima Taktu?) his grandfather (line 13), King Vima Kadphises his father, and himself King Kanishka. The inscription is engraved on a block of limestone and is known at present only from photographs. The edition of Nicholas Sims-Williams is a masterpiece of philological erudition, but there are many uncertainties and his text and translation should be studied in conjunction with the 1998 re-examination and commentary of Gerard Fussman[3] who tries to set out clearly what seems reasonably certain from what is at best hypothetical. The inscription is mostly effaced on the left side and we must take full note of all the conjecture as restorations that Sims-Williams has carefully noted in his transcription and translation.

Perhaps the most interesting feature about the inscription is the genealogy it gives of the first four Kushan kings and the claim that it reveals the name of a totally new ruler (Vimo Takto?) who is identified by Cribb with the nameless king Soter Megas, known from an extensive coinage in billon and copper. Unfortunately the first half of line 13 is almost illegible, and the reading of the new name is merely based on an imaginative restoration by Sims-Williams. Indeed the reading and translation by B N Mukherjee[4] gives a completely different name at this point—'for this grandfather Saddashkano, the Soma sacrificer'. Fussman reminds us that the Rabatak inscription by itself gives no assurance that Kanishka's grandfather bore the name of Vima Taktu. The restoration was apparently suggested not by anything visible on the stone itself but by comparison with (a) the Brahmi inscription from the devakula at Mat near Mathura in India and (b) the trilingual inscription in Bactrian, Kharoshthi and an unknown language from Dasht-e Navur near Ghazni in Afghanistan.

The Brahmi inscription of Vima from Mat

The Brahmi inscription between the feet of a seated statue of 'Vima' from the *devakula* at Mat, known since 1913, was translated by Lüders[5] from a squeeze as 'the maharaja

[1] It is with great pleasure that I dedicate this article to Ralph Pinder-Wilson whom I have known as a personal friend and colleague for so many years. In the 1950s we were both Assistant Keepers in the British Museum. We maintained our friendship through the Royal Asiatic Society and British Institute of Afghan Studies in Kabul, of which he was the Director and I was first Hon Secretary and eventually Chairman.

[2] N Sims-Williams and J Cribb, 'A New Bactrian Inscription of Kanishka the Great', *Silk Road Art and Archaeology* 4, Kamakura, 1995/96, 75-142.

[3] G Fussman, 'L'inscription de Rabatak et l'origine de l'ére saka', *Journal Asiatique* 286 numéro 2, Paris, 1998, 571-651—a persuasive article on which I have based my comments on the inscriptions.

[4] B N Mukherjee, 'The Great Kushana Testament', *Indian Museum Bulletin*, Calcutta, 1995, 1-106.

[5] H Lüders, *Mathura Inscriptions*, Unpublished Papers edited by K Janert, Göttingen, 1961.

rajatiraja devaputra the scion of the Kushans, *sahi Wema*(?)', repeating the formula inscribed on the standing headless statue of Kanishka in the nominative giving the name and titles of the personage represented on the statue. A second phrase, in normal Sanskrit word order, begins with a noun in the instrumental case, and was translated by Lüders 'By the *bakanapati* of Taksuma, Humaspala (?) a *devakula* was caused to be made, moreover a garden, a tank, and a well, an assembly hall, a gateway'. Gritli von Mitterwallner[6] (who, as Fussman points out, unfortunately knows no Sanskrit) is responsible for translating Taksumasya as an epithet attached to Vema even though the case is different from that of Vema.

The trilingual inscription from Dasht-e Navur

Sims-Williams' new edition[7] of the Bactrian version of the trilingual inscription from Dasht-e Navur DN1 reads 'year 279 of the king of kings the great salvation Vima Taktu the Kushan ...' Fussman who spent three days at the remote site in 1967 points out that the text of the Bactrian inscription was so badly damaged that conjectures are unavoidable, but they remain conjectures: and this one conflicts with the corresponding part of the Kharoshthi version at Dasht-e Navur DN4. The reading there is clear and without any conjecture reads 'vhamakushana' and is not followed by any letters remotely like Tak(to) or Takpi.[8]

The significance of the Rabatak inscription

Although there are substantial doubts about the reading of the name of Kujula's son, the inscription does give us a firm genealogy of the family of the early Kushan kings, spanning four generations from Kujula to Kanishka. Although we can never be sure how long this may cover, it suggests a period of some 60 years or more between the arrival of Kujula and the accession of Kanishka. Kanishka issued a Greek edict and then he put it into Aryan, echoing the obverse legends of his initial gold coinage where the first issue with Greek titulature was altered in the die to Bactrian, which was subsequently the regular form.[9] The edict was proclaimed to India, specifying a number of key towns—Saketa (near modern Faizabad), Kausambi (modern Kosam near Allahabad), Pataliputra (modern Patna), Campa (near modern Bhagalpur) and possibly Ujjain. There is an interesting insight into the gods to be worshipped—in addition to Nana—Umma, Aurmuzd, Strosshard, Narasa and Mihr, and the range of titles applied to Kanishka such as Soter Megas.

Fussman pointed out that the inscription does not derive from Kanishka himself- the first person is never employed; and does not date from year one of Kanishka—this is the hypothetical restoration of Sims-Williams whereas the stone is completely effaced at this point. But whatever his name there was a prince between Kujula and Vima Kadphises.

The context of the coins of Soter Megas the nameless king

It has long been recognised that there was a substantial coinage in billon and copper of a nameless king who is simply given the titulature Soter Megas (the great salvation), which follows the coinages of Kujula Kadphises and precedes the issues of Vima Kadphises. [10] This context is no longer a matter of dispute although there is no general agreement about its more precise attribution. Some scholars have argued that the coinage was issued by Kujula Kadphises in the latter part of his reign; some have regarded the coinage as an early issue of Vima Kadphises, before he introduced his main coinage with his full name and some have argued that it was the coinage of a major separate sovereign. From the Rabatak inscription we now know that there was a line of four successive princes—Kujula Kadphises, his son the new person seen in the genealogy, Vima Kadphises his grandson, and Kanishka his great-grandson. There are also four major coinages—of Kujula Kadphises, Soter Megas, Vima Kadphises and Kanishka. Cribb claims that the simplest explanation for the relationship between the new king (whom he terms Vima I Tak[to]) and Soter Megas is that he is the anonymous issuer. He does however realise that it is difficult to explain why the issue lacks the ruler's name. Cribb notes that each prince in the genealogy in the Rabatak inscription is called

---

[6] GV Mitterwallner, *Kusana Coins and Sculptures from Mathura*, Mathura, 1986, 54-62.

[7] Sims-Williams and Cribb, *ibid.*, 95-96.

[8] Fussman *op.cit.*, 618.

[9] R Göbl, *Münzprägung des Kusanreiches*, Wien, 1984, 61-63.

[10] D W Mac Dowall, 'Soter Megas, the King of Kings, the Kushana', *The Journal of the Numismatic Society of India* Volume XXX, Varanasi, 1968, 28-48.

'shao' and interprets this as a direct succession in which each member of the family had his own reign. But Fussman points out that the purpose of the construction of the Bagolango was to assert the legitimacy of Kujula's power from the favour of the gods and his own direct descent from Kujula Kadphises. The use of 'shao' after each name must be interpreted simply as a mark of respect. To show that the new king had actually ruled, it would be necessary for his name to be known with full imperial titulature 'shaonano shao'. The major alternative that Cribb does not envisage or consider is that the son of Kujula did not rule at all. Instead he proceeds to list in an Appendix 'Coins of Vima I Tak(to)'—the coins of Soter Megas and Kujula's type with the bull obverse and the Bactrian camel reverse on which he read Vima's name in 1981.[11] This of course leaves unexplained why the son of Kujula issued his coins anonymously. The alternative—that the early Kushan empire was ruled by the three kings Kujula Kadphises, Vima Kadphises (his grandson) and Kanishka (his great-grandson) known from the coins that bear their names—offers a readily understandable sequence of actual rulers if we can adequately explain why the many anonymous coins, 'the Soter Megas' series, may have been issued. Kujula Kadphises who attacked and destroyed the other four Yabghu of the Yüeh-chih is said to have died at the age of more than 80.[12] The son of any monarch who rules to an advanced age is himself likely to have a short reign of his own if any. In such cases we frequently see a king succeeded not by his son but by a grandson even though the son may have played a major role during the lifetime of his father. But why do we find the extensive coin issues without any name—the coinage of Soter Megas?

The Roman connections of the Kushans have been extensively discussed.[13] Kujula Kadphises was certainly a broad contemporary of Augustus and the Julio-Claudian emperors in the 1st century AD. Roman trade with the north west of India developed extensively after the Roman conquest of Egypt following Augustus' victory in the battle of Actium in 31 BC at the end of the civil war. In his Roman head issue Kujula Kadphises specifically copies the obverse portrait on the gold aurei and silver denarii issued by Augustus and Tiberius from 2 BC to AD 37. But we seem to have overlooked the more important way in which the Roman empire may have influenced the new Kushan kingdom—in the creation of a uniform coinage from the multiplicity of types they inherited and in the use of coin titulature designed to create a unifying image of the ruler in the new state.

The career of Kujula Kadphises

The Han-Shu (History of the former Han), covering the period 206BC to AD25, mainly compiled *c* AD80 describes in 96A 14b the five *yabghu* (tribes) of the Great Yüeh-chih, one of which, the Yabghu of Kao-fu resides at the walled city of Kao-fu (Kabul). The Hou-Han Shu (History of the Later Han ch 118), compiled by Fan Yeh (died AD 446), describes how the Yüeh-chih moved to Ta-hsia (Bactria) and divided their country into five yabghu. More than a hundred years later the Yabghu of Kuei shuang, Ch'iu-ch'iu ch'üeh attacked and destroyed the other four Yabghu and established himself as their king; the kingdom was named Kuei-shuang. This king invaded An-hsi (Indo-Parthia), took the country of Kao-fu (Kabul) and moreover destroyed P'u-ta (Pushkalavati) and Chi-pin (Kashmir) and completely possessed their territory. Ch'iu-ch'iu ch'üeh died at the age of 'more than 80 years'.[14] The principal coinages with the name of Kujula Kadphises, reflect the first stages of this conquest, but not the capture of Pushkalavati or the consolidation of his rule in Bactria. It is only when we consider the coinages of the nameless king Soter Megas that we see the complete career of Kujula Kadphises over a long reign, extending beyond his 80th year.

The coin types of Kujula Kadphises

Issues K1 to K4 have no royal title. Kujula is simply termed 'Yabghu'. He had of course begun his career as leader of the Kushan Yabghu, one of the five Yabghu of the Yüeh-Chih. Issue K5 from Kashmir, however, in the Indo-Scythian tradition, styles him 'Maharayasa rayatirayasa'. All types of Kujula were struck in virtually pure copper.

[11] J Cribb, 'A new coin of Vima Kadphises, King of the Kushans', *Coins, Culture and History in the Ancient World* (ed. M J Price and L Casson) Detroit, 1981, 333-340.

[12] Sims-Williams and Cribb, *loc. cit.*, 111-123.

[13] D W Mac Dowall, 'Numismatic Evidence for the Date of Kanishka', *Papers on the Date of Kanishka* (ed. A L Basham) Leiden, 1968, 137-149, and R Göbl, *op.cit.*

[14] Translated in E Zürcher, 'The Yüeh-chih and Kanishka in the Chinese Sources', *Papers on the Date of Kanishka* (ed. A L Basham), Leiden, 1968, 346-390. For a recent discussion of the Yüeh-chih see Lazlo Torday, *Mounted Archers. The Beginnings of Central Asian History*, Durham 1997.

Type K1—The standing Herakles type[15]

DB nos. 17-35
IGISC type 1049-1050

OX 9.17, 9.07, 9.02, 8.51, 8.18gm
BM 9.92, 9.82, 8.31, 9.30, 9.26, 9.12, 9.11, 9.06, 8.85gm

was the reverse type of the Indian copper tetradrachms of Kujula in the Paropamisadae (the province of Begram) and Arachosia (the province of Ghazni and Kandahar). Their denomination was derived from the silver tetradrachms used by the Indo-Greeks kings. After the fall of Hermaios there had been a sharp debasement.[16] The coinage retained the types and legends of Hermaios at the same Indian weight standard of 9.6gm, but the silver content was progressively reduced and eventually became copper. The copper tetradrachm remained the standard denomination of subsequent issues at Begram of Su Hermaios, the Indo-Parthian Gondophares and finally Kujula Kadphises the Kushan. Herakles type tetradrachms of Kujula are commonly found at Begram, Mir Zakah and Butkara. They are also common at Taxila where 1975 specimens were found at Sirkap—imported no doubt by Kujula's advancing armies.[17] The obverse initially retained the crude bust of Su Hermaios. Later issues substituted a bust of Kujula. Kharoshthi legends include the name of Kujula throughout.

At this period there was a serious problem with barbarous imitations, some extremely crude, with weights from 9 to 2gm or less. Any semblance of an orderly coinage with clear fractions was impossible. The remedy was to introduce a series of new types with carefully executed legends and more artistic designs struck to a tighter weight standard.

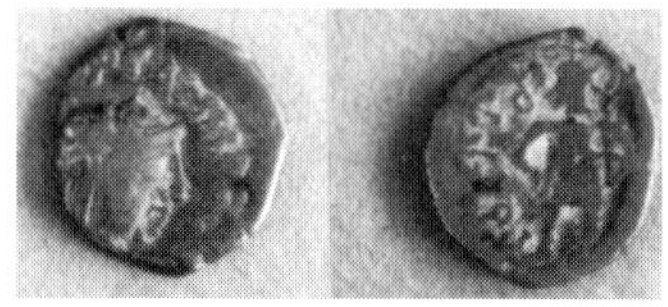

Type K2—The Macedonian soldier type

DB nos. 41-42
IGISC type 1052

OX 4.61, 4.58, 3.67gm
BM 5.44, 5.18, 4.83, 4.68, 4.56, 4.54, 4.45, 4.45, 4.20, 4.18, 4.05, 3.97gm

seems to have been struck in Gandhara—perhaps to serve as a half denomination of the copper tetradrachm. Two examples came from Hazara[18] and coins of this type were found recently in a hoard from Mardan.[19]

Type K3—The Roman head type

DB nos. 36-40
IGISC type 1053

OX 3.60, 3.44, 3.41, 3.37, 3.29, 3.17, 3.12, 3.03, 2.97, 2.87, 2.83, 2.33gm
BM 3.54, 3.46, 3.44, 3.41, 3.38, 3.37, 3.36, 3.34, 3.39, 3.29, 3.27, 3.20, 3.08, 3.05, 2.97, 2.47, 2.05gm

circulated in Taxila. 334 specimens were found at Sirkap. It copied in copper the portrait head found on Roman aurei and denarii (issued 2 BC to AD37).

---

[15] In the listing of types *DB* is an abbreviation for the catalogue R Göbl, *Donum Burns, die Kušamünzen in Münzkabinett Bern und die Chronologie*, Wien, 1993 and *IGISC* is an abbreviation for the type catalogue M Mitchener, *Indo-Greek and Indo-Scythian Coinage*, London, 1975-1976. The coins cited are the examples in the collection of the Ashmolean Museum, Oxford (OX) and the British Museum, London (BM) giving the weight in gm of each example.

[16] O Bopearachchi, 'The Posthumous Coinage of Hermaios and the conquest of Gandhara', *Gandharan Art in Context* (ed. R Allchin, B Allchin, N Kreitman, E Errington) New Delhi, 1997, 189-213.

[17] In the list of types, finds are cited at Taxila from J Marshall, *Taxila, an illustrated account of the Archaeological Excavations,* 3 volumes, Cambridge 1947, 751-863; at Begram from: Three memoirs on the ancient coins found at Beghram in the Kohistan of Kabul, *Journal of the Asiatic Society of Bengal*, Calcutta, 1834, 152-175; 1836, 1-28 and 537-547 and H H Wilson, *Ariana Antiqua*, London, 1841, 332-336 and 347-350; at Mir Zakah from R Curiel and D Schlumberger, *Le Trésor Monétaire de Mir Zakah,* Paris, 1953; at Butkara from R Göbl, *A Catalogue of Coins from Butkara I (Swat, Pakistan)*, Rome, 1976.

[18] Rawlins and Talbot, *Journal of the Asiatic Society of Bengal*, Calcutta, 1898, XIV 4-5.

[19] R C Senior, 'A note on Early Kushan Coins', *Oriental Numismatic Society News Letter* 150, London, 1996, 14-15.

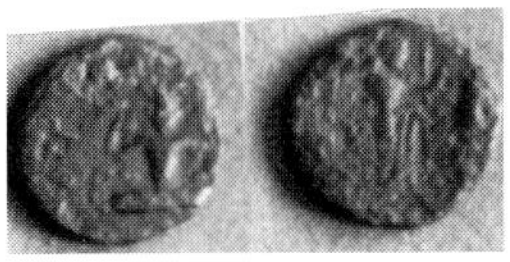

Type K4—The seated king type

DB no. 49
IGISC type 1054

OX 1.83, 1.76, 1.73, 1.46gm
BM 2.24, 2.02, 1.97, 1.74, 1.71, 1.69, 1.69, 1.67, 1.61, 1.59, 1.43gm

also seems to have circulated in Taxila. 78 specimens were found at Sirkap excavations. It seems intended as a half denomination of the Roman head type.

Type K5—The bull and Bactrian camel type

DB nos. 43-45
IGISC type 1054

OX 11.29, 10.59, 10.28, 10.20, 10.05, 10.04, 9.50, 9.15, 8.97, 8.74, 8.69, 7.81, 7.81, 7.11gm
BM 12.74, 12.71, 12.51, 11.59, 11.16, 10.95, 10.75, 10.49, 10.48, 10.48, 10.37, 10.30, 10.26, 10.26, 10.08, 9.86, 9.82, 9.66, 9.59, 9.58, 9.49, 9.26, 9.15, 9.10, 9.08, 8.91, 8.53, 8.32, 7.40gm

was struck in Kashmir copying the copper denomination of Jihonika. Cunningham noted that Kujula's coins of this type are rarely found west of the Indus.[20] 23 examples were found at Sirkap compared with 1975 coins of the Herakles type and they must belong to a different mint. All the three coins of Kujula in the museum at Srinagar[21], however, are of this type, and a hoard of these coins was discovered at Tanakpur 50 km. north of Srinagar in 1985.[22] Their Kharoshthi legends all begin with the more elaborate title of *maharaya rayatirayasa*—king of kings. Yabghu is dropped. To the basic king's name subsequent issues add first *Devaputra* and then *Khushanasa Devaputra*.

The coin types of Soter Megas

Later moves to stabilise the Kushan coinage come with the anonymous coinage of a ruler with no personal name but grand titles in Greek *Basileu Basileuon Soter Megas*. This seems to reflect awareness of the importance of Greek in international trade and of the way in which titulature had been used at Rome to heal the divisions of the Civil War.[23] After Octavian's victory at Actium in 31 BC there is no further reference to his personal name Octavian. Self-proclaimed saviour and restorer of the Roman republic, he is called simply 'Caesar Augustus, *Divi filius*, Imperator'. Circumstances are of course very different in the east, but there seems something analogous between the anonymity of Augustus and that of Soter Megas. There is the same hint of military office and prestige in *Basileu Basileuon*, as in Caesar and Imperator. Soter Megas (the great salvation) is no more a proper name than Augustus which signifies 'worthy of deference and respect'. *Deva putra* implies divine approval as does *Divi filius*. The transition was necessary. The military commander, ruler of one Yabghu, had by stages to become the leader of an empire and to create a unified currency for it all. In the coinages of Soter Megas we see the second stage of this process being implemented.

Type SM1—The horseman/Zeus bilingual type

DB nos. 53-54
IGISC types 1148-1149

OX 9.73, 9.66, 9.35gm
BM 9.84, 9.83, 9.59, 9.47, 9.36, 9.30, 8.88gm
2.05, 2.01, 1.85, 1.72gm

[20] A Cunningham, 'Coins of the Kushans part III', *Numismatic Chronicle*, London, 1892, 45-47.

[21] R C Kak, *Handbook of the Archaeological and Numismatic Sections of the Sri Pratap Singh Museum, Srinagar*, Calcutta, 1923, 153.

[22] Press cutting at Indian Institute for Research in Numismatic Studies 1985.

[23] See C H V Sutherland, *Coinage in Roman Imperial Policy*, London, 1951, *passim*.

was used for billon tetradrachms and drachms in Gandhara. They contained some 5% silver and were struck to the Indian weight standard of 9.6gm. both the obverse and reverse types are copied from coins of Sasan, the Indo-Parthian king who succeeded Abdagases (nephew of Gondophares)—and are attributed to the mint of Pushkalavati. The coinage must have resulted directly from the Kushan conquest of Pushkalavati. The use of billon was in the tradition of the preceding Indo-Parthians. With 5% silver the metal value must have been four times that of coins of the same weight in copper. A variant with the additional *aksaras Vima* at the end of the Kharoshthi legend is very rare and known from two examples only, one in the BM and one on Lahore.

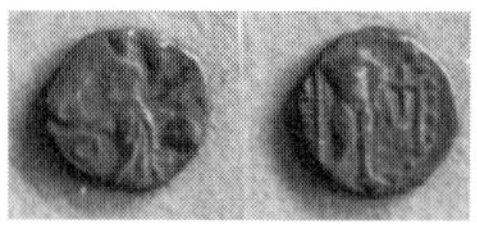

Type SM2—The Shiva/Ardoxsho type

DB no. 56

OX 1.60, 1.58, 1.23gm
BM 1.83, 1.66, 1.68, 1.61, 1.56, 1.56, 1.51, 1.50, 1.40, 1.31, 1.31, 1.19, 1.06gm

with no legends has the Soter Megas *tamgha*. It seems to have circulated at Taxila, as a half copper denomination for the Roman head type of Kujula.

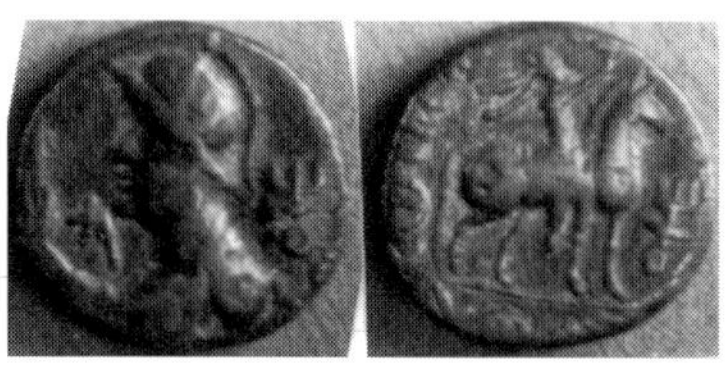

Type SM3—The helmeted head type

DB no 57

OX 13.05, 12.97, 12.57, 11.65gm
BM 12.61, 12.52, 12.51, 11.87, 11.84, 11.09gm

seems to have been the currency of Qunduz. Finds gave been reported from Balkh and Begram and the French excavators called it the 'Qunduz type' because of finds there. The type is derived from the helmeted head of barbarous copies of Eukratides. Cribb describes the denomination as a reduced Attic tetradrachm; but it is also a copper tridrachm in the Attic metrological system that was being developed by Soter Megas.

Type SM4—The Mathura type

DB no. 55

OX 4.59,4.24, 4.04gm
BM 4.36,4.34, 4.28, 4.28, 4.27, 4.26, 4.20, 4.18, 3.93, 3.88, 3.85, 3.71, 3.56, 3.53, 3.37gm

copied the obverse bust and reverse Zeus of the barbarous Heliokles coinage in the Surkhandaria valley. Struck to a weight standard of *c.* 4gm it provided a local coinage of Attic copper drachms at Mathura. Examples are commonly found there, and have been reported from Delhi, Jagdhri and Kaital—brought no doubt by an invading Kushan army.

Type SM5—The general coinage type

DB no. 55

copper coins weighing about 8.5gm and 2.1gm have a diademed bust surrounded by rays on the obverse and a horseman on the reverse. They were issued in large numbers and provided a standard currency throughout the whole Kushan empire from northern Bactria to Mathura. There are many different varieties indicating different issues and probably different mints. Some have lunate and some have square letter forms. There are different numbers of rays round the obverse bust, different forms of Tamgha (some with three and some with four prongs) and the Tamghas are found in different combinations. I have argued that the coins of this type were Attic copper didrachms and hemidrachms, the first coinage for the whole empire which was strengthened by the issue of complementary copper tetradrachms (c.

17gm) didrachms (c. 8.5gm) and drachms (c. 4.25gm) in Vima Kadphises' subsequent monetary reform.

In conclusion

While the Rabatak inscription provides important new evidence about the ancestry of Kanishka, there is no clear unambiguous epigraphic evidence for the name of Kanishka's grandfather. As Fussman has demonstrated the reading 'Vima Taktu' is based only on a conjectural restoration. Nor does the numismatic evidence establish the name of any Kushan king ruling between Kujula and Vima Kadphises. Cribb has carefully examined the Kharoshthi legends on coins of the Bull/Bactrian camel type.[24] Most are of Kujula Kadphises but some have elements of the name ofVima plus a title of some sort. His readings suggest that the type continued for a short time underVima Kadphises (the interpretation that he originally gave to his discovery). Whitehead[25] had previously noted the existence of additional aksaras at the end of the Kharoshthi legend on 2 billon tetradrachms type SM2 of Soter Megas. This is equally explicable as a short continuation of the billon denomination into the first years ofVima Kadphises. A billon tetradrachm at 9.6gm with 5 % silver would be worth the same as some 34gm in copper and be valued as an octodrachm in the Attic system promoted by Soter Megas. This does not of course give the name of Kujula's son. But the Kharoshthi aksaras in the reverse field of SM types 1-3, (the early local coinages of Soter Megas) are more promising. They follow other aksaras such as *va* on earlier Indo-Parthian coins. *Vi* cannot be interpreted as a mint mark because it occurs on SM type 1 from Pushkalavati. SM type 2 from Qunduz and SM type 3 from Taxila; but it can be regarded as the mark of a minting official—perhaps Vi[ma] and he might just be the heir apparent of Kujula responsible for the administration of the newly captured territories. But on present evidence it is premature and misleading to reattribute the coins of Soter Megas to another king. Indeed it is only when the coinage of Soter Megas is seen to be a later phase of the coinage of King Kujula Kadphises that we can make sense of the career of Kujula described in the Han-shu.

> Type K1 marks the occupation of Kaofu and Taxila
> Types K2, K3 and K4 attempt to sort out the barbarous copies
> Type K5 marks the conquest of Chi-pin
> Type SM1 follows the capture of Pushkalavati
> Types SM2, SM3 and SM4 are local coinages co-ordinated to a common pattern of Attic copper denominations; but none of those types is found in Bactria north of the Oxus.
> Type SM4 is the unifying coinage to a common pattern that circulated through the empire north and south of the Hindu Kush mountains, including the territories of the other 4 Yabghu of the Yüeh-chih.

[24] J Cribb, 'A new coin of Vima Kadphises King of the Kushans', *loc. cit*.

[25] R B Whitehead, 'Two coins of Soter Megas', *Journal of the Royal Asiatic Society* July 1913.

17 *PEM NEM:* A 16TH CENTURY DAKANI MANUSCRIPT

David Matthews

In the important volume entitled *Paintings from Islamic Lands*, edited by Ralph Pinder-Wilson in 1969,[1] Douglas Barrett contributed an article, *Painting at Bijapur*, in which he discussed at some length the miniatures contained in a hitherto unnoticed British Museum Library manuscript. The manuscript undoubtedly originated from Bijapur and could be firmly dated 999 AH/1590-1 AD. The text, which consists of 238 folios, is executed in beautiful *nastaʿlīq* calligraphy, and in the opinion of Douglas Barrett the thirty-eight paintings, which accompany the text, are among the earliest and finest, which can be attributed with certainty to Bijapur. The excellence of the miniatures and the great care, which was lavished upon the production of the text, indicate that in its time the work was regarded as being of some importance. It may well have been produced for the personal library of Sultan Ibrahim ʿAdil Shah II, who ruled Bijapur from 1580 to 1627.

In his catalogue of the Hindi, Panjabi and Hindustani manuscripts of the British Museum J F Blumhardt described the work (erroneously, as we shall see) as a version of the romance of Ratan Sen and Padmavati, written in an archaic form of Hindi, and suggested that its title was probably *Ratan Kahān* 'The Tale of Ratan (Sen)'.[2] Since Blumhardt implied that the work belonged the realm of Hindi rather than Urdu literature, it was ignored by later scholars of Dakani Urdu, who, without stopping to examine it, excluded it from their studies. Over the last eighty years or so, many books and articles have been written by Indian and Pakistani scholars on the subject of the Dakani works produced between 1500 and 1700 AD in and around the courts of Bijapur and Golkunda, but none of them contains any reference whatsoever to this important manuscript.

On closer examination of the manuscript a number of incontrovertible facts emerge. In his lengthy introduction the author clearly states that the title of his poem is *Pem Nem* 'The Rule of Love', which he had composed only after expending much effort and great care. He declares his own name to be Hasan Manju <u>Kh</u>alji and states that he has adopted the *upnām* or pen name Hans or Hans Shāh. The name Hasan Manju <u>Kh</u>aljī is itself strange and the *nom-de-plume Hans* may simply be an anagram of *Hasan*. In the final part of the poem the author states accurately that his work consists of 199 *dohas* and 999 *caupāīs*, and that it was finished in the year 999 AH/1590-1 AD. The recurrence of the auspicious figure 9 in the number of the verses and the date of composition can surely be no accident. It may further be pointed out that the introduction to the poem begins with the enumeration of the 99 names of God.

When suggesting his own title, Blumhardt was presumably led astray by the two words *ratan khān* 'jewel-mine', which occur frequently throughout the poem in verses such as:

nem yih astut šah jī jān
dhan gun sāgar ratan khān

'This section is in praise of Shah Ji; a blessed
sea of qualities; mine of jewels.'

Here it must be pointed out that the final word *khān* 'mine' can also be read as *kahān*, and until fairly recently no distinction was made in Urdu handwriting between the consonantal *choṭī he* and the aspirate marker *do-cašmī he*. Blumhardt's reasoning seems to have been: *kahān* is a variant of the common Hindi word *kahānī* 'tale'; *ratan* 'jewel' must refer to Ratan Sen, the Raja of Chitor; the 'tale of Ratan' must therefore be that of Ratan Sen and Padmavati, the best known version of which was composed by Malik Muhammad Jayasi in 1520 AD. Hence we have before us another adaptation of the celebrated medieval Hindi romance. Indeed Jayasi found many imitators in the Deccan and elsewhere, and a number of largely inferior versions of his work were produced both during and after his lifetime. It is therefore not surprising that 20th century scholars, assuming that Blumhardt's *Ratan Kahān* must be

[1] R Pinder-Wilson (ed.), *Paintings from Islamic Lands*, Bruno Cassirer, Oxford, 1969. Douglas Barrett's article begins on p. 163.

[2] J F Blumhardt, *Catalogue of the Hindi, Panjabi and Hindustani Manuscripts in the Library of the British Museum*, London, 1889, 57, no. 83, Add. 16880.

one of these, passed over it, without even examining the text or its remarkable miniatures. Douglas Barrett was, as he readily admits, an art historian and not an expert in Dakani Urdu, and for this reason he had no cause to question Blumhardt's judgement regarding the title or the subject matter of the work. A closer examination of the text, however, reveals that Hans's *Pem Nem* is an original story, invented by the author, who recounts the love of Shah Ji for his estranged beloved Mah Ji. A brief summary of the story will be given at the end of this paper.

The text of the *Pem Nem* presents a number of problems in terms of language and style, which will only be solved when it is carefully edited and studied. This can only be done by scholars, who are not only competent in Dakani Urdu, but who also possess a wide range of expertise in other medieval Hindi dialects as well as those of Gujarati and Marathi, languages which also influenced the writers of the 16th-century Deccan. Sadly editors of such texts rarely take the trouble to consult colleagues in other domains, who might well be able to shed light on apparent obscurities. When a critical edition of this text is finally undertaken such interdisciplinary collaboration will be essential.

If one can define 'Dakani Urdu' as the language of that vast body of literature, produced almost exclusively by Muslims, who flourished mainly in Bijapur and Golkunda from the beginning of the 16th to the end of the 17th centuries AD, then the *Pem Nem* can justifiably be called a Dakani work.[3] In compositions dating from this period we encounter several registers of language and style. There are many works, whose language contains a large medieval Hindi element with words strung together in a loose syntactical framework. This often leads to obscurity, which cannot always be easily resolved. On the other hand there are works dating from exactly the same time, or even composed by the same author, which have a greater Persian element and a relatively clear syntactical structure. Both kinds of texts, however, exhibit linguistic elements, which are common to all Dakani works. The language of Hasan Manju Khalji, who takes great delight in the use of excessive alliteration, falls mainly into the first category. The following two verses in praise of Shah Ji for example, are not untypical:

karak karijan kar ṝ kar kat
kāṝ khan khan khar khar kar kat
śah jal bal bal pal tal mal
pem pāyā man muṅh at

Interpretation of such lines is, to say the least, problematic, and indeed the only meaning which can be deduced from the verses given above is that Shah Ji had found love! But in spite of such localized difficulties, much of the text of the *Pem Nem* makes reasonable sense and the main drift of its contents is more or less clear.

The first Dakani texts, which can safely be ascribed to Bijapur, are the brief religious and mystical poems of the sufi, Mīrāṅ Jī Shams ul-ᶜUshshāq, who is said to have died in the region in 904 AH/1499 AD. According to his autobiographical *nasalnāma*, he arrived in Bijapur from Mecca, and was immediately obliged to come to terms with the language of his adopted country, since preaching to the masses in Arabic or Persian would have been futile. Like many of his contemporaries, who were already active in other areas of the Deccan like Bidar and Ahmadnagar, he was gracious enough to apologize for his linguistic shortcomings, and hoped that his mistakes would be forgiven by his audience. It might be argued (uncharitably) that his verse does not possess great literary merit, but at least it was comprehensible and served its purpose:

yih sab ᶜālam terā
rāziq sabhoṅ kerā
tujh bin haur na koe
na xāliq dūjā hoe
je terā hoe karam
to ṭūṭe sabhī bharam

'The whole world is Thine, O Nourisher of all. No one exists but Thee; there is no other Creator. Because of Thy grace, all secrets are revealed.'[4]

Mīrāṅ Jī established his *khānqāh* outside Bijapur, and after his death in 1499 he was succeeded by his son, Burhān ud-Dīn Jānam, who in his old age was greatly revered by Sultan Ibrahim ᶜAdil Shah II. Ibrahim, in his collection of songs, entitled *Kitāb-i Nauras*, the bulk of which was finished around 1600 AD, like most of the other poets of Bijapur pays special homage to these two great

[3] The discussion as to whether 'Dakani' works of this period should belong to Hindi or Urdu is endless and for the most part futile. The major reasons for considering them under the umbrella of Urdu are that almost all their authors were Muslim, their themes are mostly inspired by classical Persian works and they were all written in a form of the Arabic script. The present debate, of course has wide-ranging political implications, which do not concern us here.

[4] Quoted in A A Surur (ed.), *Alīgaṛh Tāṝkh-i Adab-i Urdū*, 214, Aligarh, 1962

sufis, whose compositions seem to have had a profound influence on the language and style of his own works.

Burhān ud-Dīn Jānam was a prolific writer of both verse and prose. Typically some of his works, like parts of the *Pem Nem*, are replete with Hindi dialect forms and are remarkable for their alliteration:

lokā yih mat kuch alāḋī jin būjh baxtoṅ?
lāḋī
bhau dhāt yogī kareṅ bicār gur bin na pāve?
soe
sādhū jin kī sevā lhāī toc parāpat hoe …

'O people! This doctrine is something different, and those who understand it are fortunate. Yogis have many kinds of ideas but without a guru they do not find [the truth]. Only a sadhu, who benefits from serving him (i.e. the guru) will acquire it.'[5]

In other words, if you wish to learn the truth, you must take a mentor like me. Such forms of self-advertisement are frequently found in the writings of the sufis of this period!

Other poems of Burhān ud-Dīn are, from our point of view, clearer, and with a higher proportion of Arabic and Persian words are more readily comprehensible:

allāh vāhid sirjanhār yih jag racnā racyā apār
saglā ᶜālam kiyā zahūr apne bātin kere nūr …

'God the Creator is unique; He made the creation of the world boundless. He made the whole world manifest by the light within Him.'

As we shall see, very similar words are used by Hans at the beginning of the section of the *Pem Nem* devoted to the praise of Allah.

The question as to why one and the same writer should choose to compose in two very different styles has not been resolved. Some scholars have suggested that the more 'dialectal' or 'Sanskritizing' verse must belong to the earlier period of the poet's life, while the more 'regular' and Persianizing works belong to a later period. Since, however, most of the poems cannot be dated, the theory is impossible to sustain. The choice of language may well have been determined by the nature of the audience at which the poems were directed. For unconverted Hindus, who were completely unfamiliar with Islamic doctrine, Sanskrit words such as *yogī, gurū, sādhū, sevā, parāpat* were probably deemed to be more suitable. For a converted Muslim, who was now better acquainted with basic Quranic terminology, the Arabic words *vāhid, ᶜālam, zahūr, nūr* would be acceptable.

The next substantial work produced at Bijapur was the *Kitāb-i Nauras*, a collection of *dohas* and songs, set to various *rāgas* and *rāginīs* by Sultan Ibrahim ᶜAdil Shah II. The songs, which were composed roughly between 1580 and 1600 AD (the same time as the *Pem Nem*) were written on a variety of themes, many of which are familiar to us from similar compositions found in other medieval Indian languages. As well as songs in praise of the Prophet and the *Panjtan* (Ibrahim had converted to Shiᶜism), we find compositions devoted to certain Hindu deities, descriptions of the king's favourite possessions, such as his elephant, Ātish Khān, and his tanbura, Motī Khān, as well as songs extolling the beauty of women and nature. The language and style of the *Kitāb-i Nauras*, like that of the *Pem Nem*, is chosen to harmonize with the genre, and is, as we might expect, full of 'rustic' dialect forms:

pyāre candā ākhūṅ kanth ḋīn duī dukhī
man cāhe so nis bhaī ham tum raheṅ ab
sukhī
bujhāūṅ ḋīpak koṅ tarāsūṅ ḋinkar āvegā
ghar ghar chup jāsūs sab sudh pahuṅcāvegā
poh phāṭī to dekh jā ṭāk dhāvegā
ibrāhīm na so jāg aysā pyū kahāṅ pāvegā
sandhyāṅ kar singār lob kanṭh lāvegā
rāt thoṛī madan bahut banā uṭh jāvegā[6]

'Dear moon, I'll tell you a story;
We are both unhappy by day.
The night has come in its glory;
Our cares are far away.

I'll put out the lamp, for the envious sun
Like a spy will take our news and run
Through every street and lane of the town;
Beware lest he come to announce the dawn.

Ibrahim! Wake up and rise.
Your lover is fair of face.
Deck yourself out, for the evening flies,
And fall in his embrace.
The night will be over; my passion awakes.

[5] M Hafiz Syed, *Suk Suhelā*, in Allahabad University Studies, vol. VI, Allahabad, 1931, 487.

[6] Nazir Ahmad, *Kitāb-i Nauras*, New Delhi, 1956, 102.

Your lover will leave ere the first dawn
breaks.'

Ibrahim was one of the first poets of Bijapur to compose verse on secular themes. His excessive love for the Hindu *devmālā* caused some alarm, and we are told by the author of the Persian chronicle, *Basātīn us-Salātīn*, that some prominent Islamic clerics were dispatched to his court to put the Sultan back on the straight and narrow path.[7] At exactly the same time, his contemporary, Muhammad Quli Qutb Shah, the ruler of Golkunda, was engaged in writing his Dakani *dīvān*, the ghazals of which naturally lent themselves to a more Persianizing style.

For the first time, both rulers sought vernacular poets to grace their courts and sing their praises. In Golkunda the mystic writer, Vajhi, was commissioned to compose the *masnavī, Qutb Mushstarī*, in which the lover-hero is none other than Muhammad Quli himself. In Bijapur Ibrahim invited a poet, known to us only as ᶜAbdul, to write a panegyric *masnavī*, which bore the title *Ibrahīmnāma*. Both works, though somewhat different from each other in language and style, are composed in the Persian *mutaqārib* metre. It is clear from the introduction to the *Ibrāhīmnāma* that ᶜAbdul was rather embarrassed by the king's request, saying that he knew no Arabic or Persian, but only spoke the vernacular:

zabān hindavī so hūṅ dihlavī
na jānūṅ ᶜarab haur ᶜajam masnavī [8]

'My language is Hindavi; I am from Delhi.
I do not know [the art of] the Persian and
Arabic *masnavī*.'

Notwithstanding his protests, in 1012 AH/1610 AD ᶜAbdul received the commission and set about producing a substantial work, which has much in common with the *Pem Nem*. In their introductions both Hans and ᶜAbdul wrote at length on the subject of Ibrahim's court, the magnificent city of 'Bidyapur', the Sultan's obsession with the word *nauras*, his elephant Ātish Khān and his tanbura, Motī Khān. Although Hans says nothing of his connections with the court, it is possible that he, like ᶜAbdul, was commissioned to write the *Pem Nem*, which predates the *Ibrāhīmnāma* by only fourteen years.

We may now turn to the *Pem Nem* itself, bearing in mind that the following remarks are based only on a preliminary reading of the lengthy and troublesome text. The detail must wait until the whole work has been accurately edited and studied in the context of other contemporary Dakani compositions.

As the poet states himself, the *Pem Nem* contains 199 *caupāīs* and 999 *dohas*. By *caupāī* the poet means a rhyming couplet with seven syllables with four beats to the line. The second, fourth and sixth long syllables may be resolved into two short syllables. For example:

nem yih navvad nuh nām bhed
motī cunneṅ jin nahīṅ ched

'This is the secret of the ninety-nine names
[of God]; pearls have been chosen, which
have no blemish.'

Each section of the poem begins with a *caupāī*, written in red ink. Most of the *caupāīs* begin with the word *nem* 'rule'.

By *doha* the poet means four lines with the rhyme scheme ABCB, written in an eight syllable four beat metre. Any of the eight long syllables but the last may be resolved into two short syllables. For example:

nabī yār tāre jhamkeṅ sāre
maṅh šah mardāṅ yazdāṅ šer
sar pīr pīrāṅ ammīr mīrāṅ
gardūṅ gardāṅ mazhar her

'The Prophet, our friend, shines like all the
stars, a king of men, the lion of God, the
lord of lords. See his appearance on the
revolving firmament.'

The main body of the text consists of such dohas, which are written in black ink. Although the rhyme scheme and metre are on the whole regular and consistent, in places there are slight variations in the scheme. The whole text of the work is marked with vowel signs and suprascript marks indicating gemination of consonants (*tashdīd*) and absence of vowels (*sukūn*). Retroflex consonants are carefully marked with four dots written underneath the letter. Again the consistency and accuracy of the pointing of the text indicate that this work was regarded as important.

The 199 *dohas* (of which one incidentally is missing from the text)[9] are numbered by the scribe. When these are extracted and placed together they form a summary of the whole poem. This practice was later

[7] Mirza Ibrahim Zubairi, *Basātīn us-Salātīn*, Hyderabad, 1890, 276-9.
[8] M H Khan, *Ibrāhīmnāma*, Hyderabad, 1969, 3.

[9] The *doha*, which should introduce section 150, is omitted from the text.

adopted by other writers of Bijapur. For example, the poet Nusratī (fl. 1640–80), who worked at the court of Ibrahim's grandson, Sultan ᶜAli ᶜAdil Shah, begins each section of his *masnavīs* with a rhyming couplet. When these couplets are taken together they form a *qasīda*, in which the whole *masnavī* is summarized.

The first fifty-five sections of the *Pem Nem* contain the author's introduction. This begins with the enumeration of the 99 names of God, who possesses limitless qualities. Hans, in his vain attempt to understand the true nature of the Creator, sheds tears of dejection and misery. The world is unique, and he has sacrificed himself to God, who has showered him with priceless gifts. There follows a discussion of the five elements of sky, wind, water, fire and earth along with the miraculous creation of the sun, the moon and the world. The verses describing the unity of God are strongly reminiscent of the verse of Burhān ud-Dīn Jānam quoted above:

allāh vāhid ek ankār
tirlok kartā dhan kartār
durjak se sišṭ jis bistār
sāniᶜ sāmiᶜᶜalīm sattār

'Allah is unique, one entity; the Creator, who made the three worlds. From his chest he produced the expanse of creation; the Creator, the Hearer, the Wise, who conceals sins.'

After praising the Prophet, ᶜAli, Bibi Fatima and the Four Righteous Caliphs, Hans makes mention of the two great spiritual guides, Mīrāṅ Jī and Burhān ud-Dīn Jānam:

nem yih astut muršid pīr
hans ke sirtāj dhīr gambhīr
šah mīrāṅ jī šah burhān
pitā put at jān sujān

'This is praise of the spiritual guides, the crown on Hans's head; they who have deep knowledge. Shāh Mīrāṅ Jī, Shāh Burhān, father and son; know them to be very wise.'

Several sections are devoted to the eulogy of Ibrahim ᶜAdil Shah, who is likened in splendour to the full moon. He is the very embodiment of the nine *rasas* (*nauras*, an epithet given by Ibrahim to his own book of songs, his new capital, Nauraspur, and many of his favourite things). The king is a great musician, who produces fine melodies on his tanbura, Motī Khān. But there is nothing to compare with his elephant, Ātish Khān, which is frisky and coquettish (*cancal*) and 'salty as the sea', i.e. as sweet as honey.

Finally comes praise of the *Pem Nem* itself, a work inspired by God. People sigh when they hear its exquisite verse, which inspires faith and devotion:

nem hans māṅgat daī kan dān
acchar ākhat ratan khān

'Hans asked a boon from God; he pronounced the words and revealed a mine of jewels.'

The story begins in section 55. The theme, it must be said, is a re-working of those known to us from many Indian and Persian romances. A prince falls in love with a princess, who resides in a far-off land. Suffering from the anguish of love, he goes in search of her, experiencing many adventures and adversities on his journey. Finally, however, the two lovers are united and all ends happily ever after. The art of recounting such a familiar story was, of course, to embellish it with striking and beautiful language, and to be as inventive as possible in the detail.

In the *Pem Nem* Shah Ji, a prince of peerless qualities lived in the northern kingdom of Kuldip. Mah Ji, a princess of the island of Sangaldip, was so beautiful that Yusuf would have lost his senses if he had cast his eyes upon her. Fate made them fall in love with each other, when a tortoise mysteriously conveyed their portraits to them. Separation burnt their hearts like the slow poison of a cobra. After taking advice from his courtiers, Shah Ji crosses the ocean and finally arrives on the island of Sangaldip, which by coincidence is ruled by his paternal uncle. There he is informed by a mullah that there is indeed a princess on the island, who is wasting away in her love for an unknown prince. When the two lovers meet, however, Shah Ji believes that the picture of the beloved he carries in his heart is reality, whereas Mah Ji, who stands before him, is only a reflection of it. He therefore departs in order to seek the truth by contemplation and meditation *(gyān)*. Mah Ji laments his absence throughout the twelve months of the Hindu calendar, providing the author with the opportunity to compose a lengthy *bāra-māsā* :

nem neh dukh dhan davā-das mās
bītyā khin hans dāsāṅ dās

'This is a description of the twelve moths
of love's pain, which Hans, a slave of slaves,
passed in misery.'

The theme of the *bāra-māsā*, commonplace in medieval Hindi literature, but something of a rarity among Dakani poets, was later taken up by Sultan ᶜAli ᶜAdl Shah, in his twelve stanza poem, entitled *Birhanī Mukhammas* 'An Ode on Separtation'.[10]

Finally permission is given for the marriage (*sanjog*) by Shah Ji's parents, and an auspicious date for the wedding is fixed. Mah Ji's hands are painted with henna (*meṅhdī*) and the festivities are celebrated in great style. The lovers are at last united.

Under the patronage of the ᶜAdil Shahi and Qutb Shahi Sultans, who ruled in Bijapur and Golkunda respectively from the last decades of the 16th century until the annexation of the Deccan by Aurangzeb in the 1680s, a substantial amount of verse and prose literature was produced in the vernacular. Initially the language had no particular name and was referred to variously as *dihlavī*, the speech,which had originated from Delhi, *hindī* or *hindavī*, Indian as opposed to Persian, *gujrī*, the form of the language, which had been adopted by the sufis of Gujarat, and *dakanī*, the lingua franca of the Deccan. The term Urdu, of course, only became current towards the end of the 18th century.

After the death of Aurangzeb, when Delhi became the major centre of royal patronage, poets from the Deccan, among whom Valī (d. *c.* 1707) is the most famous, brought their tradition of vernacular writing to the north, laying the foundations of what is now termed 'classical' Urdu literature. The works, which had been produced earlier in the south, were neglected, if not quite forgotten, and were rediscovered only at the beginning of the 20th century. The handful of scholars, who found them, immediately set about editing and publishing the manuscripts, which for over two hundred years had lain unread in the libraries of India and elsewhere. Unfortunately the results, owing to lack of resources and proper expertise on the part of the editors, were on the whole very poor, and the available published texts of these important works are without exception unsatisfactory.

As we have already pointed out, the treatment of a text like that of the *Pem Nem* requires much more than the efforts of one willing scholar. Such a project calls for solid team work. Given the parlous state of Urdu in present day India, whose academic institutions are in many ways best equipped to undertake such work, little can be expected from that quarter. All that one can do is to hope for a brighter future. After all, this vast body of neglected or poorly edited manuscript material, to which the *Pem Nem* belongs, constitutes the very foundations of one of the most important literatures of South Asia.

[10] Zinat Sajida, *Kulliyāt-i Shāhī*, Hyderabad, 1963, 70ff.

18 ISLAMIC GLASS BRACELETS: SOME HINTS FROM FUSTAT

George T Scanlon

In the recently published Catalogue of the registered glass objects from the Fustat Excavations of the American Research Center in Egypt (1964-1981), the authors omitted two categories of glass finds. The first was of glass coin weights and *jetons*, and the second of the fragments of glass bracelets also referred to as glass[1] bangles. It was felt that the former group would be more sensibly handled as numismatic data; the latter were for the most part surface finds and could not be fitted with any security into any of the chronological categories as defined by the archaeology of the site or stylistically paralleled in the extant literature.[2]

However, with the publication of Maud Spaer's pioneering work on the glass bracelets of Hebron, both pre-Islamic and Islamic, this exclusion concept is no longer tenable.[3] These articles set the context and parameters for any further discussion of glass bracelets, provided a typology of shapes and decoration and offered a tentative chronology based, for the Islamic period, on the excavations of Tel Dan and Khirbet El-Minyeh.[4] She then collated these materials against the holdings of 19th century Hebron glass bracelets in the Österreichisches Museum für Angewandte Kunst in Vienna to prove the continuity of shape and decoration.

The only disappointment registered with this ground-breaking research was the enormous gap, *c.* 800-1200 AD, for which she could find no artefactual materials from the excavations. It is the purpose of this paper to present the evidence that at least four fragments were manufactured before 1200 even though comparable pieces in Spaer's decorative typology would have been made through the Mamluk period. Because of such longevity of shape and decoration it behooves us at this point to consider the manufacture and utility of these glass products.

There was not much leavings from a medieval glass house inasmuch as the broken or misshapen glass from the moulds or blowpipes could simply be melted down and reused. However, one reaches a point where the original cullet has been exhausted and a new one is employed so as not to diminish the quality of the vessel. These cullet remainders (probably of various colours) could be melted down yet again and the coagulate used to make varicoloured beads or fashioned to make our bracelets/ bangles. Not much time was spared on the working or the decoration (which may already have been *inherent* in the glass) and as many were made as could be processed from the remainders. The dimensions are covered by Spaer (MS-II, p. 48); our fragments were parts of bracelets whose dimensions were not significantly different from those analyzed by Spaer.

From Spaer's analyses it would seem that in the Islamic period more opaque glass was used for bracelets than in the period back to *c.* 300 AD. As very few opaque glass vessels have been recorded for the Islamic period[5] we must consider the possibility that there were distinct glass houses for making these bracelets (and beads?) which were wholly opaque or with opaque decorative elements. A perusal of Colour plate II (herein) provides a hint of the variety of opaque glass colours.

After Spaer's research there can be little doubt that Hebron was a centre for manufacturing glass bracelets through the 19th century. However, we feel it was not the

[1] George T Scanlon and Ralph Pinder-Wilson, *Fustat Glass of the Early Islamic Period*, Altajir World of Islam Trust, London 2001, 134.

[2] The same was not as generally true for glass beads a great number of which came from datable *loci* and therefore acted as a key element of associative dating; *op. cit.*, 119-123.

[3] Maud Spaer, 'The Pre-Islamic Glass Bracelets of Palestine', *Journal of Glass Studies*, vol. 30 1988, 51-61 and *idem.*, 'The Islamic Glass Bracelets of Palestine: Preliminary Findings', *Journal of Glass Studies*, vol. 34 1992, 44-62. Hereinafter MS-I and MS-II. Mlle Stephanie Boulogne is preparing a doctoral thesis on the subject of glass bracelets under the supervision of Prof Barrucand.

[4] She studied the bracelets found by Whitcomb at Aqaba and those found by Kawatoka at al-Tur in the Sinai as well as slides of the bracelet fragments found at Fustat. (A sampling of the 1965 season which she saw can be seen in Colour pl. II.) Further she studied the collection of bracelets (the majority from the excavations of Aly Bey Bahgat at Fustat) at the Museum of Islamic Art in Cairo.

[5] The background on this question of opaque glass can be gleaned from George T Scanlon, 'Lamm's classification and archaeology', *Gilded and Enamelled Glass from the Middle East*, ed. Rachel Ward, British Museum Press, London 1998, 27-29, with particular reference to Colour Plate P and ill. 8.4-7 therein.

Colour plate II

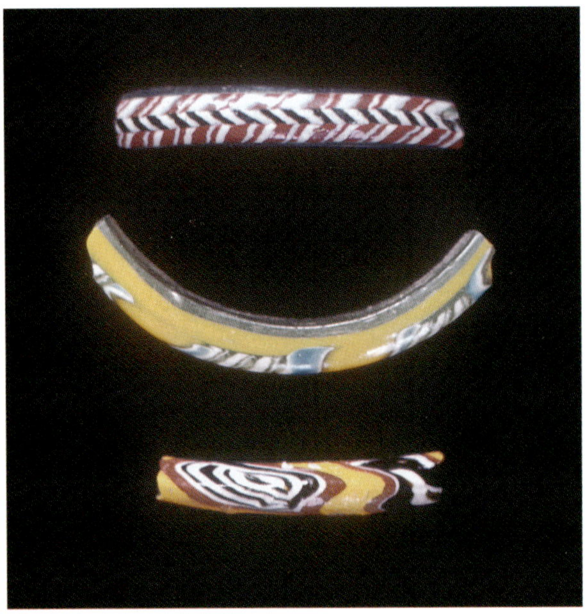

Colour plate III

[facing p. 177]

only one and that Fustat must have been equally important during the Islamic period. The presence of opaque glass slag and the fact that most opaque glass vessels have become associated with Egypt attests an equal prominence if not an equal longevity.[6]

All but four of the registered and unregistered fragments of glass bracelets found in the Fustat/ARCE excavations were surface finds. These exceptional pieces help throw some light on Spaer's long period without chronological attribution noted above. Thus they merit a fuller description:

A. (Colour plate III, lower) Fragment of glass bracelet of rough semicircular section; translucent blue glass with chevron-like decoration in alternating red-white and black-white opaque glass. Found in the fill above the gutter and cistern at H in XVI-21 (FEPR '65-1 Plan II).

Reg. no. 65.2.66. Orig. dia. 6.5cm. Akron Museum of Art.

The find-spot was part of a Fatimid installation which was signalled by an element carrying stone plaque flooring laid in herring-bone fashion. This particular *locus* also contained a portion of a Sung celadon bowl datable to *c.* 1200 AD, hence pre-Mamluk (cf. Egypt-China, pl. XVI).

Spaer's closest approximations can be seen in MS-II, fig. 23, 11-13 from Tel Dan. Approximations to our example from Khirbet al-Minyeh can be found in MS-II, fig. 25, 15 and 16. Spaer would have these Mamluk and later, but the very fineness of the design and execution on our fragment points to a late 12th century dating if not earlier.

B. (Colour plate III, middle) Fragment of glass bracelet of rough semicircular section; translucent blue-green glass with applied opaque yellow half-cane containing patch patterns in light blue, white and black opaque glass. Found at the foundation level in XVI-16' west of the long N-S street (FEPR '65-I Plan II).

Reg. no. 65.2.80 Orig. dia. 6.5cm. Kelsey Museum/Ann Arbor.

A 30 m. cut was made into the mounds at this extremity of the concession to ascertain the route of the street. The finds at the foundation levels on the other side of the street and within the pits pointed to an occupancy from *c.* 700-1200, a chronology paralleled by the stratigraphical cuts into the street itself. Thus it would seem the same applied for the long cut we took to the west of the street. Hence once again this beautiful specimen which lay on the *gabal* points to a late 12th century dating if not earlier.

Spaer's counterparts can be seen in MS-II, fig. 11 and Table 3, Type D-1-d(a) which she concludes are mainly Ottoman. Even were our example to be a surface find it is doubtful if it could be Ottoman (cf. Shard Count, *passim*).

C. (Colour plate III, upper) Fragment of glass bracelet of rough semicircular section; core of black glass with concentric ellipsoidal patch patterns in opaque yellow, red and white. Found in the fill and around base of kiln in XVI-11' (FEPR '65-I Plan II).

Reg. no. 65.2.76 Orig. dia. 6.6cm. Islamic Museum/Cairo.

Again the *locus* is on the west side of the long N-S street with a chronology comparable to that found on the east side. As two Byzantine coins were found in *loci* adjacent to our find spot it seems again that our example must have been made long before the finale of the 12th century.

Spaer's nearest parallels can be seen in MS-II, fig. 12, all of which are flat sectioned. Our ellipsoidal patterns are too large to be mistaken for Spaer's mosaic eye pattern; both patterns are assigned to the Mamluk-into-Ottoman chronology. However, her examples and ours are too finely wrought not to have had a much earlier origin.

D. (Fig. 18.1-a and pl. 18.1-A) Fragment of glass bracelet of rough semicircular section; core of translucent dark manganese glass with inset mosaic eye patterns in opaque white and turquoise plus some 'drag' of the white opaque glass. Found in the fill of X in XVI-13 (FEPR '65-I Plan II).

Reg. no. 65.3.15 Orig. dia. 6.5cm. Akron Museum of Art.

The find spot was within a very large domicile containing three courtyards. Originally Tulunid, most of the complex was incorporated in a later Fatimid

[6] This discussion is rehearsed in the article cited in n. 5 *supra*.

structure. Our example we believe to be from the latter incorporation, hence before 1100 AD.[7]

Spaer's mosaic eye examples can be seen in MS-II, fig. 10.
The motif is much smaller in hers than in ours leading to her statement: 'Superior mosaic eye ornamentation is encountered in Egypt' (MS-II, p. 54). At least for Egypt the motif's origin can be dated well before the Mamluk period.

A surface find at Fustat (fig. 18.1-b and pl. 18.1-C) introduces a new decorative concept into the Islamic bracelet. Made of a translucent cobalt glass of an odd section (as of a flattened ellipse), its outer surface is incised with a scroll pattern with small traces of red and yellow enamel. If the latter be true enamel there can be little doubt that we are looking at a new and more 'artistic' type of Mamluk glass bracelet, one involving the latest decorative technique—polychrome enamelling. (Reg. no. 65.3.88. Orig. dia. 6.5cm. Islamic Museum/Cairo.)

In Spaer's typology there is not apparent an example of a simple marvered bracelet paralleling the beautiful run of marvered glass beads found at Fustat.[8] Such an example was found within the surface fill at Fustat (fig. 18.1-c and pl. 18.1-D). It is circular in section, made of translucent manganese glass with opaque white trailed decoration. One may imagine the complete marvered bangle complementing a string of marvered beads. (Reg. no. 65.3.87 Orig. dia. 5.1cm. Kelsey Museum/Ann Arbor.)

Another surface find presents a rather more complicated decorative pattern. Onto a translucent light blue glass rod is worked another core of opaque yellow glass sided by a chevron design in opaque white and red glass; the combination gives a semicircular section. Then asymmetrically placed prunts, alternately of opaque white-and-red and opaque turquoise-and-white, complete the composition (fig. 18.1-d and pl. 18.2-A). Spaer's only example (MS-II, fig. 9) is not as 'finished' as is our fragment. But for the prunt group as a whole she assigns an ambiguous chronology '9th cen onwards' (MS-II, Table 3 D-1-b) then gives as her second example a 19th century example from Vienna (MS-II, fig. 26 b). We would assign our example a dating of before 1200 AD because of the intricate working of the opaque glasses and the herring-bone border which associates it with our example in Colour plate II lower (Reg. no. 65.4.16 Orig. dia. 6.6cm. Princeton Museum).

Our last example is but a contribution to the buzzing argument between Spaer and Richard Ettinghausen over using 'Kufesque' as a chronological diagnostic (Colour plate II, top middle row and pl. 18.2-B). They both published an almost complete example from the L A Mayer Institute in Jerusalem (MS-II, fig. 18) which Ettinghausen assigned to the ll/12th century while Spaer felt that such bracelets could not have been made 'before the late 13th century' (MS-II, p. 56 and note 34 therein) However, the example she appeals to from the upper level at Khirbet al-Minyah (MS-II, fig. 25-16) lacks entirely the Kufesque element in the Mayer Institute bracelet and of which our example has one half. It seems to us that Ettinghausen is probably correct in that those examples we have cited here bearing 'full Islamic style' were made before 1200 AD though the stylistics may have continued after that date.[9] Further, it seems to us that these 'Kufesque' bracelets are very close in spirit to objects whose manufacture involved the *millefiore* technique. Thus we are inclined to think them as a class even earlier than Ettinghausen surmised.

ABBREVIATIONS

Egypt-China George T Scanlon, 'Egypt and China: Trade and Imitation', *Islam and the Trade of Asia*, ed. D S Richards, Oxford and Philadelphia, 1971, pp. 81-95.

FEPR '65-I George T Scanlon, 'Fustat Expedition Preliminary Report 1965. Part I', *Journal of the American Research Center in Egypt*, V (1966), pp. 83-112.

---

[7] Within the same fill of the same find spot as our bracelet fragment a number of matching shards of an FFS bowl came forth including within the straight ring foot the name 'Mubarak' which signified either the potter or the owner (Pl. I-B). For the significance and chronology of the FFS genre, see George T Scanlon, 'Fustat Fatimid Sgraffiato: Less than Lustre', *L'Egypte Fatimide*, ed. Marianne Barrucand, Presses de l'Univesité de Paris-Sorbonne, Paris 1999, 263-283.

[8] For marvered beads see reference in note 1 *supra*, pl. 47 f-h and figs. 47 f-h.

[9] Three last registered surface finds complete this survey of bracelet fragments form the Fustat/ARCE excavations. Comparable examples can be found in Spaer's typology and they contribute nothing to the chronological arguments.

1. Reg. no. 65.4.14. Found together with the surface fill of XVI-23: a) Black glass with opaque yellow and turquoise inset patch patterns (MS-II, fig. 11); and b) dark manganese glass with yellow and turquoise loose patching (MS-II, fig. 14). Pl. 18.2-C; Akron Museum of Art.

2. Reg. no. 65.4.80 Found in the surface fill at T in XXI-1; manganese translucent glass with opaque red, white, yellow and turquoise inset patterns (MS-II, figs. 24-7 and 25-18). Pl. 18.2-D; Kelsey Museum/Ann Arbor.

3. Reg. no. 65.5.48 Found in the surface fill at D in XI-23; black glass with yellow, red and white patch pattern insets (Spaer, fig. 11). Pl. 18.3-A; Princeton Museum.

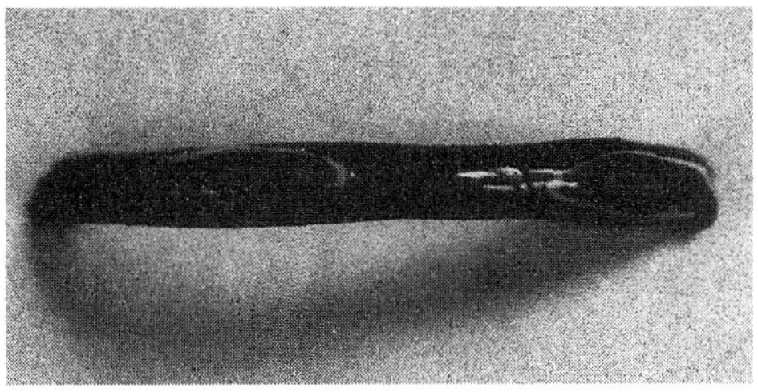

Plate 18.1A

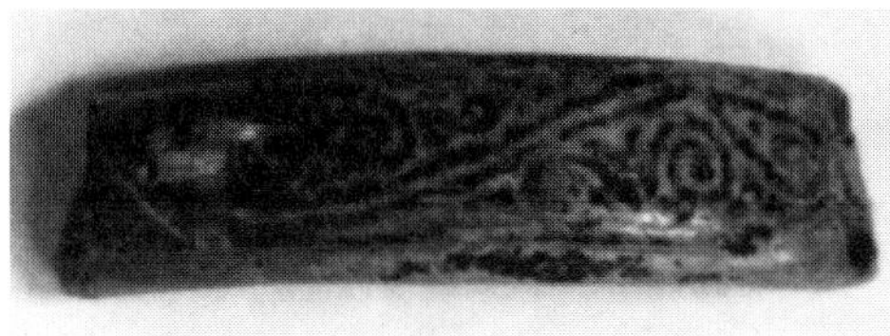

Plate 18.1C

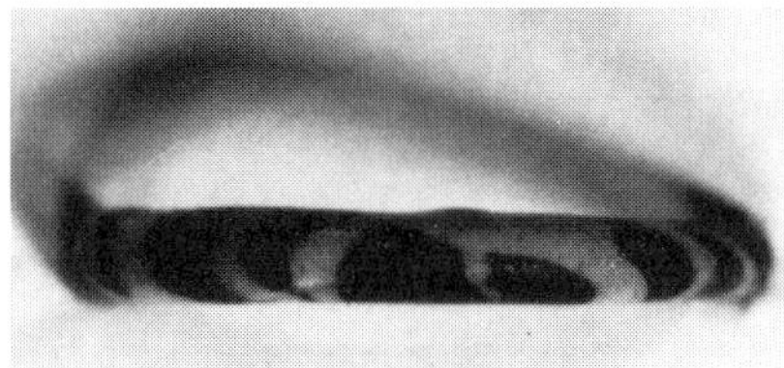

Plate 18.1D

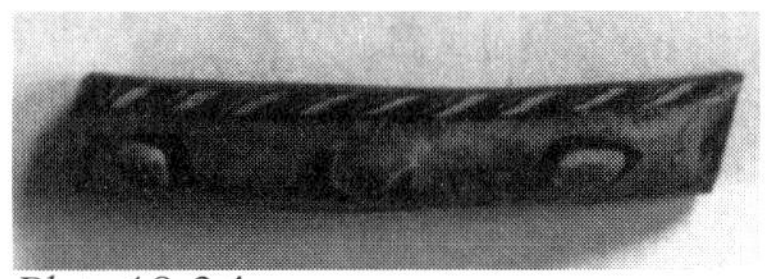

Plate 18.2A

Plate 18.2B

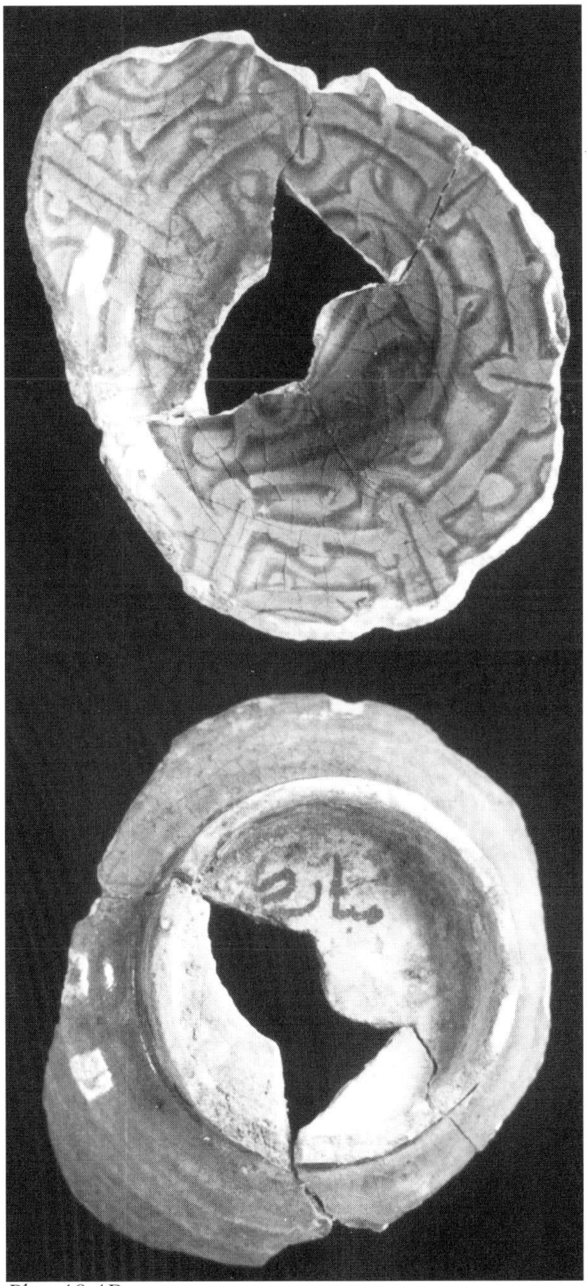

Plate 18.1B

Fig. 18.1a

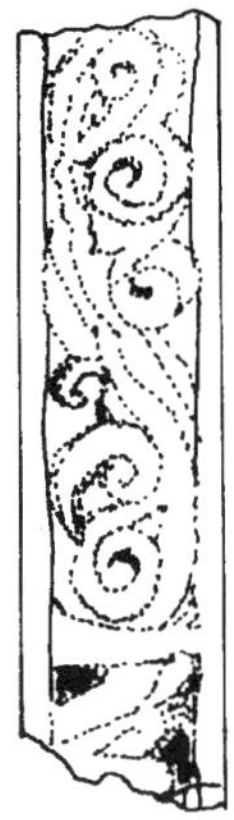

Fig. 18.1b

Fig. 18.1c

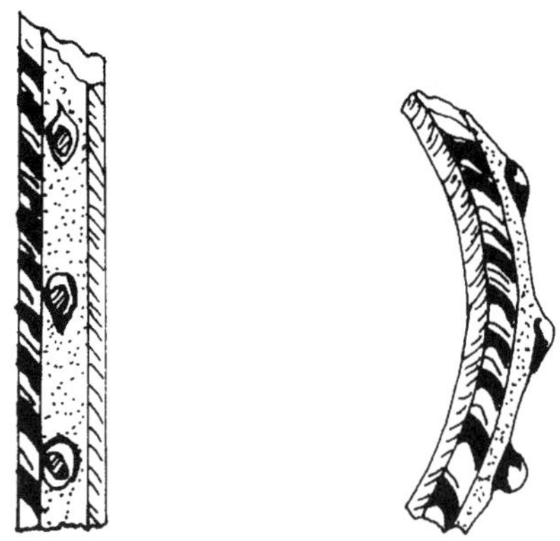

Fig. 18.1d

19 PRINCES AND HEROES OF BANDAR-I TAHERI—A LATE QAJAR FORT AND THE *SHAHNAMA*

Jennifer M Scarce

> Tahiri is interesting as being the site of the ruins of the once famous emporium of Siraf which shared with Ormuz the mercantile supremacy of the Gulf.[1]

George Curzon's exhaustive survey of Persia as the correspondent of *The Times* between November 1889 and April 1990 missed little of importance yet during his journey along the coast of the Persian Gulf from Bushire to Bandar Abbas his comments are uncharacteristically terse. He defines the scattered settlements accurately as ports and maritime villages noting distinctive features such as land access and anchorage, but is silent about any public and private buildings. His political comments, however, reveal the strategic importance of this Iranian coast of the great transit route of the Gulf. All of these modest settlements were administered by a deputy of the governor of Shiraz who in turn was ultimately responsible to the Amin-es Sultan, Mirza Ali Askar Khan, one of Nasiruddin Shah's most senior officials who included among his titles the 'Governorship of the Persian Gulf Ports'.

Bandar-i Taheri's past as the thriving medieval port of Siraf is further witness to the commercial and strategic value of the coastal settlements. Siraf, built on Sasanian foundations, was the boomtown of the 9th to 11th centuries where excavations[2] have revealed mosques and maritime, commercial and residential quarters. Arnold Wilson, a political officer in south-west Iran, noted as he passed through Taheri in 1911 on a rail and road reconnaissance mission:

> Yet this was once a famous port—SIRAF—mentioned by a score of early geographers: it antedates Hormuz, which is just as hot and desolate by many centuries. It was a port of call for Sindbad the Sailor, and it has a history far older than Islam, for we passed as we entered the town, a great number of pre-Islamic graves cut deep into the rock.[3]

Taheri is still a small village on the Iranian side of the Gulf located approximately midway between the old town of Bushire and the modern port of Bandar Abbas, in the narrow coastal strip of Tangestan at the foot of the south-east extension of the Elburz mountains in the province of Fars. Taheri is within a shallow bay divided into east and west by a spur running from the mountains to the sea. Medieval Siraf's ruins lie to the west, the sprawling houses of the village to the east while the hill of the spur is dominated by the remains of a once imposing fort whose buttressed walls and towers are 'clearly visible at a distance of about 7 miles when approaching from westward' (fig. 19.1).[4]

The fort in its heyday (pl. 19.1) was a substantial construction of both storage and residential quarters built of unfired and fired brick, mortar and plaster, the versatile materials of traditional Iranian architecture. A common wall divided the square building into two courtyards each surrounded by several storeys of rooms. The south courtyard facing the sea was entered through a massive wooden gate and functioned as the public area receiving visitors, supplies and livestock, whereas the north courtyard reached through a discreet door at the north-east corner was reserved for the Sheikh's family; both areas corresponded respectively to the *biruni* and *andarun* of a traditional Iranian home.[5]

---

1 George N Curzon, *Persia and the Persian Question*, London 1892, vol. II, 40.

2 Siraf was excavated by Dr David Whitehouse for the British Institute of Persian Studies from 1966 to 1973. See *Iran*, Journal of the British Institute of Persian Studies, vols. V-XII, 1967-74 for interim reports.

3 Sir Arnold Wilson, *South-west Persia—a political officer's diary 1907-1914*, Oxford 1941, 181.

4 *Persian Gulf Pilot*, London. Supplement 4, 1964, 26, 11th edition 1967, 146, Supplement 5, 1965, 26.

5 I stayed in the fort from October 1968 to January 1969 cataloguing the small finds of the third season at Siraf which gave me the opportunity to study the remarkable series of stucco reliefs. I acknowledge with gratitude the support of Dr David Whitehouse in supplying me with information about the background history of the fort and the set of photographs used in this article, and of the Royal Scottish Museum Edinburgh (now the Royal Museum of Scotland, National Museums of Scotland) in granting me generous study leave.

Here a single storey on the south side was a shelter for goats and gave stair access to a flat roof corner which served as a walkway to other parts of the fort. North, west and east sides each had two storeys of rooms, the lower functioning as stables and granaries, the upper as reception and living quarters. Further levels of construction are seen in a two-storeyed block at the south-east corner and in a *badgir* at the north-east corner, a tower of square section with vertical slots at each side which functioned as an air-conditioning mechanism by trapping and drawing air into the rooms below.

The most remarkable feature of the fort, however, is seen in the upper storey of the west side of the south courtyard (pl. 19.2). Here, two rooms, one with a carved stucco fireplace, open on to a colonnaded balcony elaborately decorated with eighteen moulded and carved stucco scenes (pl. 19.3) inspired by the narrative of Ferdousi's classic Persian epic poem the *Shahnama* (completed *c.* 1010) (pls. 19.3-16). This balcony may be compared in form and decoration with the columned *talar* porch which is found throughout Iran in the *biruni* of palaces and wealthy households as a place for the reception and entertainment of guests.[6] As yet no known parallel with this extraordinary pictorial narrative has been identified in the remains of forts along either the Iranian or the Arab coasts of the Gulf. It is surprising that neither Curzon nor Wilson referred to such a prominent feature of the Taheri landscape. Wilson, in particular, had visited Hatim Khan, one of the Al-Nasouri sheikhs of Arab origin who controlled extensive areas of the coast around Taheri. His descendants continued to use the fort as their residence until it was abandoned sometime during the 1980s.[7]

The presence of such sophisticated narrative scenes in the interior decoration of Taheri's fort poses many questions especially about the status of Taheri. It is easy enough to dismiss the village as an obscure place with scant natural and human resources. It is, however, well-located with a bay once the site of the great medieval port town of Siraf and had a good and plentiful water supply. The balcony scenes in themselves demonstrate access to sufficient financial resources and to master craftsmen. Here a critical survey of official records of the Gulf yields facts which contribute to a reasonably clear picture of Taheri in the 19th and early 20th centuries. Taheri's ruling family at that time were the Al-Nasouri sheikhs descendants of migrants from Nejd[8] in central Arabia who in turn had developed a network of Arab contacts in the neighbouring villages of Kangan and Asalu and further afield in Bahrain and Muscat. The population of Taheri consisted of about 200-300 people[9] mainly of Arab origin (Shafiʿi Sunni) and some Iranians (Shiʿa) and a few Baluchi tribesmen.[10] They made the most of such precious resources as the permanent supply of well water[11] to cultivate wheat and barley, dates and vegetables; they also tended sheep and cattle.[12] Trade was another source of income as Taheri was the port for the inland districts of Jam and Galehdar connected by a camel and donkey route through mountain passes[13] along which charcoal, salt fish, pomegranates and grapes were bartered and sold.[14] Taheri's merchants also ran their own boats up to Basra and across to Oman and Arab Gulf ports.[15] Additionally there was a steady flow of emigration to Basra, Oman and India. These external contacts together with a profitable arms smuggling trade justified the presence of a post of the Imperial Persian Customs at Taheri.[16]

Taheri, therefore, enjoyed some success as a trading port, communication route and centre of agricultural production and permanent official residence. The buildings were correspondingly substantial with the Sheikh's fort overlooking a settlement of about 150 houses.[17] A reconstruction of the historical background and building sequence of the fort is essential to establish the date of the *Shahnama* reliefs.

The fort was one link in a chain of strongholds extending along the coast from Bushire to Bandar Abbas whose size and importance indicated the relative power of the local rulers who had built them.[18] These structures were known from the early 19th century onwards to the European officials, political agents, merchants, surveyers and naval personnel who used the sea route to Iran entering through the port of Bushire. Their references to Taheri

6 For example the Ali Qapu and Chihil Sutun Palaces of 17th century Isfahan, and the Gulestan Palace and Narangistan of 19th century Tehran and Shiraz respectively.

7 I am grateful to Warwick Ball for information on the present condition of the fort.

8 The Al-Nasouri sheikhs of the Munasir tribe reputedly migrated from Nejd to the Persian side of the Gulf in the 16th century.

9 Captain Arthur W Stiffe, 'Ancient trading centres of the Persian Gulf I Siraf', *Geographical Journal*, Vol. VI, 1895, 167, notes from his journal of 1857; *Persian Gulf Pilot*, 1st edition 1864, 197; 3rd edition, 1890, 262.

10 J G Lorimer, *Gazetteer of the Persian Gulf, Oman and Central Arabia*, Calcutta 1908, vol. II, pp 1853-1854.

11 Persian Gulf Pilot 1864, 197.

12 Lorimer *op. cit.* 1853.

13 *Ibid.*

14 Wilson *op. cit.* 183.

15 Lorimer *op. cit.* 1853.

16 *Ibid.*

17 *Ibid.*

18 There were forts also at Asalu, Charak and Kangan all close to Taheri.

offer an intriguing at times confusing record both of its existence and their own standards of accurate observation.

The earliest 19th century observer of Taheri was James Morier who accompanied Sir Harford Jones mission to Iran of 1808-09. Morier sailed from Bombay on 12 September 1808 and anchored at Bushire on 14 October. There is no evidence that he stopped at Taheri during his voyage but as he sailed along the coast he noted:

> At Tauhrie (or Tahrie) a port just below Congoon, are extensive ruins and sculptures, with the Persepolitan character. The land-marks for the entrance of the harbour are two large white spots on the summit of a mountain which the people of the country affirm to have been made by the hand of man; on which, on the same traditional authority, are said to have been formerly covered with glass.[19]

During his second visit, accompanying Sir Gore Ouseley's mission of 1810-16 he disembarked at Taheri and explored both the village and the ruins of Siraf between 25 and 26 February 1811. 'The most conspicuous object that met our eyes was an octagonal tower, surrounded by a high wall, which some took for a fortification, others for a mosque. On a hill commanding the town we discovered walls, and three round towers.'[20] The accounts of later visitors prefer sober fact to the exotic image of Persepolitan sculptures flanked by the sparkling lanterns of two lighthouses.

After Morier two Indian navy surveyors visited Taheri—Captain Kempthorne in 1835 who noted that 'it is defended on the western side by an insignificant fortress or rather wall with loop holes for musketry, flanked at every six yards or so with round towers.'[21] and Captain Arthur Stiffe who from 17 to 18 October 1857 both confirmed the location of the fort and described the ruins of Siraf. Entries in various editions of the Persian Gulf Pilot, a navigational reference aid, from 1864 to 1898 confirm the continued presence of Kempthorne's fort of 1835. After 1898, however, the situation changed as the supplement of 1905 to the Persian Gulf Pilot states: 'The square fort on the hill has been pulled down, and a new one erected at the east end of the village.'[22] Thereafter all editions of the Pilot from 1908 to 1967 refer to the east fort. Since the fort containing the *Shahnama* stucco reliefs is definitely to the west of Taheri it must be of 20th century date but when exactly did it replace the demolished structure? How does it—if at all—relate to the fort at the east? The most convincing answer here is found in early 20th century official topographical and archaeological records of the Gulf. The first clue is provided by J G Lorimer, British Political Agent at Bushire, who toured both Arab and Iranian coasts of the Gulf between 1904 and 1905 with a team of surveyors, collecting information for a definitive gazetteer. He travelled the standard route from Bushire to Bandar Abbas and noted the square fort to the west of Taheri;[23] this is clearly to be identified with the fort recorded as demolished in the Pilot supplement of 1905 and is evidence that it was still standing as late as 1904. The first account which identifies the present fort is in the Pilot of 1922: 'on a small hill westward of the village is a large fort with square wind tower and a large conspicuous round tower with a white band near the top and a flagstaff pole from which the Khan's flag is flown.'[24] This entry continues in following editions of the Pilot together with that of the fort at the east of Taheri.[25] The evidence suggests, therefore, that the fort was constructed some time after 1905 and at the latest by 1922.[26] As Arnold Wilson made no reference to it during his visit of 1911 it is possible to estimate a building period of at most ten years from 1912 to 1922. The fort was certainly fully established by 1933 when Aurel Stein, on archaeological survey work, camped in Taheri from 11 to 19 June 'on an old walled up terrace below the fortified mansion of Sheikh Hatim, the local chief'.[27] The building in his accompanying photograph corresponds exactly to the present fort.[28]

Assuming that the *Shahnama* stucco reliefs are contemporary with the fort, they are remarkable examples of the survival of a traditional form of decoration and iconography themes well into the 20th century. The

[19] James Morier, *A journey through Persia, Armenia and Asia Minor to Constantinople in the years 1808 and 1809*, London 1812, Chapter IV, 48-49.

[20] James Morier, *A second journey through Persia, Armenia and Asia Minor to Constantinople between the years 1810 and 1816*, London 1818, 34.

[21] Captain G B Kempthorne, *Transactions of the Bombay Geographical Society*, Vol. XIII, March 1856-1857, 127.

[22] *Persian Gulf Pilot*, Supplement to 4th edition, 1905, 24.

[23] Lorimer *op. cit.*, 1853.

[24] *Persian Gulf Pilot*, Supplement 7, 1922, 250.

[25] The east fort has long since disintegrated. It was certainly not there during my visit.

[26] Sheikh Naser Nasouri who occupied the fort during the 1960s claimed in 1967 that it was built by his grandfather with British money at during the 1914-18 war. Anecdotal information given to me by Dr Whitehouse, letter of 7th July 1969.

[27] Sir Aurel Stein, *Archaeological Reconnaissances in North-western and South-eastern Iran*, London 1937, 202.

[28] *Ibid.*, pl. 60.

Pl. 19.1 Taheri Fort, general view (Photo: W Ball).

Pl. 19.2 Taheri Fort, west side of south courtyard (Photo: W Ball).

Fig. 1 Sketch map of Taheri showing the Sheikh's fort. 1933. (Adapted from Stein, Archaelogical Reconnaissances in North-western and South-Eastern Iran, *1937, Plan 17).*

Pl. 19.3 Taheri Fort, colonnaded balcony (Photo: W Ball).

Pl. 19.4 Taheri Fort, stucco scene 1, Rustam killing Esfandiyar.

Pl. 19.5 Taheri Fort, stucco scene 3, Sohrab seeks the identity of Rustam.

Pl. 19.6 Taheri Fort, stucco scene 4, Rustam killing Sohrab.

Pl. 19.7 Taheri Fort, stucco scene 5, Rustam rescuing Bizhan from the pit.

balcony which they adorn, of a simple rectangular plan, is entered through a door at the top of the stairs of the south-west corner of the fort, which leads into a long vestibule open on the east side overlooking the courtyard. The long west side is interrupted by five evenly spaced pairs of wooden doors each surmounted by a semicircular fanlight of coloured glass within a wooden frame. On the east side four equally spaced full columns and two semi-engaged columns support five arches. The columns, all varied in form and shape are covered with moulded and carved stucco; the central pair are octagonal with vertical bands, while the outer and semi-engaged ones are circular with oblique fluted bands. All have elaborate *muqarnas* stalactite capitals which lead to the arches decorated on their inner surfaces with stucco panels of floral motifs and foliate tendrils. The stucco itself is formed from a fine-textured buff plaster applied over a mortar base covering the original brick and then moulded, carved and incised according to the requirements of the design. The most intricate work, however, is reserved for the inner walls of the balcony where a carefully articulated scheme of rich foliage ornament frames the *Shahnama* panels. Common to all three sides is a deep cornice of repeated pairs of winged flying figures holding bouquets of flowers above a continuous garland of swagged and beribboned roses carved in prominent relief. Below the cornice foliage is trained into bouquets and sprays of carnations and poppies with birds perched among them, to fill the spandrels and borders around the panels. Here the stucco has been worked in a combination of moulding and carving on various levels to create a rich naturalistic effect emphasised by incised detail on petals and leaves. There is also a dado of approximately one third of each wall's height covered with stucco lightly carved into a pattern simulating either neat courses of brickwork or a crazy paving of interlocking triangles. There are no traces of colour on the stucco which relies for effect on the contrast between light and shade through different levels of relief.[29]

The eighteen narrative panels are aligned in vertical pairs within the decorative frame:

1. 1-2 and 3-4 on each side of the door of the south wall
2. 5-6, 7-8, 9-10, 11-12 flank the three central doors of the west wall
3. 13-14, 15-16, 17-18 are along the north wall Each panel has a simple shape; a rectangular (2, 4, 14, 16, 18), semicircular (1, 3, 13, 15, 17) or a vertical cartouche (5-12) all within a coiled or ribbed moulded border. All of the scenes are identifiable with either episodes, principal characters and associates of the *Shahnama*:

1. *Rustam killing Esfandiyar* (pl. 19.4). Rustam shoots arrows into the eyes of Prince Esfandiyar, son of Shah Goshtasp, a legendary king of Iran.
2. The death of Rustam. Shahgad, Rustam's treacherous half-brother. lures Rustam into a trap lined with knives and swords. Before dying Rustam kills Shagad by shooting an arrow into his heart.
3. *Sohrab seeks the identity of Rustam* (pl. 19.5). Sohrab, Rustam's son, leads the Turanian army against the Iranians. He asks an Iranian soldier the names of his leaders in order to identify Rustam.
4. *Rustam killing Sohrab* (pl. 19.6). Rustam has defeated Sohrab in single combat, each unaware of the other's identity. Rustam recognizes his dying son too late from an amulet inscribed with his name.
5. *Rustam rescuing Bizhan from the pit* (pl. 19.7). The Iranian Bizhan has fallen in love with Manizha, daughter of the Turanian king Afrasiyab. As punishment he is thrown into a pit. Rustam here pulls him up with a rope.
6. *Rustam kicking the rock* (pl. 19.8). Bahman, the son of Esfandiyar, discovers Rustam feasting and drinking. He tries to kill Rustam by rolling a rock down on him. Rustam simply kicks it away, proof of his enormous strength.
7. Key Khosrau enthroned. Key Khosrau was the son of the Iranian prince Siyavosh and the Turanian princess Farangis. His reign was famous for justice and mercy.
8. *Rustam and his father Zal* (pl. 19.9). Rustam's ancestry is illustrious. Zal is ruler of the eastern province of Sistan and the son of the great warrior Sam. Rustam's mother, Rudaba, is the daughter of the ruler of Kabul.
9. *Prince Siyavosh hunting* (pl. 19.10). Prince Siyavosh goes to the court of

[29] During the later part of the reign of Nasiruddin Shah Qajar (1848-96) monochrome stucco fashioned into very elaborate designs of flower bouquets and garlands became very fashionable. Good examples of this style are in the Gulestan palace, and the Bagh-i Ferdous—a garden pavilion in the north of Tehran.

Pl. 19.8 Taheri Fort, scene 6, Rustam kicking the rock.

Pl. 19.10 Taheri Fort, stucco scene 9, Prince Siyavosh hunting.

Pl. 19. 9 Taheri Fort, stucco scene 8, Rustam and his father Zal.

Pl. 19.11 Taheri Fort, stucco scene 12, Rustam killing the White Elephant.

Pl. 19.12 *Taheri Fort, stucco scene 14, The Div Akhvan throwing Rustam into the ocean.*

Pl. 19.14 *Taheri Fort, stucco scene 16, The meeting of Ferdousi with Sultan Mahmud's court poets.*

Pl. 19.13 *Taheri Fort, stucco scene 15, Mahmud of Ghazna (998-1030) enthroned.*

Pl. 19.15 *Taheri Fort, stucco scene 17, Key Kavus and his grandson Key Khosrau seated.*

Afrasiyab, ruler of the Turanians, and eventually marries his daughter Farangis. He displays his skill in both playing polo and hunting.

10. Giv and Gaudarz. Giv and Gaudarz, warriors at the courts of the rulers Key Kavus and Key Khosrau, are secondary but important characters who ensure that the main story continues.

11. Prince Siyavosh's ordeal by fire. Sudaba, stepmother of Siyavosh son of the Iranian ruler Key Kavus, falls in love with him. When accused Siyavosh and his horse emerge unharmed from the fire thus proving his innocence.

12. *Rustam killing the White Elephant* (pl. 19.11). Zal's white elephant runs wild. Rustam kills it using the mace of his grandfather Sam.

13. Anushiravan enthroned. Anushiravan, like Key Khusrau, ruled justly and reformed Iran's tax system.

14. *The Div Akhvan throwing Rustam into the ocean* (pl. 19.12). One of Rustam's seven heroic deeds. He tricks Akhvan into throwing him into the ocean rather than hurling him on to a mountain.

15. *Sultan Mahmud of Ghazna* (998-1030 AD) *enthroned* (pl. 19.13). Sultan Mahmud ruled territories extending from Isfahan to Lahore. Firdausi, after 35 years of work, completed the Shahnama *c.*1010 A.D. and presented it to Mahmud in the hope of patronage.

16. *The meeting of Ferdousi with Sultan Mahmud's court poets* (pl. 19.14). This refers to an event recorded in the biography of Ferdousi compiled by Prince Baisunqur in the early 15th century. Ferdousi joins the three poets in a garden. They shun him until he completes a line of verse, which is inscribed on the plaque which he holds. They then welcome him and later introduce him to Sultan Mahmud.

17. *Key Kavus and his grandson Key Khosrau seated* (pl. 19.15). Key Khosrau was crowned as ruler of Iran during his grandfather's lifetime. Here they are shown as equal in status and the scene probably refers to their meeting to discuss the problem of their joint enemy Afrasiyab.

Pl. 19.16 Taheri Fort, stucco scene 18, Rustam's combat with the White Div.

18. *Rustam's combat with the White Div* (pl. 19.16). This is the last of Rustam's seven heroic deeds. He rescues the ruler Key Kavus from the White Div who had kidnapped and blinded him.

All of the figures are conveniently identified by name and caption written in Persian in a squat *nasta'liq* script within circular or square medallions placed above or beside them.

The scenes invite many lines of discussion concerning artistic technique and convention, identification and importance of scenes, source and date. All of the figures and inscriptions have been moulded in bold relief against a smooth plain ground. Bevelled edges, however, soften the abrupt transition between levels while details of calligraphy, features, textures and folds of clothing are worked in shallow relief and boldly incised strokes. This technique enables the characters to be depicted clearly and the space used to best advantage. A flat cartoon-like treatment has been chosen for the figures, with frontal poses and little regard for perspective and proportion in relation to the size of horses and elephants. Compositions are formal and static focused on the principal character with supporting figures grouped symmetrically around him. Available space is exploited by foreshortening animals or by depicting them in part only; thus in the scenes with Rustam and Sohrab (4) only the front halves of their horses are shown.

The scenery and action around the figures is streamlined and simplified; rocks and tents are treated as triangular peaks in outline and parallel strokes. Bizhan's and Rustam's pits are enclosed loops (2, 5). Onlookers peer down at the main action from behind rocks (6) or from windows (11, 12) sometimes with hands raised in the classic gesture of astonishment. There is little attempt at individual treatment of features. All have long narrow eyes and prominent noses; seasoned warriors have handlebar moustaches (e.g. 1, 4), young men may be clean shaven (9.11), while clothing also aids identification – rulers and dignitaries wear crowns, turbans and long robes, warriors have armour of a type worn from the 17th to early 19th centuries and a range of helmets. Rustam is immediately identified by his long forked beard, his leopard cap, bow, quiver and bull-headed mace (e.g. 6, 8, 12). Skilful use of moulds to duplicate certain features is a time and effort-saving device. Here, for example, Rustam and Zal (8), Giv and Gaudarz (10) are seated in identical poses on identical chairs.

The presence of this remarkable stucco panorama of the *Shahnama* at such a late date in the Qajar period and in such an apparently unlikely place, is an impressive witness to the vitality of the great epic as a continuing pictorial source for a robust popular art. Although, however, the *Shahnama* mingles myth, romance, heroism and historical narratives of Iran's Sasanian kings in an inexhaustible choice of subject to artists and craftsmen, certain themes are repeated constantly because they have a strong narrative and emotional appeal, and can be depicted effectively in pictorial form. Rustam, the national hero, famous for his miraculous birth, his superhuman strength and his endless battles on behalf of Iran is the most popular and celebrated hero. He is also a flawed tragic figure who abandons his wife Tahmina, kills his son Sohrab and stupidly falls into the trap set by Shahgad. The choice here apart from the two scenes of the presentation of Ferdousi's poem to Sultan Mahmud (15, 16) is devoted to the *Shahnama* in a balance between action and repose. Eleven of the scenes depict *Shahnama* episodes (1-6, 11-12, 14, 18) of which eight directly feature Rustam as the man of action (1-2, 4-6, 12, 14, 18) and three the young men Sohrab, Bizhan and Siyavosh (3, 5, 11). He is shown both in his great moments of courage and sacrifice—rescuing Bizhan (5) outwitting wild animals and demons (12, 14) his victory over the White Div (18) and in his failures—the killing of Sohrab (4) falling into Shahgad's trap (2); even here he makes one last effort and summons up the strength to kill his betrayer. The action of these main scenes is tempered by the two prefaces and five more tranquil scenes which although they feature important mythical and historical characters, such as Anushiravan and Key Khosrau—enthroned and seated do not stress any specific event (7-10, 13, 17). Within this sequence of alternation of action and repose the placement of each scene does not follow the order of the poem; for example, Rustam's killing of the White Elephant and his combat with the White Div are respectively first and second in the poem and twelfth and eighteenth in the reliefs. The two preface scenes (15, 16) are framed between two of Rustam's deeds (14, 18). This arbitrary order means that the scenes can be 'read' as a sequence in either direction or as self-contained stories according to the viewer's choice.

The stucco reliefs in terms of their technical and artistic accomplishment are the confident product of a patron and craftsmen who had access to a sophisticated illustrated source. Although the *Shahnama* was so widely admired in Iranian cultural life at all levels, illustrated editions were luxury products reserved for a narrow elite circle. The introduction, however, of the process of lithography into Iran during the 1840s drastically changed the situation enabling copies of the classic texts to be produced quickly and cheaply and widely circulated.[30] The *Shahnama* was an obvious case for treatment and many lithographed editions were printed during the 19th and early 20th centuries in Tabriz and Tehran and also copied in India—at Delhi, Bombay and Lucknow. Two of the most important and copiously illustrated editions were printed in 1849 one in Tehran, the other in Bombay.[31] These in turn were frequently reprinted including a re-lithographed edition of 1913 at Bombay.[32] In comparing the stucco scenes with the illustrations of various editions it is clear that those printed in Bombay supplied the main sources, which however were adapted and interpreted rather than

[30] See B W Robinson, 'The Tehran Nizami and other Qajar lithographed books in Islam' in the *Balkans and Persian Art and Culture of the 18th and 19th centuries*, Edinburgh 1979 (ed. Jennifer Scarce), 61-74, for an excellent account of this change.

[31] Lithographed editions of the *Shahnama* in the British Library: Tehran 1849/50 copied by Mustafa Quli b. Muhammad under the direction of Hajji Muhammad Husayn Tehrani, 596 folios, 57 illustrations by Ali Quli Khoyi (2 signed) (reg. no. 757.1.4); Bombay 1849, illustrations by Ali Akbar (reg. no. 14807.h.4). I am grateful to B W Robinson for suggesting lithograph illustrations as a possible source.

[32] Bombay 1913, Lithograph from the original manuscript and paintings of Aga Awalia Sami Shirazi compiled by Irani Amuzanda Shirmand Nauzar, 10 Frere Road and 218 Bazaar Gate Street, Fort, Bombay (India Office Library London reg. no. 306.34.G.16).

Pl. 19.17 Shahnama. *Ferdousi before Mahmud of Ghazna and his court poets. Lithograph illustration from the Bombay edition of 1849.*

directly copied. Features in the 1849 edition such as the style of crowns, turbans and robes, treatment of faces and placement of figures have been observed and then simplified to suit the techniques and limitations of stucco moulding and carving where the fine hatched and shaded detail of the lithograph could not be reproduced.

An analysis of some of the principal scenes indicate how the text illustrations have been interpreted. Detailed treatment of interior furnishing, clothing, ornament and the outdoor scene has been eliminated. Ferdousi's audience with Sultan Mahmud and his court poets has been sharply divided into two scenes by a fringed lattice border (pls. 19.12-13 and 17) and the composition is static with two attendants flanking Mahmud to fill the space and balance the figures below. Rustam's exploits are similarly varied. His killing of the White Elephant (pls. 19.10 and 18) keeps the asymmetry of the illustration but the figures are cut and aligned to suit the vertical format of the panel. The treatment of Rustam's killing of Sohrab (pls. 19.6 and 19) has effectively reduced the original to the minimum. Rustam's victory over the White Div (pls. 19.15 and 20) has also been reduced to a vertical composition of the two protagonists, their positions have been reversed and the bewildered Div grasps at a bulbous tree for support. Despite the obvious debt of the stucco reliefs to the Bombay edition of the *Shahnama* which version was used? The illustrated lithographed text was deservedly popular requiring continual reprinting both of the original and other revised and embellished versions such as the Bombay edition of 1913. While retaining the format and composition of the early editions this one crowds the scenes with extra figures and fussy detail but is closer to the stucco reliefs in interpretation. In the context of the date of the fort, which was built between 1912 and 1922, and the close contact of Taheri's inhabitants with India it is reasonable to assume that a copy of the 1913 edition was acquired either directly in Bombay or from Bushire still at that time the main port of entry for merchandise from the sub-continent.

Many questions still remain unanswered such as the circumstances which led to the commissioning of these elaborate stucco reliefs, the financial resources allocated to the project, the identity of the craftsmen and their terms of employment. The intentions of the patron are tantalisingly elusive. It seems probable that the balcony was a display area of both the family's status and connections where guests would be suitably impressed by the cultural references of the *Shahnama*.

Pl. 19.18 Shahnama. *Rustam killing the White Elephant. Lithograph illustration from the Bombay edition of 1849.*

Pl. 19.19 Shahnama. *Rustam killing Sohrab. Lithograph illustration from the Bombay edition of 1849.*

Pl. 19.20 Shahnama. *Rustam's combat with the White Div. Lithograph illustration from the Bombay edition of 1849.*

20 A MANUSCRIPT OF MĪR-ᶜALĪ AL-KĀTIB:[1] A POEM ON THE DUTIES OF PRAYER

Annemarie Schimmel

> *A poem, composed by himself, on the duties of prayer; it contains notes and seals from Jahāngīr to Shāh ᶜĀlam as well as seals of later* nawwābs.

Who would not be overjoyed when he finds an original work by Mīr-ᶜAlī of Herat, the famous calligrapher whose writing was and still is highly appreciated by museums and individuals in East and West? Even greater are both surprise and joy when one discovers not only a single page but rather an entire booklet penned by the great master of Herat. That happened to me thanks to Daniel Walker who, many years ago, took me to a private collector's house in Cincinnati. The owners of the manuscript most generously permitted me to have the manuscript photographed and—finally—published.

The little treasure is a *muqaddimat aṣ-ṣalāt*, an introduction to the duties of the believer, in particular prayer and fasting. This genre of literature was popular in the eastern Islamic countries from the Middle Ages, at least from the days of Abū Laith as-Samarqandī (d. *c.* 1000) and one finds such treatises in different languages, including Sindhi, as children and converts had to learn their ritual duties in a simple way.

This Cincinnati manuscript is written on goldflaked yellowish paper and has a number of wormholes; it contains 24 folios with eight lines in the page in large, clear *nastaᶜlīq*. The title page is beautifully decorated with elegant flowers, each letter being surrounded by a thin line. The title, *muqaddimat aṣ-ṣalāt*, is inserted in a yellow cartouche with arabesques in the centre of a dark blue ground with tiny flower arabesques.

The poem itself consists, according to its author, of 170 verses in ten chapters in the metre *khafīf*, and Mīr-ᶜAlī writes (p. 8.):

> I strove as much as possible;
> I covered the *fiqh* with the mantle of poetry.

We know quite a number of short fragments, ghazals, rubāᶜiyyāt and also chronograms from Mīr-ᶜAlī's hand; they date mainly from time when he lived at the Shaybanid court in Bukhara where he had been brought from his hometown Herat after the Uzbek conquest of Herat in 1529. Understandably, he felt homesick in Bukhara and expressed his longing for freedom in numerous verses which are preserved in many *muraqqaᶜs*, including 'The Emperors' Album' in the Metropolitan Museum New York.

Poetical art was not required in the *muqaddimat aṣ-ṣalāt* as the poem was meant as an schoolbook for his young son. The colophon states:

> It was completed by the poorest of calligraphers, ᶜAlī al-Ḥusaynī—may God cover his faults!—in 933 of the Prophet's *hijra* (=1526-7) in the city of Herat for his child Muḥammad Bāqir, may God give him a long life!

Muḥammad Bāqir was probably about seven or eight years old—an age when a Muslim child should be introduced to his religious duties. It is possible that Bāqir was the one who took a great number of his father's calligraphies from Bukhara to other parts of the Muslim East, especially to India, where Mīr-ᶜAlī's work was highly admired.

The manuscript gives also a clear proof of the calligrapher's religious affiliation. One might be inclined to regard him as a Shiᶜa (as I did in my chapter on Mīr-ᶜAlī in 'The Emperors' Album'), for his name and that of his son are common among Shiᶜites, and it is known that he wrote some inscriptions for the sanctuary at Mashhad, one of the spiritual centres of Shiᶜa Islam. Yet, the fact that the final eulogy does not mention the Prophet's family but only his companions shows his Sunni persuasion. Even more: at the end of the introductory praise-poem for the Prophet (p. 5) he writes in a strictly Sunni phrase:

---

[1] About Mīr-ᶜAlī: A Schimmel in the introduction to: S. C. Welch *et al.*, eds., *The Emperors' Album*, The Metropolitan Museum, New York, 1987.
My thanks are due to Dr Zia A Shakeb, London, who helped me with deciphering some of the seals and notes and identified some of the persons mentioned there.

We are of his community, *umma*, and his friends
and the friends of his four friends (the first four caliphs).

Furthermore, he refers twice (pp. 26, 33) to Abū Ḥanīfa Nuᶜmān as the master of jurisprudence whose guidelines he follows in his booklet—the Hanafi *madhhab* was widely spred in the Turkish areas.

The ten chapters of the booklet are short and consist mainly of the enumeration of a believer's duties, of what is *farḍ*, 'duty' and what is *sunna*, 'traditional acts' and mentions also what is considered reprehensible.

After a *naᶜt*, a eulogy for the Prophet (p. 4) the actual text begins on p. 5, lines 5-6:

O praying person, come, purify yourself
and build up the house of your religion!

Chapter 1 deals in four paragraphs with ablution, *wuḍū'*; Chapter 2 mentions things that nullify ablution, while Chapter 3 (p. 16) deals in three paragraphs with *ghusl,* the major ablution, and the amount of water to be used for *wuḍū'* and *ghusl.*

Chapter 4 (p. 20) speaks of the acts that require *ghusl* (sex, childbirth, contact with dead people), and Chapter 5, (p. 23) explains that *tayammum*, the purification with sand, is permitted only when the next watering-place is $^{1}/_{3}$ *farsang* = *c.* one mile, away from the person.

Then follow chapters about ritual prayer (p. 26 f.) On p. 31 the author deals with the *sijda-i sahw*, when one has missed parts of the prayer. p. 29 speaks of daily and nightly acts of worship as mentioned in the *sunna*, Chapter 9 (p. 41) is devoted to fasting in Ramaḍān, and Chapter 10 (p. 44) to the penance for missing the fast and things that invalidate fasting.

On p. 46 follows the author's closing remark:

Whosoever reads this with sincerity
Knows the necessary duties and the supererogative rules of God.
God's mercy may extend over the reader,
over the one who repeats it and carries it out.
I request a prayer from everyone who reads it,
for I am a sinful slave.

* * *

The manuscript ends on p. 47 with blessings for the Prophet.

The discovery of such a manuscript would be a very happy occasion in itself, but its value is enhanced beyond description by the fact that inscriptions and seals on the first and last page prove that the manuscript belonged to the Imperial Mughal library from the days of Jahāngīr (ruled 1605-1627) to those of Aurangzēb ᶜĀlamgīr (ruled 1659-1707). Later it came into the possession of the Bangash rulers of Farrukhabad.

The front page contains thirteen, the back page thirty-four inscriptions and seal, the original paper is covered in various places with diaphanous paper or is repaired in such a way that in most cases the original writing is still legible.

The front page contains in large *nastaᶜlīq* the Persian saying: 'A few days were given on loan to us', a line certainly inspired by the verse quoted at the end of the page by Nawwāb Shujāᶜalmulk.

After the *Allāhu akbar* on the left side a note by Jahāngīr follows:

On Tuesday the beginning of ... it was entered into the library of this petitioner at the Divine Court. Written by Nūraddīn Jahāngīr on the lucky day of year 2 of the *julūs* (enthronement).
This treatise ... so that with this beauty ... very very special, value ... 2 (partly illegible)

On the right side:

ilāhi ... In the name of God ...
on the date of 23 Bahman corresponding to 8 Jumādā al-Ākhira 1037
hijrī (= 15 February 1628) it entered the library of this petitioner at the Divine Court. Written by Shihābaddīn Khurram Shāh Jahān Pādishāh ibn Jahāngīr Pādishāh ibn Akbar Pādishāh.

Close to the writing one sees Shāh Jahān's almond-shaped seal with a *nastaᶜlīq* inscription.

The date is interesting as a note by Shāh Jahān for another Mīr-ᶜAlī manuscript, an anthology of Persian epic poetry, now in the Sālār Jung Museum Hyderabad, is dated the same day.

On the lower left side we find a verse by Ḥakīm Sanā'ī (d. 1131). It is barely legible but can be identified as the first lines of the *Ḥadīqat al-Ḥaqīqat.*

In the middle of the page an almond-shaped seal of Aurangzēb ᶜĀlamgīr is found. On a piece of paper that seems to be added later, one reads the Persian line:

By its writer:
We wrote a letter on a rose petal—
Maybe the zephyr brings it to the door!

The longest inscription is found on the lower right:

On the blessed 12 Jumādā al-Ūlā 1263 (= 29 April 1847), Wednesday, this manuscript (beginning with the words) *nām-i Ḥaq* entered the library of the petitioner at the Divine Court, Badraddin Shujāᶜalmulk Muḥammad Saᶜādatmand Khān Bahādur Asad Jang ibn Nawwāb Amīnaddaula Muḥammad Khiradmand Khān Bahādur Bābur Jang, the true successor of Nawwāb Shamsaddaula Muḥammad Khiradmand Khān Bahādur Ghazanfar Jang Governor of Farrukhābād …

… Nawwāb Muḥammad saw (it) and mentioned only this verse:

It is on loan just like our life,
its owner is no one but the Lord of the
world.

A rectangular seal of the Nawwāb with exquisite arabesques in the background of the fine *nastaᶜlīq* text is found twice on the manuscript: once besides his remarks and also besides the *Allāhu akbar* on the left upper corner.

Thanks to the numerous notes and seals on the last page we can find out when the manuscript was shown to the Emperor. That dates are sometimes given in *hijrī* years, sometimes in *julūs* (enthronement) years.

The dates—all from Shāh Jahān's time—are as follows:

1 (=1628), 3 (=1631), 5 (=1633), 6 (=1634), 7 (=1635), 9 (=1636), 11 (=1638), 1048 *hijrī* (=1638-9), 13 (=1640), 1053 *hijrī* (= 1643), 16 (= 1644), 19 (=1647), 1061 *hijrī* (=1651), 1063 *hijrī* (=1653), 21 (=1649-50)

Emperor Aurangzēb ᶜĀlamgīr saw the manuscript in Shāhjahānābād in 1089 hijri (=1678)

A considerable number of seals of courtiers or grandees to whom the manuscript was entrusted or who owned it during the Bangash rule fills the last page of the booklet and could offer additional information about the Mughal and Bangash nobility. Thus, the *muqaddimat aṣ-ṣalāt* is not only a beautiful piece of calligraphy but a valuable historical source.

Pl. 20.1 Muqaḍḍimaṭ aṣ-Ṣalāṭ, *fly leaf at front*

Pl. 20.2 Muqaḍḍimaṭ aṣ-Ṣalāṭ, *page 1*

Pl. 20.3 Muqaḍḍimaṭ aṣ-Ṣalāṭ, *last page*

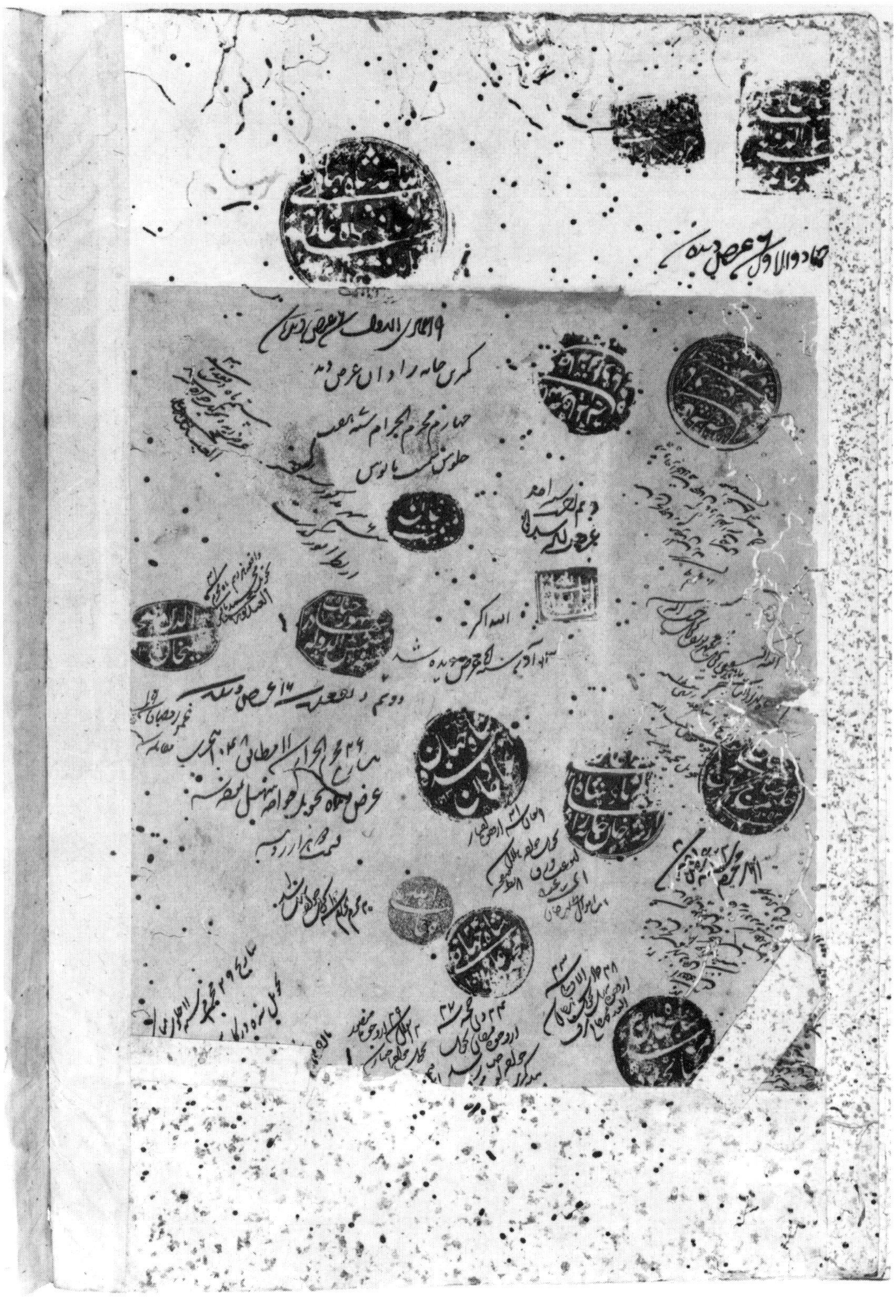

Pl. 20.4 Muqaḍḍimaṭ aṣ-Ṣalāṭ, *end fly leaf*

21 THE OVAL AGATE PLATE OF THE BOOK COVER OF THE BAMBERG APOCALYPSE[1]

Avinoam Shalem

This paper examines the agate plate, which is kept at present in the treasury of the Residenz in Munich and which was once mounted on the book cover of the famous Bamberg Apocalypse (completed at the very beginning of the 11th century). The suggested provenance of this plate is rather controversial: Pharaonic, Late Antiquity, Byzantine and Fatimid. Examining the style of carving of this plate and comparing it with several other oval plates carved out of precious stones, such as jade and rock crystal, a late Sasanian or early Islamic date is suggested. In addition, the history of this piece in its Christian setting is also discussed.

The superb chalcedony plate (pl. 21.1) kept at present in the Schatzkammer of the Residenz in Munich (Inv. Nr. Res. Mü. Schk. 6WL), reached the treasures of the Reiche Kapelle of the Residenz during the secularization, most probably in 1803.[2] According to literary sources, this piece is known to have formerly been kept, at least as early as 1608, in the Kollegiatstift St Stephan in Bamberg forming part of the lavish decoration of the book cover of the Bamberg Apocalypse.

It is a relatively huge piece of oval shape. It measurements are: length 23 cm., width 16 cm., and height

Pl. 21.1 Agate plate once mounted on the book cover of the Bamberg Apocalypse (front side). Munich, Schatzkammer der Residenz (inv. no. Res. Mü. Schk. 6WL). (Photo: courtesy Bayerische Verwaltung der Staatlichen Schlösser, Gärten und Seen.)

[1] The author would like to thank Dr Sabine Heym, chief curator in the Bayerische Verwaltung der Staatlichen Schlösser, Gärten und Seen, Mr Klaus Oelke, restorer of the Schatzkammer der Residenz in Munich and Dr Rupert Hochleitner from the Mineralogische Staatssammlung in Munich for their kind assistance, stimulating suggestions and for sharing their knowledge with me while studying this piece in the Schatzkammer der Residenz in Munich. This study was made for the commentary volume of the facsimile edition of the Bamberg Apocalypse. See Avinoam Shalem, 'Die Achat-Platte vom ursprünglichen Einband', in Gude Suckale-Redlefsen and Bernhard Schemmel (eds.), *Das Buch mit 7 Siegeln. Die Bamberger Apokalypse*, Faksimile Verlag Luzern, Luzern, 2000, 169-173.

[2] For the history of the Münchner Kunstkammer, see Lorenz Seelig, 'Die Münchner Kunstkammer: Geschichte, Anlage, Ausstattung', *Jahrbuch der Bayerischen Denkmalpflege*, vol. 40, 1986, 101-138.

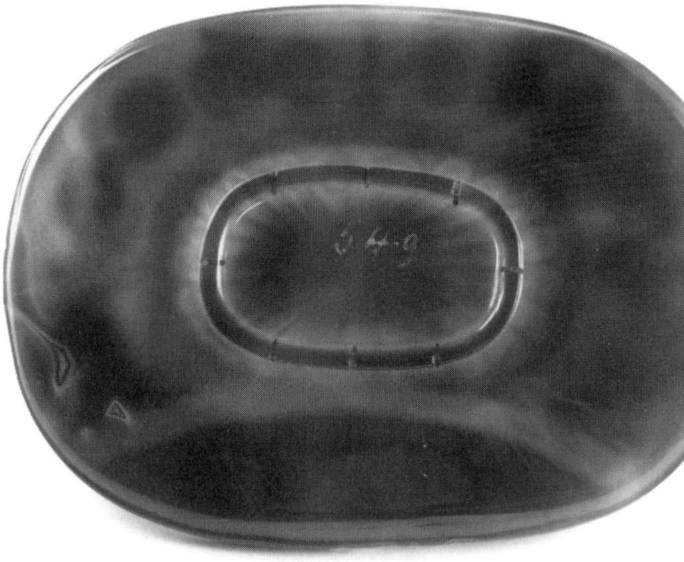

Pl. 21.2 *Agate Plate (rear side). (Photo courtesy Bayerische Verwaltung der Staatlichen Schlösser, Gärten und Seen)*

circa 1.5cm. It weights 670 grams. The plate is cut out of a huge piece. It has a finely polished surface and its colours are rich and varied. They range from almost honey white to various shades of brown, reddish-brown through honey-coloured to dark brown. The pattern is irregular. The reddish-brown and honey-colours swirls and patches are interspersed on the brown background creating a cloudy spotted pattern. The plate is highly translucent; with the light shining through in differing degrees of intensity caused by the varied depths of carving, the general effect is one of great delicacy and fineness.

As far as its material is concerned, the plate has been mentioned in the literature as made of onyx, sardonyx, agate smoky topaz, (Rauchtopaz) and smoky quarz (Rauchquarz).[3] It should be noted that agate, onyx and sardonyx are all subvarieties of chalcedony. The latter is specified as a microcrystalline translucent variety of fine-grained quartz with a fibrous microstructure. Thus, the different names associated with the material of this piece are quite understandable. Moreover, to the best of my knowledge, the piece has been examined by mineralogists only twice. The first examination was made in the fifties by a specialist, Professor W F Eppler, who described it as smoky quarz (Rauchquarz).[4] Lately, Dr Hochleitner, a mineralogist in the Mineralogische Staatssammlungen in Munich, has examined the plate and suggested that it is made out of a superb piece of chalcedony, most probably agate. He has pointed out the two small crystalline raised areas of irregular shapes, which appear on the rear side of the plate, next to its outer rim, and which bear the typical agate's crystalline pattern with its concentric milky white swirls (pl. 21.2).

The carved decoration on the front side of this plate is arranged in two main fields: an inner oval one, which is located at the very centre of the piece, and a relatively wide rim which encircles it. When compared with the rest of the plate's surface, the inner oval section is somewhat shallow. However, it is less likely that it has any functional purposes, and it is more likely that it was done for pure aesthetic reasons. The fact that the oval section is slightly deeply carved enriches the beauty of this piece because two levels of transparency are achieved, and thus the colour of the two main decorative fields are subtly different. The decoration of the inner oval area consists of two shell-like motifs, or perhaps two double palmettes, which face each other and which are clearly divided at the centre by three vertical lines. Each of the shell-like motifs consists of elongated segments; eleven segments appear on one side and twelve on the other. The upper ends of the four segments at the very centre are curled inward; it must be noted that the shell-like motif somewhat recalls a stylised honeysuckle flower, a motif which usually appears in a common Greek and Roman ornament called anthemion. The wide rim is decorated by a row of pointed leaves and tendrils, which

---

[3] Alois Fauser, *Die Bamberger Apokalypse*, Frankfurt a. M, 1958, 5.

[4] *Ibid*.

encircle the central oval area. They are organised in four groups. Each group consists of three pointed leaves and four spiral-formed tendrils. The three pointed leaves are marked by a relatively deep carved lines. The leaf at the very centre points straight up outwards, and the two others gently bend at each side towards the curved tendrils. The leaves and the curved tendrils appear in a slightly higher level of the rim's surface and are clearly marked by roughly carved lines. The border of the plate's rim is also indicated by a carved narrow edge. The latter is a bit higher than the surface of the plate's rim and also marked by a carved line. The border between the central oval section and the wide rim is marked by a roughly carved line. A narrow and oval ring base is carved on the rear side of the plate. The ring base is merely higher than the surface of the plate's bottom. It should be added that, since the central oval section is slightly thinner than the rim, the ring base could also be seen on the front side of the plate. It appears as a slender dark line in the centre of the relatively translucent oval section.

Kahsnitz has recently discussed this piece.[5] He explains that the fact that the carved decoration consists of simple motifs deters scholars from suggesting a definite date or provenance for this piece.[6] Although Kahsnitz has gathered the different suggestions concerning the provenance and dating of this plate,[7] it would be worth reviewing again the scholarly debate about this artefact. The plate was firstly discussed in 1914 by Bassermann-Jordan, who proposed that the central motif is most probably an Egyptian, or at least Egyptianised, double palmette motif and thus ascribed it to the Antique period.[8] Until the early fifties the Egyptian origin was usually accepted.[9] However, in 1952, Messerer argued that the plate is of Egyptian origin but dated it to the Late Antique era.[10] Since 1958, the plate has been also associated with Fatimid art and is usually dated around the year 1000.[11] But, as Kahsnitz has stressed, the Fatimid carving style of rock crystals, as well as cut glass vessels, is evidently different; the cut is usually sharp, straight and relatively deep, and, above all, Fatimid vegetal motifs, like palmette leaves and scrolls, are remarkably elegant and finely carved. Moreover, Kahsnitz concludes: 'Auch die den fatimidischen Arbeiten vorausgehenden, möglicherweise im Iran oder im Irak, jedenfalls im arabischen Gebiet entstandenen Werke, die stärker sassanidischer Hartsteinschlifftechnik verpflichtet sind, erweisen sich nicht als so ähnlich, daß sie eine überzeugende Lokalisierung der Münchner Platte ermöglichen könnten.'[12] Kahsnitz evades, therefore, discussing the dilemma of the plate's provenance and doubts its Late Antique dating.

A small group of relatively flat dishes which are made of carved rock crystal and other valuable stones such as jade and agate and which are usually assigned to the late Sasanian or early Islamic periods, namely between the 7th and the 10th centuries, might throw some light on the puzzling question concerning the provenance and date of the plate. The group consists of two dishes, a rock crystal and a jade one, which are kept in the Louvre, and another two dishes, made of rock crystal and agate, in London.[13] In comparison with the plate from Munich, these dishes are relatively small, but they bear a striking resemblance in shape, decorative programme, and even style of carving to the plate from Munich. Moreover, the two dishes from the Louvre were excavated in Iran, in

[5] Reiner Kahsnitz, 'Chalzedoneplatte,' in *Rom und Byzanz. Schatzkammerstücke aus bayerischen Sammlungen*, exhibition catalogue, the Bayerisches Nationalmuseums in Munich, Munich, 1998, 83-84, cat. no. 8.

[6] *Ibid.*, 83.

[7] *Ibid.*

[8] Ernst Bassermann-Jordan and Wolfgang Schmid, *Der Bamberger Domschatz*, Munich, 1914, 49 (no. 198) and fig. 64. It should be added that the plate was already mentioned in a catalogue of the treasury of Munich published in 1879. See Emil von Schauss, *Historischer und beschreibender Catalog der königlich bayerischen Schatzkammer zu München*, Munich, 1879, 224 (D. 20).

[9] Fritz Haeberlein, *Schatzkammer der Münchener Residenz. Amtlicher Führer*, Bayerische Verwaltung der Staatlichen Schlösser, Gärten und Seen, Munich, 1937, 138, no. 549; *Ars Sacra. Kunst des frühen Mittelalters*, exhibition catalogue, Bayerische Staatsbibliothek München, Munich, 1950, 6, no. 11.

[10] Wilhelm Messerer, *Der Bamberger Domschatz in seinem Bestande bis zum Ende der Hohenstaufen-Zeit*, Munich, 1952, 29 and 44, no. 1 and fig. 1.

[11] Hans Thoma, *Schatzkammer der Residenz München*, Bayerische Verwaltung der Staatlichen Schlösser, Gärten und Seen, Munich, 1958, 20, no. 6; Herbert Brunner, *The Treasury in the Residenz Munich*, Bayerische Verwaltung der Staatlichen Schlösser, Gärten und Seen, Munich, 1967, 5, no. 6; *Schatzkammer der Residenz München, Amtlicher Führer*, Bayerische Verwaltung der Staatlichen Schlösser, Gärten und Seen, Munich, 1981, 5, no. 6.

[12] Kahsnitz, 'Chalzedoneplatte', 84.

[13] For the rock crystal and jade dishes from the Louvre see: Maurice Pézard and Edmond Pottier, *Les Antiquités de la Susiane*, Paris, 1913, 175, no. 403; Roman Ghirshman, *Parthes et Sassanides*, Paris, 1962, 222, fig. 264; Pierre Amiet, 'Nouvelles acquisitions: Antiquités parthes et sassanides', in *La Revue du Louvre*, vol. 17, 1967, 273-282, especially 277-278, figs. 10 und 11; Prudence Oliver Harper, *The Royal Hunter. Art of the Sasanian Empire*, exhibition catalogue, Asia House Gallery, New York, 1978, 85, cat. no. 29. *Le trésor de Saint-Denis*, exhibition catalogue, Musée du Louvre, Paris, 1991, 82, fig. 2; *Splendeur des Sasanides*, exhibition catalogue, Musées Royaux d'Art et d'Histoire, Bruxelles, 1993, 231, cat. no. 82. The rock crystal dish from London, formerly in the Mansur Gallery in London and at present in

Pl. 21.3 Rock crystal dish with gold mounting, excavated in Susa, Iran, circa 7th century AD. Paris, Musée du Louvre (inv. no. Sb 3795). (Photo courtesy Musée du Louvre)

Susa. The rock crystal one (Sb 3795) was found during the excavations made in the late 19th and early 20th centuries by Jacques de Morgan, and was acquired by the Louvre in 1912. The jadeite piece (Sb 3792) was excavated by de Macquenem in Susa in 1928 and reached the Louvre later.[14]

Since the four vessels are almost identical, I have chosen to compare only one of them with the plate from Munich, namely the rock crystal dish from the Louvre. The rock crystal dish (Length 8.9 cm., width 6.6 cm., height 1.7 cm.) which is set within an elaborate and wide gold mount (pl. 21.3), is quite shallow and has an elegant oval form. The decoration is similarly carved in low relief and organised within two main fields: a central oval one which was left undecorated, and the one encircling it which is decorated with plant forms and cross-hatched lines. The plant forms strongly recall the vegetal ornament of the plate in Munich. They consists of three pointed leaves with a spiral volute at either end. It should be added that the dish's rim and the border of the inner oval field are similarly accentuated by thin lines and are also slightly raised above the dish's surface. The assured Susa provenance of the two Louvre dishes, as well as the alleged Iranian provenance of the rock crystal dish in London, suggests a West Iranian or Iraqi provenance for the group as well as for the Munich plate. The dating, however, is more problematic.

As there are no certain Sasanian objects of carved valuable stones,[15] the Sasanian attribution remains to be proven. However, the historical evidence might suggest a rather late Sasanian or early Islamic dating. The city of Susa was destroyed already in the 4th century by Shapur II (309-379) and only partially populated by the end of the Sasanian period, namely around 600. However, it flourished again in the early Abbasid period.[16] The slightly rigidity and the less refined carving of the spiral tendrils and the shell-like motifs of the plate in Munich suggest then a late Sasanian or early Islamic date, namely between 600-800.

It should be stressed, however, that the specific group discussed here as well as other rock crystal vessels found in Iran, suggest that it is possible to locate a school

a private collection, was first published in 1985. See 'An Important Abbasid Rock Crystal Dish 9th-10th Century', in *Arts and the Islamic World* vol. 3/3, 1985, 2-3. The Jadeite dish from London is unpublished. I would like to express my thanks to Mr Nasser Mokhtarzadeh from the Mansur Gallery in London who provided me with a photograph of this piece.

14 Amiet, 'Nouvelles acquisitions', 277-278.

15 For this problematic issue see mainly, Kurt Erdmann, *Die Kunst Irans zur Zeit der Sassaniden*, Mainz, 1969, 116-121; Joseph Philippe, 'Le cristal de roche et la question byzantine', in *26 Corso di Cultura sull'arte ravennate e bizantina*, Ravenna 6/18 May, 1979, Ravenna, 1981, 227-247.

16 Prudence Oliver Harper et al. (eds.), *The Royal City of Susa. Ancient Near Eastern Treasures in the Louvre*, exhibition catalogue, The Metropolitan Museum of Art, New York, 1992.

of rock crystal and hard stone carving in the eastern Islamic lands, most probably in Iraq or Iran.[17] Moreover, medieval literary sources hint at the possibility of the existence of an Iranian or an Iraqi school for carving rock crystals and hard stones already in the early Abbasid period. For example, according to the 11th-century scholar al-Biruni, the last Tahirid governor of Khurasan (deposed in 873) had expensive rock crystal vessels in his treasury.[18] And the Abbasid author al-Suli (d. 946), tells us that the Abbasid caliph al-Radi (r. 934-940) was one of the great rock crystal collector of his time.[19] Other medieval sources claim that the Abbasid caliph al-Amin (r. 809-813) was also a rock crystal collector.[20]

The question concerning the original function of the plate cannot be easily answered. The fact that the plate is extremely flat suggests that it might have been used as a cover for a luxuriant vessel, be that of chalcedony or any other precious metal—it is tempting to suggest that the two shell-like motifs, which decorate the inner oval section of the plate, recall several Sasanian silver bowls with elliptical and fluted, or rather segmented, bodies. But it is also possible that it was simply used for decorative purposes. In that case it might have had a lavish mounting attached to its rim, like the wide gold mounting of the rock crystal dish in the Louvre.

It is unknown in which vein this piece reached the West.[21] But it is plausible that like other remarkable objects, which usually wandered from one royal court to another, this plate might have had a similar peregrination.[22] Chalcedony vessels were extremely valued in the medieval and Renaissance periods and were a sought after objects in church treasuries and cabinets of art and curiosities.[23] Perhaps the best examples illustrating in which esteem these chalcedonic objects were held, is the famous chalice of Abbot Suger (the National Gallery, Washington, Widener collection, C-1), or the 'Tazza Farnese' (Museo Archeologico, Naples).[24] Nonetheless, there are at least another three examples for using Islamic precious stones for decorating medieval book covers, but their biographies before they reached the West are also left in the dark.[25]

The chequered history of the agate plate from Munich in its Christian context has been lately revealed by Baumgärtel-Fleischmann, who has gathered the specific archive documents relating to the book cover of the

[17] For example, a pre-Fatimid dating, either Tulunid (868-905) or Ikhshidid (935-969), for rock crystals was already suggested by Kurt Erdmann. See Kurt Erdmann, 'Fatimid rock crystals', in *Oriental Art*, vol. 3, 1951, 142-146, especially 145.

[18] For the account of al-Biruni, see Al-Beruni, *Kitab al-Jamahir fi Ma'rifat al-Jawahir*, Hyderabad, 1936, 178; for the English translation see Al-Beruni, *The Book Most Comprehensive in Knowledge on Precious Stones*, trans. Hakim Mohammad Said, Islamabad, 1989, 162-163.

[19] Abu Bakr Muhammad b. Yahya al-Suli, *Akhbar ar-Radi wa Muttaki from the Kitab al-Awrak*, ed. by J Heyworth Dunne, London, 1935, 20.

[20] The accounts about the love of al-Amin for rock crystal vessels appear in varied literary sources, see for example Ibn ʿAsakir, *Tarikh Madinat Dimashq wa Zikr Fadlaha wa-Tasmiyat man Hallaha min al-Amathil aw Ijtaza bi-Nawahiha min Waridiha wa-Ahlaha*, ed. by Salah al-Din al-Munaggid, Damascus, 1954, vol. 2, 45-46; Al-Ghuzuli, *Mataliʿ al-budur fi manazil al-surur*, Cairo, 1882-83, vol. 2, 284; Al-ʿUmari, *Masalik al-absar fi mamalik al-amsar*, ed. A Zaki Pasha, Cairo, 1924, vol. 1, 193-94.

[21] It has been suggested that this piece might have reached Germany via Constantinople, as part of the dowry of the Byzantine princess Theopano who married Otto II in 972. But the lack of any evidence leaves us in a rather speculative domain. See Hans Wenzel, 'Das byzantinische Erbe der ottonischen Kaiser. Hypothesen über den Brautschatz der Theophano', in *Aachener Kunstblätter*, vol. 32, 1972, 15, fig. 12.

[22] For the travelling of Islamic objects to the West, especially in the Middle Ages, see Avinoam Shalem, *Islam Christianised*, Frankfurt am Main, second edition 1998, especially part I, 17-125 and *idem.*, 'Jewels and Journeys: The Case of the Medieval Gemstone called al-Yatima', in *Muqarnas* vol. 14, 1997, 42-56.

[23] For Hellenistic chalcedonic objects as well as for their acceptance in medieval and Renaissance periods, see mainly Hans-Peter Bühler, *Antike Gefässe aus Chalcedonen*, PhD thesis, Julius-Maximilian Universität in Würzburg, 1966; *idem.*, *Antike Gefäße aus Edelsteinen*, Mainz, 1973; Klaus Parlasca, 'Neue Beobachtungen zu den hellenistischen Achatgefäßen aus Ägypten', in *The J Paul Getty Journal*, vol. 13, 1985, 19-22; Mariarita Casarosa Guadagni, 'The Medici Collection of Gems during the Fifteenth and Sixteenth Centuries', in Cristina Acidini Luchinat (ed.), *Treasures of Florence. The Medici Collection 1400-1700*, Munich, New York, 1997, 73-92.

[24] For the chalice of Abbot Suger see mainly, *Le trésor de Saint-Denis*, exhibition catalogue, Musée du Louvre, Paris, 1991, 173-176, cat. no. 28 (with extensive bibliography); *The Royal Abbey of Saint-Denis in the time of Abbot Suger (1122-1151)*, exhibition catalogue, The Metropolitan Museum of Art, New York, 1981, 108-111, cat. no. 25; Erwin Panovsky, *Abbot Suger, on the abbey church of St.-Denis and its art treasures*, Princeton, New Jersey, 1979, 78. For the 'Tazza Farnese' see, Ernest Babelon, *La gravure en pierres fines, camées et intailles*, Paris, 1894, figs. 106-107; Bühler, *Antike Gefäße*, 41-43, cat. no. 13, pls. 4, 5; Klaus Parlasca, 'Neue Beobachtungen', 21, figs. 3a, 3b; Burchard Brentjes, 'The 'Tazza Farnese' and its way to Harat and Naples', in *Oriente Moderno*, n. s. vol. 15, 1996, a monography: *La civiltà timuride come fenimeno internazionale* (ed. by Michele Bernardini), Naples, 1997, vol. 1, 321-324; Horst Blanck, 'Eine persische Pinselzeichnung nach der Tazza Farnese', in *Archäologischer Anzeiger*, vol. 26, no. 2/3, 1964, 307-312; Ulrico Pannuti, 'La 'Tazza Farnese', datazione, interpretazione e trasmissione del cimelio', in *Atti del Convegno di Ravello*, 13-16 nov., 1987, Louvain-la Neuve and Rixenart, 1994, 205-214.

[25] Shalem, *Islam Christianized*, cat. nos. 277, 278, 280. See also Geerto A S Snijder, 'Antique and medieval gems on bookcovers at Utrecht', in *The Art Bulletin*, vol. 14, 1932, 5-52.

Bamberg Apocalypse.[26] It seems that the plate was first mentioned in an inventory dated 1608: 'Ein ander Euangelium Buch Apocalypsis genandt mit einem grosen braunen Stein geschmuckt' (Staatsarchiv Bamberg, Rep. B 115, Nr. 80);[27] but it is very possible that this inventory copied the one of 1605. In an inventory dated 1799, the plate is mentioned again as part of the lavish decoration of the book cover of the apocalypse: 'Ein mit 46 verschiedenen Steinen besetztes Buch, worinn der Apokalipsis und die Evangelien auf Bargement geschrieben sind, und wo auf einer Seite der Decke ein Onix, auf der anderen Seite goldene Sternlein sich befinden' (Staatsarchiv Bamberg, Rep. b 115, Nr. 214).[28] The inventory of 1803 describes how, after the secularisation, the precious stones including the *onix* were transported to Munich: 'Die Steine von der Bücherdecke, worin der Onix sich befand, und welcher zurückbehalten und besonders aufbewahrt wurde' (Staatsarchiv Bamberg, Rep. K. 202, Nr. 102, S. 9).[29] In 1805, the Bamberg Apocalypse received a new book cover. In the inventory of the Kurfürstlich Library dated to 1805, the plate is mentioned again. This time as being already in the treasury in Munich: 'nachdem der grosse, auf der vordern Decke angebrachte, wellenförmig geschliffene Sardonyx wegen seines ausserordentlichen Werthes in den Schatz zu München gebracht worden war'.[30]

The records concerning the agate plate suggests that the piece was highly admired for its beauty and value. The inventory of 1799 clearly asserts that the plate was mounted on the front side of the book cover, most probably at the centre. The other 46 precious stones mentioned in this inventory were probably mounted on both sides of the book cover, flanking the 'Onix' plate on the front and the gold 'Sternlein' on the rear. The eight drilled holes which appear on the rear side of the plate, running through the oval ring base (pl. 21.2), suggest that the piece was firmly secured to the book cover, most probably by metal wires.

It is almost impossible to answer whether, or if at all, the existence of an agate plate on the book cover of the Bamberg Apocalypse had a specific meaning. Generally speaking, like many other antique and medieval gems mounted on book covers, the agate plate might have also been associated with medieval ideas referring to light symbolism, and its red-fire colour might be an allegory to the fearful nature of God.[31] But, it should not be ruled out that carved precious stones were also chosen to be mounted on book covers for the healing and even the magical power they were believed to possess.[32] For example, the magical lore associated with agate tells that it has the power of making man to be loved by man and God alike;[33] it is tempting to suggest that the appearance of a huge oval agate on the Bamberg Apocalypse might have reinforced existing prejudices and folk tales concerning the talismanic or even protective virtues of this precious stone, and that its oval shape might rouse the idea that the plate metaphorically operates as a guarding shield. But these suggestions are mere speculative.[34] It is much more likely that, in the first place, the agate plate was chosen to be mounted on the book cover for the superior quality of its material, preciousness and the aesthetic values relating to its colours, translucency and carved decoration.

[26] Published in Bernhard Schemmel, *Staatsbibliothek Bamberg, Handschriften, Buchdruck um 1500 in Bamberg, E T A Hoffman*, exhibition catalogue, Bamberg, 1990, 64-67, cat. no. 26. See also Renate Baumgärtel-Fleischmann, 'Der Einband' in Suckale-Redlefsen und Schemmel (eds.), *Die Bamberger Apokalypse*, 165-167.

[27] Schemmel, *Handschriften, Buchdruck um 1500*, 64.

[28] *Ibid.*, 64-65.

[29] *Ibid.*, 65-66.

[30] *Ibid.*, 66.

[31] See mainly William S Heckescher, 'Relics of Pagan antiquity in medieval settings', in *Journal of Warburg Institute*, vol. 1, 1938, 204-220; Christel Meier, *Gemma Spiritalis: Methode und Gebrauch der Edelsteinallegorese vom frühen Christentum bis ins 18. Jahrhundert*, Munich, 1977, part 1, especially 120-121; Ulrich Henze, 'Edelsteinallegorese im Lichte mittelalterlicher Bild und Reliquienverehrung', in *Zeitschrift für Kunstgeschichte*, vol. 54, 1991, 428-51.

[32] For this topic see John Evans and Mary S Serjeanston, *English Medieval Lapidaries*, London, 1933; John Evans, *Magical Jewels of the Middle Ages and the Renaissance particularly in England*, Oxford, 1922, 30-50; George F Kunz, *The Magic of Jewels and Charms*, London, 1915, especially 118-60; Urban T Holmes, 'Medieval Gem Stones', in *Speculum*, vol. 9, 1934, 195-204.

[33] Evans and Serjeantson, *English Medieval Lapidaries*, 129.

[34] An interesting motif is that of Christ apotheosis, in which Christ appears on an agate-like cloud. See Ursula Nilgen, 'Das Himmelfahrtsbild im Perikopenbuch Heinrichs II', in *Sancta Treveris. Beiträge zu Kirchenbau und bildender Kunst im alten Erzbistum Trier, Festschrift für Franz J Ronig zum 70. Geburtstag*, ed. by Michael Embach *et al.*, Trier, 1999, 467- 490.

22 THE TOMB OF GHIYĀTH AL-DĪN AT TUGHLUQABAD: PISÉ ARCHITECTURE OF AFGHANISTAN TRANSLATED INTO STONE IN DELHI

Mehrdad Shokoohy and Natalie H Shokoohy

The tomb of Ghiyāth al-dīn—a square domed chamber in the courtyard of a small octagonal fortified island south of Tughluqabad—is among the few early sultanate tombs in India, and shows a strong architectural influence from Afghanistan and Central Asia. Its sloping walls—displaying close analogies with the pise architecture of rural Afghanistan—became a characteristic of Tughluq architecture, not to be seen in any other period except perhaps in the fortification walls. In this tomb the simple form of a domed chamber is transformed to a colossal monument of marble and red sandstone, standing as a landmark in the middle of a royal lake.

The well-known tomb of Ghiyāth al-dīn—a square domed chamber in the courtyard of a small octagonal fortified island south-west of the citadel of Tughluqabad—is the only monument at Tughluqabad which is well preserved and is mentioned in most general works.[1] The monument is also included in the list of touristic sites of Delhi, but it is rather far from the other sites, and only the more intrepid travellers take the trouble of visiting the building. The tomb stands to the south of Tughluqabad town which together with its fort and citadel was constructed by Ghiyāth al-dīn Tughluq (r. 720-725/1320-1325) early in his reign. In spite of the relative proximity of Tughluqabad to Delhi, the town itself and the ruins in the fort and the citadel (fig. 22.1) have remained unstudied until recently,[2] but

[1] For a list of the general works mentioning this monument and other features in Tughluqabad see Saiyid Ahmad Khan, *Āthār al-ṣanādīd*, Delhi, 1854, chapter 2, 19-22, Lucknow, 1876, 11-15, figs. 1-7; 'Report of the proceedings of the Archaeological Surveyor to the Government of India for the season of 1862-63', *Journal of the Asiatic Society of Bengal*, XXXIII, 1865, Supplementary Number (addenda to the main number), lxix-lxxv; *Archaeological Survey of India* (Cunningham series) (*ASIR*), 1862-5, Report of 1862-3, 212-17; J D Beglar, 'Report on Delhi for the half year ending September 1871', *ASIR*, IV, 1874, 76-8; James Ferguson, *History of Indian and eastern architecture*, revised edition by James Burgess (Indian Architecture) and René Spiers (Eastern Architecture), II, London, 1910, 215; John Marshall, 'The monuments of Muslim India', *Cambridge History of India*, ed. W Haig, III, Cambridge, 1928, 585-6; Percy Brown, *Indian Architecture (Islamic Period)*, 1942, 7th reprint, Bombay, 1981, 20-1; Sidney Toy, *The strongholds of India*, London, 1957, 116-21; P L Madan, 'Adilabad: a dream of Muhammad bin Tughluq', *Islamic Culture*, XXXVII, 1963, 49-51; John Burton-Page, entry under Delhi in the *Encyclopaedia of Islam*, New ed., London-Leiden, II, 1965, 257-8; Tatsuro Yamamoto, Matsuo Ara and Tokifusa Tsukinowa, *Delhi, architectural remains of the sultanate period* (3 vols.), Tokyo, I, 1967, 52, 64, 102, 111-12; R Nath, *History of sultanate architecture*, New Delhi, 1978, 52-5; R Nath, *Monuments of Delhi*, New Delhi, 1979, 4-5, 35, pls. 2, 22; Y D Sharma, *Delhi and its neighbourhood*, ASI, New Delhi, 1982, 24-5, 101-4; Anthony Welch and Howard Crane, 'The Tughluqs: master builders of the Delhi sultanate', *Muqarnas*, I, 1983, 127-8. K V Soundara Rajan, *Islam builds in India*, Delhi, 1983, 76-7.

[2] The town and its well preserved walls, its street layout and the remains of its buildings provide us with the earliest existing example of Indo-Muslim urban planing and its architectural components. Some restoration work and clearance has been carried out on the walls of Tughluqabad early in this century. During this time some of the monuments may have been surveyed but they have not been published and no records are known to have survived. See *Annual Progress Report of the Superintendent, Muhammadan and British Monuments, Northern Circle* (*ASINC*), 1914, 40, pl. 27; 1921, 14, 35, pls. 9-17; *Archaeological Survey of India Annual Reports* (*ASIAR*), 1904-5, 18-19; 1913-14, i, 3; 1920-1, 3; 1921-2, 4; 1922-3, 7; 1923-4, 141; 1924-5, 5, 9; 1925-6, 199, 1926-7, 254. For a more detailed study of the town the present authors have so far carried out six seasons of fieldwork between 1986 and 1999, during which the fortification walls, the remains of the palaces, the royal square and other buildings in the citadel and the fort were surveyed. In the old town the outline of the remains of the residential buildings, the Jāmiᶜ mosque and other structures were established and outlined in the town plan, and the remains of the Jāmiᶜ mosque, the market, a *madrasa* and two houses were surveyed in some detail. The project has been supported by the British Academy and the Society for South Asian Studies. For the authors' earlier reports see: Tughluqabad, the earliest surviving town of the Delhi Sultanate, *Bulletin of the School of Oriental and African Studies University of London* (*BSOAS*), LVII, 1994, 516-550, pls. I-XVI; 'The Dark Gate, the Dungeons, the Royal Escape Route and more: survey of Tughluqabad, second interim report', *BSOAS*, LXII, 1999, 423-61, pls. I-XI; 'Pragmatic city versus ideal city: Tughluqabad, Perso-Islamic planning and its effect on Indian towns', *Urban Design Studies*, V-VI, 1999-2000, 57-84.

Fig. 22.1 Tughluqabad, plan of the town and its surroundings also showing the Tomb of Ghiyāth-al-dīn Tughluq situated on the fortified artificial island in the middle of the lake to the south-west of the citadel.

Key:
1 Citadel gate
2 Gate leading to the causeway of Ghiyāth al-dīn's tomb
3 Postern gate
4 Quarry made into a tank
5 Stepped pyramidal platform with remains of the Jahān-nāmā pavilion above
6 Basement chambers at both sides of a corridor
7 Main reservoir of the citadel
8 Small mosque
9 Royal square
10 Ruins of gateway with a standing arch
11 Walled area
12 Courtyard with standing arcade
13-14 Streets
15 Forecourt
16 Gate house
17 Court of public audience
18 The audience īwān
19 East court connecting the southern buildings to the audience īwān
20 Street
21 Court south of the palace complex
22 Courtyard with two halls
23 Larger hall
24 Building with square court and a smaller hall
25 Reservoir
26 Six basins known as Hāthī Kund
27 Pavilions in the open area of the fort
28 Probable site of an urban square
29-30 Wells and step-wells
31-32 Two buildings, probably mosques, orientated towards the qibla.
33 Building, probably a madrasa, around a courtyard within a larger compound.
34-35 Probable sites of market squares
36 Tunnel under wall
37 Prayer ground, probably on the site of an old shrine
38 House
39 Royal escape route

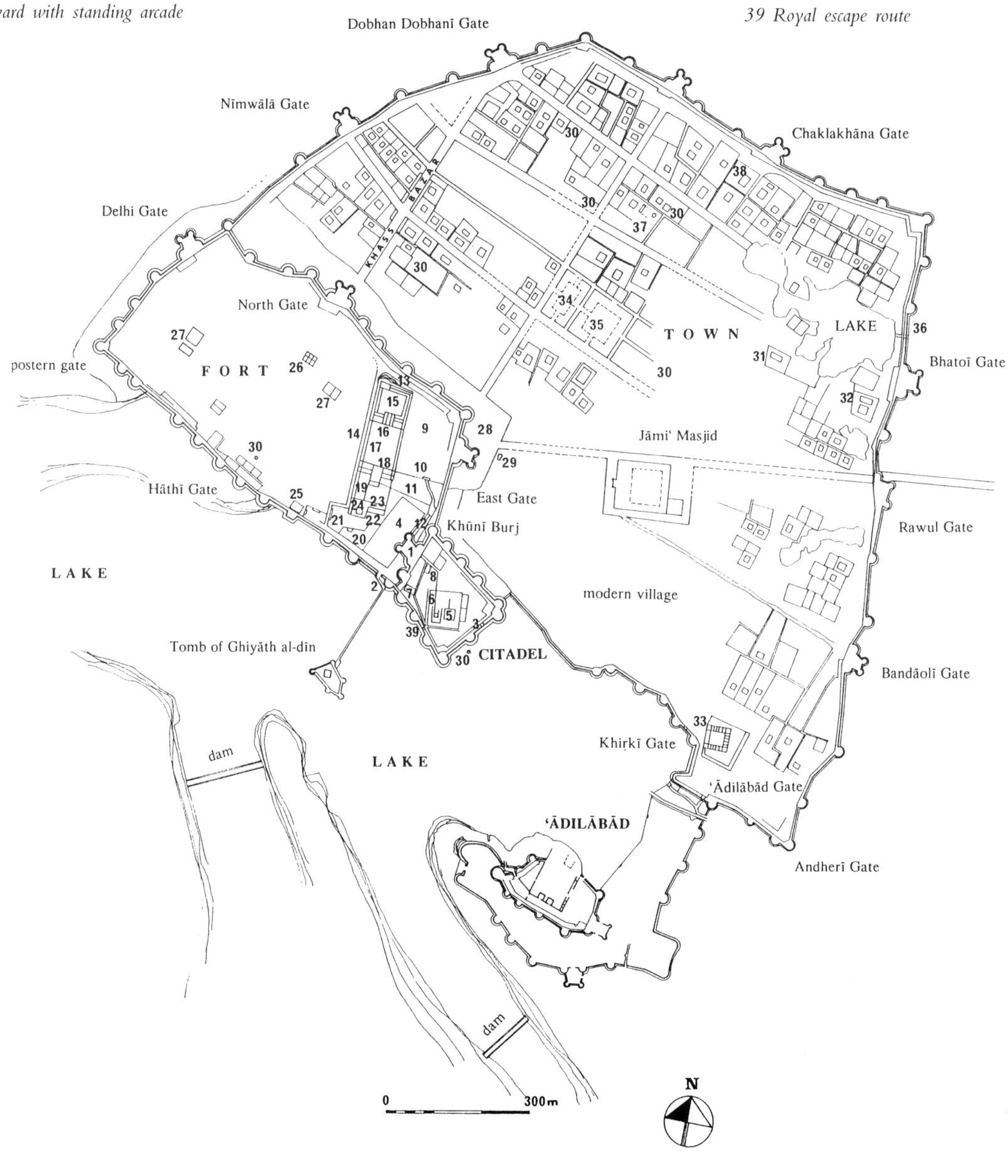

the tomb has been surveyed many times, first by Cunningham[3] and Page,[4] and later in some detail by Wetzel[5] and Yamamoto.[6] A reason for the attention paid to this building is partly its good state of preservation, but its grand design, the delicate use of different coloured stone in its construction, and above all its imposing structure contribute to its recognition as an outstanding sultanate monument. The spirit of the tomb was perhaps best evoked by Fergusson[7] as early as 1876.

> His tomb, which was finished at least, if not built, by his successor, instead of being situated in a garden, as is usually the case, stands by itself in a strongly-fortified citadel of its own, surrounded by an artificial lake. The sloping walls and almost Egyptian solidity of this mausoleum, combined with the bold and massive towers of the fortifications that surround it, form a model of a warrior's tomb hardly to be rivalled anywhere, and in singular contrast with the elegant and luxuriant garden-tombs of the more settled and peaceful dynasties that succeeded.

However, there is little reason to believe that the building was not constructed by Ghiyāth al-dīn himself.[8] Not only does the design of the building and its site as an island in the middle of the lake (fig. 22.1, pl. 22.1) seem to be integral to the master plan of the town, but there is other historical evidence to confirm this. Ibn Baṭṭuṭa[9] informs us that when the sultan died his body and that of his young son Maḥmūd were brought to the tomb which had been constructed by the sultan himself, but the main evidence comes from an inscription of Ghiyāth al-dīn in the building. The epigraph (pl. 22.2) belongs to the tomb of Ẓafar Khān, an army commander of Ghiyāth al-dīn who died during the reign of the sultan. Ghiyāth al-dīn ordered his body to be buried in the northern tower of the perimeter walls of the tomb, apparently already completed. This is the only inscription of Ghiyāth al-dīn found in Tughluqabad. The text is in Persian, carved on the lintels of the entrance of an octagonal chamber in the northern tower:[10]

On the outer face of the lintel:

بنا این عمارت خیر در عهد همایون مجلس اعلی خدایگان
عالم غیاث الدنیا و الدین ابوالمظفر تغلق شاه ناصر امیر
المومنین خلد الله ملکه

On the inner face:

1 .... ارکان برای ترتیب ضبط اقلیمی مخصوص گردانید
و خان مرحوم ظفرخان را عرصه ظفراباد

2 داد خان مرحوم هم در ایام صغر تا سرحد لکهنوتی در
چند روز بگشاد و ولایتی دیگر ضبط می آورد ناگاه بتقدیر
آسمانی زخم چشم زمانه بدو رسید و از دار فنا بدار بقا
رحلت کرد مجلس اعلی این بنا خیر دارالامان را از برای
خان مرحوم عمارت فرمود

> This sacred building was erected during the auspicious reign of his majesty (*majlis-i aʿlā'*), the lord of the world, Ghiyāth al-dunya wa al-dīn Abu'l Muẓaffar Tughluq Shāh, the king and the bearer of victory for the prince of the believers (the Caliph) (*nāṣir-i amīr al-mu'minīn*) may God make his reign everlasting ... [His majesty] putting the affairs of the country in order had given the late noble, Ẓafar Khān, the region of Ẓafarābād. The late Khān, who was still a minor, also took over lands as far as the borders of Lakhnautī in a few days, and, while he was engaged in the seizure of another region, suddenly, by heavenly decree, received a wound from the evil eye of fate and left this transitory world for the eternal abode. His majesty ordered

---

3 *ASIR*, 1862-5 (Report for 1862-3), 213-14; A Cunningham, 'Report of the proceedings of the Archaeological Surveyor to the Government of India for the season of 1862-63', *Journal of the Asiatic Society of Bengal*, XXXIII, 1865, Supplementary Number (addenda to the main number), lxxii-lxxiii.

4 Maulvi Zafar Hasan and J A Page *et al.*, *Monuments of Delhi, lasting splendour of the Great Mughals and others* (four volumes); Archaeological Survey of India, Northern Circle (ASINC), 1920, reprinted Aryan Books International, New Delhi, IV, 1997, 2-5. Hasan and Page, as well as Cunningham, give only some measurements, but no sketches or drawings.

5 Friedrich Wetzel, *Islamische Grabbauten in Indien*, Ausgabe, 1918, reprinted Osnabrück, 1970, 24-32.

6 Tatsuro Yamamoto *et al.*, *Delhi, architectural remains of the sultanate period*, Tokyo, II, 1968, 34-56 and pls. 32-4 at the end of the book.

7 Ferguson, *op. cit.*, 215.

8 The view that the tomb was not built by the sultan is also expressed by Cunningham without giving any evidence, see *ASIR*, I, 1862-5, 213. This view was later corrected by Marshall who states rightly that the building is by Ghiyath al-dīn. See Marshall, *op. cit.*, 585-6.

9 Muḥammad b. ʿAbd'ullāh called Ibn Baṭṭūṭa, *Tuḥfat al-nuẓẓār fī gharā'ib al-amṣār wa ʿajā'ib al-asfār*, known as *Raḥla* ed. Talal Harb, Beirut, 1987, 461.

10 Text is given after Hasan and Page; also see Yamamoto, II, 38.

Pl. 22.1 The tomb of Ghiyāth al-dīn Tughluq standing in the former lake, seen from the Jahān-nāmā pavilion in the citadel.

Pl. 22.2 The opening line of the inscription on the lintel of the entrance of the tomb of Ẓafar Khān. The other lines are on the other side of the lintel facing the interior.

Pl. 22.3 The tomb of Ghiyāth al-dīn, general view of the courtyard looking north-west and showing the royal tomb chamber, the entrance to the compound and the tomb of Ẓafar Khān to the right, and the colonnade of the mosque to the left, behind the tomb.

this sacred edifice to be erected for the
late Khān (in) the *dār al-amān*.

A number of points in the inscription are of historical interest. While a few inscriptions of the time of Ghiyath al-dīn are to be found in different regions of India, only this one is written at his own order, and gives his full title. The title *nāṣir amīr al-mu'minīn* was commonly used by the sultans of Khurāsān in the 11th and 12th century and also by the early sultans of India. However, after the Mongol conquest of Baghdad and the fall of the house of the Abbasid caliphs, the title was no longer current in the Islamic world. The use of the title by Ghiyāth al-dīn may be regarded as a mere continuation of an older tradition, but it is also well known that the Tughluq sultans attached great importance to acknowledging the caliphate of the powerless descendants of the Abbasids.[11]

In spite of the inscription mentioning only one person, there are two tombs (pl. 22.7), different in shape and size, the larger one near the wall, and the smaller one, possibly of the young Ẓafar Khān, beside it, but the identity of the second personage is not known. There is no date on the inscription, but it seems likely that Ẓafar Khān had taken part in the sultan's campaign to Lakhnautī. If this

[11] Ibn Baṭṭūṭa, *op. cit.*, 423, 474, 478-9; Ḍiyā' al-dīn Barnī, *Tārīkh-i Fīrūz Shāhī*, Calcutta, Bibliotheca Indica, Asiatic Society of Bengal, 1862, 491-2; Shams Sirāj ᶜAfīf, *Tārīkh-i Fīrūz Shāhī*, Calcutta, Bibliotheca Indica, Asiatic Society of Bengal, 1891, 273-6; also see: Hilary Waddington, "ᶜĀdilābād, a part of the "forth" Delhi', *Ancient India*, no. 1, 1946, 75, coin no. 2: a copper coin of Muḥammad b. Tughlaq, struck in the name of the Abbasid Caliph Al-Ḥākim II, who conferred upon him the title of Nāṣir Amīr-al-Mu'minīn in AH 744 (AD 1343-44).

Pl. 22.4 Courtyard of the tomb looking south-east towards the arcades, with the entrance to the semi-circular chamber to the left, the blank wall of the southern tower in the centre, and the entrance to the chamber with a latrine to the right behind the tomb. The engaged column of the eastern entrance of the tomb chamber can also be seen.

was the case he must have died only a few months before the sultan himself. From the inscription it is clear that Ẓafar Khān died some distance away from the capital, perhaps as far away as Bengal. Carrying his body in the heat and humidity of India must have been a difficult and unusual task, particularly with regard to Muslim traditions, which require the dead to be buried without much delay. However, this is not the only known occasion and as we shall see, similar arrangements were made for the body of Muḥammad b. Tughluq, who is also buried in this complex.

The phrase *dār al-amān* (sanctuary) in the inscription is particularly worthy of attention. Ibn Baṭṭūṭa notes that a building by this name had been constructed some generations earlier by Sulṭān Balban, who was later buried there.[12] In the Islamic world the shrines of saints usually acquire the status of sanctuaries, often respected even today. In India it seems that the sultans themselves built their tombs to function as sanctuaries during their life, and with the hope, perhaps, that this function would continue after their death, giving their tombs the status of shrines. This expectation was not always unjustified, as Ibn Baṭṭuṭa[13] notes that at his time the tomb of Īltutmish's daughter, Sulṭān Raḍiya (d. 634/1236) was a sacred shrine, and today in South India the tombs of the Maᶜbar sultans in Madura and Tiruparangundram are amongst the most revered Muslim shrines of the region.[14] The tomb of Ghiyāth al-dīn remained known as *dār al-amān* throughout the Tughluq period, and, as noted, when Muḥammad b. Tughluq died in 752/1351 during his campaign to Thatha in Sind, his body was brought to Delhi, and was buried in the *dār al-amān* by the grave of his father. Fīrūz Shāh refers to the building by the same name and records:[15]

[12] Ibn Baṭṭūṭa, *op. cit.*, 447. Ibn Baṭṭuṭa mentions that the building was called *dār al-amn* (or *dār al-amān*), and was founded by Sulṭān Balban himself as a place of refuge for those in debt, or oppressed by a person in power, or even for murderers seeking to make a settlement with the family of the victim according to Islamic law. After his death the sultan was buried there. For descriptions of the building see Percy Brown, *op. cit.,* 15, pl. 101, fig. 1; Yamamoto, *op. cit.,* I, 71-2.

[13] Ibn Baṭṭūṭa, 446.

[14] M Shokoohy, 'Architecture of the Sultanate of Maᶜbar in Madura and other Muslim monuments in South India', *Journal of the Royal Asiatic Society* (*JRAS*), Third Series, I, 1991, 45, 74.

[15] Fīrūz Shāh Tughluq, *Futūḥāt-i Fīrūz Shāhī*, ed. Shaikh Abdur Rashid, Aligarh, 1954, 14-16.

در دارالامان که مضجع و مرقد مخدومان است درها از چوب صندل ساخته و بر قبور آن خداوندگاران از پرده های در خانهٔ کعبه سائبان افراخته ... دیگر از حضرت ذوالجلال و قادر پر کمال این بندهٔ عاصی توفیق یافت که اشخاصیکه در عهد خدایگان مغفور و مرحوم محمد شاه السلطان طاب ثراهُ که خداوندگار و مخدوم و مربی من بود به تقدیر الله تعالی کشته شده بودند و کسانی که اعضای ایشان از چشم و بینی و دست و پا ناقص گشته ورثه ایشان از قبل پادشاه مرحوم مغفور استرضا نموده و هر یکی را به اموال راضی نموده خطوط خوشنودی موکد به شهود مستند در صندوق کرده به دارالامان مقبرهٔ سلطان مغفور مرحوم نورالله مرقده جانب سر داشته تا حق تعالی به کرم عمیم خویش آن مخدوم و مربی ما را غریق رحمت گرداناد.

> In the *dār al-amān* which is the resting place and the tomb of my masters, I fitted doors of sandal-wood and over the graves of those kings erected canopies made from curtains of a door of the House of Kaᶜba ... Also with the help of the most glorious Lord and the most perfect Almighty this dissident slave [of God] succeeded in obtaining on behalf of the late king Muḥammad Shāh—who was my lord, my master and my teacher—deeds of forgiveness from survivors of those who, by Divine decree, had been killed, and from those who had been maimed in the eye, nose, arm or leg. I made each one of the survivors and heirs satisfied by providing them with riches, and obtained their written deeds of satisfaction duly attested by witnesses and deposited them in a box and put them in the *dār al-amān* over the head of the grave of the late sultan, may God illuminate his grave, so that by His all-encompassing mercy our master and teacher be submerged in His forgiveness.

Inside the royal tomb chamber there are three simple tombstones (pl. 22.9), covered with plaster and without any inscription. The central tomb is believed to be that of the sultan himself, and that to its east of his son Muḥammad, but the identity of the third, which is smaller in size, is not entirely clear. Some of the earlier reports[16] speculate that it may belong to Ghiyāth al-dīn's wife and Muḥammad's mother, Makhdūma Jahān (Mistress of the World). This is not entirely unlikely, as we know from the account of Ibn Baṭṭūṭa[17] that the Queen enjoyed exceptional privileges, and it is possible that after her death[18] she was buried next to her husband. Furthermore the tombstone has a flat top which may be an indication that it belongs to a woman as opposed to the solid pointed arch which is considered to indicate men's tombstones.[19] However, the personage who is known to have been buried there is the prince Maḥmūd, the favourite son of Ghiyāth al-dīn, who was apparently a child, and as already noted, was killed at the same time as his father. Although it is possible that the second grave in Ẓafar Khān's tomb chamber may be that of Maḥmūd, it is unlikely that the son of the sultan would be buried beside the grave of a commander rather than that of his father, unless Ẓafar Khān, also a minor, were a close relative, which is not known.

The monument and its fortified enclosure has another significance in that it is amongst the very few

Pl. 22.5 The arched causeway to the tomb from the south-east with the postern gate to the Fort in the background. In this photograph, the floodwater of the 1994 monsoon gives an impression of how the lake would appear, but normally the site of the lake no longer retains rainwater.

16 *ASIR*, 1862-5, 216; Hasan and Page, *op. cit.*, 2.

17 Ibn Baṭṭūṭa, *op. cit.*, 515-16.

18 Makhdūma Jahān died in Delhi during the later years of Muḥammad b. Tughluq's reign, at the time when his commanders were revolting against him (c. 1345-6). Barni, *op. cit.*, 482-3, records that she died when Muḥammad was a few stages away from Delhi on his way to put down the revolt at Multan, but does not mention where she was buried.

19 The question of whether the form of the 14th century tombstones of North India indicates the gender of the deceased is not yet fully studied. While the general rule noted above might apply in most cases, it is possible that the grave of an immature boy could have also been surmounted by a tombstone with a flat top. The form was apparently later stylised in 15th century Gujarat, where all sultanate tombstones have flat tops, but those of the men have a small solid feature with a pointed arch carved on the top near the head of the slab.

Pl. 22.6 The exterior of the entrance portal to the compound seen from the causeway to the north-east, and showing the battlements and loopholes.

Pl. 22.7 The octagonal tomb of Ẓafar Khān, interior looking north and showing the dome which rests directly on the arches and corbel-stones set at the corners of the octagon. The outer and inner arches all bear religious inscriptions. The two tombs inside the chamber can also be seen.

sultanate monuments where the architect can be identified. The architect of Tughluqabad was Aḥmad b. Ayāz, a nobleman of Anatolian origin (*rūmī*),[20] expert in design, structural engineering and geometry. Ghiyāth al-dīn appointed him in charge of the royal buildings and later, at the time of Muḥammad b. Tughluq, he rose to the rank of grand vizier with the title Khwāja Jahān. However, Ibn Baṭṭūṭa[21] records the contemporary rumours that Ayāz had been responsible for the death of Ghiyāth al-dīn Tughluq. It occurred at the end of Rajab 725/12th July 1325 when a pavilion collapsed over the sultan's head while he was reviewing the troops on his return from the Lakhnautī campaign. The pavilion was designed and constructed in three days by Aḥmad b. Ayāz under the order of Muḥammad b. Tughluq. Naturally, the formal accounts of

Pl. 22.8 The colonnade in front of the western tower, interior view looking south. The colonnade seems to have been a mosque, with the qibla marked by the opening to the inner chamber, seen on the right, instead of by a miḥrāb.

[20] Ibn Baṭṭūṭa, *op. cit.*, 432.

[21] *Ibid.*, 461.

the Tughluq court,[22] although tainted with suspicion, record the event merely as an accident.

The royal tomb chamber is set at the north side of a pentagonal fortified courtyard (fig. 22.2, pl. 22.3). The fortification is similar in details to that of the town, but is smaller in scale, rising over 13m from the present floor of the lake up to the crenellations, and about 11m above the water level when the lake was fairly full.[23] The fortification has three large circular towers at the main corners, and two smaller towers: that at the eastern angle is semi-circular, and that at the south-western angle is rectangular. The square tower has a small covered balcony supported by stone corbelled brackets. A hole in the floor of the balcony indicates that it was a latrine (fig. 22.3). This is the only example of its kind found in Tughluqabad, but such arrangements for latrines were common in Tughluq forts and a good example can be seen in Hisar.[24] Around the fortification walls run vaulted arcades which are about 2m wide (pl. 22.4). They are smaller than similar features which run around the fortification walls of Tughluqabad. However, unlike in Tughluqabad here the arcades do not open directly into the towers, leaving the chambers accessible only from the courtyard. As a whole most of the other details are also scaled down versions of those in Tughluqabad, keeping the courtyard, the tomb, and the whole complex in proportion.

The causeway which links the postern gate of the fort to the tomb (pl. 22.5) is in the form of a bridge 180m long, which originally had 27 arches, several of which were demolished some time ago to give way to the Delhi-Gorgaon road. During the last decade the road has been widened but the old gap in the causeway has been retained at the same size and no other arches have been demolished. The causeway joins the northern tower of the tomb complex, and skirts round it arriving at the entrance of the enclosure (figs. 22.4-7) just to the south-east of the tower. The causeway is about 9m below the level of the crenellations and 5.5m below the level of the courtyard. The arched portal (pl. 22.6) of the entrance is once again a scaled down version of the Tughluqabad portals, but the interior is different. Four steps ascend from the causeway to the portal, which opens to a corridor with a niche at the north and another at the western side, but at the south side a flight of steps ascends to a small hall at the level of the courtyard. The entrance to the courtyard is a simple opening at the west side of the hall. The circulation, as with the main gates of Tughluqabad, takes a dog-legged form, but the stairs for the tomb entrance are inside the portals, rather than being on the exterior.

We have already noted the tomb of Ẓafar Khān (figs. 22.5-7, pl. 22.7) being in the octagonal chamber within the northern tower. The chamber is domed with a nearly hemispherical dome standing on eight arched piers, with Quranic inscriptions running round the interior of the arches. A hemispherical dome is not a common feature in India, as the form of true domes, which had been imported a few generations earlier from Khurāsān, has the profile of a pointed arch. On the other hand, hemispherical domes, originating from Byzantine architecture, cover most of the Islamic buildings of Anatolia. The dome of the tomb may be one of the rare occasions when a direct influence from Anatolian architecture is seen in India. On the exterior, the dome is faced with white marble, a contrast to the red sandstone of the structure itself. A similar chamber also exists in the western tower, but the interior arrangement is slightly different and the original roof has been lost. It is likely that there was a third chamber in the southern tower, but only the shell of this tower has survived and the original arrangement of its interior is not clear.

The location of the two tombstones in the Ẓafar Khān chamber is worthy of attention as they are set at one side rather than in the centre, probably to leave room for other graves. The chambers in the other towers could have also been intended to house more graves. If this were so, it may be a further indication that the *dār al-amān* was conceived as a shrine, which like that of a saint would be surrounded by the tombs of followers, or in this case nobles. Muslims attach great importance to being buried near (*mujāwir*) the shrine of a saint or a descendent of the Prophet. However, if this was Ghiyāth al-dīn's intention, it seems that his son did not fulfil the desire of his father and no other personages were buried there.

The western tower has yet another significance. It is orientated toward the *qibla* and in front of it is a colonnaded structure of red sandstone with a flat roof on finely carved monolithic columns. This building, which is attached at both sides to the arcade of the perimeter walls,

[22] Barni, *op. cit.*, 452-3; M Shokoohy, *Haryana I, the column of Fīrūz Shāh and other Islamic inscriptions from the district of Hisar*, Corpus Inscriptionum Iranicarum, Part IV Persian Inscriptions down to the early Safavid Period, Vol. XLVII, India: State of Haryana, London 1988, 21. Also see Yaḥyā b. Aḥmad al-Sihrindī, *Tārīkh-i Mubārak-Shāhī*, Bibliotheca Indica, no. 254, Calcutta, 1931, 96. The date of Ghiyāth al-dīn's death varies in the published copies of the histories, but the most reliable date, given above, is as appears in the inscription of the column of Fīrūz Shāh, one of the main aims of its erection being to record this particular event.

[23] The area of the lake has silted up to at least 2m above the original level, and the lower parts of the arched piers of the causeway are now buried under sediment.

[24] M Shokoohy and N H Shokoohy, *Ḥiṣār-i Fīrūza, sultanate and early Mughal architecture in the district of Hisar, India*, Monographs on Art, Archaeology and Architecture, London, 1988, 28, fig. 10, pl. IIc.

Fig. 22.2 Tughluqabad, the Tomb of Ghiyāth al-dīn Tughluq, plan of the compound, showing the main tomb in the courtyard protected by five towers, and the octagonal tomb chamber with the tomb of Ẓafar Khān in the northern tower, adjacent to the causeway across the lake to the fort. Other features include the arcade running along the fortification walls, the mosque and the octagonal chamber by the western tower, as well as the latrine in the form of a balcony behind the colonnade in the square tower at the south.

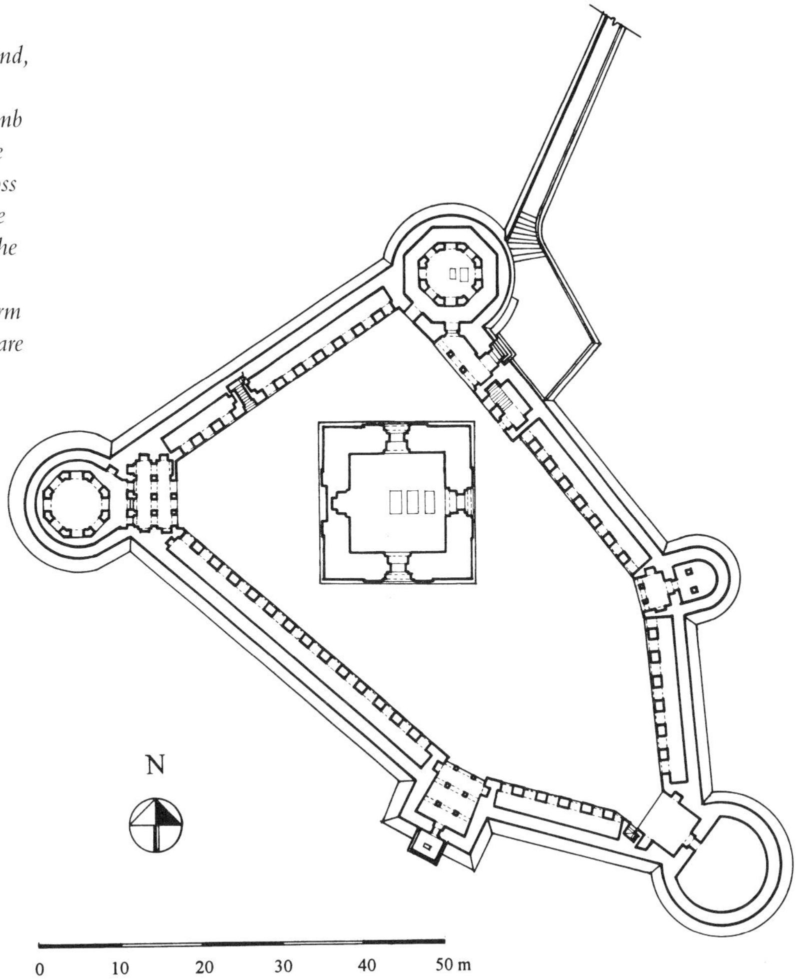

is designed as a small mosque (fig. 22.2, pl. 22.8), with its *miḥrāb* in the form of a doorway to the chamber of the eastern tower. In India the compound of most tombs includes a small mosque or prayer wall for visitors. The mosque here could, therefore, be seen as part of this tradition, but opening the *miḥrāb* as a door to a chamber is unusual and appears only in a very few Islamic buildings in the world—often for an exceptional reason. No such condition is apparent in the tomb of Ghiyāth al-dīn. However, the chamber could have been intended to house the resting-place of a religious personage—an inner shrine for the mosque similar to that of the shrine of Sikandar Shāh in South India.[25] A saintly tomb in the compound of Ghiyāth al-dīn would have guarantied its status as a shrine. It is also possible that the room, which is also orientated towards Mecca, was designed as the private prayer chamber of the sultan himself.

The most important feature in the compound is the royal tomb chamber itself (figs. 22.8-10, pls. 22.3 and 9). It is square in plan, measuring on the exterior 11.70m high to the top of the walls below the crenellations, and 18.80m wide at each side. The chamber has three entrances but at the *qibla* side instead of a door is a *miḥrāb*. The thick walls are pronouncedly battered on the exterior, but vertical on the interior, measuring at base about 3.50m thick making the interior 11.75m square. At the top, however, the walls are only about 2.00m thick, giving the walls a slope of 7°. The sloping walls seen in this tomb are characteristic of Tughluq architecture, and apart from where they are used for fortification walls appear neither in pre-

[25] M Shokoohy, 'Architecture of the Sultanate of Maʿbar in Madura and other Muslim monuments in South India', *JRAS*, Third Series, I, 1991, 68, 73, fig. 11.

Tughluq buildings nor in the architecture of the later dynasties.[26] This battering more than all other details gives Tughluq architecture its archaic or 'ancient Egyptian' look. However, battered walls are also a characteristic of pisé structures, where unbaked clay is the only load bearing material. When laying the clay in layers the lower layers are thicker than the ones above to ensure that the weight of the wall is well supported. Pisé was used extensively in the domestic architecture of ancient Khurāsān and can still be seen in the villages of Afghanistan. The true reason for the introduction of battered walls to Tughluq architecture is not known. It could be yet another innovation of Aḥmad b. Ayāz, to give the monuments a sense of majesty and solidity, but it could also be a choice of Ghiyāth al-dīn himself—a nostalgia, perhaps, for the architecture of the homeland he had left behind.[27]

Pl. 22.9 The interior of the tomb of Ghiyāth al-dīn Tughluq, interior looking north-west and showing the miḥrāb, the squinched transitional zone of the dome, and two of the tombs, probably that of Ghiyāth al-dīn in the middle, and that of Muḥammad b. Tughluq to the right.

The arches and the dome have a slightly pointed and nearly two-centred profile, but the radius of the upper segment of each arc is slightly greater than that of the haunch below. The arches also have a slightly ogee form on the crown, and the outer arches of the *miḥrāb* and the exterior of the doors have decorative spear shaped fringes. The form of the arches is not unusual in India and follows closely those of the time of Balban and of the Khaljīs. It is also like the 11th and 12th century arches of Khurāsān, except for the ogee form which was not common there. In the 13th and early 14th century, however, four-centred arches—which could cover wider spans with lower heights—became more fashionable in Khurāsān, while in India the older form still remained a dominant feature in the 14th century.

---

26 This prominent Tughluq feature has always attracted the attention of scholars. Percy Brown was among the first to note the feature and related it to the tombs of Multan (*op.cit.* pp. 21-2, 33). For several decades Brown's work was regarded as a main source on the Muslim architecture of India and his view has reverberated in practically all modern publications including tourist guide-books. Brown, perhaps unaware of the structural properties of pisé architecture, argued that the form must be related to the brick structures of Multan and Panjab. This suggestion is not entirely satisfactory as the few remaining early brick temples in Sind, Multan and Swat do not have battered walls nor do the surviving walls of Ribāt-i ʿAlī Karmak (also known as the Tomb of Khālid Walīd) which may date from the Ghaznavid period. There is no evidence, therefore, that battered walls appeared in the brick monuments of the region before the mid-13th century. The tomb of Shāh Yūsuf Gardizī (1152) does have battered walls but the present structure is not a domed chamber and has apparently been reconstructed later (Marshall, *op.cit.* 598). The tombs with battered walls noted by Brown to be the prototype of the tomb of Ghiyāth al-dīn are those of Shāh Bahā al-Ḥaqq (d. 1262), Shams al-dīn Tabrīzī (d. 1276), Shādnā Shahīd (d. 1270) and Rukn-i ʿĀlam. All these tombs were built shortly before or during the period when Ghiyāth al-dīn was the governor of the region. The tomb of Rukn-i ʿĀlam was built by the order of Ghiyāth al-dīn. The Multani form should perhaps be described as being related to Tughluq architecture rather than *vice versa*. The question remains as to whether the pisé tradition was brought from Afghanistan by the builders employed by the Delhi governors of the region, themselves from Afghanistan, or already existed in Multan in the vernacular architecture of the villages. For the monuments of Multan also see: A Cunningham, *The ancient geography of India*, London, 1871, 230-41; V V Mirashi, 'Three ancient and famous temples of the sun', *Pūrāṇa*, viii, 1966, 38-51; A Nabi Khan, *Multan: history and architecture*, Islamabad, 1983; H Edwards, 'The Ribāt of ʿAlī Karmak', *Iran*, XXIX, 85-93.

27 According to Shams Sirāj Ghiyāth al-dīn Tughluq and his two brothers were from Khurāsān, and came to India at the time of ʿAlā al-dīn Khaljī. In the words of Ibn Baṭṭūṭa (p. 458) they came from the mountainous region between Sind and Turkistan, i.e. modern Afghanistan. See Shams Sirāj, *op. cit.*, 36; Ibn Baṭṭūṭa, *op.cit.*, 458.

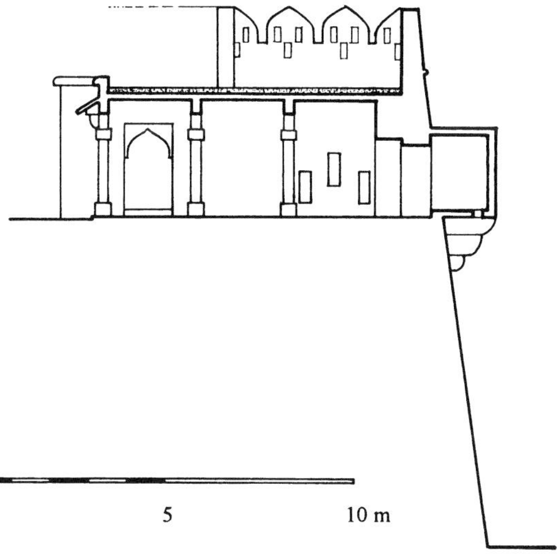

Fig. 22.3 Compound of the Tomb of Ghiyāth al-dīn , southern rectangular tower, section through the colonnade within the tower and the latrine.

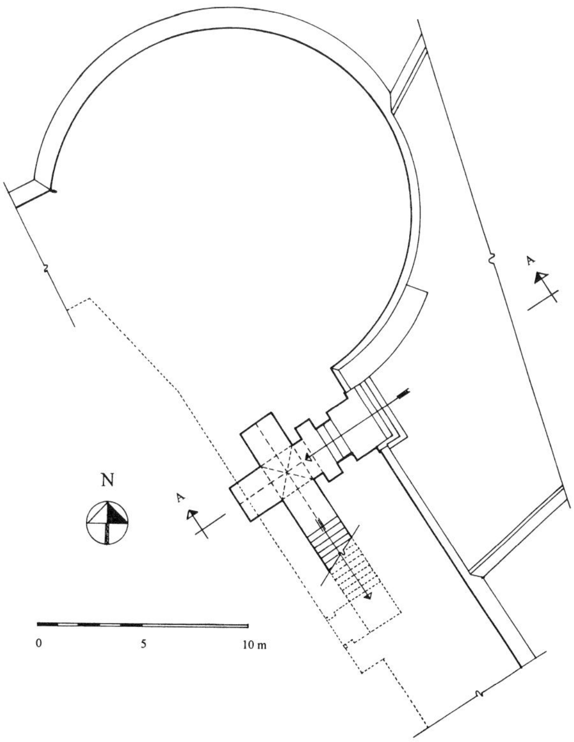

Fig. 22.4 Compound of the Tomb of Ghiyāth al-dīn, detailed plan of the entrance and the northern tower, lower level.

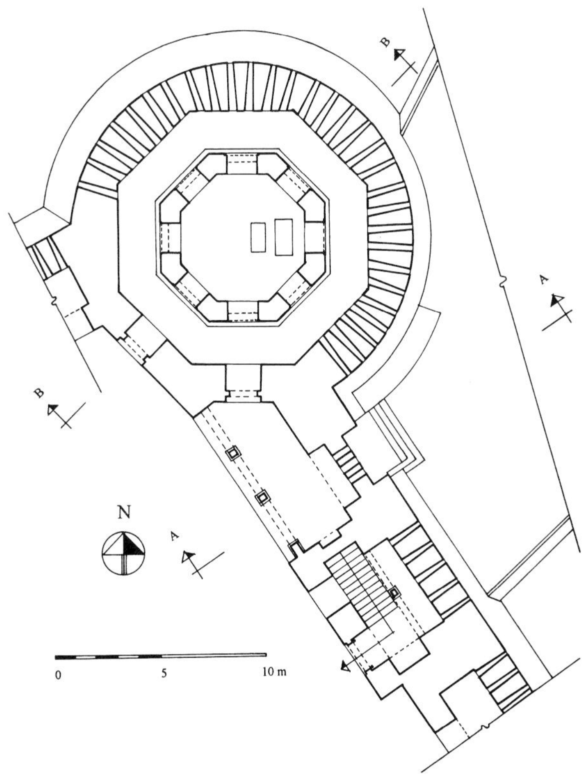

Fig. 22.5 Compound of the Tomb of Ghiyāth al-dīn, detailed plan of the upper level of the entrance and the northern tower housing the tomb of Ẓafar Khān.

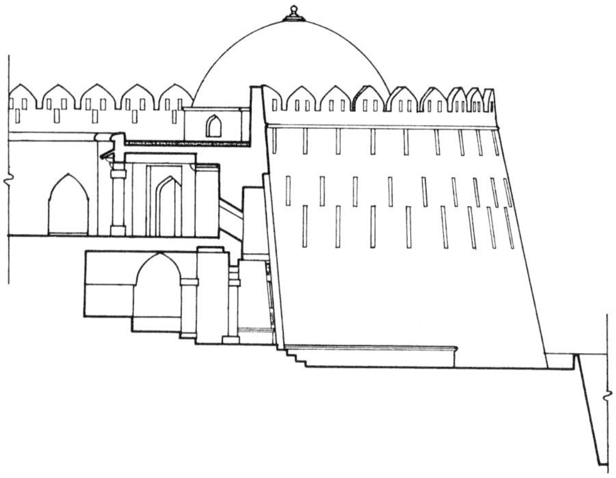

Fig. 22.6 Section A-A through the entrance, also showing the elevation of the northern tower and tomb of Ẓafar Khān.

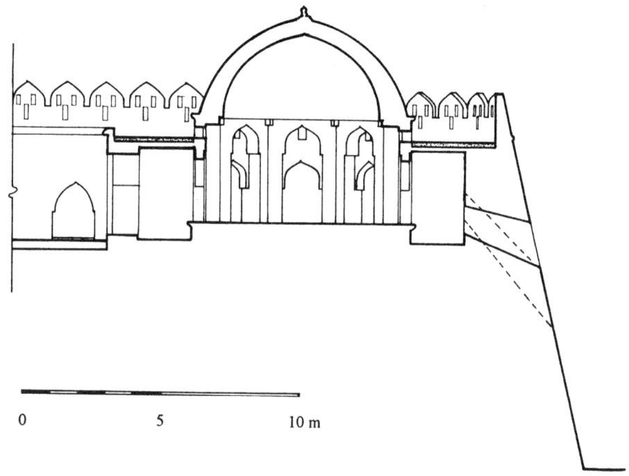

Fig. 22.7 Section B-B though the northern tower and octagonal tomb chamber of Ẓafar Khān.

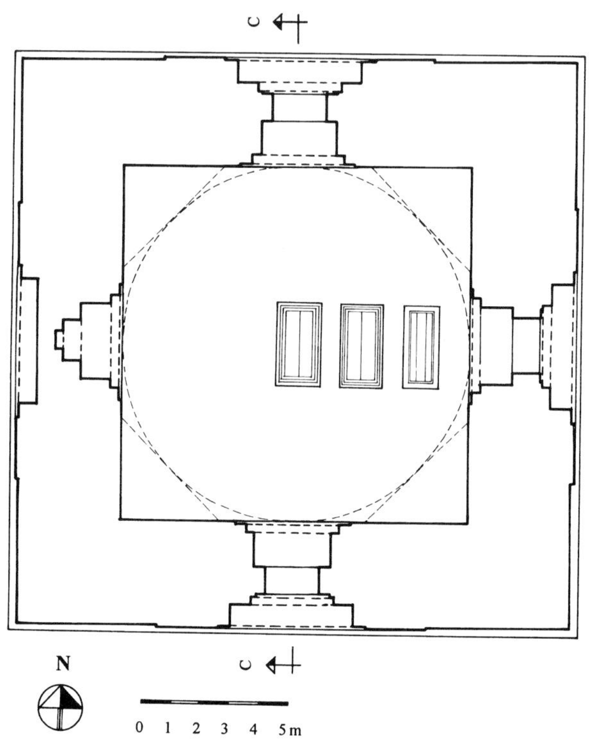

Fig. 22.8 Tomb of Ghiyāth al-dīn, plan.

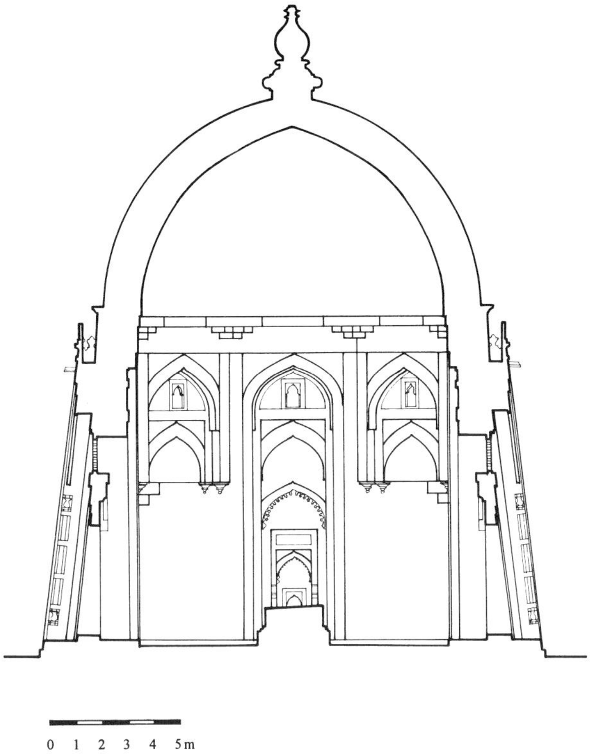

Fig. 22.9 Tomb of Ghiyāth al-dīn Tughluq. Cross Section C-C, looking towards the miḥrāb.

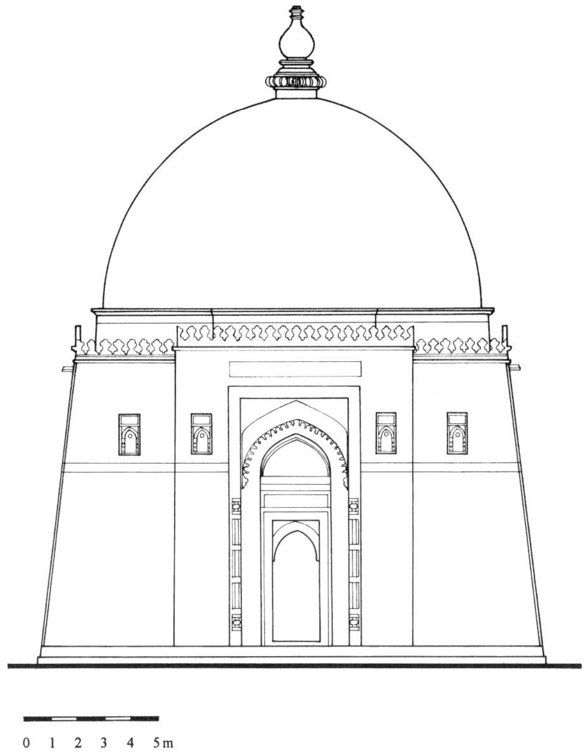

Fig. 22.10 Tomb of Ghiyāth al-dīn Tughluq, east elevation.

The dome needs particular attention, as in the chronology of Indian Islamic architecture it is one of the few surviving true domes preserved in its original condition. The technology of true domes, raised on squinched transitional zones, had been imported from Khurāsān to India at least half a century earlier, and traces of such domes are found in several early buildings including the tomb of Balban. However, the only standing domes earlier than that in Tughluqabad are those of the ᶜAlā'ī Darwāza[28] in the Quwwat al-Islām complex, and also the Jamāᶜat Khāna Masjid[29] in the shrine of Niẓām al-dīn Awliyā', both dating from the time of ᶜAlā al-dīn Khaljī. These domes are similar in form, but the earlier ones are slightly less imposing. All are raised on squinches,[30] and in the tomb of Ghiyāth al-dīn the transitional zone appears on the exterior as a relatively squat octagon, while in the ᶜAlā'i Darwāza this zone is absorbed into the walls and is not apparent at roof level. This early method of assimilating the zone is responsible for the squat appearance of the dome on the outside. During the later periods the height of the octagonal zone was gradually increased—sometimes for aesthetic reasons only—to give the dome an even higher elevation.

The profile of the dome of Ghiyāth al-dīn is similar to the form of the arches in the building. As a result, the dome appears at first glance as a hemisphere, again perhaps an aim of the architect, but when examined closely the height is slightly greater than the radius, giving the dome an elevated and well-proportioned appearance—more pronounced than in the tomb of Ẓafar Khān. This height is further emphasised by a pinnacle in the stylised form of a vase or a pitcher (*kalaśā*) over a fluted circular cushion or 'flattened melon' (*amalaka*) (figs. 22.9-10). These features are clearly Indian in origin and are taken from temple architecture.[31] They were introduced to Muslim buildings in the early days of the Islamic conquest if not

[28] J A Page, *An historical memoir on the Qutb, Delhi*, Memoirs of the Archaeological Survey of India, no. 22, Calcutta, 1926, 14-15, pls. 2, 7.

[29] Maulvi Zafar Hasan: *A guide to Nizamu-d Dīn*, Memoirs of the Archaeological Survey of India, X, Calcutta, 1922, 14-16, pls. 1, 4.

[30] For the comparison of the squinches of these buildings see Brown, *op. cit.*, pl. 17 facing p. 9.

[31] The features are an integral part of the *śikhara* of an Indian temple, see Rāmachandra Kaulācāra, *Śilpa Prakāśa, medieval Orissan Sanskrit text on temple architecture*, tr. and annotated by Alice Boner and Sadāśiva Rath Śarmā, Leiden, 1966, Sanskrit text, 43-5, tr. 62-3, pl. 33.

earlier,[32] and appear in the corbelled domes of the Ghurid mosque of Aṛha'ī din kā jhoṇpṛa at Ajmer.[33] Instead of the *amalaka*, sometimes the form is further stylised to represent a lotus. It seems that by the time true domes were introduced to India these early motifs had been fully accepted by Muslims as an integral part of the decoration of a dome, and with the exception of a few buildings they appear on all Muslim domes in India. More interesting is that in around the 14th century the idea of the pinnacle was exported from India to the rest of the Islamic world. The *amalaka* or lotus motif was not adopted but the stylised vase—often made out of brass and sometimes gilded—appears on many domes in Iran[34] and is called *kalāsh*.

Ghiyāth al-dīn's tomb would have been a striking architectural feature merely for its design and proportions, even without the use of colour, but a carefully chosen colour scheme executed with different stones has added to its grace and elegance. The walls are constructed with red sandstone and the arches of the doors are filled with white marble lattice screens. At the springing line of the arches a wide band of white marble runs around the building, and above this band are small arched niches within a rectangular frame executed in white and black marble. These niches are patterns borrowed from the 13th century architecture of Khurāsān,[35] themselves derived from openings around the roof of the 10th and 11th century tomb chambers, and first seen in the tomb of Ismāᶜīl the Samanid in Bukhara.[36]

On the exterior of the tomb of Ghiyāth al-dīn further bands of marble appear below the decorative battlements of the wall as well as around the octagonal transitional zone, but the bold effect of the red and white colour is achieved by the marble dome against the red walls, with the pinnacle of the dome also executed in red sandstone. A similar contrast is achieved on the interior (pl. 22.9) with the lower part of the walls being red, changing to white just below the foot of the squinches. The *miḥrāb* is also executed in white marble, with slabs of black marble filling the spandrels and set as a rectangular panel above the main arch.

The use of coloured stone in the tomb of Ghiyāth al-dīn follows an earlier tradition in India first seen in the ᶜAlā'ī Darwāza and to a lesser extent in the Jamāᶜat Khāna mosque already noted. Ibn Baṭṭūṭa also mentions the use of coloured stones in the Khaljī buildings and notes:[37]

و كان السلطان قطب الدين أراد أن يبني أيضاً مسجداً جامعاً بسيري المسماة دار الخلافة فلم يتم منه غير الحائط القبلي و المحراب و بناؤه بالحجارة البيض و السود و الحمر و الخضر ولو كمل لم يكن له مثل في البلاد و أراد السلطان محمد اتمامه و بعث عرفاء البناء ليقدروا النفقة فيه فزعموا أنه ينفق في اتمامه خمسة و ثلاثون لكا فترك ذلك استكثاراً له و أخبرني بعض خواصه أنه لم يتركه استكثاراً لكنه تشائم به لما كان السلطان قطب الدين قُتل قبل تمامه

> Sultan Quṭb al-dīn (Mubārak Shāh Khaljī) ordered another *jāmiᶜ* to be constructed in the town of Sīrī, which is called the capital, of which only the *qibla* wall and the *miḥrāb* were built. The building was of white, black, red and green stone, and if it had been completed it would have been unrivalled in the world. Sulṭān Muḥammad (b. Tughluq) decided to complete the building, and when the experts were asked to estimate the cost of completion they averred that it would be 35 *lakhs*. The sultan found it too expensive and abandoned the scheme. However, some of the close confidantes of the Sultan told me that the heavy cost of the building was not the reason for abandoning the project, but that he took it as a bad omen that Sulṭān Quṭb al-dīn had been killed before the building was completed.

Ghiyāth al-dīn's tomb therefore seems to represent a continuing tradition, well-developed and widespread at the time. Its elegance and majesty should not be regarded as an exception intended by the architect to be presented to the sultan as a masterpiece amongst

[32] A simpler version of the feature appears on the corbelled dome of the pre-conquest Shine of Ibrāhīm at Bhadreśvar, see M Shokoohy *Bhadreśvar, the oldest Islamic monuments in India*, Leiden-London-New York, 1988, 16, 18, figs. 6-8.

[33] J A Page, *An Historical Memoir on the Qutb: Delhi*, Memoirs of the Archaeological Survey of India, no. 22, Calcutta, 1926, pl. 19a.

[34] See for example the domes of the Pir-i ᶜĀlamgīr at Damghan, Jāmiᶜ of Yazd, Masjid-i Shāh and Madrasa Mādar Shāh at Isfahan, in A U Pope, *A survey of Persian art*, London-Tokyo, 1964-5, VIII, 339, 438, 465, 470 respectively.

[35] M Shokoohy, The Shrine of Imām-i Kalān in Sar-i Pul, Afghanistan, *BSOAS*, vol. VII, 1989, 312-14.

[36] Eric Schroeder, 'Standing monuments of the first period', *A survey of Persian Art*, ed. A U Pope, London-Tokyo, 1964-5, III, 945-9; VIII, 264.

[37] Ibn Baṭṭūṭa, *op. cit.*, 440.

the other structures of Tughluqabad. The choice of stone rather than plaster finish was undoubtedly to give the building a longer life, but otherwise the building was just one amongst many other grand edifices of Ghiyāth al-dīn's capital. Furthermore, for a tomb the architecture would be expected to be relatively restrained. The palaces, with their cut stucco, oiled and carved wooden columns and ceilings, 'golden bricks'[38] (probably lustre glazed) and a skyline of colonnades and domed pavilions must have looked far more elaborate and ornamental. In short, its religious nature safeguarded the tomb from destruction, but in its time it presumably appeared as an elegant—but sober—punctuation mark among the now lost treasures of Tughluqabad architecture.

[38] *Ibid.*, 461.

23 THE ILLUSTRATIONS OF BAGHDAD 282 IN THE TOPKAPI SARAYI LIBRARY IN ISTANBUL

Eleanor Sims,
with a contribution by Tim Stanley

One of the most imposing Timurid manuscripts to have come down to us has no formal title. Instead, this large gathering of historical works is most often referred to as Baghdad (Bağdat) 282,[1] a name serving merely to identify the pavilion of the Ottoman Palace in Istanbul in which the manuscript was stored before it was catalogued for the general library of the Topkapı Palace Museum. Yet B. 282 is a volume of signal importance to historians and art-historians alike: to the former for the importance of the texts it contains, and to the latter for the interest of its illustrations and the superlative quality of its abundant illumination.

The manuscript has 938 folios measuring 422mm in height and 315 in width; the written surface is 289 x 215mm and a normal text-page has 31 lines of *nastaᶜliq* writing. 32 folios have illuminations, as *shamsas* or *ᶜunwans*, and the manuscript also contains 20 large paintings. As it lacks a final colophon, we do not know exactly when this huge gathering was finished, although the richly illuminated oval medallion on folio 10r avers that it was done 'in the days of the reign of Shahrukh Bahadur Khan' and therefore at some point between 807/1405 and 851/1447.

Textual research by Felix Tauer, in the 1930s, had narrowed the probable period of its production down to a point in the second decade of Shahrukh's reign;[2] more recently, dates of 818/1415 and 819/1416 have been noticed for the completion of later sections of this large and imposing manuscript.[3]

B. 282 is essentially a volume of historical texts in Persian, and it is so described in the earliest Topkapi catalogues: *kulliyat-i tarikhi*. It contains the *Ta'rikh al-rusul wa'l-muluk*—the *Annals*, of Abu Jaᶜfar Muhammad ibn Jarir al-Tabari, in the Persian translation of Abu ᶜAli Muhammad ibn Muhammad al-Balᶜami; the *Jamiᶜ al-Tavarikh*, or *Compendium of Histories* of the great Ilkhanid vizier, Rashid al-Din; and the earlier *Zafarnama*, or *Book of Victory*, the panegyric history of Timur compiled from chronological records by Nizam al-Din Shami, here supplemented by Shahrukh's court historian, known as Hafiz-i Abru, to bring the history of the Timurids up to the date of 819/1416.

The 20 illustrations are found only in the *Annals* of Tabari. All are square (or squarish) and large, occupying about ²/₃ of the page; all are of different sizes but measure

[1] In chronological order, the manuscript has been discussed by: Mehmet Aga-Oglu, 'Preliminary Notes on Some Persian Illustrated Manuscripts in the Topkapu Sarayi Müzesi, Part I', *Ars Islamica*, I, 1934, 192, and figs. 8-9 (abbreviated as *A-O*, 1934); Felix Tauer, 'Les manuscrits persans historiques des Bibliothèques de Stamboul: I', *Archiv Orientalni*, III, 1931, no. 32, 97-98; *idem.*, 'Vorbericht über die Edition des Zafarnama von Nizam Sami und derwichtigsten Teile der Geschichteswerke Hafiz-i Abru's', *Archiv Orientalni*, IV, 1932, 250-256; *idem.*, 'Continuation du Zafarnama de Nizamuddin Sami par Hafiz-Abru, editée d'après les manuscrits de Stamboul', *Archiv Orientalni*, VI, 1934, 429-465; C A Storey, *Persian Literature: A Bio-Bibliographical Survey*, vol. I, part I, London, 1927-39, reprinted 1970, 86-88 (abbreviated as Storey); Ivan Stchoukine, *Les peintures des manuscrits Timurides*, Paris, 1954, MS XXX, 51; Felix Tauer, 'Analyse des matières dans la première moitié du Zubdat al-Tavarikh de Hafiz-i Abru', *Charisteria Orientalia*, Prague, 1956, 345-373; Fehmi Edhem Karatay, *Topkapı Sarayı Müzesi Kütüphanesi Farsça Yazmalar Kataloğu*, Istanbul, TKS, 1961, 51-53, no138; Eleanor G. Sims, *The Garrett Manuscript of the Zafar-Name: A Study in Fifteenth-Century Timurid Patronage*, Doctoral dissertation, New York University, 1973 (unpublished thesis available through University Microfilms, Ann Arbor), 70-71; Ernst J Grube, *Miniature Islamiche nella Collezione del Topkapi Sarayi Istanbul*, Padua, 1975, 127-128, pl. 64 A-B; Ernst J Grube, Filiz Çağman, and Zeren Akalay, *Topkapı Sarayı Collection: Islamic Painting*, Tokyo, 1978, 162-3 (in Japanese), pls. 72-73 (abbreviated as Grube *et al*, 1978); Ernst J Grube and Eleanor Sims, 'The School of Herat from 1400 to 1450', *The Arts of the Book in Central Asia*, ed. Basil Gray, Paris and London, 1979, 146-178 (abbreviated as *ABCA*, 1979); Ernst J Grube, *La Pittura dell'Islam*, Bologna, 1980, no. 27; Joseph Gutman and Vera Basch Moreen, 'The Combat Between Moses and Og in Muslim Miniatures', *Bulletin of the Asia Institute*, n.s., I, 1987, 112, fig. 4 (abbreviated as *BAI*, 1987); Thomas W Lentz and Glenn D Lowry, *Timur and the Princely Vision: Persian Art and Culture in the Fifteenth Century*, Los Angeles, 1989, cat. 46, 132, 135, 338-39, 372 (abbreviated as *TPV*, 1989); B W Robinson, '"Zenith of his Time": The Painter Pir Ahmad Baghshimali', *Persian masters: five centuries of painting* (Marg), 1990, 15, figs. 16-17 (abbreviated as *BWR*, 1990).

[2] All quoted in n. 1 above; it should also be noted that the analysis of the content of B. 282 provided by Karatay is neither correct nor complete; a full listing is instead to be found in both Tauer, *A-O*, IV, 1932, 251, and Storey, 87-88.

[3] By Lentz and Lowry, *TPV*, 1989, one on folio 652r.

approximately 200 x 300 mm, not counting the extensions which often break through the picture-frame. All have the distinctively wide gold margin, the hallmark of painting done for Shahrukh's wayward nephew, Iskandar ibn ʿUmar Shaykh, in and around Shiraz between 810/1407 and his blinding in 817/1414, but none of the paintings of B. 282 are signed and none are dated. Most have later annotations[4] in red ink, found above the pictures, by someone writing in Ottoman Turkish: the texts summarise the action of the picture and sometimes identify the principal personages. The illustrations are clearly the work of more than one painter whose styles, collectively, resemble pictures in manuscripts made for a number of bibliophile Timurid princes. In addition to the earlier Shiraz painting of Iskandar, the illustrations in B. 282 clearly anticipate the styles and the subjects of later painting in Herat, as this is found in copies of some of the historical texts commissioned by Shahrukh as well as those in some of the illustrated manuscripts made for his sons Ibrahim-Sultan and Baysunghur.

The Illustrations in B. 282

1. folio 16r (II), 'The Angels Prostrating Themselves Before Adam'
   195 (204) x 272mm
   Published: *A-O*, 1934, fig. 8; Grube, 1975, pl. 64A; Grube *et al.*, 1978, pl. 72 in colour; *ABCA*, 1979, pl. XLIII in colour; *BWR*, 1990, fig. 16

2. folio 23r (IV), 'Noah and the Giant ʿUj'
   178 (295) x 299mm
   Published: Grube, 1980, fig. 27 in colour

3. folio 27v (V), 'Salih and the Camel'
   1 68 (303) x 269 (286)mm
   Published: *ABCA*, 1979, pl. XLIV in colour

4. folio 30r (I), 'Nimrud Casts Abraham into the Flames'
   190 (199) x 212 (263) mm (pl. 1)

5. folio 31v (I), 'Nimrud Ascends to Heaven'
   191 (225) x 212 (270) mm (pl. 2)

6. folio 35v (I), 'The Sacrifice of Abraham'
   188 x 209 mm

7. folio 41r (VI), 'Yusuf Appears Before Zulaykha and Her Maidens'
   190 x 213mm
   Published: *BWR*, 1990, fig. 16 in colour

8. folio 51v (III), 'Moses' Rod Becomes a Snake'
   190 x 212mm

9. folio 54v (VII), 'The Magi of Pharaoh Prostrate Themselves Before Moses'
   201 x 242mm
   Published: Grube *et al.*, 1978, pl. 73 in colour; *ABCA*, 1979, fig. 84

10. folio 65r (IV), 'Moses Strikes the Giant ʿUj'
   266 (300) x 212 (281) mm
   Published: Gutman-Moreen, *BAI*, 1987, fig. 4

11. folio 74r (II), 'Balqis Brought to Sulayman by an Angel'
   198 x 212 mm
   Published: *Islamic Art*, I, (1981), fig. 258

12. folio 78r (III), [A Man in a Garment of Leaves Rescues Another From a Stream]
   185 x 209mm

13. folio 85r (VII), 'The Building of the Wall Against Gog and Magog'
   @ 190 (250) x 213 (226)mm

14. folio 89v (V), 'Jesus Restores Shem, Son of Noah, to Life'
   152 (356+) x 289mm
   Published: *A-O*, 1934, fig. 9

15. folio 105r (III), 'Bahram Gur Kills a Lion and an Onager With One Arrow'
   191 (217+) x 212mm

16. folio 154r (VIII), 'The Angels Assist the Prophet Muhammad in the Muslim Victory at the Battle of Badr'
   187 x 114mm

[4] The Ottoman annotations have been read by Tim Stanley, as a preliminary to a longer joint monographic article on this manuscript: it is a pleasure to express my gratitude to him.

17. folio 169r (VII), '^c^Ali Uses a Door as His Shield in Storming a Redoubt during the Battle of Khaybar'
212 (261+) x 300mm
Published: *TPV*, p. 132 in colour

18. folio 171r (VII), 'The Prophet Muhammad in the Ka^c^ba'
190 (261) x 210 mm

19. folio 178r (VII), 'The Death of the False Prophet Musaylima at the Battle of ^c^Akraba' '
190 x 214mm

20. folio 214r (VIII), [A Battle Scene]
190 x 274mm

Looking at the entire illustrative complement of B. 282, instead of at only one of its more striking pictures, certain features stand out with some force. One is its stylistic variety. Another is the difference between the rulings of the paintings and those of the written surface throughout the manuscript: the paintings' wide gold margins contrast with the thinner text-rulings, a gold band and an outer blue line. Of nine squarish pictures with profiles of no complexity, even those that most approximate the width of the written surface actually exceed it by several millimetres, almost certainly because of the greater width of the picture's rulings. The paintings may have been executed after the text was copied—not infrequently the case with princely Islamic manuscripts. Indeed, the time-lag would deserve no comment were it not for the fact that many of the smaller illuminated *^c^unwans* of B. 282 are still in the Shiraz style predating the Timurid arrival in Fars, whereas the larger and more resplendent illuminated passages, including that with the name of Shahrukh on folio 10r, are in the more polychromatic Herat style of the 15th century. These observations suggest that perhaps B. 282 was also a manuscript begun in Shiraz—the text copied, its illumination partially executed, and spaces left for 20 illustrations—but only completed in Herat, having been brought there in the baggage of members of Iskandar's *kitabkhana* who then found employment with Shahrukh, along with other manuscripts that include the little Cartier *Khamsa*.[5] A complete re-examination of B. 282 would be necessary to confirm—or deny—such an assertion, although the stylistic divergences among its illustrations already add weight to the balance.

[5] Eleanor Sims, 'A Timurid Manuscript of Nizami's *Khamseh* From the Library of the Timurid Sultan Shah Rukh ...', *Bonhams, Oriental and European Rugs and Carpets and Islamic Works of Art*, October 15-16, 1996, Lot 491, 57-68.

To this observer, the illustrations in B. 282 appear to fall into eight different groups. The first three evoke prior styles of Timurid painting and its formative periods in both Shiraz and Baghdad. Group I consists of nos. 4, 5, 6 (folios 30r, 31v, and 35v) and is derived from some of the finest of Iskandar's Shiraz pictures, having wide golden skies, relatively large figures, and related compositions. 'Nimrud Casts Abraham Into the Flames' (fig. 23.1) is a subject virtually unique; sequentially, it illustrates the moment preceding one of the more beautiful paintings in the large Anthology of 812/1410, a beatific Abraham seated in the fire which has miraculously turned into roses.[6] 'Nimrud Ascends to Heaven' (fig. 23.2) is memorable for many reasons. One is the adoption of the vehicle of the foolish shah Kay Ka'us—a box-throne with corner-posts on which legs of meat were impaled, continuous bait for four rapacious birds tethered to the base of the throne—for Nimrud's flight. The image is clearly borrowed from prevailing *Shahnama* iconography, although contemporary parallels, for the moment, are lacking and even 14th-century models are few.[7] Another is the pictorial emptiness of the picture: there is nothing, save an empty landscape and a few trees on the horizon, between the astounded onlookers, grouped at the bottom left of the painting, and the image of Nimrud soaring out of the painting and into the upper right margin, calmly seated in his 'flying machine' with his bow and arrow at the ready and four flapping eagles beneath him. Such quantities of empty space are unusual in the finest of Persian paintings but not uncommon in B. 282, a feature that might be considered intentional but could, equally, argue that its painters were dealing with given spaces to be filled with a given subject, for which there were few pictorial models of size and shape to fit into the blanks left for illustrations.

The second group comprises two pictures that are a large and dramatic mix of early Timurid Shiraz and the best of Jalayirid Baghdad, nos.1 and 11 (folios 16r and 74r). 'The Angels Prostrating Themselves Before Adam', with Iblis malevolently glaring at the left, is among the more impressive of Islamic paintings. The third group consists of three pictures that most bring to mind certain of the simpler paintings in the Cartier *Khamsa*, nos.8, 12, 15 (folios 51v, 78r, 105r), in their squarish shapes with no

[6] Basil Gray, *Persian Painting*, Geneva, 1961, 79.

[7] From the 1341 Inju (Shiraz) *Shahnama*, folio 46r: Sadruddin Agha Khan Collection, IR.M.6/B (unpublished); and the denouement, from the Schulz-Gutman *Shahnama*, Isfahan, about 1340: MMA 1974.290.9, illustrated in colour, 91, in M L Swietochowski *et al.*, *Illustrated Poetry and Epic Images: Persian Painting of the 1330s and1340s*, New York, 1994.

extensions, their golden skies, and the high, rounded horizon of 8 and15, as well as the figure of Moses in no. 8—very similar in pose and in headgear to the Cartier 'Shepherd Who Hanged His Dog'.[8]

The next two groups instead look forward to the most typical painting done for Shahrukh, presumably in Herat and in the period when his court historian, Hafiz-i Abru, was working on his continuation of the great historical texts of Rashid al-Din. 'Group' IV is two pictures, nos. 2 and 10 (folios 23r and 65r), that could almost be assigned to the copy of a dispersed *Majmu'a-i Tavarikh* usually considered to date between 1425 and 1430[9] were it not for their shape and size. Both depict the giant ᶜUj ibn ᶜAnaq, shown as a huge pale figure, nude but for a green skirt and with a notably oval face. He is first shown as a beardless 'youth' menacing Noah's ark as it rocks on a (now tarnished) silver sea, and then older—bearded, stumbling to his death under the weight of the stone around his neck. Both subject and image were used, but altered, in the dispersed Hafiz-i Abru manuscript:[10] the composition reversed, the flaming aura and the crowd of vividly astonished Israelites done away with, and the dynamic posture of ᶜUj simplified. It provides another comparison arguing an earlier date for the pictures of B. 282. The two very fine paintings of Group V add still further weight to this proposition. They are nos. 3 and 14 (folios 27v and 89v), 'Salih and the Camel' and 'Jesus Restores Shem, Son of Noah, to Life'. Again, the subject of the former was used in the dispersed Hafiz-i Abru manuscript, and again the picture was reduced and simplified.[11] Moreover, the fundamental coarseness of the execution of paintings in the dispersed volume is emphasised by the exceptionally fine quality of that in B. 282, as well as that of its companion: these pictures are highly sophisticated in their compositions and their placement on the pages, masterful in their figural drawing, and exquisite in their finish. Indeed, they adumbrate some of the finest of Baysunghuri painting in Herat and well serve to introduce the next 'group'—a single painting, no. 7 (folio 41r).

It illustrates a favourite story in Islamic literature, the appearance of the captive Yusuf to Zulaykha and her ladies who, seeing him as they were eating fruit at a deliberately staged gathering, were so astonished at his beauty that they cut their hands instead of the fruit they were holding. The incident is already found in the *Qur'an* (XII, 31) and was related by many later writers, al-Tabari among them. As celebrated as is Jami's late 15th-century poem *Yusuf u Zulaykha*, this single image of the beautiful youth and his effect upon Zulaykha's women came to epitomise the entire Yusuf story.[12] So it is notable that the Timurid illustration to Tabari's text, in B. 282, appears to be the earliest depiction that is presently recorded. The composition is a usefully neutral, if princely, garden-setting, and it was adapted by a painter working on an Anthology completed for Baysunghur in 830/1426-27[13] although it rarely appears again, even in later Timurid princely painting.

The seventh group most deserves its appellation, for it includes five paintings: nos. 9, 13, 17, 18, 19 (folios 54v, 85r, 169r, 171r, 178r). In them may be seen some of the features of Shiraz painting as it was evolving under the patronage of Ibrahim-Sultan, who ruled there from 817/1414-1415 until his death in 838/1435. 'The Magi of Pharaoh Prostrate Themselves ...' partakes of the aesthetic of resounding emptiness to illustrate the divine power of Moses, whose rod has become a snarling dragon in the foreground; both the particular blue of the sky, and its large figures in empty space, recall some of Ibrahim's better pictures rather than Iskandar's Shiraz paintings. 'The Building of the Wall Against Gog and Magog' has the same blue for the sky but its more complex vertical composition is more typical of Ibrahim's paintings, as is also the explosive mass of rock with the characteristic 'piecrust' edge, at the upper right margin.[14] Illustrations 17 and 19, specific incidents in early Islamic history, were essentially new subjects requiring new compositions in which architecture and armies ought—ideally—to be integrated in some logical manner; moreover, unlike so many of the preceding pictures, neither would be understandable without reading the text underneath (or the Ottoman gloss above it). In both pictures the same formula has been adopted, a tall structure at one margin surrounded by a curving moat. Relatively infrequent thereafter—not even found in

---

8 Sims (n. 5 above), illustrated in colour, 61, min. 7.

9 Storey (n. 1 above), 87-88.

10 Ernst J Grube, *Muslim Miniature Paintings*, Venice, 1962, 51-56, cat. 40.

11 *Op. cit.*, 53-54, cat. 38.

12 Two notable mural examples are the 'cut-out' stucco murals in a 16th-century house in Nayin, and the 17th-century painting (rather badly damaged and thus unpublished) in Room P3, one of the smaller side rooms in the Chihil Sutun in Isfahan. For the Nayin mural, see Ingeborg Luschey-Schmeisser, 'Der Wand- und Deckenschmuck eines safavidischen Palastes in Nayin', *Archaeologische Mitteilungen aus Iran*, n.f. 2, 1969, 183-192, pls. 71, 72, 2.

13 'The Games of Backgammon and Chess', folio 50v: Richard Ettinghausen, *Persian Miniatures in the Bernard Berenson Collection*, Milan, 1961, pl. V, in colour.

14 R H Pinder-Wilson, *Persian Painting of the Fifteenth Century*, London, 1958, pl. V in colour.

Ibrahim-Sultan's illustrated *Zafarnama*, it is used to good effect in several post-Ibrahim pictures of the 1430s.[15] 'The Prophet Muhammad at the Kaᶜba' evokes the style of Ibrahim-Sultan's Shiraz paintings by the shapes and features of men's faces and facial hair, rather than by the simplicity of the asymmetrical composition, whose formal organisation does recall a double-page painting of Mecca and the Kaᶜba in Iskandar's smaller Anthology of 813-14/1410-11.[16] The varied tents in the foreground of no. 19 can be seen as a more stylised variation on the tents in the earlier Shiraz picture.

The last 'group' includes the two least interesting pictures of B. 282, nos.16 and 20 (folios 154r and 214r): both are undifferentiated battle-scenes with the same blue skies and high, rounded horizons. Such a formula can already be seen in Shiraz painting earlier by at least half a century[17] and might be considered an indication of the pictorial conservatism that is almost always apparent in any complex Timurid illustrative project. Nonetheless, 'The Angels Assist ... at the Battle of Badr' is not without interest: it illustrates a signal victory early in Islamic history that was rarely depicted;[18] and the angels' weapons are maces, one with an ox-head, while the Muslims use spears alone. Perhaps this is another way the painters of B. 282 relied upon *Shahnama* imagery when they were required to invent new iconographies for new subjects.

What manuscripts these might have been is, then, one of many questions raised by B. 282: princely Timurid *Shahnama* volumes are rare although there is a plethora of other 15th-century examples, and the dozen or so 14th-century copies—dispersed though they are—are among the best-known of all illustrated Persian manuscripts.[19] But we should not overlook the fact that lesser-known copies of related texts were also produced around the same time, and their illustrative programs will surely prove relevant to the issue.[20] And Nimrud's most unusual conveyance (fig. 2) may well owe some of its details to the parallel story of Alexander the Great who also journeyed 'through the sky in a vehicle drawn by griffins lured upward with a bait of meat'[21]—as the dedicatee of this volume will of course have recognised. Details like this, and their ramifications, are but one feature testifying to the iconographical importance of B. 282 while, together with the much smaller Cartier *Khamsa*, the varied styles of its 20 illustrations represent an important—if heretofore overlooked—transitional phase in the development of classical Timurid painting in Herat.

---

15 In the ex-Dufferin-and-Ava *Shahnama*, 840-41/1436-37, folio 316v: illustrated in colour on the cover of the most recent auction sale, at Sotheby's, October 16, 1996; and in the *Tarikh-i Jahan-Gushay* of 841/1438, Paris, BN, suppl. Pers. 206, folio 149v: E Blochet, *Musulman Painting*, London, 1929, pl. XCIV.

16 Gray (as in n. 6 above), 73.

17 *Op. cit.*, 63.

18 In the fragmentary 14th-century *Jamiᶜ al-Tavarikh* in the Topkapi Saray Library, H. 1653, fol. 165r, and illustrated—although not identified—by M S Ipşiroğlu, *Painting and Culture of the Mongols*, New York, 1966, 50, fig. 10.

19 M S Simpson's *The Earliest 'Shahnama' Manuscripts*, London/New York, 1979, is thorough, for the material she covers, but does not deal with the second half of the 14th century: *passim* and Appendix I, 347-350. For the 14th century, the best survey still remains Ernst J Grube, 'Persian Painting in the Fourteenth Century: A Research Report', Supplement 17, *Annali*, 38, 4, 1978, 15-29; figs. 18-26, 33-38, 45-46, 48; reprinted, in *Studies in Islamic Painting*, Ernst J Grube, London, 1995, as essay VII. 15th-century manuscripts are discussed by this writer, 'The Illustrated Manuscripts of Firdausi's Shahnama Commissioned by Princes of the House of Timur', *Ars Orientalis*, XXII, 1993, 43-68, the appendices of particular interest.

20 B W Robinson, in early 1997, kindly permitted me to look at photographs of a copy of the *Qisas al-Anbiya*, completed in 828/1424 and originally containing over 100 illustrations; those (at least that I was able to look at, hurriedly) were either in a poor Shiraz style or in the more ordinary Shahrukh 'historical' style; especially relevant is that many of the Old Testament figures depicted in it—Abraham, Nimrud, Salih, Yusuf—also appear in B. 282.

21 Victor M Schmidt, *A Legend and its Image: The Aerial Flight of Alexander the Great in Medieval Art*, Groningen, 1995, 1.

Pl. 23.1 Nimrud Casts Abraham into the Flames. *Painting in the* Kulliyat-i Tarikhi, *Istanbul, TKS, B. 282, folio 30r.*

Pl. 23.2 Nimrud Ascends to Heaven. *Painting in the* Kulliyat-i Tarikhi, *Istanbul, TKS, B. 282, folio 31v.*

24 THE ETHNOGENESIS OF THE PASHTUNS

Willem Vogelsang

Introduction

The Pashtuns, or Pathans as they are traditionally called in the Indian subcontinent, constitute an ethnic group of some twenty million people, most of them Sunni Muslims, who live along both sides of the border between Afghanistan and Pakistan.[1] Many of them are still tribally organised and enjoy a large degree of autonomy, both in Afghanistan and in Pakistan. Pashtun society is generally regarded as a particular example of a so-called segmentary lineage organisation. This is an abstract structure based on descent groups whereby the various units, such as nuclear families, sub-clans, clans, tribes and confederations of tribes, together constitute some sort of pyramid with the (eponymous) ancestor placed on top. The Pashtuns are generally well aware of their place in the Pashtun kinship pyramid, and therefore answer this model fairly well. However, such an anthropological model also harbours the danger of over-simplification and tends to provide a petrified picture of an otherwise far more fluid process, as will be discussed below.

In popular books the Pashtuns are often portrayed, in the true Orientalist fashion, as *noble savages*, as people whose way of life is fully governed by their *pashtunwâli*, the Pashtun code of honour, in which hospitality (*malmastiyâ*), asylum (*nanawâtay*) and revenge (*badal*) play important roles.[2] Their stubborn resistance against British encroachments in the 19th and early 20th centuries provided them with a romantic aura of purity and manliness. This image was strengthened in the 1980s when the peoples of Afghanistan, including the Pashtuns, managed to defeat the Marxist Kabul regime and their Soviet puppet-masters. However, with the rise of the Pashtun-dominated *Talibân* in Afghanistan and the emergence of comparable movements among the Pakistani Pashtuns, the Western image of the Pashtuns changed again. They are now broadly regarded as heroin-dealing bigots who are keen on taking their country back to the Middle Ages.[3]

Whatever the changing image of the Pashtuns, which anyhow tells more about the outside world than about the Pashtuns, there is a wide-spread and age-old belief among the Pashtuns, and many others, that they constitute a homogeneous ethnic group and that they all descend from one eponymous ancestor. This self-perception is closely linked to the type of society that the Pashtuns have built for themselves. However, perceived truth is not necessarily identical to absolute truth. In the present paper I want to question in general terms the fallacy of this belief of a homogeneous nation. I want to describe the ethnogenesis of the Pashtuns as a continuing process of fission and fusion, whereby various groups at some time in their history adopted 'Pashtunhood', while others (although this is of course more difficult to demonstrate), lost their 'Pashtunness'. This process, as I hope to show, received an important impetus in the late 15th and 16th centuries. At that time the Afghanistan/Pakistan borderlands became the common frontier area of three emerging empires, namely those of the Safavids in Iran, the Uzbeks in Bukhara and Samarkand, and the Mughals in the Indian subcontinent. This situation led to a growing outside influence upon the Pashtun tribes and consequently an increased stratification of Pashtun society and a concomitant intensification of inter-tribal contacts and ultimately, in the face of a hostile outside world, an awareness and self-definition of Pashtunhood.

The position of Pashto

One of the most defining aspects of Pashtunhood, in particular in the eyes of the Pashtuns themselves, is the

1 This is the so-called Durand Line of AD 1893. It cuts straight through the tribal lands of the Pashtuns and ever since its demarcation has been a source of conflict between Afghanistan and British India/ Pakistan.

2 Compare Imran Khan's book, *Warrior Race*, published in 1993.

3 Although a comparison with the Middle Ages seems superseded by recent events. The Taliban mayor of Kabul has recently announced the rebuilding of Kabul according to megalomaniac plans from the 1970s that will turn the city into an amalgam of the architectural geniuses of Stalin, Albert Speer and Le Corbusier. Progress indeed!

language, called Pashto.[4] Pashto is an Iranian language closely related to *Fârsi* (Persian). Together the Iranian languages constitute a branch of the Indo-Iranian language family. The other main Indo-Iranian branch is Indo-Aryan, represented in India and Pakistan by Hindi, Urdu, Bengali, and a host of other languages. Possibly a third branch is formed by the so-called Nuristani languages that are spoken in modern Nuristan (ancient Kafiristan), which lies north-east of Kabul, Afghanistan's capital.

Indo-Iranian forms part of the much larger family of Indo-European languages, which include Balto-Slavonic, Greek, Hittite, Germanic, Italic, Celtic, etc.[5] By the third millennium BC, Indo-Iranian speaking groups had moved east from the supposed Indo-European homeland in the Ukraine. They spread across the Urals onto the steppes of Kazakhstan. By the second millennium BC, some of them moved south towards the Iranian Plateau. They travelled along ancient routes that lead east of the Caspian and connect Central Asia with the Near East. The migrants thus arrived in the north-eastern parts of the Iranian plateau, in present-day north Afghanistan and north-east Iran, from about the early second millennium onwards. Hence some of them moved on, either voluntarily or pushed on by others that moved behind them. They moved west, along the southern foothills of the Elburz towards west and north-west Iran.[6] Others moved south, through the so-called Herat corridor towards Sistan in modern south-west Afghanistan, or they migrated south-east, across the Hindu Kush mountains to the Kabul Valley and hence to the Indus valley and the Indian subcontinent.

This process continued for many centuries. It is likely that the first Indo-Iranians to arrive on the Plateau were Indo-Aryan speaking groups, who were later pushed south-east across the Hindu Kush mountains in Afghanistan by their Iranian-speaking kinsmen. The earliest Indo-Aryan documents (the Vedic texts) correspondingly date to the late second or early first millennium BC and may geographically be placed in the north-west of the Indian subcontinent, south of the Hindu Kush watershed. By that time Iranian speaking groups had arrived on the Plateau, soon to spread to the west and south. The first clear references in Assyrian sources to the (Iranian) Persians and Medes in modern west and south-west Iran date to the late 9th century BC. The composition of many of the Zoroastrian texts of the (east) Iranian prophet Zarathustra, now contained in the *Avesta*, should also be dated not much later than the early first millennium BC.

The immigration of Iranian-speaking newcomers onto the Plateau, including those of the equally Iranian-speaking Scythians and related groups, continued until the early first millennium AD, when Altaic-speaking peoples originating from the Mongolian plains occupied most of Central Asia. From that moment on, the Iranian Plateau and the Indian subcontinent were subject to recurring waves of Altaic-speaking peoples (the Huns, Turks, Mongols, Uzbeks, etc.). The introduction of (proto) Pashto on the Iranian Plateau should therefore be placed within the larger context of the Indo-Iranian, and in particular the Iranian migrations. The speakers of (proto) Pashto apparently migrated together with the other Iranian groups and at some stage in their history moved south-east to the Indo-Iranian borderlands. Here they replaced Indo-Aryan speakers who had moved there before them, and perhaps others who had lived there from before the time of the Indo-Iranian migrations.[7]

Within the Iranian language family, Pashto is generally classed as a north-east Iranian language, since it is closely related to a group of isolated Iranian languages spoken in the mountains of Badakhshan in south Central Asia and neighbouring districts.[8] As a north-east Iranian language it probably represents a later wave of Iranian migrants. The language is differentiated from other Iranian languages, including *Fârsi* (Persian) that is generally classed as a south-west Iranian language. Persian, which was originally spoken only in the south-west of the Iranian Plateau (Fars province) far away from the north-east where the Iranians first emerged, probably represents an earlier wave of Iranian immigrants.

The north-east Iranian languages are generally linked to the Iranian-speaking Scythians and Scythian related groups that moved onto the Plateau in successive waves from the early first millennium BC onwards. An attractive theory as to the origin of the Pashto speakers was recently put forward by the late Sir Harold Bailey, who suggested that their name should be linked to the Pasianoi, a Scythian-related group who in the late 2nd century BC migrated from the north onto the plateau.[9]

---

4 In the north, Pashtun and Pashto are pronounced Pakhtun and Pakhto. Compare also the name of the northern Pashtun capital, Peshawar, generally pronounced Pekhawar.

5 For the Indo-Europeans, see Mallory 1989.

6 The earliest Indo-Iranian migrants who moved west may have exercised some influence on the Mitanni of northern Syria in the mid-second millennium BC.

7 The Brahui speakers of Baluchistan, who speak a Dravidian language akin to the Dravidian languages of south and Central India, may constitute a group that survived the Indo-Iranian migrations.

8 See especially Morgenstierne 1958: 167-169.

9 Bailey 1994: 10.

Comparable indications, namely that Pashto was introduced to the Plateau after the arrival of earlier Iranian immigrants, are found in Afghanistan and Pakistan. In the area where Pashto is now spoken, there are pockets of people speaking other Iranian languages. These include Ormuri and Parachi, which are generally classified as south-east Iranian languages and which are spoken in isolated areas south of Kabul, and in and around Kaniguram, in neighbouring Pakistan.[10] The classification of these languages and the continuing pressure upon these residual languages from the side of Pashto speakers would indicate an on-going process of Pashtunisation, or at least a Pashto-isation, that has been going on for many centuries. A similar process can be observed among the Wanetsi speakers north of Quetta. According to Morgenstierne, this Iranian language is closely related to Pashto, but certainly not identical. It was spoken in a much larger area than at present, but over the years Pashto gradually replaced it.[11]

Apart from these Iranian languages, there are also Indo-Aryan languages being spoken in this part of the world, namely the so-called Dardic tongues. The most important of these is Pashai, still spoken by a sizeable group of people living dispersed in a number of side-valleys of the Kabul plain.[12] Dardic may well represent the common Indo-Aryan language spoken in the Kabul valley and beyond before the arrival of Iranian speaking groups. Persian Achaemenid and Classical sources from the mid-first millennium BC indicate a strong Indian presence in the Kabul valley and the borderlands. The process of 'Iranisation' of the area was by that time clearly still continuing, as, in fact, it still is to the present-day. The on-going Pashtun encroachments upon the land of the Pashai and Nuristanis further north not only lead to a replacement of Pashai speakers and Nuristanis by Pashtuns, but also to the adoption of Pashto by many of the autochthonous population.[13]

To the south, the Pashto speaking area is bounded by Baluchistan and the Baluch, who speak Baluchi, another Iranian language. The Baluch probably derive from north-west Iran and arrived in these barren lands in the late medieval period. In recorded history the spread of the Pashtuns and the whole process of Pashtunisation was in general directed towards the west and north from the central Indo-Iranian borderlands, but not towards the south. The city of Quetta traditionally marks the transition from the Pashtun-dominated north to the Baluch and Brahui dominated south.

Afghans and Pashtuns

Most of the Pashtuns have traditionally described themselves as the Afghans *par excellence*, and the name of modern Afghanistan was consequently coined after the dominant ethnic group of the country, the Pashtuns/ Afghans.[14] However, the relationship between the two names, and their history, is far from clear.[15] Although the Pashtuns claim an ancient pedigree, there is remarkably little known about their ancestry from before the 16th century. Afghans, however, are mentioned in various Persian and Arabic documents from at least the 10th century onwards. They are described as living in the lands between the Central Afghanistan mountains and the Indus valley. However, the name of the Afghans is not Pashto, but probably Persian in origin, and obviously a blanket name given by outsiders to those inhabiting the borderlands.[16] In other words, Iranian and Arabic outsiders would not have differentiated between Pashto speakers and those using another language, as for instance those speaking Ormuri or Parachi. In this way (proto-) Pashto speakers were generally coined as 'Afghans', but not all 'Afghans' were Pashto speaking.

Something similar happened in the Indian subcontinent, where the peoples inhabiting the borderlands were called 'mountaineers', or Rohillas, as the Pashtuns are still often named.[17] However, as in the case of the Afghans, this term does not denote a specific ethnic affinity, but a habitat, and does not inform us directly about the history of the Pashtuns.

All this information would undermine the absolute relevance of Pashto as a defining characteristic of the Pashtun nation in ancient and modern times. The one-to-one relationship between Pashtunhood and Pashto is an artificial construct that does not allow for the still continuing process of Pashtunisation. People may adopt Pashto as their language, but this of course does not mean that their long-dead ancestors also suddenly become Pashto

[10] For a good survey of these languages, see Morgenstierne 1979 and Orywal 1986.

[11] Morgenstierne 1932: 12-14.

[12] Orywal 1986: 54-56.

[13] Compare Vogelsang 1992, esp. pp. 140-141, 194-197.

[14] The name of Afghanistan is therefore regarded by many non-Pashtun inhabitants of Afghanistan as a misnomer and a symbol of the traditional Pashtun domination of the country (compare Mousavi 1998: 2-13).

[15] A distinction between the epithets of Afghan and Pashtun was also brought forward by Caroe (1958:xiv-xv).

[16] Compare Elphinstone 1815: 151.

[17] Compare Caroe 1958:xvi, 118 and Gommans 1995: 9-10.

speakers. *Vice versa*, it is very possible that some Pashto speakers adopt another language. In fact this is what has happened, and is still happening in west and south-west Afghanistan, where many Durrani Pashtuns have adopted Persian as their every-day language. Similarly, the Gaduns east of the Indus in northern Pakistan have also dropped their original Pashto language. They even hardly remember that they used to be Pashtuns.[18]

The Indian connection

Although the Pashtuns and Afghans are not generally mentioned as such in medieval Indian sources, it is quite clear that the people from the Indo-Iranian frontier played a major role in the history of the Indian subcontinent from at least the time of Mahmud of Ghazni (AD 998-1030) onwards. Under his command, hillmen from the borderlands, including undoubtedly the ancestors of the modern Pashtuns, carried out annual raids on the rich Indian plains and cities to the east. From that time onwards, the northern parts of the Indian subcontinent were deeply affected by Islam and Islamic culture and were politically being dominated by Islamic dynasties. These in their turn generally relied heavily upon mercenaries from the borderlands. The Islamic dynasties of Delhi included two that were of apparently Pashtun origin: the so-called Lodi dynasty (AD 1451-1526) and the Sur dynasty (AD 1539-1555).

For all those years, the relationship between the borderland tribes and Indians was close, although not always particularly peaceful. For the Indians, the Rohillas constituted a limitless supply of mercenaries and at the same time the accursed homeland of ferocious marauders. For the men west of the Indus, the Indians and their land formed a welcome source of income, urgently needed to eke out their meagre existence in the barren hills of the borderlands.

The names of the two apparently Pashtun dynasties, and their tribes, are known, and the Lodis and the Sur nowadays form part of the Pashtun nation. The name of the Pashtuns, however, as an overall designation is lacking. The *Bâburnâma*, which contains the memoirs of Babur, the Mughal conqueror of India in the early 16th century, likewise does not refer to the Pashtuns, although he crossed their lands many times. Instead we find general references to the 'Afghans' and to the names of various tribes, nowadays known as being Pashtun.[19]

[18] Caroe 1958: 19.

[19] The *Bâburnâma*, transl. by A S Beveridge (1922).

Consequently, the idea of 'Pashtunhood' seems, at least on the basis of outside sources, to be of fairly recent date. Outsiders did not describe the Pashtuns on the basis of one of their alleged characteristics, namely their language, but instead used more specific names to indicate the various tribes, or they applied blanket terms (Afghans, Rohillas) of unspecified connotation.

The legendary past

In the early 17th century, a Pashtun scholar in Delhi called Ni^cmat Allah compiled the so-called *Makhzan-i Afghâni*, in which he described the origins and genealogical relationships of the Pashtuns.[20] By that time, the borderland people had been a dominant political and military factor in the north of the Indian subcontinent for many centuries. In the first half of the 16th century they had to give way to Babur and his son, Humayun, who founded the Mughal dynasty, but for many years the Rohillas retained their importance in India as local landholders and middlemen in the administration of the vast Mughal empire. Proud of their history and perhaps to counterbalance their reduced prestige under the Mughals, they developed a sharp awareness of their own standing and position, of their background in the borderland mountains and their distinctiveness from the autochthonous Indians. They felt different, and no doubt superior to the Indian natives. The *Makhzan-i Afghâni* reflects this awareness. Ni^cmat Allah's work is based on oral history and describes the relationships between the various confederacies, tribes, sub-tribes, clans and families in which the Pashtuns, according to the author and his sources, are divided. It is a proud story, taking the ancestry of the Pashtuns back to the Israelites in far-away Palestine.[21]

Ni^cmat Allah differentiaties between three main groups of Pashtuns, namely the descendants of Sarban, Bitan and Ghurghusht. They were the three sons of the putative ancestor of all Pashtuns, Qays ^cAbd al-Rashid Pathan, a contemporary of Muhammad and a descendant of Biblical Saul. Most important of the three sons, at least in the eyes of Ni^cmat Allah, was the eldest, Sarban. His descendants, via his son Sharkhbun, are nowadays mainly found in south Afghanistan, and via his other son Kharshbun in the Peshawar Valley. Those in south Afghanistan include the Abdalis, who

[20] Ni^cmatullah, transl. by B Dorn.

[21] The Jewish exile in Babylonia may well have had a comparable influence upon the ethnogenesis of the Jewish nation as the Pashtun expatriate community in northern India upon that of the Pashtuns of the borderlands.

since the mid-18th century are called the Durranis.[22] Those in the east include the Yusufzay who live north of Peshawar, and many other tribes in the same area.

The relationship between the descendants of Sharkhbun and Kharshbun is of great interest. If Niʿmat Allah is correct it indicates historical connections and migrations. In this context the spread of another group, namely the offspring of a man called Kasi, is intriguing. Kasi was also a descendant of Kharshbun, Sarban's son. Kasi's descendants include the Shinwaris, who nowadays live in the Jalalabad area west of Peshawar. But they also include two other Pashtun tribes who live far to the south, in the Quetta region south-east of Qandahar, namely the Kasis themselves and the Ketrans. A particular relationship between the Pashtun tribes in south Afghanistan and those living much further to the north, in the Kabul valley and the Peshawar plains, is therefore a distinct possibility.

The descendants of the second brother, (Shaykh) Bitan, constitute the second Pashtun branch. According to Niʿmat Allah, Bitan's daughter, called Bibi Mato, married an outsider called Shah Husayn of Ghur (in Central Afghanistan). This marriage resulted in the large confederacy of the Ghaljis (Ghilzay)[23] and other tribes, living in the lands between Ghazni in Afghanistan and the Indus river in Pakistan. The Ghaljis themselves descend, according to Niʿmat Allah, from a son of Bibi Mato and Shah Husayn, who was conceived before they were married. Whatever really happened, Niʿmat Allah seems to have held a low opinion about this branch and especially about the Ghaljis!

The third brother, Ghurghusht, was the ancestor of a number of tribes that live throughout the land of the Pashtuns. The largest of these are the Kakars, who inhabit the rather poor lands north of Quetta, in modern Pakistan. Another group of the same branch is that of the Safis, who live far away from the Kakars, to the north-east of Kabul. If these groups are related, and there is no reason to doubt it, this would again indicate large-scale migrations. Since the lands in and around Kabul are known in the main to have been inhabited, as they still are, by non-Pashto speaking people, the Safi presence is clearly intrusive and they may well originate from the far south, from near the Kakars.

There is a fourth branch of Pashtuns, namely the descendants of Karran. The native genealogists do not agree as to whether he was a foundling who was adopted by Qays, or whether he belonged to one of the three branches mentioned earlier. Whatever the case, Karlan is the reputed ancestor of most of the Pashtun groups in modern Pakistan and in particular in the inaccessible lands south of the Peshawar Valley. They include the Afridis, the Khataks, the Mangals, the Wazirs, the Bangash, the Mahsuds, and many others.

Of course Niʿmat Allah's account should not be read as a sound historical document. It does tell us, however, something about the Pashtun self-image. The Pashtuns in Niʿmat Allah's circle regarded themselves as belonging to one nation, as descendants of one ancestor. In doing so they probably reproduced the self-image of many of the borderland Pashtuns, but since there are hardly any references to the Pashtuns as a nation from before that time, the idea of Pashtun ethnic unity may well have been rather underdeveloped among the Pashtuns themselves. This is shown by a number of features.

In spite of their attempt to produce the image of a homogeneous nation, the Indian Pashtuns were clearly forced to accept some generally known 'facts' among the Pashtuns. They had to differentiate between 'true' Pashtuns, namely those who descended directly from their eponymous ancestor, and others with a more dubious genealogy. Apparently Niʿmat Allah and his group were clearly aware of gradations of Pashtunhood. The descendants of Sarban were clearly regarded as 'good' Pashtuns. The descendants of Bibi Mato, however, and especially the Ghaljis, were somewhat suspect, and so were the many tribes inhabiting the hills south of Peshawar, namely the descendants of Karran.

Fusion and fission

Gradations of Pashtunhood are reflected in the process of fusion and fission that I referred to before. A modern example of 'fusion' may be the southern groups of the (non-Pashtun) Taimani and Maliki Aimaq in west Afghanistan, who feel affiliated to the Pashtuns and have adopted Kandahari Pashtun culture and language.[24] On the other hand, 'fission' may be indicated by the Persian speaking (Pashtun) Nurzai Durranis in south-west Afghanistan, who feel more related to non-Pashtun groups.[25]

[22] The Durranis are named after Ahmad Shah Durrani, the founder of the Kingdom of Afghanistan in the mid-eighteenth century.

[23] The name Ghilzay is the Persianised form of the name they give themselves: *Ghalji* (*sg. Ghaljai*).

[24] They are known for their typical black tents that resemble that of the Pashtuns (Szabo and Barfield 1991:48-50).

[25] See Roy 1990:111 for the affiliation of Persian speaking Nurzai with the (mainly Tajik) *Jamʿiyyat-i Islâmi* resistance organisation in the war against the Soviet Union. Their Pashto speaking kinsmen sided with another (Pashtun) organisation.

In 19th-century literature there are, within the same context, frequent references to the non-Pashtun background of certain 'Pashtun' tribes. Mountstuart Elphinstone tells of the Nasir Ghaljis, a tribe of wandering *Kuchis* or Powindahs who live along the Afghanistan/ Pakistan border. According to him: 'The Hotukees [Hotaki Ghaljis] say that the Naussers have been their Humsauyahs [clients], but not their kindred: some even represent them as sprung from the Beloches [Baluchis]; and though they speak Pushtoo, and strenuously maintain their descent from the Afghauns, their features and appearance certainly indicate a race distinct from that nation.'[26]

The critical years

The complex structure of relationships between the various Pashtun and affiliated groups indicates a history of migrations and of Pashtunisation. The spread of the Abdali Pashtuns to south-west and west Afghanistan dates back to historical times, to the 16th and 17th centuries.[27] The influx of the Pashtuns into the Peshawar plains also seems to date back to approximately the same time, namely the late 15th and early 16th centuries.[28] These were the Yusufzay and their kinsmen.

The turn of the 15th and 16th centuries thus emerges as a critical period in the history of the Pashtuns. Before that time, the Pashtuns were virtually unknown as such to the outside world. People had heard of various tribes that in later years formed part of the Pashtun nation, but there is no evidence that all of these tribes in ancient times spoke Pashto, or were otherwise linked to the *Pashtunwâli* of later years.

Throughout the 15th century, the borderlands had been under nominal control of Timurid princes and their governors. They dominated the scene as a result of the conquests of Timur in the late 14th century and that of the Mongols in the 13th century. The advent of Chenghiz Khan in the 1220s had led to a demise in the power of the major cities in the area, and a concurrent rise of the influence of the various mainly Turco-Mongolian tribes that came to roam the plains and mountain valleys of Afghanistan and neighbouring lands. In the early 15th century this led to the political division of much of Afghanistan among a number of Turco-Mongolian tribes, whose source of power was the military might of their following, rather than the wealth produced by trade and manufacture in the cities. In east Afghanistan, the Negüderi and Qara'unas were particularly powerful.[29] The rise of Timur from among the Turco-Mongolian *ulus* changed this situation. His continuous warfare brought little peace to the country and any attention to city dwelling and building activities was more or less limited to Samarkand and nearby Shahr-i Sabz, north of modern Afghanistan. An important development, in the context of the present paper, was the gradual demise of the power of the Turco-Mongolian tribes, including those in east Afghanistan, which were firmly brought under Timurid control.

With the death of Timur the throne was ascended by his son Shah Rukh, who until his death in March 1447 reigned the ever-crumbling empire of his father from the city of Herat, which was much embellished. After Shah Rukh's death, political decline set in that resulted by the early 16th century (AD 1507) in the fall of Herat and much of the rest of south Central Asia to another wave of newcomers from the far north, namely the Uzbeks. They not only defeated the Timurid princes of Herat, but sometime earlier they had forced another Timurid prince to flee from Samarkand to the south. This was Babur, who in AD 1504 successfully claimed Kabul from a local princeling of the Arghun family, who had succeeded Babur's uncle two years before.

Babur in later years went on to India and founded the Mughal empire. Before that time however, he first was forced to protect his rearguard and make sure that another major town in Afghanistan, Kandahar, was under his control. His first move on the city was made in AD 1507, when he took the city and dispelled its rulers, the Arghunids, who had been installed years before by the Timurid princes of Herat as governors of Kandahar. However, soon after the Uzbeks took Herat they subsequently also moved to Kandahar where they reinstated the Arghunids. Babur could only finally defeat the Arghunids in May 1522, when he took Kandahar again.

By that time, the place of the Uzbeks in west and south Afghanistan was taken by the rising power of the Iranian Safavids, who in AD 1510 had defeated the Uzbeks and were slowly consolidating their position in the area. Soon, the Mughals in India and the Safavids in Iran would start their long struggle for the control of Kandahar. The city changed hands many times. Both parties were desperately seeking support in the region, and they inevitably turned to the Pashtuns. The influx of prestige

[26] Elphinstone 1815: 461. See also Janata 1987 for the apparently non-Pashtun background of the Jajis and Turis.

[27] Noelle 1997: 233.

[28] Compare Caroe 1958: 168-192.

[29] Compare Manz 1989.

titles and wealth led to a change in the traditional equality of the Pashtuns. The local leaders were no longer *primi inter pares*, but developed into sometimes very willing, and sometimes very unwilling and rebellious middlemen who exploited their position between the king in far-away Isfahan or Delhi on the one hand and their local kinsmen on the other. It should be noted that this development particularly took place among the tribes that resided along the major roads of communication between Iran and India, namely those living in the Peshawar valley and in east and south Afghanistan. One of these local leaders was the famous Khushhal Khan Khatak (AD 1613-1689), of the Khatak tribe south-east of Peshawar, who as no other before him extolled the *nang* ('honour') of the Pashtuns (or in his case, the Pakhtuns). In this way he greatly contributed to the self-awareness of the Pashtuns who still, to this very day, know his songs. Another middleman was the famous Sado, an Abdali Pashtun from south Afghanistan, who became the ancestor of the royal house of Afghanistan (the Sadozai).

In the end, by the beginning of the 18th century, this development led to the unification of the Ghaljis of south-east Afghanistan under the Ghalji Hotaki leader, Mir Wais, and the subsequent Pashtun conquest of Iran by his son, Mir Mahmud.

The ethnogenesis of the Pashtuns

Discussing the ethnogenesis of a nation, as may be clear from the preceding pages, may be compared to finding the origins of the Amazon. Many small currents together constitute a major stream. Some of the water may be diverted elsewhere, and along its path the river may meet various physical obstacles that determine its course. The Pashtun nation is likewise the result of a number of contributing factors, both internal and external. One of these factors is the ongoing process of migration and expansion, and the other is that of Pashtunisation, or the growing awareness among the Pashtuns of their own special identity.

There are various stories among the Pashtun tribes south of Peshawar that testify to a general east to west movement, from along the banks of the Indus upland into the mountainous borderlands and the Iranian Plateau.[30]

This movement is also expressed in the east to west migrations of the Abdalis, who in historical times came to inhabit south and south-west Afghanistan. It is also found in the apparent migrations of some Pashtun tribes from the south to the Kabul valley and beyond in the north. One of the major Pashtun groups that moved from the mountain valleys along the Indus valley onto the Iranian plateau are the Ghaljis. Their habitat and that of their kinsmen now stretches from west of Ghazni in Afghanistan to the banks of the Indus in the east. The important point is that the Ghalji expansion to the west continued until very recent times at the cost of the Turco-Mongolian Hazaras of central Afghanistan. The recent study by Dr Mousavi describes the plight of this much-oppressed people at the hands of the Pashtuns.

The expulsion of the Hazaras from their ancestral lands in recent years can consequently be regarded as part of a much longer historical process that in the late medieval period removed the Turco-Mongolian tribes from eastern Afghanistan. It cannot be a coincidence that the Ghaljis are given a somewhat dubious genealogy, and that their name resembles that of the Turkish tribe of the Khalaj that inhabited this part of Afghanistan from the late first millennium onwards.[31] The Ghalji confederacy obviously contains a large amount of Turkish blood! Something similar occurred in the 16th and later centuries when the Abdali Pashtuns occupied the plains of south-west Afghanistan and subsequently moved into the mountains east of Herat for summer pasturage. There they came into contact with the ancestors of the Turco-Mongolian Aimaq tribes, some of whom are closely related to the Hazaras. Certain Aimaq groups adopted Pashtunhood, while others were forced to move away. The Pashtun 'push' was, however, never strong enough to totally dislodge the Aimaqs from the hills of western Afghanistan, contrary to the advent of the Pashtuns in east Afghanistan.

These observations would clearly locate the Pashtun 'homeland' in the borderland mountains west of the Indus, in modern Pakistan. This is in fact the area, generally described as that of the Sulaiman mountains, where many Pashtuns and outside observers have placed the origins of the Pashtuns.[32] From here, the process of migrations must have started at some time before about AD 1500. In the late medieval period the Baluch were advancing via Baluchistan in the south into Sind along the Indus and they were slowly encroaching upon the foothills of the Sulaiman mountains. Whether this was an important contributing factor in the spread of the Pashtuns remains impossible to tell. What we do know is that for many years the Rohillas had been amassing wealth and fame in the Indian subcontinent. This led to social

[30] Compare Janata 1987.

[31] See B A Litvinsky and M H Zamir Safi 1996: 179-182.

[32] Compare Elphinstone 1815: 151.

differentiation and further demographic pressure upon the rather unproductive lands west of the Indus. With the decline of the Turco-Mongolian tribes in eastern Afghanistan the road was open to expansion to the west. A possible Baluch pressure from the south may have triggered this movement. Many Pashtuns and others from the borderlands suddenly found themselves in the relatively rich plains of south and south-east Afghanistan and the green fields around Peshawar.

The migrations of the mid-second millennium of course do not fully explain the emergence of the Pashtuns as a nation. What it does indicate is that by around AD 1500 the ethnic constellation of the region was drastically altered. The migrations brought about new alliances of people who up till then had no relationships whatsoever. But the same migrations also dispersed kinsmen over large distances. Many of the wandering groups were ready to adopt a new background. Pashto was the dominant language and slowly replaced the Turco-Mongolian and other languages spoken in this region. This period of migrations apparently coincided and was followed by a process of Pashtunisation that received a strong impetus from external developments. New wealth and prestige were acquired from the competing neighbouring empires. By the late 16th century, most of the ethnic groups inhabiting the borderlands and by then speaking the same language perceived themselves as being different from the Shi^cite Safavids to the west, the Turkish Uzbeks to the north and the Indian Mughal rulers to the east. And they were proud of it.

BIBLIOGRAPHY

Bailey, Harold, 'Asiani and Pasiani', *Bulletin of the Asia Institute* 7, 1993, 9-10.

Bellew, H W, *The Races of Afghanistan: being a Brief Account of the Principal Natives inhabiting that Country.* Calcutta and London, 1880; reprint Graz, 1973.

Idem., *An Inquiry into the Ethnography of Afghanistan.* Woking, 1891; reprint Graz, 1973.

Caroe, O *The Pathans. 550 B.C.-A.D. 1957.* London and New York, 1958.

Dupree, L, *Afghanistan.* Princeton 1973. Revised edition 1980.

Elphinstone, Mountstuart, *An Account of the Kingdom of Caubul. An Account of the Kingdom of Caubul, and Its Dependencies in Persia, Tartary, and India, comprising a View of the Afghaun Nation; A History of the Dooraunee Monarchy.* London, 1815; second edition, 1839.

Gazetteer of Afghanistan. Vol. IV: Kabul and South-eastern Afghanistan Calcutta (reprint Graz, 1985)

Gommans, Jos J L, *The Rise of the Indo-Afghan Empire, c. 1710-1780.* Leiden/New York/Köln, 1995.

Janata, A, 'Constituents of Pashtun ethnic identity: The Jaji case', *Studia Iranica* 16, 1987, fasc. 2, 201-214.

Khan, Imran, *Warrior Race. A Journey Through the Land of the Tribal Pathans.* London, 1993.

Litvinsky, B A and M H Zamir Safi, 'The later Hephthalites in Central Asia', in: *History of Civilizations of Central Asia*, Vol. III. Paris, 1996, 176-183.

Mallory, J P, *In Search of the Indo-Europeans. Language, Archaeology and Myth.* London, 1989.

Manz, Beatrice Forbes, *The Rise and Rule of Tamerlane.* Cambridge 1989.

Morgenstierne, Georg, *Report on a Linguistic Mission to North-Western India.* Oslo, 1932.

Idem., 'Neu-Iranische Sprachen', in *Handbuch der Iranistik, Iranistik/Linguistik.* Leiden, 1958, 155-178.

Idem., 'The linguistic stratification of Afghanistan', *Afghan Studies* 2, 1979, 23-33.

Mousavi, S A, *The Hazaras of Afghanistan. An Historical, Cultural, Economic and Political Study.* Richmond, 1998.

Ni^cmatullâh, *Makhzan-i Afghâni*, translated by B Dorn. London, 1829-1836.

Noelle, Christine, *State and Tribe in Nineteenth-Century Afghanistan. The Reign of Amir Dost Muhammad Khan (1826-1863).* Richmond, 1997.

Orywal, Erwin (ed.), *Die ethnischen Gruppen Afghanistans. Fallstudien zu Gruppenidentität und Intergruppenbeziehungen.* Wiesbaden, 1986.

Raverty, Henry George, *Notes on Afghanistan and Baluchistan.* London, 1878 (reprint Lahore 1976).

Ridway, R T I, *Pathans.* Calcutta, 1910.

Roy, O, *Islam and Resistance in Afghanistan* (second edition) Cambridge, 1990.

Steul, Willi, *Paschtunwali. Ein Ehrenkodex und seine rechtliche Relevanz.* Wiesbaden, 1981.

Szabo, A and T J Barfield, *Afghanistan. An Atlas of Indigenous Domestic Architecture.* Austin, 1991.

Vogelsang, Willem, *The Rise and Organisation of the Achaemenid Empire. The Eastern Iranian Evidence.* Leiden/New York/Köln, 1992.

Vogelsang, Willem, *The Afghans.* Oxford (in press).

25 ECHOES IN A LANDSCAPE—WESTERN AFGHANISTAN IN 1989

Bruce Wannell

Between September 1989 and January 1990, I travelled, mostly by horse, in the historic areas of Ghur, Gharjestan, Chesht and Herat.[1] As I crossed the landscape of the medieval Ghurid heartland, I came across many legendary echoes and archaeological remains consisting in three main types of buildings: defensive towers rendered with mud-plaster at Nili and Qaisar; elaborate kiln-burnt brick prestige structures at Jam, Jawand and Chesht; and fine stone masonry at Larwand. These probably date from what has been called the 'Ghurid Interlude', after the Ghurids took Ghazni in 1150 to 1214 when they were finally defeated by the Khwarazmshah.

These short notes aim to give an account of these 'echoes in a landscape', in the hope of encouraging further scholarly investigation, in the administrative areas *(uluswali)* of Purchaman, Taiwara, Shahrak, Jawand, Auba/Chesht, Farsi/Shindand and Zendejan/Enjil.

In **Larwand**,[2] where the Mushkan river runs on its way to the Purchaman valley, stands a small ruined stone mosque surrounded by *khenjak* wild pistacchio trees (pl. 25.1). It is called Ziyarat-e Malekan, and is of fine stone masonry carved in an Indo-Muslim style associated with North-West India. Shehabeddin Ghuri ruled in Ghazni from 1173 and in Ghur after his brother's death from 1203 till 1206 when he was assassinated by Isma^cili heretics. The capture of Lahore in Punjab from the last Ghaznavid ruler in 1186 established the Ghurids in the Subcontinent—they further expanded with campaigns against Hindu rulers in 1192 when they took Ajmer and Delhi and in 1194 when they took Benares and Kannauj. These are likely dates for sending Indian prisoners of war to build a victory memorial in the rural homeland. Above the entrance arch is carved a heraldic device of horned candlestick, or crescent moon on a cone. As the motif was in shadow, I was unable to obtain a photo of it, and only realised later when I saw the same repeated on a mud-plaster defensive tower that it might be significant (cf. pl. 25.5).

The Khwaja Khezr irrigation tunnel on the pass between Larwand and Tuli is built of fine stone masonry, well-cut and ordered as if placed by demons, *div-chin*, that is, by the artisan-demons commanded by the Prophet Sulaiman. The stones are blackened by coal-dust in the water that gushes out of the mountain.

One of the striking features of the otherwise bare landscape of Ghur is the number of medieval towers of rough masonry rendered with mud-plaster carved in quite elaborate detail, which stand at the mouth of every gorge and along every valley.[3] Locals attribute them to Zuhhak, the legendary pre-Islamic ancestor of the Shansabi rulers of Ghur. Ghur was one of the last areas of Iran-Afghanistan to be islamised: is there a certain anti-Zoroastrian element in this putative genealogy? Zuhhak was not only a tyrant (or a dragon, as this name has the same etymology as modern Persian *ezhdeha*), but also an Arab. The Al-e Shansab were originally chieftains of the Ahangaran area east of Jam and were raised to greater power after Mahmud of Ghazna's campaigns against the pagans of Ghur in 1010. The circular ornaments around the slit-windows are inspired (cf. pls. 3-4), I was told, by the traditional Ghur speciality *khalawak*: dumplings with a hole in the middle, made of rain-fed hill barley flour boiled in water and a plant-potash, *ishghar-e ushnan*, served with the classic whey-sauce, *qorut,* and clarified butter, *roghan-e zard*. The sickle-shaped hollows on the walls are a warning, my host told me, that 'All who live in this harsh land must work the land and live frugally, for only barley will grow here.'

The castle of **Qaisar**,[4] known as Qal^ca-ye Dokhtar—the daughter's fort (*Tochter, dokhtar* and daughter

[1] In 1985, I was offered the post of running an aid agency for displaced Afghans in Peshawar, Pakistan. That lasted till 1987 when I parted company with the London-based NGO and travelled to Hazarajat and Faryab in Afghanistan, monitoring aid projects for a group of European NGOs. Two years later, I travelled again to monitor a variety of projects in agriculture, education and health, in the historic areas of Ghur, Gharjestan, Chesht and Herat. I travelled mostly by horse with one Afghan colleague, from the beginning of September 1989 to mid January 1990, with introductions to local khans, mujahedin commanders and religious elders.

[2] Warwick Ball, *Archaeological Gazetteer, of Afghanistan*, 2 volumes, Paris 1982, Site number 683 and references (henceforth *Archaeological Gazetteer,* followed by Site No.).

[3] See also Warwick Ball, this volume.

[4] *Archaeological Gazetteer*, 875.

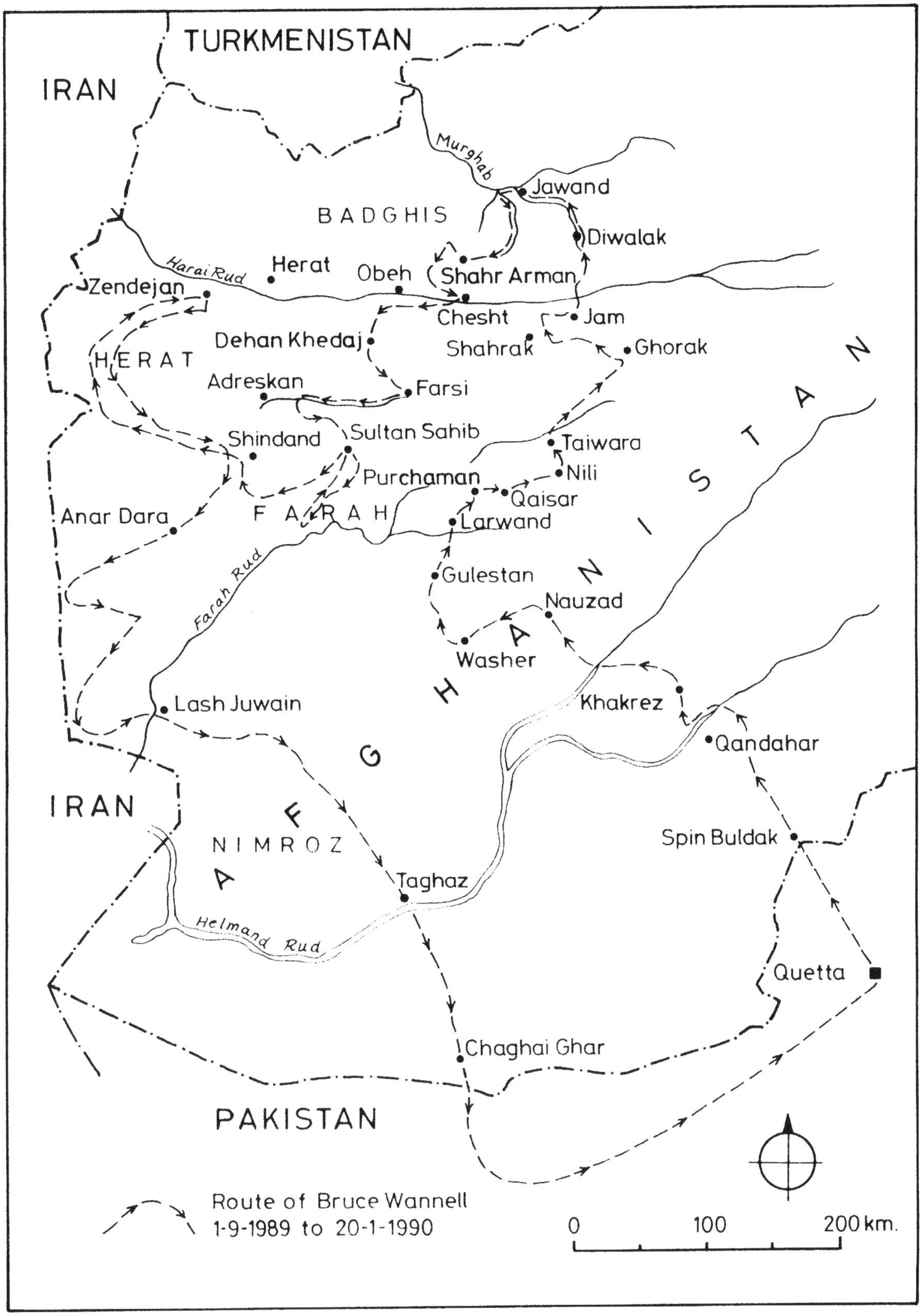
TURKMENISTAN
IRAN
Murghab
Jawand
BADGHIS
Diwalak
Harai Rud
Herat
Obeh
Shahr Arman
Zendejan
Chesht
Jam
Dehan Khedaj
Shahrak
Ghorak
HERAT
Adreskan
Farsi
Sultan Sahib
Shindand
Taiwara
Purchaman
Nili
Qaisar
Anar Dara
FARAH
Larwand
Gulestan
Farah Rud
Nauzad
Washer
AFGHANISTAN
Khakrez
Lash Juwain
Qandahar
IRAN
Spin Buldak
NIMROZ
Taghaz
Helmand Rud
Quetta
Chaghai Ghar
PAKISTAN
Route of Bruce Wannell
1-9-1989 to 20-1-1990
0
100
200 km.

Fig. 25.1

have the same etymology), commands the whole valley largely populated by Mongols; its mud-rendered walls are carved in the form of dumplings and sickles (pls. 25.2-4). Similar ornaments are found on the towers at Mullaha, Galla Cheshma and Sarmazur in Nili,[5] at Kaji in Chahar Dar and at Yakhan Bala in the upper Taiwara valley.[6] These towers were therefore no doubt built at the same time and by the same people—whether the feudal lords of the Ghurid tribes or the conquering Mongols who destroyed the Ghurid and Khwarazmian empires in the 13th century. The tower at Sarmazur at the top of the Nili valley (pl. 25.5) has a motif of horned candlestick/sickle moon astride a cone almost identical to that above the arched door of the Ziyarat-e Malekan in Larwand, so most probably these mud-rendered towers are Ghurid. According to Professor David Bivar these heraldic motifs could be derived from Sasanian cattle-brands, *neshan*.

I heard of other towers at Yaman and Warkash, as well as at Ahangaran and Bamyan,[7] which are identified in local popular tradition with Malek ᶜAntar from the *Malek ᶜAntar* epic cycle[8] and Gulshah from the *Warqa o Gulshah* romance.[9] The more classical literary tradition probably has had less effect on the names of the Ghur landscape than the popular chap-book/ballad tradition, which conflates the two epics, with lithographed editions published in Kabul with crude line drawings. My Afghan colleague, Gul Agha of Logar, later obtained for me an undated damaged copy of just such a popular version of *Warqa o Gulshah*. Our host in Larwand told us that in the days before radios, the winters were spent reading verse romances such as *Warqa o Gulshah* which, though situated among the desert tribes of Arabia, has given names to features of the landscape of Ghur, just as the hero of Islamic chivalry, Hazrat ᶜAli, has given his name to countless sites where dragons are supposed to have been slain, where ridges of rock pierce the earth or hot springs gush out of the ground.

At **Sarmazur** at the top of the Nili valley,[10] we were guests of Commander Khalil Ghuri of the Sardar-Khail descended from the former rulers of Ghur; he showed me finds from local digs, including rough medieval earthenware, a silver bracelet with paired birds in roundels and cursive Arabic script engraved illegibly, and a remarkable bronze tripod vase with three elaborately curving horned ibex heads, comparable to Bactrian and Lurestan finds from the Bronze Age[11] In the family mosque further down the valley at Mahalla, he showed me frescoes (pl. 25.6) by his uncle Aghay Mash'al the famous Herat miniaturist, and also a beautifully calligraphed manuscript of the family history claiming descent from the Al-e Shansab.

I was struck throughout this region, from Larwand to Jam to Chesht, that the local dialect pronunciation of 'father', *pedar* in Persian, is *piyar*; I had already noticed this in Quetta where I came across an annotated edition of the 12th century Qur'an commentary written for Ghiyatheddin Ghuri, known as the *Tafsir-e Torbat-e Jam*—this shows a dialect continuity of 800 years.

We arrived from the village of **Jam**[12] down a narrow boulder-filled valley at dusk to see the top of the minaret appearing between a crack in the mountains: when we reached the minaret in the dark, the full moon was rising in the east along the Harai Rud. We stayed over on the north bank of the river at the shrine of Seyyed Hasan Bokhari, where the *khalifa* was also a miller and operated a ferry and had grown rich on the sale of *zir-khaki* finds

[5] Compare a similar near-by site, *Archaeological Gazetteer,* 775.

[6] Cf. *Archaeological Gazetteer*, 1130 and 1236.

[7] *Archaeological Gazetteer,* 1239, 1234, 15, 238 and 100.

[8] ᶜAntar, cf. Lane *Manners and Customs of the Modern Egyptians*, London 1836, chapter XXIII: 'There is in Cairo a third class of reciters of romance called ᶜAnatireh or ᶜAntareeyeh (in the singular ᶜAntaree) ... the chief subject of their recitation ... is the romance of ᶜAntar (Seerat 'Antar) ... the reciters read it from the book. They chant the poetry, but the prose they read in the popular manner ... the modern Muslims of Egypt have sufficient remains of Bedawee feeling to take great delight in hearing tales of war.'

Based on the chivalrous exploits of the pre-Islamic poet-warrior ᶜAntara bin Shaddad who was the son of an Abyssinian black slave mother by a chief of the 'Abs tribe; he won his freedom by his bravery and wooed his paternal cousin ᶜAbla, as well as composing one of the prize-winning odes enshrined in the collection of the 7 or 10 *Muᶜallaqat*. His role in tribal raids and skirmishes became a pattern of chivalry, and the cycle of stories was reworked in the process of largely oral transmission, partly in 14th century Mamluk Egypt. It was published in Cairo in 32 volumes, and translated in 1820 by T Hamilton as *ᶜAntar, a Bedoueen Romance* and again in 1980 by W Norris as *The Adventures of ᶜAntar.*

[9] *Warqa o Gulshah* survives in a unique early 13th century manuscript in the Topkapi Library, Istanbul, which was published by Zabibullah Safa in 1964 and translated by Assadullah Suren Melikian-Chirvani in 1970. Warqa of the Bani Shayba tribe is about to marry his cousin Gulshah when she is kidnapped by a rejected former suitor on her wedding night; he tries to rescue her, but is captured and is only saved from execution by Gulshah's timely murder of her captor; Warqa is told to make his fortune before the marriage can take place, so goes off to his uncle the king of Yemen; meanwhile Gulshah is married off to the king of Syria; the cousins manage to find each other again, but die of grief until resurrected for a happy ending through the intercession of the Prophet Muhammad.

[10] Cf. *Archaeological Gazetteer*, 775 and 987.

[11] Which he offered to swap for my tape-recorder. I regret that I didn't accept the offer: the tape-recorder was of poor quality, so the recordings were unusable by the BBC, and later it was stolen from my saddle-bags on the return journey! The photographs I took of this remarkable object were unfortunately bleached and useless.

[12] *Archaeological Gazetteer*, No 468.

from digs in the area. Recently a bronze statue of a seated bearded man with one hand raised as if teaching had fetched a good price in Dara Takht market. Next to the shrine the *khalifa* kept a *khergah* tent, white with bands of coloured appliqué work, pointed as in Taimurid and Safavid miniatures, now specific to the Allahyar and Zai-Reza Firuzkuhi. The saint's tomb was covered in fragments of carved white marble, probably looted from the dado of a ruined palace or mosque.

In the morning, we re-crossed to the south of the river and visited the minaret of Jam, the outstanding monument of Ghur at the confluence of the Harai Rud and Jam torrent. It was erected in 586/1190 for the greatest of the Ghurid rulers, Ghiyatheddin Abu'l-Fath Muhammad bin Sam Ghuri who ruled from 1163 to 1203 and is buried by the Great Mosque in Herat, which he had had rebuilt in 577/1181. It stands perhaps as a victory tower where the Ghurids had their summer capital Firuzkuh—which was important enough as a centre of trade to attract a Jewish community which left Hebrew inscriptions dated between 1153 and 1203. Interlaced bands of Kufic epigraphy carry the text of the *Sura Maryam* (Chapter of Mary) and inside the minaret is a fine double spiral brick stair, which allows people to climb up without crossing those coming down. When I walked north of the river up to the ruined fort overlooking the minaret, fragments of glazed pottery crunched underfoot at every step. There were traces of solid brick embankments on the bank opposite the minaret; the *khalifa* told me the tradition that there had once been another minaret facing the surviving one and that the Harai Rud had been covered with a brick platform to make a mosque.

On the banks of the Baidan torrent opposite Jam were more kiln-burnt brick, *khesht-e pokhta,* ruins. As we rode on, we passed more such ruins, at **Diwalak**, where a small brick wall with windows and machicolations blocked a hollow high up the cliff. *Sorud-khana-ye parian*, 'the fairies' music-hall!' explained my guide. More probably a guard-post to secure the route of the Ghurid royal progress from Larwand, Purchaman to Shah Mashhad, Jawand, which would have happened if/when they weren't too busy campaigning away.

Further, at **Dara Asya** in the Allahyar area,[13] and at **Sharshar-e Ab-e Garm**, we passed more plaster and masonry walls with machicolations high up the cliffs. These almost inaccessible rooms cut into the cliff-face may have been reused later as shelters during the Mongol reign of terror. By a waterfall in **Zanu**, we passed the shrine of Hazrat ᶜAli's footprint, *Qadam-Gah-e Hazrat ᶜAli.*

[13] Cf. *Archaeological Gazetteer*, 27.

Jawand[14] has a spectacular landscape of deep canyons between honey-coloured sandstone walls. Its most important monument is the Madrasa Shah-e Mashhad just beyond the confluence of the Kucha and Murghab rivers. It is dated to the month of Ramadan in the year 571 and carries the text of the *Sura al-Fath*, the Victory chapter, beginning on the three bays of the south east tower, which probably continued over the 9 bays of the facade, though the four western bays have crumbled into rubble; the arch of the central bay of the entrance has collapsed since it was discovered by Bernt Glatzer and Michael Casimir almost 30 years ago (pls. 25.7-9). The lower left side of the entrance arch carries benedictions in Arabic to a female patron: as shown by the feminine possessive pronoun suffix *-ha*: *wa khalada mulka-ha* may God perpetuate her reign, etc. Many of the flat baked bricks have migrated to cover tombs in the local cemetery or to build the walls of the farmhouses of recently arrived Pushtuns. I saw traces of coloured plaster in the remaining *muqarnas* vaults and was told that a *shamsa* disc of tile-mosaic had fallen off the facade after a storm. On the slopes above the madrasa, commanding a fine view of the sweep of the Murghab through the valley, is the ruin of a fort or palace with heaps of baked brick and carved unglazed tiles.

Just above the confluence of the two rivers, my Pushtun hosts pointed out a cave in the cliff-face with two mouths, saying that it had been the home of a demon called Shadnam who loved a miller's daughter called Gulnaz—they also pointed to the ruins of her mill on the opposite banks crowning the cliff—probably another Ghurid fort defending the approach to Shah-e Mashhad.

The 12th century heresiographer Shahrestani[15] mentions the Karrami sect which under the Ghaznavids was widespread in Ghur and Gharjestan among the recently islamised tribes with their barbarous dialects. The Ghurid rulers adhered to the sect until they took power in Herat where they adopted the Shafei *madhhab* (rite and canon law), and in Ghazna where they adopted the Hanafi *madhhab*. The 13th century historian Menhaj Seraj Jauzjani grew up in the household of Ghiyatheddin's daughter and spent the years of the Mongol invasion at the castle of Tulak before fleeing to the originally Ghurid court at Delhi where he wrote his *Tabaqat-e Naseri* circa 659/1260 for the Muezzi ruler Nasereddin Mahmud Shah who ruled from 1246 to1266. In his history, he mentions the wisest of the Karrami divines working during the reign of Ghiyatheddin, Sadreddin ᶜAli Haitham of Naishapur, who

[14] *Archaeological Gazetteer*, 1023.

[15] Abu l'-Fath Muhammad b. ᶜAbd al-Karim b. Ahmad al-Shahrastani, *Kitab al-Milal wa 'l-Nihal*, e. Badran, 2 vols, Cairo, 1370-5/1951-5.

Pl. 25.1 *Ziyarat-e Malekan, Larwand*

Pl. 25.2 *Qalᶜa-ye Qaisar*

Pl. 25.3 *Qalᶜa-ye Qaisar – detail of decoration*

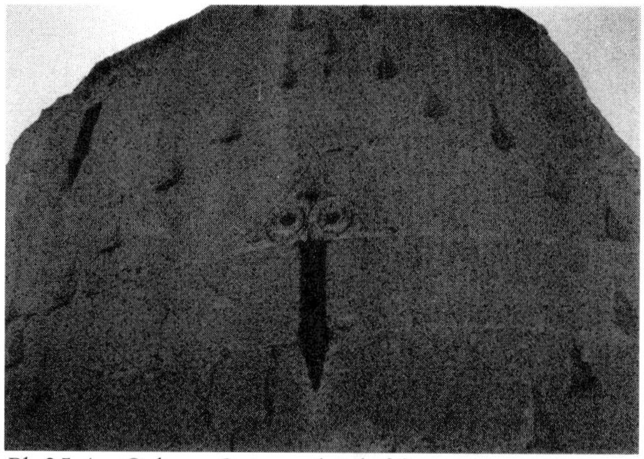

Pl. 25.4 *Qalᶜa-ye Qaisar—detail of decoration*

Pl. 25.5 *Sarmazur in Nili*

Pl. 25.6 Mosque at Mahalla in Nili

Pl. 25.7 Shah Mashhad, Jawand

Pl. 25.8 Shah Mashhad, Jawand

Pl. 25.9 Shah Mashhad, Jawand

had an important madrasa at Afshin, the capital of Gharjestan. Stylistically, the madrasa Shah-e Mashhad fits in with other brick buildings built between 1163 and 1203 during the reign of Ghiyatheddin at Jam, Heart and Chesht. Could the madrasa on the Murghab be that of Sadreddin the Karrami, endowed by a princess of the royal house in the capital of the province of Gharjestan, to celebrate the Ghurid conquests of Seljuq Herat and Isma^cili Multan in the same year 571/1176?

In Sheberghan of **Yalanta**, our host showed us a horde of 120 silver coins of Shah Rukh Mirza, dated 827-48/1424-45, which his workmen had just found while clearing a water-channel at the base of the cliff behind his house. He said a bronze bucket with many embossed figures had recently been sold to Jawand's wealthiest shopkeeper for 3 lakhs Afghanis, and had later been sold on to antique-dealers in Herat for 95 lakhs!

Shahr-e Arman[16] is one of the most beautiful sites I have seen in Afghanistan, a perfectly enclosed valley (pls. 25.10-11) with narrow exits along the valley to Kucha in the north, to Ghurghuri in the east, to Zakak in the south and the forested slopes of Ab-e Barik to the west. In the centre of the small valley with its pink and dove-grey rock walls is the mound of a once prosperous city and castle, which has been tentatively identified with the second city of Gharjestan, Shurmin.[17] Near the river stands a large smooth rock with 'runic' inscriptions which, my local guide mentioned, Russian scholars had compared to other such inscriptions in Central Asia. The site of the city had been totally worked over by treasure-hunters, and the ruined castle had become a mujahedin guard-post. Large earthenware amphorae with swirling black patterns, others with claw-like fingers pendant from the handles, fragments of thick blue- or green-glazed earthenware littered the ground by the freshly dug trenches (pls. 25.12-15). Our host the Arbab showed us the roof of his outhouse, where next to his Dashaka artillery was a collection of Seljuq fritware bowls, mostly smashed in the clumsy digs, and a fragment of a purple crystal globe vase with ribbed sides and small round neck—a lovely piece even though half was missing. There were green and brown splashed wares, sgraffiato under thick green glazes, buff pottery with turquoise glaze that all have a long and continuing craft tradition. Yet the layer of charred wood and ash that lay half way down the trenches implied that all these pieces pre-dated the (Mongol?) cataclysm when the city was burned and never recovered. I was told of a bronze plaque with figures of milkmaids milking cows and ploughmen driving teams of oxen and farmers clipping vines, as if they were almost alive: I was unable to see it as it had been taken for safe-keeping to the far end of the valley at Ghurghuri. I was shown a damaged cauldron with flanged lip on which the maker had inscribed his Shiite-sounding name *ʿamal ʿAli bin Haidar*. All these were due to be sold to the dealers of Dara Takht and Herat.

At **Chesht**,[18] we came to the two surviving brick domes (pl. 25.16) of the madrasa built probably at the order of Sultan Ghiyatheddin Ghuri for the son of Sultan Maudud Cheshti, Ahmad Mushtaq, who died in 577/1182, the last of that family mentioned in Jami's collected sufi hagiographies *Nafahat al-Uns*. These domes were said, by my local guide, to have originally numbered a dozen, housing up to 1,000 students—perhaps Sultan Ghiyatheddin was aiming to legitimise his conquest of Herat by patronising the province's oldest religious family. Executions and imminent upheavals at Dara Takht left me no time to attempt to read inscriptions in the interior of the domes, which have also been interpreted as funerary monuments.

Though the Cheshtis were an influential descent group between Tagau Ghaza and Dara Takht, (and in the Kuhestan of southern Faryab, where I met several respected religious teachers of the Cheshti Saiyed lineage in 1987), I could not find any trace of the Cheshti sufi *tariqa*: I was told that if there was any *tariqa* at all, it was Naqshbandi. The Cheshti *tariqa* as a formal congregation came into being in India no earlier than the late 13th century, the writings attributed to Khwaja Muineddin Cheshti are agreed to be spurious,[19] and the Cheshti *tariqa* remained chiefly Indian in its sphere of influence, distinct from the family of Sultan Maudud Cheshti who enjoyed Ghurid patronage. The Cheshti *khanegah* in Kabul's Kucha-ye Kharabat came into being in the 19th century as a result of importing Indian court musicians who belonged to this order.[20] Like the Mevlevis in Turkey, the Cheshtis favoured music to draw potential converts. Notably they promoted *Qawwali* devotional singing to rival the attractions of Hindu music.

Sebarz[21] in the Harai Rud valley had been the home of the head of the Cheshti saiyeds in 1912 according to Adamec's 1980s re-edition of the *Gazetteer of Western Afghanistan*. But I was told that the land had been sold in the 1920s to descendants of the charismatic religious figure

16 *Archaeological Gazetteer*, 1033.

17 Jonathan Lee, in conversation.

18 *Archaeological Gazetteer*, 212.

19 P Mark Currie, *The Cheshti Shrine at Ajmer*, OUP, Oxford, 1985.

20 John Baily, in conversation.

21 *Archaeological Gazetteer*, 961.

Pl. 25.10 Shahr-e Arman

Pl. 25.11 Shahr-e Arman

Pl. 25.12 Objects excavated from Shahr-e Arman

Pl. 25.13 Objects excavated from Shahr-e Arman

Pl. 25.14 Objects excavated from Shahr-e Arman

Pl. 25.15 Objects excavated from Shahr-e Arman

of the 18th century Gandom ᶜAli, who had performed the useful miracle of filling the town's empty grain store for the new Pushtun monarchy of the Abdali. An octagonal brick pavilion on the hill above the orchards was said to be named after Khwaja Nezameddin Cheshti: when I went to examine it, I found only a rather grand marble tombstone of a mid-15th century Taimurid prince, Ghiyatheddin Jamshid bin ᶜEzzeddin Muhammad. The current descendants of Gandom ᶜAli had become big landowners, but were driven by mujahedin exactions to side with the Communist government to preserve themselves: at their oath-taking ceremony in the spring of 1990, shortly after I visited the area, they were, however, blown up by the mujahedin commander Ismaᶜil Khan.

Dehan-e Khedaj on the way up to Taghan Kuh is the home of lineal descendants of the last great classical Persian poet and Naqshbandi sufi, Nureddin Abdu Rahman Jami. Though he was buried in Herat, such was the fear of Shiite hostility to this revered figure of Sunni Islam after the Safavid conquest of Herat in 1510, that his son Ziaeddin Yusuf and disciple Abdul Ghafur Lari took the body to the highlands and buried it at Arf-e Haft Galla in the upper reaches of the Kaughan Rud: the grave is still visited at Jauzestan. Fifty families descended from the poet still live at Dehan Khedaj, Arf-e Haft Galla, Haji Bagh and Ushan. My host was supervising the harvest, standing by the threshing floor wearing a green *chapan* and holding a long staff—33 year old Abdu Rahman Jami was also a poet, as had been his father Bahaeddin Qased, who was the last to teach the *tariqa*. A quotation from one of his poems caught my eye: *ensaf ᶜain-e shariᶜat ast*—'fairplay is the essence of the Divine Law'—both of which seemed to be in abeyance in these parts! The family had bought land from Tajik iron miners in Taghan Kuh in the 1930's. When the Russians advanced and looted their home and burned books, manuscripts and title deeds, the Jami family fled to Farsi; it was only a few months since they had returned to their home. I noticed that they were referred to as Saiyed and asked if they were descended from the Prophet: my host said no, they were descended from Shaibani Arabs settled at Jam in Khorasan, but that with the passage of time creeping 'saiyedization' had occurred, and they were addressed by this title out of respect for their religious learning and spiritual authority.

Haji Bagh was where we met another Abdu Rahman Jami, a cousin of our host in Dehan Khedaj, who pointed to a hillock known as Negar-Khana, where ruins with pictures and frescoes had been found: the name on the map, as often, was inaccurate—Naqqara-Khana would imply an orchestra in these barren windswept uplands!

Tazarbaid (not, as on the map, Keysarbeg) at the mouth of the Tangi Azau gorge[22] has ruins known as Shahr-e Malek ᶜAntar, where medieval metalwork had been dug-up. The area had long been a centre for iron-mining. Of the objects offered for sale, I bought a long-handled spoon made of a hard un-corroding metal-alloy which I used for the rest of the trip to scrape out honey from the supply we had bought in Wardak months previously—it had lasted longer than our horses, which were almost washed away in the fast flowing river and soon after had to be abandoned! I don't know if the site has any relation to the other Malek ᶜAntar sites in Ghur, other than the winter-reading of the chap-book romance.

In **Kuh-e Zur**, I stayed in the black goats-hair tents of Haji Saidu Jan, one of the former notables of Shindand, now leading the jehad from near the tomb of his ancestor, Sultan Ibrahim Qattal. I walked a few hours to see the tomb, as the Qattali saiyeds descended from the saint were still influential throughout the area from Purchaman to Shindand and Herat. That they were recognised as genuine saiyed descendants of the Prophet is shown by the exemption of the entire Qattali lineage from taxes and military service, after Saiyed Ismaᶜil Qattali applied for confirmation of their status to the court of Amir Abdu Rahman Khan in the late 19th century.

According to the legend, the saint's ancestor, Saiyed ᶜAli Shah, had settled in Hamadan during the persecutions by the Umayyad governor al-Hajjaj; his descendants migrated to Afghanistan: Saiyed Ahmad to Pasaband in Ghur; Saiyed ᶜAli to Kunar; Saiyed Ibrahim to Chesht, where Sultan Qutbeddin Maudud Cheshti sensed an imminent rival and sent him to convert the pagans of Kuh-e Zur in the wild hinterland of Farah. His name 'Qattal'—'one who fights energetically'—and that of a neighbouring shrine, Khwaja Sar-bor—'Reverend Decapitator'—imply a less than peaceful penetration of Islam in these regions. Eventually, the Zuris of Kuh-e Zur were persuaded with much fighting and decapitating to abandon their pagan worship of fire. The saint is buried by a spring of fresh water in a grove under the sturdy four-arched dome-chamber of what looked to me like a Sasanian fire-temple. His first convert, the Zuri Mulla lies at his feet.

I was told that three large inlaid brass candlesticks given by the 15th century Taimurid Sultan Husain Baiqara and a large Qu'ran had been stolen and sold in Kabul's Chicken Street some fifteen years previously by one Saiyed Hashem Qattali. His sacrilegious disrespect for his ancestor's shrine did not go unpunished, as he shortly afterwards

[22] Cf. *Archaeological Gazetteer,* 1144, where mention is made of Hebrew inscriptions from *c.* 1300.

went mad. His family in penance paid for the shrine to be re-plastered in 1353/1974. When I visited, there was nothing to identify the site other than the histories given by my guides, who pointed out the three tombs lacking any inscription, and the *Chella-Khana* where the saint had fasted and gone into seclusion—now used as tent and fodder store by the Zuri villagers. The portico could be 15-16th century provincial, but the massive piers of the dome-chamber reminded me of Sasanian fire-temples in Iran. It would be interesting to know which auction house ever handled these candlesticks, to have at least some evidence to anchor these tales in history.

In **Zendejan**, once known as Pushang/Fushanj,[23] I was taken to see the shrine of Muhammad Ghazi in the Mahall-e Sar Mazar—a sturdily built brick dome and portal. It shelters a partly ruined tomb with elaborate decoration of glazed tiles in turquoise and lapis blue and manganese purple, deep-moulded or carved in high relief with large Arabic text on the lower frieze and a Persian *ghazal* on the narrow upper band in a free and elegant *ta*ʿ*liq* script. This decoration reminded me of 14th century Central Asian work but, if the local antiquarian Fekri Seljuqi is right, could be older: after floods damaged the shrine in the 1960s, he removed the tomb-slab with the main inscriptions to Herat, and in his *Resala-ye Mazarat-e Herat* attributes the tomb to Nasereddin Muhammad Alap Ghazi, son of the Seljuq prince Qara Arsalan who married Sultan Ghiyatheddin Ghuri's sister and died in 600/1204. I was not allowed much time to decipher the *ghazal* from the scattered tiles and managed only a few rhymes with the repeated *na-darad*:

... hayat-ash, darigha, darigha, baqa'i na-darad
... saheb-qerani ... hajat rawa'i na-darad
*... jehan naser al-haqq wa 'l-din .. haq kadkhoda*ʿ*i na-darad*
... husn nema'i na-darad
*... du*ʿ*a'i na-darad*

It would be interesting to check in the *divan* collections of contemporary poets to see if such a *ghazal* or *marthiya* can be found—which could then help in reassembling the fallen tiles.

South of Zendejan, in a narrow valley between the Kaftar Khan and Keshmarun ranges, lies the shrine of **Robat-e Pai** (pl. 25.17). It has a double brick dome surrounded by pine and pistachio trees and the tombs (again according to Fekri Seljuqi) of Khwaja ʿAbdullah Ansari's teacher and two Bokhara princes as well as a Nasereddin Tughril bin Shamseddin who died in 756/1355. The shrine probably has pre-Islamic origins and was known locally as a second Kaʿba—which echoes the mention in the *Tarikh-e Sistan* of the 9th century Yaʿqub bin Laith decreeing a second Kaʿba in Sistan. I hired a jeep and organised a *khairat* thanks-giving picnic after surviving ambush, bombing and tank-shelling over Christmas in Enjil. On the rocks leading to the shrine, I was shown the hoof-marks of Duldul, Hazrat ʿAli's mount, and inside on smooth black rock the hand and foot marks of Bibi Fatema, who had sheltered in the cave to give birth to a child. These holy imprints in the rock resemble those of the Buddha's feet once venerated in Swat—the diffusion of Buddhism from the Nau-Bahar temple at Balkh was perhaps not so distant, though overlaid with legends reflecting the ʿAlid or Shiite sympathies of the population during the Safavid domination. In Maqdisi's *Ahsan al-Taqasim fi Macrifat al Aqalim*, mention is made of the imprint of Abraham's foot in a rock kept in a box in the Haram in Mecca which was opened and exhibited to the faithful at prayer times[24]—so the veneration of imprints associated with prophets and holy personages goes beyond the range of the historical expansion of Buddhism.

Another folk superstition was that the many fossils of small sea-creatures that littered the valley floor were in fact birds which came to life on Friday eve and fluttered around the shrine till Friday dawn, when they once again turned to stone!

While monitoring aid projects in Enjil, I had persuaded some Shiite friends to show me the Taimurid mosque at **Hauz-e Karbas**: we searched among the ruins of the villages and after several false trails clambered down over a heap of rubble to examine what remained of the exquisite tile-work. A panel once placed above a doorway had fallen to the ground: what was not shattered contained Persian verses from the end of the *Dibacha* introduction of Saʿdi's *Golestan*:[25]

Bemanad sal-ha in nazm o tarkib
ze ma har zarra khak oftada ja'i
gh(araz) naqsh(ist) k'az ma baz manad
ke hasti-ra ne-mi-binam baqa'i
magar saheb-deli ruzi be rahmat
*konad dar kar-e meskinan do*ʿ*a'i*

and the date in Arabic *tammat hadhih al-*ʿ*imarat al-mubaraka ...fi shuhur sinna 845* = 1441 AD, towards the end of the

[23] *Archaeological Gazetteer*, 1259.

[24] Ed. de Goeje, 1874, 73, and in the offset by Madbuli's, Cairo.

[25] My thanks to Sandy Morton for pointing out the source.

Pl. 25.16 *Chesht*

Pl. 25.18 *The Taimurid mosque at Hauz-e Karbas*

Pl. 25.17 *Robat-e Pai*

Pl. 25.19 *The Taimurid mosque at Hauz-e Karbas*

reign of Shah Rukh Mirza (pls. 25.18-19). The magnificent tiled mehrab was almost detached from the wall and looked about to crumble after the building had been hit by missiles again only a few days before. The outer band of calligraphy contained the Throne verse 255 of *Sura Baqara*, the Chapter of the Cow, and the inner panel the beginning of verse 39 of *Sura Al Imran*, the Chapter of the Family of Imran: *fa-nadat-hu 'l-mala'ikatu wa huwa qa'imun yusalli fi'l-mihrab* when the angels announced the news of John's birth to Zacharia while he was praying in the sanctuary apse-niche. The colours of the tiles, turquoise and lapis blue, white, deep buff, sage green, were the most beautiful I have seen and the *thulth* calligraphy of the highest quality.

The destruction of Herat and Afghanistan's cultural heritage cannot be sufficiently deplored and condemned, as part of that greater human and economic destruction perpetrated by a government prepared to wage total war against its own citizens.

A personal note

Ralph was away when I arrived in the late summer of 1979 to stay at the embassy compound with Peter Barker, the Oriental Secretary in Kabul. Peter and I had been hill-walking in the Oshtoran Kuh in Iran the previous spring and he had pressed me to visit him in his new posting on my way back from India. At the gates of the embassy guarded by tall Pathans nestled the British Institute. When I went to use the library, Lavinia Davies, then working in the library, told me he was travelling in the south west looking at archaeological sites.

Shooting around the Presidential Palace that night was followed the next morning by a rapid removal of all portraits and posters of the deposed/murdered communist leader Tarakki. I returned by air to teach in Isfahan.

It was Lavinia who finally introduced me to Ralph when I had a musical evening at home in Islington with an Afghan *robab*-player—that was in 1982 shortly after Ralph's return to London: I was impressed that his sympathy for the culture and the people of Afghanistan was unshaken by his recent ordeal in Kabul. That was the beginning of a friendship, with Ralph's unfailing courtesy, hospitality and encouragement nurturing my own enthusiasm for Persian Islamic culture.

These notes taken from my reports were incidental to the main purpose of my mission which was monitoring humanitarian assistance, rather than surveying the pillage and devastation of an invaluable cultural heritage. But as I came to know and love the Afghans, I realised that without their history and their culture, they would truly be dispossessed. People like Ralph have helped preserve and illumine the artefacts of that culture, and it is with respect and admiration for his work and his person that I offer this *pa-ye malakh* to him—*Pa-ye malakh nazd-e Sulaiman bordan ʿaib ast, wali hunar ast ze muri!*

A note on transcription of names

Place and personal names are given as heard rather than according to any strict transliteration system.

26 TWO IVORY PLAQUES IN THE BRITISH MUSEUM

Rachel Ward

This article is unapologetic about narrowing the focus to consider two ivory plaques in the British Museum. Ralph Pinder-Wilson has always concentrated on the less studied areas of Islamic art: ivory, jade, rock crystal, glass and metal. While he was in the Department of Oriental Antiquities at the British Museum he greatly expanded the collections of these materials and acquired some spectacular objects (including the Hedwig glass, Whitehouse, this volume, no. 13). Ralph Pinder-Wilson was following in the tradition of the great 19th century curator Augustus Wollaston Franks: looking through the museum registers, it is striking how Islamic ivories, jades, rock crystals, glass and metal were first acquired during Franks curatorship in the 19th century and next entered the museum in the 1950s, when a fruitful combination of Ralph Pinder-Wilson's interest and funds from the department's benefactor, P T Brooke Sewell, enabled these sections to expand once more.[1]

Ivories were foremost amongst the many gifts that Franks made to the museum. In a letter to Birch of 19 April 1866 with reference to a medieval ivory he had purchased he wrote: 'I am not quite sure whether the museum had better buy it or I present it. I should like my name attached to a few tidy things to preserve some recollection of me when I am gone and ivories are rather favourite subjects of mine.'[2] In 1874 he donated the two plaques that are the subject of this paper (pl. 26.1).

The plaques are carved from pale elephant ivory. They are tall, thin rectangles and originally had the same dimensions: height 28.2cm (the broken plaque now measures 17.6cm), width 2.9cm and depth 0.6-0.7cm. The complete plaque has five holes irregularly positioned so as to remain invisible from the front. Two holes may be the result of damage but the other three were intentionally drilled and must have been used to attach the plaque to a larger object. However, the broken plaque has no drilled holes, which suggests that the original method of fixing was glue rather than nails. They are deeply carved but not pierced. Dark material in the recesses and on the flat ground may just be dirt but could be remains of black-blue paint intended to give the impression that the plaque was pierced.

The unbroken plaque is carved with three figures on a ground of scrolling arabesques. The top figure is shown frontally but looking to the left. He wears a calf-length tunic decorated with an ogival palmette medallion design and decorated hem over a plain tight sleeved undergarment with *ṭirāz* bands. A cape hangs from a decorated circular collar around his shoulders and is slightly longer than his tunic. There is a tasselled girdle around his waist. His head is shown in profile with shoulder-length hair and a pointed hat of a soft fabric which is decorated with a cross. His boots are decorated with motifs that are now too abraded to distinguish. He holds a long staff terminating in a Byzantine double-barred cross. He must be a Christian ecclesiastic, perhaps a bishop.

The middle figure is shown walking to the left. He wears a calf-length tunic with a front pleat, neck opening and short sleeves ending in *ṭirāz* over a plain tight-sleeved undergarment. The tunic is decorated with a Y-design which may be intended to represent chain mail and has a patterned hem.[3] His boots are decorated with a star motif. There is a girdle around his waist from which hangs a rosette and a sword with a decorated scabbard and circular pommel of European type.[4] His head is shown in three-quarter view with shoulder-length hair and a three-pointed crown. There is a circular object in his right hand which is raised as if in offering; his left hand grasps the hilt of his sword. The crown, sword and short tunic suggest that this is a Christian ruler in military attire. The circular object could be an orb, but an orb is usually held by an

[1] R Ward, 'Islamism—a difficult matter' in M Caygill and J Cherry (eds), *A W Franks, Nineteenth Century Collecting and the British Museum*, BMP, 1997, 272-285.

[2] M Caygill, 'Franks and the British Museum—the Cuckoo in the Nest' in M Caygill (ed), *A W Franks*, 95.

[3] In East and Central Asian art this Y-pattern is used to represent armour or mail.

[4] Swords with circular pommels are associated with the Crusaders: see the mid-13th century miniature of a Crusader by Matthew Paris in the British Museum: M Pfaffenbichler, *Armourers*, BMP, London, 1992, fig. 9. Arab swords generally had straight or angular hilts (see fig. 5).

enthroned monarch. This is more likely to be a bag of money, often seen in the hands of standing rulers in Byzantine donor portraits.[5]

The bottom figure is also shown walking to the left. He wears a calf-length tunic with a front pleat, neck opening and short sleeves ending in *ṭirāz* over a plain tight-sleeved undergarment. It is decorated with a star-design and patterned hem. He wears an articulated belt. His boots are decorated with a diaper motif. He is bare-headed with a central parting and shoulder-length hair. From his left hand he swings a hemispherical incense burner of the type used in the Christian liturgy and in his right hand is a small crucifix which he holds up in front of him. He appears to be a sacristan.

The broken plaque is missing its top figure and the central figure is cut off at the chest. However the remaining section shows him walking to the right and wearing a calf-length tunic with a front pleat and short sleeves ending in *ṭirāz* over a plain tight-sleeved undergarment. It is decorated with a swirling palmette and arabesque design and has a patterned hem. He wears an articulated belt with sash ends and plain boots. His forearms are raised in front of him as if carrying something large.

The bottom figure is also shown walking to the right. He wears a calf-length tunic with a front pleat and undulating hem over a plain tight-sleeved undergarment with *ṭirāz* bands. The tunic is decorated with hexagon-framed rosettes and triangular infills. He wears an articulated belt and boots decorated with a Y-motif. He has long hair down his back and a tall turban tied around a protruding cap with the end left loose. In his left hand he holds a long-necked bottle with a decorated frieze around the body and in his right hand is a tall conical object, decorated around the rim, which may be a beaker or drinking horn. His turban and the bottle suggests that he is secular, probably a court attendant. His turban has encouraged scholars to assume that he is a Muslim, but he could equally be a Christian as turbans were worn by both.[6]

The curious combination of Christian and Muslim influences in the plaques has encouraged a wide range of theories as to their date and provenance. Franks, writing in the museum registers, gave no indication of their previous history or where he had acquired them, just noting that they are probably Coptic. Dalton suggested that they are Persian, 16th century.[7] He gave no reason for this curious theory; presumably the slightly effete pose of the turbanned attendant reminded him of paintings of Safavid fops. Kühnel acknowledged their indebtedness to the Fatimid tradition of ivory carving but suggested that the particular combination of Frankish and Muslim influences was more likely to have been produced in 13th century Sicily.[8] Kühnel also mentioned a personal communication from Ralph Pinder-Wilson suggesting that they could be late medieval Coptic, perhaps the frame of a Christian icon. Suggestions of provenance on record cards in the Department of Oriental Antiquities include Southern Italy, Sicily and Spain.

It is nothing new in the field of Islamic art to have such wildly divergent theories of provenance (in this volume, see Anna Contadini's article on the Pisa griffon or David Whitehouse on the Hedwig glasses) but this is as diverse as any of them—Spain, Italy, Sicily, Egypt, Iran, 13th-16th century. At the installation of the John Addis Islamic Gallery in 1989 I put them on display with Mamluk material of the 14th century. This paper gives me an opportunity to justify that attribution.

The British Museum plaques share important features with the well-known series of Fatimid plaques attributed to 12th century Egypt, including those from a double-sided book cover now divided between the Museum für Islamische Kunst in Berlin (pl. 26.2) and the Louvre in Paris.[9] Like them they are rectangular plaques designed for attachment to a larger object and have been deeply carved with courtly figures one above the other on a scroll ground. But the British Museum plaques are markedly different in style and detail: they are much thinner and not pierced. The foliate scroll is in tight circles and placed behind the figures like wall paper, whereas in the Fatimid plaques it winds itself around the figures both framing and interacting with them and includes realistic bunches of grapes and vine leaves. The figures are almost flat and move across a single plane whereas the Fatimid

---

5 For example, the 11th century mosaics of Byzantine emperors in the south gallery of St Sophia, Istanbul offer round bags of money to the central Christ or Virgin: A Grabar, *Byzantine Painting*, Skira, Geneva, 1979, 98-99.

6 Describing the early Mamluk period, Mayer writes: 'The essential point is that but for the belts of the Christians the only distinction between the "people of the Book" and the Moslems was the colour of the turban. Sartorially their clothes were exactly the same.' L A Mayer, *Mamluk Costume*, Switzerland, 1952, 65.

7 O M Dalton, *Catalogue of the Ivory Carvings of the Christian Era, with examples of Mohammedan art and carvings in bone in the Department of British and Medieval Antiquities and Ethnography of the British Museum*, London, 1909, nos. 570 and 571 on page 174 and pl. CXXIII. The Dalton catalogue numbers are painted on the back of the plaques.

8 E Kühnel, *Die Islamischen Elfenbeinskulpturen VIII-XIII Jahrhundert*, Berlin, 1971, no. 139 and pl. CIX.

9 Kühnel *op. cit.*, nos. 68-69, 88-89. E Hoffman, 'A Fatimid Book Cover: Framing and Re-framing Cultural Identity in the Medieval Mediterranean World' in M Barrucand (ed.), *L'Egypte fatimide, son art et son histoire*, Sorbonne, Paris, 1999.

figures are curvaceous and often project out to create a sense of three dimensional movement. The tunics are tight-fitting, belted and three-quarter length not loose and long, and their sleeves are short and narrow not long and wide. Some of the textile designs are similar but others (palmettes in ogival medallions, star patterns) are unparalleled in Fatimid art. The courtier's turban is conical rather than wide and flat, and his hair is long whereas the Fatimid fashion was for bobbed hair with prominent sideburns.

If the plaques are later examples of the Fatimid ivory carving tradition these similarities and differences could be reconciled. But post-12th century figural ivories, which might have supplied evidence of this continuing tradition in Egypt and Syria, are virtually unknown.[10] They must have existed. There were highly skilled and prolific ivory carvers working in both Egypt and Syria and large numbers of non-figural plaques were made for the architectural fittings of the mosques and other religious buildings of the Ayyubids and Mamluks. Figural decoration occurs on Ayyubid and Mamluk objects of all media, and it would be extremely surprising if there were not a similar range of figural ivories. They probably have not been recognised or have been mis-attributed to the better known workshops of the 12th century.[11]

Despite their non-figural decoration, the background treatment of inscribed or patterned ivory plaques made for known patrons or buildings, provides valuable assistance in the attribution of these two plaques. The flat, spiralling scrolls with their roughly hatched palmettes and half-palmettes and distinctive small curling tendrils placed with monotonous regularity along the stem can be seen on ivories dating to the 14th century, including four ivory panels made for a building commissioned by the Mamluk Sultan Muḥammad ibn Qalāwun (1293-1341) (pl. 26.3).

Comparisons for the figural decoration on the plaques can be found in other media of the 14th century. The proportions of the figures with their low waists, defined hips, large heads and small feet, their askew facial features and beauty spots and their short-sleeved tunics with *ṭirāz* bands and folded back front panel worn over plain long-sleeved undergarments and boots can be compared to the Mamluk horsemen in a Furūsiyya manuscript dated 767/1366 (pl. 26.4).[12] The turban of the courtier at the bottom of the broken plaque is tied in the same way as that of the Mamluk horseman, with a length of fabric wound in two directions around a low *qalūta* cap and then diagonally across the front before being tucked in with its end left loose on top (earlier depictions of turbans do not normally show the *qalūta* cap beneath the fabric and the ends of the fabric are tucked out of sight). Like the horseman he has long hair flowing down his back and an articulated metal belt (rather than a sash) around his waist. David James provided some evidence that the manuscript was produced in Cairo, but the style was also current in Damascus, where at least two copies of the manuscript were made in the 1370s.[13]

The short-sleeved tunic is especially relevant to the date of the plaques. A short-sleeved tunic (*qabā salārī* or just *salārī*) is said to have been invented (or made fashionable) by the amir Salār (d.1310).[14] It was worn throughout the 14th and 15th century and came to be considered typical Mamluk dress. Pictorial representations are notoriously slow to adapt to fashions in costume and short-sleeved tunics are not depicted in art before the 1330s or 1340s, and the Chester Beatty Furūsiyya manuscript is the first dated (1366) depiction known to me.

The figures can also be compared to those on the Baptistère, a metal basin in the Louvre, made in Syria between about 1340 and 1360 (fig. 1).[15] On both they walk in a single plain against a ground of formulaic foliate scroll. Their rounded faces, flat noses, beauty spots and fringe of hair at the top of the forehead are similar as is their costume of three quarter length tunic with tight (and sometimes short) sleeves, *ṭirāz* bands and a fold of material in front and the repertoire of textile patterns used to decorate them. But the most striking parallel between the

[10] Atıl refers to unpublished late 13th century ivory plaques with figural decoration which she attributes to the early Mamluk period: 'A few ivory plaques made in the second half of the thirteenth century are decorated with humans and animals, following the figural style of the age. These are extremely rare and include the plaques on the doors of a cupboard in Cairo, Coptic Museum and another door in a private collection.' E Atıl, *Renaissance of Islam, Art of the Mamluks*, Smithsonian exhibition catalogue, Washington DC, 1981, 197.

[11] Ivory chess pieces have also tended to be attributed to the 12th century, but a recent article proves that there was a continuous tradition right into the Ottoman period: A Contadini, 'Islamic Ivory Chess Pieces, Draughtsmen and Dice', in J W Allan (ed.) *Islamic Art in the Ashmolean*, Oxford Studies in Islamic Art X, part one, 111-155.

[12] D James 'Mameluke painting at the time of the "Lusignan Crusade", 1365-70, a study of the Chester Beatty Nihāyat al-Su'l wa'l-Umniya ... etc MS of 1365' in *Humaniora Islamica 2*, 1974, 73-87.

[13] Topkapi Saray Library A.2651 dated 775/1373, copied by Aḥmad al-Miṣrī in Damascus. British Library Add 18886 dated 773/1371 copied by the same scribe, presumably also in Damascus. James *op. cit.*, 66 and 75, Haldane, *Mamluk Painting* 58 and 66.

[14] Mayer, *op.cit.*, 23-25.

[15] R Ward 'The Baptistère de Saint Louis—a Mamluk basin made for export to Europe', in *Islam and the Italian Renaissance*, N Mann and A Contadini (eds), Warburg Institute, London, 113-132.

two objects are the curious motifs decorating the boots, which are not known from other objects or paintings.[16]

The range of textile designs seen on the plaques, which include hexagonal and ogival divisions, stars, palmettes and Y-shaped fillers, are all seen in the Mamluk period.[17] Some of them can be traced back to the Fatimid period but the ogival medallions of the top Christian figure is not seen before the 14th century in any media. The first example known to me is the short-sleeved tunic of the hunter on the glass pilgrim bottle in the British Museum which was probably made in mid-14th century Syria.[18]

Other comparsions with Mamluk paintings and objects could be made. They all suggest that the plaques were produced within the Mamluk Empire, probably in Syria, in the middle of the 14th century.

The plaques were obviously intended to be part of a larger ensemble. The dimensions, technique and style of both are virtually identical and they were acquired together, so it seems reasonable to assume that they were attached to the same object.[19] Eva Hoffman has produced convincing evidence that the Fatimid plaques in Berlin (pl. 26.2) and Paris were intended as two sides of a book cover. In a footnote she mentions that the British Museum plaques might have been used in the same way.[20] This seems the most likely explanation of their format, which is so different from other known Mamluk plaques and totally unsuited to the radial designs of Mamluk architectural fittings. They were probably arranged in a similar way to the Fatimid ones (pl. 26.2), with these plaques placed either side of a central panel and horizontal plaques of the same width across top and bottom. The undamaged plaque is 28.2cm high and so the total height of the cover would have been 34cm, which is an appropriate size for a book cover (the height of illustrated Mamluk mss ranges from *c.* 25 to 40cm).

Like the Fatimid plaques, the figures all look inwards which is consistent with the idea of a central scene.

Pl. 26.1 Ivory plaques with figural decoration, British Museum, Department of Oriental Antiquities, 1874.3-2.6 and 7.

What was on the central plaque? The figures gaze towards a place just above mid-point, their bowed heads, offering gestures and generally subservient demeanour suggests that the central plaque featured an important figure. The king in the side plaque makes it unlikely that the central plaque contained another Christian secular authority. It is possible that the figure was the Mamluk sultan and that the whole scene was intended to demonstrate the subsidiary status of a local Christian king and his subjects. But no such theme occurs elsewhere in Mamluk art and the prominent position accorded to the potent symbol of the cross and it

[16] D S Rice identified them as blazons, but they are too simple and repetitive to represent specific Mamluk blazons and are more likely to be ornamental. D S Rice, *Le Baptistère de Saint Louis*, Paris, 1951, 17 and 'The blazons of the Baptistère', Bulletin of the School of Oriental and African Studies 13, 1950, 377-78.

[17] Haldane, *Mamluk Painting*, 32-38.

[18] R Ward 'Glass and brass: parallels and puzzles', in *Gilded and Enamelled Glass from the Middle East*, R Ward (ed.), BMP, London, 1998, 30-34.

[19] Narrow rectangular ivory plaques mounted on a Spanish altar are similar in shape, but they are mounted sideways so appear to have been reused from somewhere else and are anyway quite different in style and attributed by Kühnel to 11th century Spain. Kühnel, *op. cit.*, no. 50 and pl. XLII-XLIII.

[20] Hoffman, *op. cit.*, note 36.

Pl. 26.2 Ivory plaques with figural decoration, part of a book cover, Berlin, Museum für Islamische Kunst, I 6375.

being held aloft as if in the act of blessing makes this theory implausible. The most likely subject for the central plaque is a religious scene, which often forms the main feature of Christian book covers. The arrangement of the figures around the space and the inclusion of a courtier with bottle and beaker or napkin, suggests that an enthronement scene would have been the most appropriate, perhaps a Madonna and Child or Christ in Majesty.

The horizontal plaques would have been too low to feature full scale figures, but might have had a series of busts. A 12th century north Italian metal bookcover has just such an arrangement with two full figures one above the other in the side panels, busts in the upper and lower panels and Christ with Peter and Paul in the central panel.[21] They might otherwise have had a frieze of racing animals—a leitmotiv of Mamluk art. The narrow frame of the frontispiece to the Histoire Universelle of the later 13th century discussed by Hoffman consists of a frieze of animals.[22]

[21] Paris, Musée National du Moyen Age, Cl.22653: A Erlande-Brandenburg, *Guide to the collections*, Paris, 1993, no. 82.

[22] British Library Add. 15768. Hoffman, *op. cit.* fig. 86.

Pl. 26.3 Ivory plaques from a building commissioned by Muḥammad ibn Qalāwun (1293-1341). British Museum, Department of Oriental Antiquities, 1880.6-7.1-4.

Pl. 26.4 Mamluk horseman, illustration to a manuscript of Nihāyat as-Su'l *dated Jumādā I 767/January 1366, Dublin, Chester Beatty Library, Ar. 5565, f. 134v. (Reproduced by kind permission of the Trustees of the Chester Beatty Library, Dublin)*

A king from an east Christian state where Muslim-Byzantine fashions were accepted is the most likely patron for such an object.[23] An obvious contender is Hugh IV of Lusignan, King of Cyprus (1324-59), who is known to have commissioned fine metal vessels from Mamluk metalworkers and may well have commissioned objects in other media also.[24] He had established strong trading links with the Mamluk empire which enabled him to make specific requests of the craftsmen. The metal vessels are unusual in being decorated with his own arms and translations of his titles or appropriate poetic inscriptions in Arabic, whereas most export metalwork simply carries generalised inscriptions and an empty heraldic shield ready to be filled by the unknown purchaser. He would certainly have been able to request a book cover designed to his own specifications.

In 1971 Ralph Pinder-Wilson suggested that these plaques come from the frame of a late medieval Christian icon.[25] The evidence presented here confirms and builds on his suggestion: they are from the outside frame of a book cover for a Bible or other Christian religious text designed and made between 1340 and 1370, probably in Syria, and on commission from a foreign Christian ruler, perhaps Hugh of Lusignan, King of Cyprus (1324-59).

[23] A west European ruler is certainly not out of the question. There was extensive commissioning of Mamluk metal vessels with European arms in the mid 14th century, especially via the Italian merchant network. As Hoffman observed, Middle Eastern motifs were used in Europe to give a sense of physical context to Christian images. The Fatimid ivory plaques were re-used in the early 14th century to frame an Italian image of Christ in Majesty which was bordered with imitation Kufic script. Hoffman, *op. cit.*, 407.

[24] Basin in the Louvre (MAO 101): D S Rice, 'Arabic inscriptions on a brass basin made for Hugh IV de Lusignan', in *Studi Orientalistici in onore di Giorgio Levi della Vida II*, Rome, 1956, 390-402. Bowl: sold at Christie's May 23 1966, lot 134.

[25] Kühnel, *op.cit.*, no. 139.

Fig. 26.1 Drawing of a panel on 'Le Baptistère de Saint Louis' in the Louvre, (after Rice, Baptistère, fig. 7).

27 A NOTE ON HEDWIG GLASSES

David Whitehouse

Hedwig Glasses (*Hedwigsgläser*) is the collective name of a small and unusually coherent group of glass vessels (pl. 27.1; appendix). The objects, which vary in height from 8.6cm to14.7cm, are beakers with a plain rim, a straight, tapering side and a foot with a horizontal flange. In many cases, the foot resembles a rudimentary cogwheel with notches that facilitated the attachment of a metal mount. The glass is transparent, and it varies from colourless to very pale brown, a tint usually likened to smoky topaz. The walls of the beakers are thick. The decoration was cut, ground and polished. It is in relief and consists mainly of from two to four motifs: lions, eagles, griffins, the tree of life (sometimes identified as two crowns, one above the other), crescents, palmettes and other elements (the glasses and their ornament are listed on pages 257-58; throughout my paper, numbers in parenthesis refer to this list).[1]

Scholars have explained the origin of Hedwig Glasses in several ways: that they were made in Europe and most of them are modern, or that they are medieval and were made in central or eastern Europe, the Islamic world, Byzantium, or southern Italy.

We may safely reject the explanation that they are modern. Iulia Scapova asserted that a fragmentary vessel excavated at Novogrudok in Belarus (15) had been relief-cut by hand, but that two complete examples she had examined were cut on a water-powered wheel.[2] The water-powered cutting wheel was introduced by Martin Winter in 1686 and Scapova conjectured that the complete Hedwig Glasses are 17th- to 18th-century versions of a lost medieval original. Evidently, she was not aware that seven of the glasses have 13th- to 15th-century metal mounts, and she could not have known that excavations would yield additional examples from medieval contexts. The view that the glasses are modern, therefore, is untenable.

Equally, despite their distribution and the existence of what appears to be a blank at Hinnenburg in Germany, the explanation that Hedwig Glasses were made in the Middle Ages in central or eastern Europe fails to convince. Various European origins have been claimed by B A Shelkovnikov, who concluded that all Hedwig Glasses were made at Novogrudok; by Rosemarie Lierke, who maintained that they were made in Germany; and by Samuel Kurinsky, who asserted that the technique and chemical composition of Hedwig Glasses were developed in Iran and carried to Silesia by the Khazars.[3] In fact, the three examples that have been analysed are made of soda-lime glass,[4] and this alone would make them very unusual if they were made in Europe in the medieval period, when glassmakers habitually produced potash glasses. Moreover, no relief-cut glass vessels (indeed, no cut glass vessels of any kind) are known to have been made in Europe between the fifth and the 16th centuries.

We are left, therefore, with the suggestions that Hedwig Glasses are medieval and Islamic, Byzantine, or Italian.

The most durable conjecture about Hedwig Glasses is that they were made in the Islamic world in the

---

1 The pioneer studies of Hedwig Glasses are: Eugen von Czihak, *Schlesische Gläser: Eine Studie über die schlesische Glasindustrie früherer Zeit*, Breslau, 1891, 184-206; Robert Schmidt, 'Die Hedwigsgläser und verwandte fatimidische Glas- und Kristallschnittarbeiten', *Schlesiens Vorzeit in Bild und Schrift*, NF, vol. 6, 1912, 53-78; and Carl Johan Lamm, *Mittelalterliche Gläser und Steinschnittarbeiten aus dem Nahen Osten*, Verlag Dietrich Reimer/Ernst Vohsen, Berlin, 2 vols., 1929-1930. For a detailed description of all the complete Hedwig Glasses and several archaeological finds, see Francis N Allen, *Hedwig Glasses: A Survey*, the author, Hayattsville, Maryland, 1987. Note also the judicious summary in Erwin Baumgartner and Ingeborg Krueger, *Phönix aus Sand und Asche*, Klinkhardt and Biermann, Munich, 1988, 86-88.

2 Julia Scapova, 'À propos des coupes dites de Sainte Hedwige', *Annales du 7e Congrès de l'Association Internationale pour l'Histoire du Verre*, Berlin-Leipzig, 15-21 août 1977, the association, Liège, 1978, 255-269.

3 B A Shelkovnikov, 'Russian Glass from the 11th to the 17th Century', *Journal of Glass Studies*, vol. 8, 1966, 95-115, esp. 109-112; Rosemarie Lierke, *Antike Glastöpferei: Ein vergessenes Kapitel der Glasgeschichte*, Verlag Philipp von Zabern, Mainz am Rhein, 1999, pp. 140-145; Samuel Kurinsky, *The Glassmakers: An Odyssey of the Jews. The First Three Thousand Years*, Hippocrene Books, New York, 1991, 340-341.

4 Allen (note 1), pp. 22-23; see also Robert H Brill, *Chemical Analyses of Early Glasses*, The Corning Museum of Glass, Corning, New York, 1999, vol. 1, 100 and vol. 2, 203, sample 1009.

11th or 12th century. A strong tradition of relief cutting existed in Egypt and the Middle East, and the remains of hundreds of glass vessels and dozens of rock crystal objects attest to the skill of Islamic glass cutters and lapidaries. While some scholars have suggested that Hedwig Glasses were made in Egypt, others have opted for Iran, in part because Egypt and Western Asia are the only regions, from which we have unequivocal evidence for the relief cutting of glass in the Middle Ages. However, Hedwig Glasses break one of the most persistent 'rules' of the medieval Muslim glass cutter and lapidary: the beakers are chunky, whereas craftsmen in the Islamic world usually aimed at delicacy rather than mass. The Corning cameo glass ewer (pl. 27.2) and its rock crystal counterparts, for example, have thin walls and fine lines; Hedwig Glasses do not.

One variation on the Islamic hypothesis, advanced by Axel von Saldern, attempts to explain why Hedwig Glasses are so untypical.[5] Von Saldern suggested that the beakers were made in the Holy Land at the time of the Crusades, and they were taken to Europe by crusaders, pilgrims, or merchants. He noted that tradition associates the two Hedwig Glasses at Namur (11 and 12) with Jacques de Vitry, bishop of Acre between 1216 and 1226; and that a fragment excavated on the site of the royal palace in Budapest (18) *might* (my italics) have been brought home by King Andrew II, who collected relics in the Holy Land in 1217.

The conjecture that Hedwig Glasses are Byzantine was championed most recently by Joseph Philippe.[6] Byzantine emperors surrounded themselves with treasures and filled their churches with luxurious liturgical objects. Eyewitness descriptions of the scale of the looting of Constantinople in 1204 are breathtaking, and the Treasury of San Marco in Venice provides a dazzling glimpse of Byzantine luxury. Moreover, the treasures in San Marco include a number of relief-cut glasses. Unfortunately, only of these objects even remotely resembles a Hedwig Glass (it is a bowl decorated with lions) and in any case scholars are still undecided about the date and origin of many of the San Marco glasses.

One further conjecture about the origin of Hedwig Glasses was advanced by the late Basil Gray at a number of colloquia in 1980s and has since found its way into publications. Gray believed that the technique used to finish the beakers was derived from the Islamic tradition of relief cutting. At the same time, he was puzzled by the wholly un-Islamic distribution of the surviving examples. Consequently, Gray sought an origin in another of the melting pots of Mediterranean cultures: southern Italy.

In the 11th century, the Normans conquered Muslim Sicily and established a dynasty that ruled a population of great cultural diversity: Greek, Muslim, and western European. In the capital, Palermo, monuments might be inscribed in combinations of Latin, Greek, Arabic, and Hebrew—occasionally, all at once! After a century of Norman kings, the Sicilian throne was inherited by a German family, the Hohenstaufen, whose most powerful ruler, Frederick II, reigned from 1192 to 1250. Hedwig Glasses, Gray maintained, were made in the reign of Frederick II, either in Sicily or on the mainland of southern Italy.

When we turn from the problem of where the Hedwig Glasses originated to the question of when they were made, we reach firmer ground. The beakers at Namur have mounts attributed to Hugo d'Oignie, also known as Hugo de Walcourt (d. about 1240) and the fragment from Novogrudok was found in an archaeological deposit attributed to the late 12th century. Hedwig Glasses, therefore, were in circulation not later than the decades around 1200.

Despite the similarities that unite the Hedwig Glasses, their ornament falls into at least two groups. The thirteen complete examples and the fragment from Novogrudok (1-13 and 15) may be divided into Group A: eight beakers decorated with, *inter alia*, one or two lions, usually with an eagle and/or a griffin (1-6 and 11, 13); and Group B: five beakers decorated with palmettes, crescents or geometric motifs, but neither animals nor birds(7-10 and 12). Three of the beakers in Group A (1, 6 and 13) also have a tree of life and three of those in Group B (7, 9 and 10) have an intermittent cross-hatched border near the top of the wall. The fragments from Weinsberg (14) and Budapest (18), and perhaps the fragment from Göttingen (17) belong to Group A, while the fragment from Pistoia (16) belongs to Group B. 21, which is known only from a 15th-century description, appears to be a lost example of Group A. All told, therefore, we are aware of at least ten and possibly twelve examples of Group A and six examples of Group B. .

Let us focus for a moment on Group A. The various motifs have been likened to ornament on Islamic glass and rock crystal, Byzantine textiles, and Italian sculpture; but few students appear to have asked what the motifs might signify. Granted that they are not simply

5 Axel von Saldern, 'Early Islamic Glass in the Near East: Problems of chronology and provenances', *Annales du 13e Congrès de l'Association Internationale pour l'Histoire du Verre*, Pays Bas, 28 août-1 septembre 1995, the association, Lochem, 1996, 225-246, esp. 239-242.

6 Joseph Philippe, *Le Monde byzantin dans l'histoire de la verrerie (Ve-XVI siècle)*, Casa Editrice Riccardo Pàtron, Bologna, 1970, 125-141.

decorative but convey messages, can we understand these messages and, if so, do they help us to understand the beakers themselves?

The lion has a multitude of meanings in different contexts, but in medieval churches it represented Christ the King, who wields power on earth through his faithful subjects. The eagle also has many meanings, but in churches it stands for the resurrected Christ. The griffin became a Christian symbol because it combines the physical characteristics of a lion and an eagle, and therefore it represents both Christ the King and the Risen Christ. Even that age-old motif the sacred tree became a Christian metaphor. The First Psalm contains the verse: 'And he shall be like a tree ... that bringeth forth his fruits in his season; his leaves also shall not wither; and whatsoever he doeth shall prosper' (Ps. 1,3). The Church Fathers repeatedly identified the subject of this verse as Christ. Saint Augustine, for example, explained, 'that tree is Our Lord' (*Enarrationes in Psalmos* 1, PL 36,680) and Saint Ambrose wrote that the Lord Jesus 'is the tree of life' (*Enarratio in Psalmum* 1, PL 14,941B).[7]

Thus, the four most common motifs on Hedwig Glasses had significance for medieval Christians. Indeed, the motifs had specific Christological significance: that is, they represented different theological aspects of the person and work of Jesus Christ. For this reason, I find it difficult to avoid the conclusion that the intended owners of the glasses in Group A were Christians, not Muslims.

This conclusion is reinforced by the fact that six of the complete glasses in Group A (1, 2, 4, 6, 7, and 11) are known to have served as chalices or reliquaries by the 15th century and the feet of three others (5, 9 and 10) have notches to facilitate mounting, as does the foot of the fragment from Novogrudok.

Although the ornament on the beakers in Group B is without overt religious significance, one of the complete examples (12) is mounted as a chalice or reliquary and three others (7, 9 and 10) have notched feet, as does the fragment from Pistoia (which was found in a bishop's palace!).

Hedwig Glasses, it seems, are not only un-Islamic in form and execution; they are also non-Islamic in purpose. Indeed, so appropriate are the form and (in Group A) the decoration for incorporation in chalices, it is logical to infer that this was their primary function. Thus, while we are still ignorant about the makers of the Hedwig Glasses, we may reasonably suspect that the patrons were Christians commissioning liturgical objects.

Appendix: an inventory of Hedwig glasses

This is a checklist of all Hedwig Glasses that are known to have survived above ground, all published fragments from excavations and one description of a lost object, which may have been a Hedwig Glass.[8]

(I) Beakers that survived above ground

1. Minden, Germany. The cathedral treasury contains a beaker, H. 9.8cm, decorated with a lion, an eagle and a 'tree of life.' In the second quarter of the 13th century, it was turned into a monstrance by the addition, in Germany, of silver-gilt mounts.
2. Kraków, Poland. The cathedral treasury contains a beaker, H. 11.2cm, decorated with two lions and an eagle. It was mounted as a chalice in the 15th century.
3. Amsterdam, Netherlands. The Rijksmuseum owns a beaker, H. 14.7cm, decorated with two lions and an eagle (acc. no. HM 712). An inscription engraved on the base records that it was presented to Louis-Philippe, the count palatine, in 1643.
4. Nuremberg, Germany. The Germanisches Nationalmuseum has a beaker, H. 9.5cm, decorated with two lions and a griffin (acc. no. KG 564). It was mounted as a chalice in the 15th century.
5. Corning, New York, United States. The Corning Museum of Glass owns a beaker, H. 8.7cm,

[7] For the Christological significance of the eagle, griffin and lion, see Engelbert Kirschbaum SJ, ed., *Lexicon der christlichen Ikonographie*, Herder, Rome, Freiburg, Basel and Vienna, 1968-76, s.v. *Adler*, *Greif*, and *Löwe*; and Maria Angiola Romanini, ed., *Enciclopedia dell'arte medievale*, Istituto dell Enciclopedia Italiana, Rome, 1991-2000, s.v. *Aquila*, *Grifo* and *Leone*. For a recent study of the Christological significance of the tree, see Constantine P Charalampidis, *The Dendrites in Pre-Christian and Christian Historical-Literary Tradition and Iconography*, Studia Archaeologica, v. 73, 'L'Erma' di Bretschneider, Rome, 1995, 55-67.

[8] The list is based on Allen (note 1). For additional finds from excavations, see: T Platz, 'Burg und Stadt Hilpoltstein, Baugeschichte und Bedeutung,' in *Ausgrabungen—Schicht für Schicht ins Mittelalter*, exhibition catalogue, Bamberg, 1998; R Friedrich, *Die mittelalterlichen Glas- und Keramikfunde der Burg Bommersheim in Oberursel*, in press, quoted by Lierke (note 3), 143.

decorated with two lions (acc. no. 67.1.11). It was removed from the cathedral at Halberstadt, Germany, in 1820.

6. Wroclaw, Poland. Until it disappeared in 1944, the Silesian Museum of Antiquities possessed a beaker, H. 12.3cm, decorated with a chalice surmounted by a crescent and a star, two lions and a 'tree of life' (acc. no. 5613). It had 15th-century silver mounts.

7. Halberstadt, Germany. The cathedral treasury contains a beaker, H. 8.9cm, decorated with a band of cross-hatching and four crescent-like motifs (acc. no. 69). In the 14th century, the object was mounted as a monstrance for relics of the apostles James and Thomas.

8. Asseberg, Germany. This beaker, now lost, was 10cm high and it had an overall pattern of six conjoined heart-shaped panels, three with small, upward-pointing palmettes and three with larger, downward-pointing palmettes with volutes. The object had a 14th- or 15th-century leather case. According to a family history, it was once at Meisdorf in Saxony-Anhaldt.

9. Nysa, Poland. The museum at Nysa owns a beaker, H. 10.6cm, decorated with a band of cross-hatching and four stylized palmettes. The object was mounted as a chalice in the 18th century.

10. Coburg, Germany. The collection at Veste Coburg includes a beaker, H. 10.3cm, decorated with a band of cross hatching punctuated by eight circular bosses, and with four downward-pointing palmettes alternating with four pairs of volutes. In 1331, the beaker was at the Franciscan friary at Eisenach in Thuringia.

11. Namur, Belgium. The treasury of the Soeurs de Notre Dame contains a beaker, H. 8.0cm, decorated with a lion and a griffin. The beaker is believed to have been given to the monastery of Saint-Nicholas d'Oignie by Jacques de Vitry, bishop of Acre between 1216 and 1226. Its 13th-century mounts are attributed to Hugo d'Oignie, also known as Hugo de Walcourt, (d. about 1240).

12. Namur, Belgium. A second beaker in the treasury of the Soeurs de Notre Dame, H. 9.0cm, is decorated with four crescents and other geometric motifs. It, too, is believed to be a gift of Jacques de Vitry and it has mounts attrributed to Hugo d'Oignie.

13. London. The British Museum has a beaker, H. 14.2cm, decorated with a lion, an eagle, a griffin and a tree of life.

(II) Fragments from archaeological excavations

14. Weinsberg, Germany. Two small fragments, one decorated with the leg of a lion and the other with the tail of an eagle, were found during the excavation of Burg Weibertreu in 1959-1960.

15. Novogrudok, Belarus. Two-thirds of a beaker, H. 12.0cm, decorated with a lion and a griffin, were found in 1960 in a deposit attributed to the late 12th century.

16. Pistoia, Italy. Three fragments, which make approximately one-third of a beaker with geometric ornament. The fragments were found in the former bishop's palace in 1978-1980. They came from an archeological deposit attributed to the decades around 1300.

17. Göttingen, Germany. One small fragment, decorated with part of a tree of life, was found in 1984 during excavations on the site of the castle of the Welfs.

18. Budapest, Hungary. One small fragment decorated with the breast and wing of an eagle was found during excavations in the royal palace at Buda.

19. Hilpoltstein, Germany. Fragments of up to three beakers were found during excavations in the guest quarters at Burg Hilpoltstein in 1989-1995.

20. Oberursel, Germany. One fragment was found in 1988 during excavations at Burg Bommersheim.

(III) A Lost Hedwig Glass?

21. An undated inventory of the possessions of Philip the Good, duke of Burgundy (d. 1447), and of his son Duke Charles the Bold (d. 1477) includes, among Charles's belongings, the following object: 'Item, ung voirre taillié d'un esgle, d'un griffin et d'une double couronne, garny d'argent, moictié doré et moictié blanc, pesant: I m. III o. V est.' ('a glass cut with an eagle, a griffin, and a double crown').[9]

---

[9] Le Compte de Laborde, *Les Duc de Borgogne: Études sur les Lettres, les Arts et l'Industrie Pendant le XVe Siècle*, Plon Frères, Paris, 1851, vol. 2, pt. 2, 96, no. 2753, quoted by Allen (note 1), 17-18.

DEPARTMENT OF COINS AND MEDALS
BRITISH MUSEUM

50

London, W.C.1

25th. February 1983

Sir,

I beg to acknowledge with thanks the receipt of a Philippines Central Bank 5 Piso note

which you have been so good as to present to the Trustees of the British Museum.

I am, Sir,

Your obedient Servant

Virginia H. Hewitt

for KEEPER

Dr. D. MacDowall,
Admont,
Dancers End,
Tring,
Hertfordshire.

Pl. 27.1 Hedwig Glass, H. 8.7cm, The Corning Museum of Glass, 67.1.11. Photo: the museum.

Pl. 27.2 Cameo glass ewer, about AD 1000, H. 16cm. The Corning Museum of Glass, 85.1.1, Clara S. Peck Endowment. Photo: the museum.